Law and the Family in Ireland, 1800–1950

Palgrave Modern Legal History series

Series Editors

Rebecca Probert, School of Law, University of Warwick, UK
Catharine MacMillan, Dickson Poon School of Law, King's College, London, UK

Law and the Family in Ireland, 1800–1950

Edited by

Niamh Howlin
Sutherland School of Law, University College Dublin, Ireland

Kevin Costello
Sutherland School of Law, University College Dublin, Ireland

macmillan education palgrave

First published 2017 by
PALGRAVE

Palgrave in the UK is an imprint of Macmillan Publishers Limited, registered in England, company number 785998, of 4 Crinan Street, London, N1 9XW.

Palgrave® and Macmillan® are registered trademarks in the United States, the United Kingdom, Europe and other countries.

ISBN 978–1–137–60638–9 hardback
ISBN 978–1–137–60635–8 paperback

This book is printed on paper suitable for recycling and made from fully managed and sustained forest sources. Logging, pulping and manufacturing processes are expected to conform to the environmental regulations of the country of origin.

A catalogue record for this book is available from the British Library.

A catalog record for this book is available from the Library of Congress.

Contents

List of Tables

Acknowledgements

This has been a project of two parts. The first was a round table event hosted by the Sutherland School of Law at University College Dublin (UCD) in March 2015. We wish to express our gratitude to everyone who participated in this event and helped to make it a success: Professor Maria Luddy, Mr Paul Ward, Dr Mark Coen, Dr Thomas Mohr, Mr John O'Dowd, Professor Mary O'Dowd, Dr Maebh Harding, Dr Deirdre McGowan, Dr Lindsey Earner-Byrne, Mr Michael Sinnott, Dr Karen Brennan and Dr Elaine Farrell. Particular thanks are due to Ms Sinead Hennessy, Events Manager at the Sutherland School of Law, for organizing the event so seamlessly. The papers presented and the ensuing discussions formed the basis for the second part of the project, this edited collection of essays. We also wish to thank Dr Simone McCaughren, Professor Fred Powell and Dr Diane Urquhart for agreeing to participate and contribute to this part of the project. In compiling and editing the essays, we have been greatly assisted by our editor, Ms Aléta Bezuidenhout, the series editor, Professor Rebecca Probert, and the two anonymous reviewers who rigorously considered our book proposal and provided valuable insight and commentary.

We are grateful to the UCD Seed Funding (Horizon Scanning) Scheme and the UCD School of Law Research Competition for providing the financial support for this project. The Sutherland School of Law's Research and Innovation Managers, Ms Deirdre Norris and Ms Suzanne d'Arcy have provided practical and administrative support. We also wish to thank our Head of School, Professor Joe McMahon and our College Principal, Professor Colin Scott, for their support both for this project and for the activities of the UCD Legal History Research Group more generally.

List of Abbreviations

Ab Not Cas	Abridged Notes of Cases
AC	Appeal Cases
AG	Attorney General
CB	Chief Baron
B	Baron
BANK	Belfast Court of Bankruptcy
Batty	Batty's King's Bench Reports
BL	British Library
Bro CC	Brown's Chancery Cases
C & P	Carrington and Payne's Nisi Prius Reports
CJ	Chief Justice
Cl & F	Clark and Finelly's House of Lords Cases
CL	Common Law
Cox CC	Cox's Criminal Cases
CP	Common Pleas
Cr & Dix	Crawford and Dix
DDA	Dublin Diocesan Archives
DPP	Director of Public Prosecutions
DSPCC	Dublin Society for the Prevention of Cruelty to Children
ECHR	European Convention on Human Rights
EHRR	European Human Rights Reports
ER	English Reports
ESRI	Economic and Social Research Institute
Ex	Exchequer Reports
GDA	Galway Diocesan Archive
HC	High Court *or* House of Commons
HL	House of Lords
IEHC	High Court of Ireland
IESC	Supreme Court of Ireland
ILRM	Irish Law Reports Monthly
ILTR	Irish Law Times Reports
Ir Eq Rep	Irish Equity Reports
ILRM	Irish Law Reports Monthly
IR	Irish Reports
J	Justice
Jebb & B	Jebb and Burke's Queen's Bench Reports
Jebb CCR	Jebb's Crown Cases Reserved
KDA	Kerry Diocesan Archive
Law Rec	Law Recorder
LCB	Lord Chief Baron

LCJ	Lord Chief Justice
LRC	Law Reform Commission
M & Rob	Moody and Robinson's Nisi Prius Reports
MS	Manuscript
NAI	National Archives of Ireland
NLI	National Library of Ireland
NSPCC	National Society for the Prevention of Cruelty to Children
P	Probate Reports
PRO	National Archives (UK)
PRONI	Public Record Office of Northern Ireland
QBD	Queen's Bench Division
SC	Supreme Court
UCD	University College Dublin

Notes on Contributors

Karen Brennan is a lecturer in law at the University of Essex. Her research primarily focuses on historical, social and gendered aspects to the criminal justice response to infanticide, and, linked with this, the purpose and contemporary relevance of gender-specific infanticide laws. This chapter was written as part of a new project focusing on other family killings.

Kevin Costello is a senior lecturer in the Sutherland School of Law, University College Dublin. His publications include monographs on *The Law of Habeas Corpus in Ireland* (2006) and *The Court of Admiralty of Ireland 1575–1893* (2011) as well as articles on aspects of English and Irish legal history published in English, Irish and American journals. His principal current research interest is in the history of judicial review of administrative action in English law between the seventeenth and twentieth centuries.

Lindsey Earner-Byrne is a lecturer in modern Irish history in the School of History at University College Dublin. She has researched and published widely on gender, health and welfare in modern Ireland with a focus on mothers, widows and children. Her most recent book, *Letters of the Catholic Poor: Poverty in Independent Ireland, 1920–1940* (Cambridge University Press, 2016), explores the experiences of the Irish Catholic poor in the first two decades after Irish independence.

Elaine Farrell is a lecturer at Queen's University Belfast where she researches and teaches crime and gender in nineteenth- and early twentieth-century Ireland. Her first monograph, *'A Most Diabolical Deed': Infanticide and Irish Society, 1850–1900* (Manchester University Press, 2013), won the National University of Ireland Publication Prize in Irish History (2016). She has published articles in *Social History*; *Irish Economic and Social History*; *Women's History Review*; and *Journal of Women's History*. She is Co-Investigator of the Arts and Humanities UK research project 'Bad Bridget: Criminal and Deviant Irish Women in North America, 1838–1918'.

Maebh Harding is Associate Professor at the School of Law, University of Warwick, where she lectures family and child law. Maebh has a keen interest in Irish legal history and has published a number of pieces on the history of marriage regulation in Ireland. In 2013 she won the W. N. Osborough Composition Prize in Legal History and has published in international journals on the history of marriage regulation in Ireland. She sits on the council of the Irish Legal History Society and has presented on the history of Irish marriage law at *Who Do You Think You Are? Live*.

Niamh Howlin is a lecturer at the Sutherland School of Law, University College Dublin. Her teaching at UCD includes courses on property law, jury trials, international crime and criminal justice history. She sits on the Council of the Irish Legal History Society (www.ilhs.eu) and was the first head of the UCD Legal History Research Group. Niamh has published articles on Irish legal history in the *Journal of Legal History, Law and History Review* and *Comparative Legal History*, and is the author of *Juries in Ireland: Laypersons and Law in the Long Nineteenth Century* (Four Courts Press, 2017).

Simone McCaughren is a lecturer in the School of Applied Social Studies, University College Cork. She is the course director for the Bachelor of Social Work programme and the deputy course director of the PhD in Social Work. Her main research interests include adoption law, policy and practice and children's rights. She has written a number of articles on the subject areas of both domestic and international adoption and regularly engages in media discussion and debates.

Deirdre McGowan is a lecturer and the Head of Law at the School of Languages, Law and Social Sciences at Dublin Institute of Technology. She is the author of *The Normalising Power of Marriage Law: An Irish Genealogy 1945–2010* (Maynooth, 2015).

Thomas Mohr is an assistant professor at the School of Law, University College Dublin. He is Honorary Secretary of the Irish Legal History Society and Book Review Editor of the *Irish Jurist*, Ireland's oldest law journal. His publications on Irish legal history range in subject from the medieval Brehon law to the law of the independent Irish state in the twentieth century. His latest publication is *Guardian of the Treaty – The Privy Council Appeal and Irish Sovereignty* (Four Courts Press, 2016). This concerns an important aspect of the Irish Free State's relationship with the British Empire in the interwar years.

Mary O'Dowd is Professor of Gender History in Queen's University Belfast. She is author of *A History of Women in Ireland, 1500–1800* (2005) and is co-author of a forthcoming study of marriage in Ireland, 1660–1925.

Fred Powell is Professor of Social Policy and former Dean of Social Science at University College Cork. His most recent book is *Dark Secrets of Childhood: Media Power, Child Abuse and Public Scandals* (co-authored with Margaret Scanlon) (Policy Press, 2015).

Michael Sinnott is a recent graduate of University College Dublin and the University of Cambridge. He works in the Banking and Financial Services Group of Matheson, a Dublin-based law firm, and is also a company law tutor at the Sutherland School of Law, University College Dublin. His main current research interests include the constitutional and judicial relationships between the kingdoms of Ireland and Great Britain during the eighteenth century as well as the scope of public law in modern Irish law.

Diane Urquhart is a reader in modern Irish history at the Institute of Irish Studies of the University of Liverpool. She is a graduate of Queen's University, Belfast and a former postdoctoral fellow of the Institute of Irish Studies at Queen's. She has published widely on women and political activism and legislative reform. She is the author of *The Ladies of Londonderry: Women and Political Patronage, 1800–1959* (I. B. Tauris, 2008) and *Women in Ulster Politics, 1890–1940: A History Not Yet Told* (Irish Academic Press, 2007). She is the editor of *The Papers of the Ulster Women's Unionist Council and Executive Committee, 1911–40* (Irish Manuscripts Commission, 2001) and co-editor of *Irish Women at War: The Twentieth Century* (Irish Academic Press, 2010); *Irish Women's History* (Irish Academic Press, 2004); *The Irish Women's History Reader* (Routledge, 2000) and *Coming Into the Light: The Work, Politics and Religion of Women in Ulster, 1840–1940* (Institute of Irish Studies, 1994). Diane is currently completing a history of Irish divorce.

1
Introduction

Niamh Howlin and Kevin Costello

In the course of the House of Commons debates on the enactment of the Divorce and Matrimonial Causes Act 1857, the Cambridge MP and barrister Loftus Wigram observed how social attitudes to family law differed between Ireland and England. The 'position of society as regards this question was very different in England from what it was in Ireland',[1] he said. While, in the nineteenth and early twentieth centuries, England and Ireland shared the same legal tradition, and while the legal framework governing the family was similar, there were differences. In Ireland, the penal laws had left their mark into the early nineteenth century. Some inter-religious marriages celebrated by Catholic and Dissenting ministers remained either illegal or doubtful up to the mid-nineteenth century. The match system of marriage negotiation endured in Ireland into the twentieth century, and dowries were still being transferred between families in rural Ireland into the 1940s. The English nineteenth-century divorce reforms, and the Divorce and Matrimonial Causes Act of 1857, were never extended to Ireland. Legislation regulating adoption was enacted later in Ireland than it had been in England. Article 41 of the 1937 Constitution imposed a constraint on State intervention into married life quite unlike anything known to English law. The causes of action for breach of promise of marriage and criminal conversation remained available in Ireland into the 1980s, long after they were abolished in England. The Irish family has, in some respects, had its own distinct legal history.

These 12 essays began life as contributions to a small round table workshop on the history of the Irish family, organized by University College Dublin's Legal History Research Group in 2015, with the object of placing the legal doctrine in a socio-historical context and covering the principal stages of married life, starting with engagement and the legal formalities of marriage up to the breakdown of marriage.

The topic of divorce is the subject of three essays. Mary O'Dowd's account of marriage breakdown in the eighteenth century (Chapter 2) sets the

1 *Hansard 3 (Commons)* CXLVII 755 (30 Jul 1857).

context in which the nineteenth-century law operated. The evidence of marriage breakdown in eighteenth century is scattered and very incomplete. O'Dowd shows how women in particular used the church courts to obtain divorces *a mensa et thoro* and the higher-grade *a vinculo matrimonii*. Elopement notices placed in newspapers by wounded husbands provide even more valuable evidence that married life was not as stable as it is sometimes supposed.

The second of the divorce studies, Diane Urquhart's essay on marriage dissolution in Ireland from 1850 to 1950 (Chapter 7), describes the range of legal processes available to deal with marriage breakdown in the nineteenth century and early twentieth century: parliamentary divorce, the separation *a mensa et thoro*, the nullity action and the separation deed. The parliamentary divorce, available in Ireland up to 1925, was 'a truly aristocratic indulgence'. Up to the 1880s the grounds of divorce discriminated between men and women: men could obtain divorce on grounds of adultery. Women petitioners carried the heavier burden of proving aggravated, incestuous adultery or adultery coupled with bigamy or cruelty. The grounds of parliamentary divorce were liberalized when the bill promoted by the pioneering Irish petitioner, Louisa Westropp, in 1886 established desertion and marital cruelty as grounds of divorce. But the numbers availing of the parliamentary procedure remained tiny. The possibility of parliamentary divorce disappeared with the birth of the Irish Free State, leaving unhappy couples with even less recourse. Similarly, the numbers petitioning for an order of separation and alimony, originally from the ecclesiastical courts and, after 1871, from the High Court, were also negligible. Physical violence was a factor in most of these applications, which were overwhelmingly wife-initiated. Irish and English practice and social attitudes were now evolving in different directions. While full, court-sanctioned divorce *a vinculo matrimonii* was available in England from 1857 onwards, the Irish courts offered only the weaker remedy of separation, and while no more than 30 Irish spouses annually petitioned for separation in the first decade of the twentieth century, the number of spouses in England seeking divorce was near 800. The reluctance to use legal processes led many people in dysfunctional relationships to remain living together, despite incompatibility or even abuse. Others simply abandoned their spouses. Marital desertion, according to Urquhart, may also have been a motivating factor in Irish emigration.

Deirdre McGowan (Chapter 8) continues into the twentieth century the theme of marriage breakdown, exploring the links between marriage breakdown, poverty and social disorder. In post-independence Ireland, marriages were frequently entered into on the basis of economic necessity rather than mutual affection. McGowan describes rural marriages in particular as economic transactions involving the settlement of land and the transfer of money and spouses from one household to another. As such, marriage breakdown was almost inconceivable, given the difficulties involved in undoing the financial arrangements and the undesirability of subdividing rural land. Nevertheless, alternative practices evolved, such as childless wives returning to their families of origin, men seasonally migrating for work, or couples simply living separate lives under one roof. Legal remedies were largely ignored. Uniquely, McGowan also constructs the experience of the urban and middle classes who experienced marital difficulties, using the law reports as a sociological resource. Finally, this chapter considers the implication of relationship breakdown in poorer, urban families. Without the safety nets of either money or land, these were the families which suffered most severely. Financial support for deserted wives was minimal and discretionary, and many such women and their children ended up being institutionalized.

Maebh's Harding's paper (Chapter 3) addresses two themes in the law of marriage formation in early nineteenth-century Ireland: the clandestine marriage and the mixed marriage. The probability is that marriage *per verba de praesenti* – the exchange of vows in words of the present tense – was neither widely practised nor legally recognized in late eighteenth- and early nineteenth-century Ireland. Instead, the demand for clandestine marriage in early nineteenth-century Ireland was met by the couple beggar – degraded clergy who had been deprived of a benefice and who carried out semi-legal marriages for a fee. As many as 37,000 couple beggar marriages were recorded as having been celebrated in South Dublin in the first half of the nineteenth century. While these marriages were regarded as legally valid, the legal validity of some varieties of mixed marriage was less secure. A particular problem in Ulster was the status of a mixed marriage between a Dissenter and a member of the Established Church, and officiated by a Non-Conformist minister. The issue divided the House of Lords in 1844 in *R v Millis*, and led to the enactment of the first marriage reform act of the nineteenth century, the Marriages Act 1844.

Michael Sinnott (Chapter 4) contextualizes the legal action of breach of promise of marriage amongst the range of 'enforcement mechanisms of the social structures of nineteenth-century Ireland'. The social institution which it maintained was the marriage engagement. In the first half of the nineteenth century when the action was at its height, the breakdown of a woman's engagement was life shattering. While a man, as Daniel O'Connell explained in 1823, 'had a thousand chances and a thousand occupations', the woman 'had only one prize in the lottery of life – the chance of a husband'. A fascinated public flocked to the courts to attend breach of promise trials, and the newspaper accounts of breach of promise actions provide a rich source of information, not merely about the litigation strategies devised by the lawyers managing these cases, but, also about the intimate romantic lives of the nineteenth-century Irish middle class. By the 1870s a reaction was beginning to set in; some viewed breach of promise as an 'engine of legalized plunder'. While breach of promise continued to be litigated into the twentieth century, its popularity was in decline.

A second legal process which served as a moral enforcement mechanism was the action by way of criminal conversation taken by cuckolded husbands against the men who seduced their wives. Niamh Howlin's study of criminal conversation (Chapter 6) shows how, soon after the surge of actions for criminal conversation in England in the 1790s, a similar phenomenon occurred in early nineteenth-century Irish courts. In Ireland, actions for criminal conversation were usually tried before special juries, and, as in England, pleaded on the case, since this avoided 'the potential unpleasantness of having to delve into the specific details of the extramarital intercourse'. Originally damages were awarded penally, to punish the seducer; by the nineteenth century the object of damages had shifted. Damages were being awarded to recognize the hurt to cuckolded husband, the harm caused by the infidelity to the marriage as a whole, and the disturbance to relations with the couple's children. After its peak in the early nineteenth century, the action entered a decline; but unlike England, where it was abolished in 1857, it both remained in place and was used until the late twentieth century.

The economic liberties of married women is the subject of Kevin Costello's essay on married women's property (Chapter 5). Married women were denied even the right to their own property by the common law rule that a married woman's property vested in her husband. It is sometimes claimed that in nineteenth century England wealthy families protected their daughters by using the marriage settlement trust (a legally recognized device through which money could be channelled to the wife free from her husband's claims). But an examination of marriage settlements made by landed upper-class families in mid-nineteenth-century Ireland indicates that, while the device was used, it was not standard. Law reform came in 1870 and 1882. Progressive circles in Ireland played a part in this law reform movement: the campaign was initiated at the 1867 Belfast Conference of the National Association for the Promotion of Social Science, and branches of the Married Women's Property Association operated in Dublin and Belfast. The married women's property acts allowed women to dispose of their own property. But the legislation was premised on married women having property in the first place. Since married women remained economically dependent on their husbands, the extent to which they could exercise the economic liberties, which the 1870–1882 reforms gave them, was limited.

Family violence in twentieth-century Ireland is the subject of two essays. The secrecy surrounding relationship dysfunction features strongly in Lindsey Earner-Byrne's examination of domestic abuse in the early twentieth century (Chapter 9). In particular, she considers State responses to the sexual and physical abuse of children, which, for a variety of reasons, went largely unprosecuted. The 1937 Constitution brought with it an emphasis on the family unit, arguably at the expense of safeguarding the rights of individual family members. The second essay to pursue this theme, Karen Brennan's 'Murder in the Irish Family, 1930–1945' (Chapter 10) conducts a close study of the criminal justice system's responses to homicide which took place in a family context between 1930 and 1944. She reviews 27 cases of family homicide from the State Files and State Books for the Central Criminal Court, representing a mix of male and female victims and killers. An overview of the cases indicates, unsurprisingly, that women were more likely than men to be acquitted of murder or manslaughter charges: over 80 per cent of the women tried before juries were acquitted, while none of the male defendants were. Did the gender of the accused affect the outcome? The more lenient treatment of female killers has long been accepted. But, by closely examining the sources, Brennan demonstrates that each of these acquittals could be attributed to evidential deficiencies; many of the female defendants appear to have killed by poisoning – an inherently secretive act. A second finding is the high proportion of family homicide cases which were disposed of on the basis of an insanity-related finding (either unfitness to plead or guilty but insane). Contemporary analyses of female violence note a tendency to 'medicalize' female offenders, but Brennan demonstrates that Irish courts during this period were more likely to medicalize male offenders, possibly in an attempt to explain what otherwise appear to be inexplicable acts of extreme violence against family members. This chapter challenges a number of received ideas about gendered aspects of the criminal justice system.

The stigma attached to single motherhood in the nineteenth and early twentieth centuries led many women to take drastic steps. Women who killed their newborn babies potentially faced prosecution for murder, or for the lesser charge of concealment of birth under the Malicious Shooting Act 1803. The 1803 Act made it an offence by 'secret burying, or otherwise, [to] endeavour to conceal the birth' of a child born alive. 'Precision', declared the Lord Chief Justice, James Whiteside, in 1874 was 'essential' in proving offences under the 1803 Act and 'nobody can be convicted under our criminal law where the case is left in obscurity and doubt'. Elaine Farrell's close study of concealment of birth cases (Chapter 11) shows how defendants in birth concealment trials were assisted by the criminal courts' strict construction of elements of the *actus reus* such as the requirement of 'concealment'.

The problem of children being taken out of the country for adoption by American Catholic families underlay, in part, the enactment of the Adoption Act 1952, the topic which is the subject of 'The Fate of the "Illegitimate" Child: An Analysis of Irish Social Policy 1750–1952' (Chapter 12). McCaughren and Powell trace the social, economic and political factors which led to the passing of the Adoption Act 1952. The practice of allowing American Catholic couples to adopt Irish babies with minimal paperwork, record keeping or suitability checks was highlighted in the press and, together with pressure from the Adoption Society, appears to have forced the government to enact the 1952 Act.

The articles concerning the family are among the best known and most controversial provisions of the 1937 Irish Constitution. Their inclusion is often contrasted with the absence of any equivalent provisions in the text of the preceding 1922 Constitution of the Irish Free State. The Irish Free State Constitution of 1922 has sometimes been praised as the model of a liberal democratic constitution, while the provisions of the Constitution of 1937 in Article 41 which affect the family are seen as reactionary. But as Thomas Mohr points out in Chapter 13, the 1937 Constitution is not explained by a radical regression in values. The drafters of both Constitutions had almost identical attitudes concerning the position of the family in Irish society. He argues that the real difference between the drafters of these two Constitutions were their ideas of the proper function of a national constitution. In 1922 the drafters prioritized brevity and simplicity, were less confident in their social vision, and preferred a constitution that was functional and dealt with institutional affairs. By contrast, the 1937 Constitution enshrined ideals that were intended to inspire and direct the future development of the State. In 1922 it was considered unwise and unnecessary to enshrine the nature and position of the family in the text of a national constitution. In 1937 it was considered essential to do so.

The history of the family and family law in England and Wales has been the subject of study for some years now, thanks to scholarship by Stephen Cretney,[2] Rebecca Probert[3] and others. However, while the importance of legal institutions and norms in regulating family life and personal relationships in Ireland is generally accepted, to date there has been no systematic, interdisciplinary examination of these issues in a historical context.[4] This book is an effort to redress this deficit. But it is far from comprehensive, and there is still more work to be done. A fuller exposition of the laws and practices relating to inheritance and succession, for example, would be of considerable assistance to those researching family history, as well as the history of property law more broadly. Similarly, the form and substance of nineteenth-century ecclesiastical law is an area meriting further exploration; as indeed is the relationship between law and religion more generally.

2 For example S Cretney (2005) *Family Law in the Twentieth Century. A History* (Oxford: Oxford University Press).

3 For example R Probert (2009) *Marriage Law and Practice in the Long Eighteenth Century: A Reassessment* (Cambridge: Cambridge University Press); R Probert (2012) *The Changing Legal Regulation of Cohabitation: From Fornicators to Family, 1600–2010* (Cambridge: Cambridge University Press); R Probert (2009) 'Control Over Marriage in England and Wales, 1753–1823: The Clandestine Marriages Act of 1753 in Context', *Law and History Review*, 27(2), 413–450.

4 Although a number of works have considered the history of marriage, e.g. A Shatter (1997) *Family Law* (Dublin: Butterworths); A Cosgrave (1985) *Marriage in Ireland* (Dublin: College Press); D Fitzpatrick (1987) 'Divorce and Separation in Modern Irish history', *Past and Present*, 114(1), 172–196.

2
Marriage Breakdown in Ireland, c. 1660–1857

*Mary O'Dowd**

In 1996, when the Irish parliament passed the Family Law (Divorce) Act, it was hailed as the introduction of divorce to Ireland. Yet it had been possible for men and women to secure divorces of various kinds from the earliest times. Early Irish law permitted divorce, as did canon law. By the later medieval period, ecclesiastical courts were empowered to grant divorces, even if a divorced spouse was not always permitted to remarry. In the eighteenth century, the Irish Parliament followed the precedent set by Westminster and began to approve the dissolution of marriages by private act of parliament. In addition, the different Christian denominations each had their own distinct regulations on marital dissolution, some of which also permitted remarriage in certain circumstances. Outside of the formal structures of Church and State, men and women made their own informal arrangements to leave unhappy marriages. The aim of this chapter is to survey the different forms of divorce and marriage separation that were possible prior to the mid-nineteenth century and to suggest that married couples living apart, and even remarrying, were more common than might be assumed.

Ecclesiastical courts, which existed in every diocese until the dissolution of the Church of Ireland in 1869,[1] presided over the implementation of marriage law as defined by a mixture of statute and canon law. The officials in the court determined the validity of marriages, heard disputes between couples and considered requests for divorce. The courts permitted two types of divorce. The first, *a vinculo matrimonii* (i.e. from the chains of marriage) was, in effect, a judgment that the marriage was null and void because it had never existed in the first place. According to canon law, divorce *a vinculo*

---

* The research for this paper formed part of the UK Arts and Humanities Research Council-funded project on the History of Marriage in Ireland, directed by Professor Maria Luddy and the author. The author is grateful for the assistance of the project's postdoctoral fellows and researcher, Dr Katy Barclay, Dr John Bergin and Dr Leanne Calvert.

1 Irish Church Act 1869 (32 & 33 Vic c 42).

matrimonii could be granted if one of the partners was incapable, mentally or physically, from consummating the marriage, or if it could be proved that force was used to coerce an individual into marriage. Bigamy and marrying within the prohibited degrees of affinity and coercion were also valid reasons for voiding a marriage. The second type of divorce considered by the ecclesiastical court was a divorce *a mensa et thoro* or from 'bed and board'. Such suits were, in effect, requests for judicial separation and were frequently initiated by wives seeking maintenance from their husbands. Unlike the divorce *a vinculo matrimonii*, a divorce *a mensa et thoro* did not permit either partner to remarry.

The records of the medieval diocesan court in Armagh have survived but we have very little documentation from the early modern Irish ecclesiastical court system.[2] A collection of petitions and a court book for the late seventeenth- and early eighteenth-century consistory court at Killaloe suggests that the court regularly, if not frequently, dealt with requests for divorce and separation.[3] Details of two requests for a divorce *a vinculo matrimonii* survive among the petitions presented to the ecclesiastical court in Killaloe at the start of the eighteenth century. Both suits were initiated by women, and in each case the wife cited impotency as the reason for her request for divorce. In 1703, Catherine Butler explained to the vicar general, John Hawkins, that she had 'cohabited and bedded' with her husband William Ryan for six months but they had not had sexual intercourse. William, according to Catherine, claimed that he had been bewitched by another woman to whom he had returned, having abandoned Catherine. Catherine also alleged that William had threatened to murder her and that she was afraid to meet with either him or his brothers and sisters on the road.[4] There were clearly a number of problems in the marital relations of William and Catherine but impotency was the only ground on which a complete dissolution of the marriage could be granted. In the second case, Elizabeth Hogan explained through her Catholic barrister or advocate, Florence Macnamara, that she and her husband, David Seymer had been married in a Catholic service three years before.[5] David, however, according to Elizabeth's petition, had 'always failed to perform conjugal society'. Elizabeth claimed that she had 'with great patience' continued to receive the 'affection and embraces' of David 'in such a manner as a wife ought ... to doe but God knowes to little purpose'. Elizabeth's 'friends'

2 On the medieval court, see A Cosgrove (1985) 'Marriage in Medieval Ireland' in A Cosgrove (ed), *Marriage in Ireland* (Dublin: College Press), 25–50.

3 Papers of the Consistory Court of Killaloe, 1671–1824 (British Library, Add. MS 31,881–31,882).

4 Papers of the Consistory Court of Killaloe (BL, Add. MS 31,881, fo. 150).

5 Papers of the Consistory Court of Killaloe (BL, Add. MS 31,881, fos 138–140). Florence Macnamara, a leading Catholic barrister, signed the petition. The author is grateful to Dr John Bergin for this information.

advised her be patient for three years and then to appeal to the ecclesiastical court for a divorce.[6]

The vicar general accepted both women's petitions and gave them permission to sue *in forma pauperis*. The outcome of the two suits is unknown but the surviving records of the Irish ecclesiastical courts suggest that such cases were rare and it is likely, therefore, that a strong and convincing case would have to be presented before the court would consider a petition for this type of divorce. There are no pleas for divorce *a vinculo matrimonii* among the fragmentary diocesan court records in the National Archives of Ireland. Instead, all the cases documented relate to the second type of divorce considered by the court, a divorce *a mensa et thoro*.[7] Adultery and/or cruelty were nearly always the reasons given for such requests. In 1767, for example, Ann Grace sued her husband John for a divorce 'for cruelty and adultery and payment of alimony' in the Dublin Consistorial Court. In her statement to the court, Ann told how she and John had been married in 1757 in a Church of Ireland service in Athlone. The couple had a number of children. John was a soldier and was stationed initially in Athlone but Ann claimed that John did not provide adequately for his family and that he had physically abused her. She alleged that he had dragged her by the hair of her head and had threatened to shoot her. When John was transferred to Dublin, he did not take his family with him but Ann followed him there 'being unable to subsist at Athlone where she had been left quite destitute'. When, in 1764, Ann threatened to tell her father-in-law how his son had treated his wife, John agreed to live again with her. But within weeks, he had left her and refused to pay any maintenance for herself or her children. John subsequently began to live with another woman by whom he had children and, who, according to Ann's account, John called 'Mrs Grace and sayed she was his wife'. John did not appear in the court to answer Ann's charges. In the other divorce cases in the Dublin Consistory Court, litigation was also delayed because of the non-attendance of the husband. This may, therefore, have been a common tactic by defendants attempting to avoid a judgment that instructed them to pay maintenance to separated spouses.[8]

Ann Grace's statement for the ecclesiastical court presented her as the victim of her husband's cruelty as well as his adultery, a combination necessary to win her suit for divorce. The definition of cruelty in a marriage was, however, legally ambiguous. Legal historians have traced the changing definitions of the term in the English court system from the early modern

6 Such a plea could only be brought following three years of marriage which is why Elizabeth waited that long before presenting her request.

7 Dublin Consistory Court Cause Papers (National Archives of Ireland (NAI), Box 4/271/37); Killaloe Court and Register Book 1707–1868 (NAI, Box 4/201/31; Tuam Consistory Court Book, 1740–1742 (NAI, M 6833)).

8 *Grace v Grace*, 1768 (Dublin Consistorial Court Cause Papers, NAI, Box 4/271/37).

period.[9] In the sixteenth and seventeenth centuries, cruelty administered by a spouse (in almost all cases, the husband) was defined as life-threatening physical abuse but by the late eighteenth century, the definition was expanded to include the threat of violence or persistent verbal abuse. The Irish documentation is not sufficient to explore the ways in which Irish judges changed their understanding of marital cruelty but there are some indications that they had done so by the early nineteenth century. In 1824, John Radcliffe, the judge in the Dublin Consistory Court, warned that the court could not interfere in 'ordinary domestic quarrels' and 'that there may be much unhappiness from unkind treatment, or violent and abusive language in which no relief can be had here'. The court had to be convinced that there was 'something which renders the cohabitation unsafe or is likely to be attended with injury to a person or health of the party, in order to warrant the interposition of the court'.[10] Radcliffe did, however, acknowledge that the threat of violence could be considered within the understanding of 'cruelty'. Radcliffe also specified that 'words of menace' could be defined as cruelty if the threat behind them appeared to be real.[11]

The ecclesiastical courts, thus, provided a means through which women with abusive husbands might appeal for relief. The threat of a public shaming may have persuaded some men to agree to pay maintenance to their wives. The ability to sue *in forma pauperis* opened the facilities of the court to poor women, although it is impossible to assess how many women availed themselves of this opportunity, or if the number of women suing decreased in the course of the eighteenth century, as was the case in England.

The petition of Elizabeth Hogan indicates that the ecclesiastical court system was used by Catholic petitioners. The legal process of securing an annulment of a Catholic marriage was, however, complicated by the fact that the Church authorities might not necessarily have recognized the legal dissolution of the marriage. If the marriage of Hogan and Seymer had been dissolved by the diocesan court in Killaloe, they would still have been obliged to request a second annulment from the Catholic Church if they intended to remarry in a Catholic service.

Given the legal restrictions on the Catholic Church in the eighteenth century, it is not clear how such requests were processed but it is likely that procedures differed between dioceses and over time. In the 1750s in the diocese of Ossory, Archbishop Butler organized meetings of priests in parochial churches which acted as ecclesiastical courts to which the parties involved in a divorce case were summoned and questioned. Advocates presented arguments for the

---

9 E Foyster (2005) *Marital Violence: An English Family History, 1660–1857* (Cambridge: Cambridge University Press), pp 32–39.

10 CR Milward (1847) *Reports of Cases Argued and Determined in the Court of Prerogative in Ireland and in the Consistory Court of Dublin during the time of the Late Hon. John Radcliffe, LLD* (Dublin: Hodges and Smith), p 159.

11 Milward (1847) *Reports*, pp 159–161.

defence and the prosecution and witnesses were summoned to provide evidence.[12] In late eighteenth-century Galway, on the other hand, there is no evidence of such a regulated administrative system. Enquiries into the validity of marriages and related issues appear to have been undertaken in a more confidential fashion with parochial priests interrogating the individuals concerned and determining the judgment in private.[13]

Whether it was done privately or publicly, the Catholic clergy determining requests for marriage separation drew on the same legacy of canon law as the ecclesiastical courts. Not surprisingly, therefore, the laws for granting divorces *a vinculo matrimonii* were very similar. Impotency, the absence of consent, mental incapacity and consanguinity were valid grounds for pronouncing a marriage null and void within the Catholic Church. Among the Galway diocesan records is a document dating to the middle decades of the eighteenth century outlining the grounds for the divorce of Henry and Margaret Joyce. Henry was described as 'much older' than his wife and it was clear from her examination that Margaret had been unwilling to marry him. 'She ... opposed their marriage and openly declared her unwillingness ... She suffered ill treatment such as beating, scolding from her mother and friends in order to force her to it.' Despite the urging of her family, however, the parish priest refused to marry the couple without the consent of both partners. Eventually, however, he was summoned at night and told that Margaret had consented to marriage. The priest insisted on examining her in private and she told him that although 'she had a dislike to the man as a partner' she would agree to marry him to 'please her mother and friends'. Although the marriage ceremony took place, Margaret refused to cohabit with Henry, claiming that she had feigned her consent out of fear. In his examination, Henry revealed to the priest that he had discovered on the first night of the marriage that he was impotent and had tried without success to find a cure for the condition. There were thus two possible grounds for a divorce: the absence of consent and impotency. If, however, the divorce was granted on the failure to consummate the marriage, Margaret and Henry would be obliged, as the ecclesiastical court also required, to cohabit for three years to which, it was noted, Margaret 'can't be persuaded to agree'. The clerical recommendation was, therefore, that the divorce be granted on 'the defect of the consent on the part of the woman'.[14]

The author of this advice also implied that divorce cases were highly unusual in the diocese and that granting a divorce on grounds of impotency should be avoided as it might lead others to make similar claims that would be difficult to prove. The rarity of such cases is supported by the evidence of

12 C O'Dwyer (1975) (ed), 'Archbishop Butler's Visitation Book', *Archivium Hibernicum*, XXXIII, 1–90; XXXIV, 1–49.

13 Based on an exploration of the documents in the Galway Diocesan Archive (GDA).

14 GDA, Box 8/file 1.

the visitation book of the diocese of Ossory in which four cases of divorce are noted for the years 1750–1794. Two dissolutions were requested on the grounds of impotency and two because the couple were related within the prohibited degrees of consanguinity.[15] In the latter cases, there is a suggestion that consanguinity proved a convenient means of securing a canonically valid dissolution, a practice that had a long tradition in medieval and early modern Ireland.[16]

Of the three main Christian denominations, Presbyterianism had the most liberal attitude towards the dissolution of marriage. According to the Westminster Confession of Faith (1646), it was permissible for a person to sue for divorce if a partner committed adultery and 'after the divorce to marry another, as if the offending party were dead'. Divorce was also possible in the event of 'wilful desertion as can no way be remedied by the Church or civil magistrate'.[17] The power to permit a couple to divorce was vested in the Presbytery and surviving records suggest that while individuals were granted permission to divorce, it was a relatively rare occurrence. In 1786, for example, the Presbytery of Down agreed that Thomas Thompson could remarry because his wife had 'eloped from him and behaved very improperly'.[18] In 1840, however, when a man whose wife had deserted him, emigrated to America and remarried enquired if he too could remarry, the Presbytery was uncertain how to answer him. The clerk was instructed to look through previous minutes of the Presbytery to discover 'what had been the practice in similar cases'. The man was eventually granted permission to remarry as his wife had 'voluntarily and without cause deserted him'.[19] The hesitancy of the Presbytery suggests that such requests were infrequent. As in the other main Christian denominations, the elders and ministers in the session and the Presbytery were primarily concerned to maintain marriage bonds rather than dissolve them.

As was the case with Catholics who secured a church annulment, a man or woman granted a divorce by a Presbytery might not have been able to remarry in a ceremony that would have been recognized by an ecclesiastical court. As discussed by Maebh Harding (Chapter 3), the civil law on bigamy

15 C O'Dwyer (1975) (ed), 'Archbishop Butler's Visitation Book', *Archivium Hibernicum* XXXIII, pp 22, 23–24, 30, 32; XXXIV pp 4, 30.

16 M O'Dowd (forthcoming 2017) 'Men, Women, Children and the Family 1550–1730' in J Ohlmeyer (ed), *Cambridge History of Ireland, vol. 2* (Cambridge: Cambridge University Press).

17 *The Westminster Confession of Faith* (1646), chapter xxiv, article v, vi. See also Westminster Assembly (1764) *The Assembly's Shorter Catechism Explained, By Way of Question and Answer. Part Second. Of the Duty Which God Requires of Man* (Belfast: Daniel Blow), p 101; A Holmes (2006) *The Shaping of Ulster Presbyterian Belief and Practice, 1770–1840* (Oxford: Oxford University Press), pp 212, 223.

18 Minutes of the Presbytery of Down, 23 August 1786 (Presbyterian Historical Society Belfast).

19 Ibid., 6 Jul 1841.

permitted a person to remarry if their partner had been missing for seven years or more. If, as seems to have been the case, Presbyteries granted divorces and gave permission to remarry to individuals who had been deserted for shorter periods of time, then the second or subsequent marriages would have been deemed bigamous under civil law. Such partnerships, although illegal, appear to have been tolerated at a community level. Individuals were willing to live with marriages that were considered illegal by the State but approved by their respective churches. This presumably did not become a significant issue unless there was a disagreement between the couple or their heirs that drew legal attention to the marriage.

In summary, the laws and regulations of the State and all of the main churches were designed to discourage the breaking of marriage bonds, and permitted dissolution in very limited circumstances. Throughout the eighteenth century, however, lawyers and judges in Ireland and England began to stretch interpretations of the civil law to permit recognition of forms of judicial separation which were not regulated by the ecclesiastical courts. Divorce by private parliamentary act was a possibility from the early eighteenth century but this was an expensive and lengthy process, limited in practice to wealthy men who accused their wives of adultery and questioned the paternity of the heirs to their estates.[20] A husband, but not a wife, could petition the House of Lords for a dissolution of marriage. In order to do so, however, he was obliged to initiate law suits in both the ecclesiastical and civil courts and then participate in a parliamentary investigation into the marriage. The court cases could also attract considerable public interest with lengthy reports filling the pages of the burgeoning newspaper industry. Unsurprisingly, the number of divorce petitions was small. Bergin estimates that there were 11 petitions for private divorce acts presented to the eighteenth-century Irish parliament and about another dozen Irish petitions presented to the Westminster parliament.[21]

From the early eighteenth century, separating couples with material assets to be distributed might take some of the legal steps necessary in a parliamentary divorce without incurring either the expense or the publicity involved. Through a private deed of separation, a man might arrange for annual maintenance for his wife while at the same time declaring that she would from henceforth be treated as a *feme sole* or single woman. The change in legal status meant that the husband would no longer be economically responsible for his wife and that she could sign contracts and earn an income in her own name.[22] Additional clauses might permit the wife to keep company

20 See Chapter 7 in this volume.

21 J Bergin (2009) 'Irish Private Divorce Bills and Acts of the Eighteenth Century' in J Kelly, J McCafferty and CI McGrath (eds), *People, Politics and Power: Essays on Irish History in Honour of James I McGuire* (Dublin: University College Dublin Press), 94–121.

22 See Chapter 5 in this volume.

or cohabit with whomsoever she wished.[23] Although such agreements contradicted the legal definition of the duties and responsibilities of husbands and wives in a marriage, Stone suggests that by the late eighteenth century private deeds of separation were considered valid in equity if not in common law.[24] In 1824, a ruling in the Irish King's Bench concluded that a separation agreement was 'inveterate in the law, and cannot be questioned'.[25] By the late nineteenth century, private deeds of settlement were regularly used by separating couples.[26]

A private deed of separation may have been cheaper than a parliamentary divorce but it still involved the employment of lawyers and was beyond the means of most people who wanted to escape from an unhappy marriage. As Diane Urquhart and Deirdre McGowan explain in Chapters 7 and 8 respectively, the simplest and cheapest way for a spouse to leave a marriage was, of course, to run away or desert the marital home. And, clearly, both men and women did just that although the extent to which they did is difficult to quantify. In 1838, the Poor Law legislation[27] gave the Poor Law Guardians the authority to prosecute deserting fathers and husbands in order to compel them to pay for the maintenance of their wives and children.

Prior to the 1830s, one source which gives us some evidence of deserting spouses are the notices placed in newspapers by husbands announcing that their wives had eloped or run away. Such notices appear in Irish newspapers from the second half of the eighteenth century through to the 1830s. They can be found scattered throughout Dublin newspapers as well as some regional ones. The notices were clearly placed by both Catholic and Protestant men but there was undoubtedly a distinct concentration of elopement notices in the *Belfast Newsletter*. Between 1750 and 1800, over 900 notices were placed in the newspaper by husbands reporting the elopement of their wives. The large number of elopement notices that appeared in the *Belfast Newsletter* suggests that this was a particularly Protestant (and probably Presbyterian) phenomenon. At least two of the notices in the *Belfast Newsletter* were placed by Presbyterian ministers.[28] Many of the notices stipulate that the wife had eloped 'without any unreasonable cause' or 'unprovoked' by any action on the part of the husband. Although there were legal reasons for the inclusion of these phrases, they also echoed the Presbyterian Church's

23 D Wilson (2009) *Women, Marriage and Property in Wealthy Landed Families in Ireland, 1750–1850* (Manchester University Press), pp 134–137.

24 Lawrence Stone (1990) *Road to Divorce: England 1530–1987* (Oxford: Oxford University Press), pp 153–155.

25 *MacDonnell v Murphy* (1824) 2 Fox and Smith 279–305. I am grateful to Dr Niamh Howlin for this reference.

26 M Luddy and M O'Dowd (forthcoming, 2017), *A History of Marriage in Ireland, 1660–1925*.

27 1 & 2 Vic c 56.

28 See notices placed by Reverend James Jackson and Reverent Arthur McKee in *Belfast Newsletter*, 11, 28 Jan 1763 and 14 Oct 1783.

requirement that a divorce could only be granted if there was evidence of 'wilful desertion'.[29]

While not all men who advertised the elopement of their wives noted their occupation, of those that did most came from the middling to lower ranks of society. In the notices placed in the *Belfast Newsletter*, 62 per cent of husbands described themselves as farmers; 14 per cent as weavers or linen weavers and 12 per cent as labourers. There were also smaller numbers of craftsmen including shoemakers, blacksmiths, a baker, a carpenter, a tanner and a miller (see Table 2.1). Although the notices were placed in an

Table 2.1 Occupations of husbands who placed elopement notices in the Belfast Newsletter, 1750–1800

Occupations	*Number*
Farmer	62
Weaver	14
Labourer	12
Shoemaker	8
Blacksmith	4
Carpenter	3
Minister	3
Mariner/Sailor	3
Soldier	2
Shopkeeper	2
Flax Dresser	1
Gardener	1
Glazier	1
Goodsman	1
Huckster	1
Currier	1
Baker	1
Miller	1
Soap boiler and chandler	1
Tanner	1
Taylor	1
Mason	1
Total	125

29 See below for the legal reason for the inclusion of a clause denying the husband's liability in his wife's departure.

urban-based newspaper, there were very few merchants or businessmen in the list of occupations. The addresses of the majority of husbands were also from rural areas.[30]

In the notices placed in the *Ennis Chronicle and Clare Advertiser* there was a similar predominance of rural addresses although few of the men listed their occupations. The elopement notices placed in Dublin newspapers were inserted by locksmiths, dealers and other small businessmen with a similar lower middle-class background. Many of the men appear to have been illiterate. Forty-three per cent of the men who placed advertisements in the *Ennis Chronicle and Clare Advertiser*, for example, could not sign their name. This suggests that clerks or scribes were employed to write the notices on behalf of the men, a practice which also helps explain why some of the notices in particular newspapers denounced the departed wife in exactly the same words.[31]

The legal rationale behind the elopement notices lay in a husband's responsibility to pay for the maintenance or the 'necessaries' for his wife which was interpreted as 'food, lodging, clothing, medical attendance and medicine'.[32] If, however, a wife eloped then the husband was no longer responsibility for supporting her in this way.[33] The public notice to traders was to warn them of the wife's elopement and the husband's repudiation of any debts she might accumulate. The newspaper advertisement was, therefore, a form of insurance against claims from traders who gave a wife credit in her husband's name. Some husbands also threatened to prosecute anyone who harboured or assisted his wife. Most notices also made clear that the wife had left the marital home without provocation from her husband. The insertion of this clause was an attempt to make clear that the husband had done nothing which had led to his wife's departure. If, at a subsequent legal proceeding, a wife could argue that she left the marital home because her husband had physically abused her or had committed adultery, then she would be entitled to claim maintenance from him. An unprovoked elopement guaranteed her no such right.[34]

30 This analysis is based on a database of the notices in the *Belfast Newsletter* compiled by Rebecca Clarke and Leanne Calvert for the Arts and Humanities Research Council-funded project 'A History of Marriage in Ireland, 1660–1925'.

31 This analysis is based on notices placed in the *Belfast Newsletter*, the *Ennis Chronicle and Clare Advertiser* and a search of the Dublin newspapers available on the digital resource, 'Irish Newspaper Archive'. (www.irishnewsarchive.com). This research is part of an ongoing project to create a larger database of elopement notices in other Irish newspapers.

32 J Bailey (2003) *Unquiet Lives: Marriage and Marriage Breakdown in England, 1660–1800* (Cambridge: Cambridge University Press), p 57. See also MB Sievens (2001) '"The Wicked Agency of Others": Community, Law, and Marital Conflict in Vermont, 1790–1830', *Journal of the Early Republic*, XXI, 20–21. See also Chapter 5 in this volume.

33 Sievens (2001) '"The Wicked Agency of Others"'; I Espinasse (1794) *Digest of the Law of Actions and Trials at Nisi Prius*, 2nd edn (Dublin: E Lynch and others), pp 119–125.

34 William Blackstone asserted that the traders had to be informed about the husband's repudiation of his wife's debt although case law suggested that by the 1790s traders did not need to be informed. See Sievens (2001) '"The Wicked Agency of Others"', pp 20–21; Bailey (2003) *Unquiet Lives*, pp 56–60.

Normally the notice was inserted within weeks of the wife's elopement but in a small number of cases there was a considerable time gap between the date of the elopement and the advertisement. In December 1759, for example, Charles Jackson inserted a notice in the *Belfast Newsletter* to the effect that he and his wife, Jane Moffat, had separated three years before, 'by mutual consent and for sufficient reasons'. Jackson appeared to have suspected that Jane was still contracting debts in his name and so issued a public notice that he would not be responsible for any future debts that Jane accumulated.[35] William Kelly's wife, Catherine, had left their home near Hillsborough, 'some time ago' when he inserted a notice in 1771. William had not heard from his wife since her departure but had recently heard that she had returned to the neighbourhood. He used his notice not only to repudiate any debt that she might have accumulated but to denounce his wife's relations who had threatened him so that he feared 'damage either in body or goods'.[36]

A notice could also be inserted as part of the winding up of a business. If the wife was involved in running the business, then she might also have been acting as her husband's agent. On 5 May 1767, David Malcomson announced in the *Belfast Newsletter* that he was retiring from his business of keeping an inn and selling his premises. Less than three weeks earlier, David had inserted another notice in the newspaper denouncing his wife, Mary, who 'by her irregular conduct and bad management for many years past, has wasted, destroyed and embezzled' his property. David expressed his 'concern that she may do him further injury by taking up money and goods on credit in his name'.[37] The insertion of the advertisement was to give notice to all of his former customers that he had retired and that his wife no longer acted on his behalf. Similarly, when Robert Mathew advertised the selling of the lease on his house, he also inserted a notice that his wife Martha had eloped six times and 'carried away [a] great part of my property'.[38]

David Malcomson's anger at his wife is clear from his notice. Other advertisements also indicate that anger and revenge were strong motivating factors behind a husband's decision to shame his wife publicly in this way. Michael King admitted in 1796 that the notice that he had inserted about his wife, Mary, 'was the effect of sudden passion, and bad advice, without any real charge against her'.[39] In a passive-aggressive fashion, Peter Hamill presented himself as a patient husband who had been forced into publicly shaming his

35 *Belfast Newsletter*, 1 Jan 1760.

36 *Belfast Newsletter*, 18 June 1771. See also the notice in the *Belfast Newsletter*, 25 Apr 1769, which was placed by Archibald Curry who had separated from his wife Agnes Walker five years earlier.

37 *Belfast Newsletter*, 24 Apr 1767.

38 *Belfast Newsletter*, 29 Jul, 1 Aug 1788.

39 *Ennis Chronicle and Clare Advertiser*, 24 Nov 1796.

wife because, despite all his efforts, she had 'obstinately' refused to return to him and had threatened to contract debts in his name.[40]

Other men publicly denounced the behaviour of their spouses and presented their actions as unfeminine or demonstrating a lack of maternal affection. A phrase used in several notices in the *Belfast Newsletter* was that the wife had given the husband 'a vast deal of trouble and uneasiness which she might have prevented had she behaved better'.[41] James McCoobry, a carpenter from Belfast, used semi-religious terminology to describe the fall of his wife. He had tried the 'most tender and gentle methods to reclaim her' but had become convinced that 'reformation is not ... to be hoped for from a person so entirely abandoned to every sense of shame and gratitude'.[42] Martha Johnson was denounced by her husband for having led a 'lewd, wicked and adulterous life', while other husbands named the adulterous man with whom their wife had fled.[43] Jane Maxwell, according to her husband, Henry, eloped with Mathias Magill, a 'strolling schoolmaster' and included in the notice a detailed physical description of both his wife and her lover.[44] The abandonment of children was also publicly denounced by husbands. Samuel Cord, blacksmith, noted that his wife had left her two children behind, one of whom, he noted, she was still breastfeeding.[45] In Ennis in 1815, Patrick Mcdallogh graphically described how his wife had again walked out of the family home leaving behind four small children and her blind mother. She had 'taken up with Tim Guigan, the lame fiddler'. Patrick made it clear that he would not pay 'bite or sup' for his wife and warned his wife 'that she had better never shew the marks of her ten toes in my house again'.[46]

If anger and revenge were strong motivating factors for such notices, some men advertised their wives' elopement in the hope that she would return. Mary McComb's husband earnestly entreated her to return while Catherine Murphy's husband noted that he had 'appealed to her several times to return to her own house'.[47] Such public requests to return to the marital home and appeals to the public to encourage mothers and wives to behave in an appropriate manner may have held an implicit threat for the women concerned. Elizabeth Small's husband asserted in his notice that he was 'desirous that she and the child should return and therein live in a manner becoming the marriage state'.[48] Peter Hamill claimed that his wife Elinor had rejected all

40 *Belfast Newsletter,* 10 Dec 1771.

41 See, for example, *Belfast Newsletter,* 27 Jan 1769; 10 Feb 1769.

42 *Belfast Newsletter,* 18 Sept 1767; 31 Mar 1769.

43 *Belfast Newsletter,* 21 Mar 1769; *Belfast Newsletter,* 14 Oct 1760.

44 *Belfast Newsletter,* 4 Nov 1760.

45 *Belfast Newsletter,* 8 Jan 1754.

46 *Ennis Chronicle and Clare Advertiser,* 11 Nov 1815.

47 *Belfast Newsletter,* 2 June 1769; 16 June 1769.

48 *Belfast Newsletter,* 21 Jan 1769.

the 'intreaties made to her by her husband and other friends, yet she obstinately refuses to return to her duty'.[49]

The elopement notices presented the husband's view of the marriage. From a wife's perspective, a public notice requesting that she return home might have appeared threatening and indicative of the reasons why she had left her husband. A small number of wives responded to their husbands' notice with a printed response. Most claimed that they had left the family home because of the violent behaviour of their husband. In 1794, for example, Bridget Coughlan from Waterford responded to her husband's advertisement with a statement that he had 'attempted putting an end to my existence with a knife'. She was also sufficiently versed in the law to claim her financial entitlement as laid out in their marriage settlement in the event of the couple separating.[50]

Although a violent home may have been the reason why some women left their husbands, it is clear from the volume of elopement notices that many women abandoned their marriages at their own volition and were intent on living separate lives. Some took their children with them and, to their husbands' annoyance, some also brought from the family home cash and goods that would enable them to set up a separate home. Bridget Slevin, for example, took a guinea and a half from the house as well as a quantity of yarn and flax, while Jane Salter took a 'bedding of clothes' and a large quantity of flax and other household goods.[51] The women also seem to have been aware of their rights under the law and the fact that they could accumulate debts or take out loans in their husbands' names. Several notices refer to the fact that the wife had threatened to accumulate debts that would lead to the prosecution, if not jailing, of their husbands.[52]

The fact that so many husbands publicly advertised their marital problems suggests too that there was communal support for the separation of husband and wife. As noted already, many of the notices in the *Belfast Newsletter* could have conformed to the Presbyterian definition of 'wilful desertion' which might have permitted the husband to remarry. The infrequency of references to divorce in Presbytery minute books suggests, however, that most of the husbands who inserted notices in the *Belfast Newsletter* did not seek a formal divorce from the church. They had no qualms, on the other hand about publicly announcing their permanent separation from their wives.[53]

Some of the notices also indicate that either the husband or, more often, the wife had family or community support. John Parker claimed that his wife

49 *Belfast Newsletter,* 10 Dec 1771.

50 *Finn's Leinster Journal,* 1 Mar 1794.

51 *Belfast Newsletter,* 19–23 Jan 1787; 17 Nov 1767.

52 See, for example, *Belfast Newsletter,* 10 Dec 1771.

53 *Belfast Newsletter,* 9 Oct 1767, 15 Feb 1771.

had departed because she was badly advised by her sister.[54] Mary Templeton left at the instigation of her mother and others.[55] Ann Edwards, according to her husband, John Watson, eloped with her child due to the 'bad advice of her father and mother'.[56] Farmer John O'Neill from County Antrim claimed that his wife, Rose O'Nogher, had been prevailed upon by her stepfather and her mother to leave him and that they had refused to deliver to him certain lands and effects to which he was entitled in right of his said wife.[57]

In colonial Vermont, Sievens argued, the elopement notices were evidence of self-made divorces. The Irish documentation also suggests that individuals made their own arrangements not only to separate from spouses but also to cohabit, sometimes in a bigamous relationship with another. As noted already, the regulations of the churches and the State did not always concur on the validity of a remarriage of a separated couple. The law on bigamous marriages was, therefore, confusing and was compounded in the early decades of the nineteenth century when the judiciary began to debate the validity of marriages conducted by Presbyterian ministers between members of the Church of Ireland and Presbyterians. The abolition of the penal legislation against Roman Catholics and Presbyterians in the last quarter of the eighteenth century led to a corresponding increase in marriages of individuals from mixed religious backgrounds. The 1782 statute, 'For the Relief of Protestant Dissenters in Certain Matters Therein Contained'[58] legitimized marriages solemnized by Presbyterian ministers of two Presbyterians but not a 'mixed' marriage of a Presbyterian and a member of the Church of Ireland.[59] In practice, however, by the 1820s such marriages had become common and had received communal if not judicial recognition. The legal controversy of the 1830s and early 1840s centred on cases in which men were accused of bigamy because they had remarried following marriages conducted by Presbyterian ministers. In all the cases, the issue in dispute was that one of the partners to the first marriage was a member of the established church while their partner was Presbyterian.[60] The individuals involved in these marriages were clearly seizing the opportunity provided by the legal confusion to abandon an unhappy marriage. Henry Baily explicitly admitted in 1842

54 *Belfast Newsletter,* 30 Jul–2 Aug 1776.

55 *Belfast Newsletter,* 10 Dec 1771.

56 *Belfast Newsletter,* 21 Mar 1769.

57 *Belfast Newsletter,* 31 May 1768.

58 21 & 22 Geo III c 25.

59 See Chapter 3 in this volume.

60 See, for example, R Jebb (1841) *Cases Chiefly Relating to the Criminal and Presentment Law, Reserved for Consideration, and Decided by the Twelve Judges of Ireland, from May 1822, to November 1840* (Dublin: Andrew Milliken), pp 267–298; R Jebb (1843) *Reports of Cases Argued and Determined on Six Circuits in Ireland: Taken During the Assizes, in the Years 1841, 1842, 1843* (Dublin: Andrew Milliken), pp 289–299, 332–335; E Spencer Dix (1842) *Report of the Cases of Regina v Millis, et Regina v Carroll, in the Queen's Bench in Ireland, in Easter and Trinity Terms, 1842* (Dublin).

that hearing of the public debate on the validity of Presbyterian marriages he 'took advantage of the situation' to leave his first wife, Anna Jordon, whom he had married in a Presbyterian ceremony in Lisburn, Co Antrim.[61]

The punishment for bigamy was initially the death penalty but this was subsequently commuted to seven years' transportation or two years' imprisonment.[62] Despite the severity of the punishment, it is clear from newspaper reports and scattered ecclesiastical records that remarriage following separation from a first spouse was not uncommon. In the absence of regular record keeping on the part of clergymen of all denominations before the 1840s, it could be difficult to prove that someone had been married before and that a former spouse was still alive at the time of their subsequent marriage. Apart from the 'mixed' marriage cases noted already, the majority of bigamy cases prosecuted in the civil courts before the mid-nineteenth century related to a first marriage conducted by a couple beggar. The latter was a clergyman who was not attached formally to a specific church but could, nevertheless, conduct legally valid marriages, usually at a much cheaper rate than that charged by a more orthodox minister. Couple beggars were particularly common in Dublin and other towns in the late eighteenth and early decades of the nineteenth century. Men and women who participated in such marriages and later married again argued that they had not realized that a marriage by a couple beggar was legally valid. In Dublin in 1842, for example, Patrick Byrne was accused of marrying Mary King when his first wife, Mary Connors, was still alive. Byrne, a Catholic, explained that he and Connors, also Catholic, had been married by the Lutheran minister, Schulz, in Cullenswood in Dublin in 1838. Byrne had lived with Connors for three years and had two children with her but he claimed that he did not think the marriage was valid in law. The couple had 'come to a mutual understanding that they should each be free to marry again as they did not well agree'. The court, however, deemed the first marriage conducted by Schulz as valid and Byrne was sentenced to seven years' transportation.[63] Schulz may have encouraged the couple to believe that they could separate if they wished. In another case, a couple described how Schulz 'pronounced a divorce' by tearing up the certificate of marriage.[64]

The statistics are not sufficient to identify the number of people who remarried while an existing spouse was still alive. Catholic canon law which prohibited remarriage under any circumstances unless there was proof that a former spouse was dead may have encouraged some to take their chances in the hope that their former marriage might not be discovered. In 1752, parish priests in the diocese of Ossory reported five cases of bigamy which suggests

61 *Freeman's Journal*, 11 Aug 1842.

62 Offences Against the Person (Ireland) Act 1829 (10 Geo IV c 34), s 26.

63 *Dublin Evening Mail*, 12 Aug 1842

64 *Freeman's Journal*, 2, 14 Feb 1838.

that while it was not prevalent it was not an uncommon phenomenon.[65] There were also accusations that itinerant priests were willing to marry couples whose spouses were still alive. In late eighteenth-century Galway, a man applied to the local parish priest to marry him. He acknowledged that he had been married before and that his first wife was still alive but living with another man. When the priest refused to marry him, the man complained of the 'hardship' of church law and announced that 'he would marry and though he acknowledged the impropriety of his act he said he would do penance before he would die'. To the local priest's annoyance, the man was subsequently married by an itinerant priest.[66] In another incident which also reflected an impatience with Catholic regulation on remarriage, Father John O'Sullivan, looking back in 1850 on his experience as a parish priest in earlier decades, recalled that he had spent four years denouncing a woman who had cohabited with a man whose wife had emigrated to America 14 years before and 'was never heard of since'. O'Sullivan noted that:

> It was very difficult to get them to separate for they with no small share of plausibility contended that the fair presumption was in favour of the wife being dead when she had not been heard of directly or indirectly for the space of fourteen years.[67]

The Presbyterian church authorities were more sympathetic to bigamous individuals than their Catholic counterparts. This may have been because desertion was considered a valid reason for divorce. In 1730, for example, when James Turner admitted to the Aghadowey session that his first wife was still alive when he married the second, the elders and minister were forgiving, and noted that 'as the fact was committed so long ago as the wars and his being in the army took him away from where his first wife found it convenient to stay, it is agreed that he only shall stand once Sabbath day'.[68] Military service also led to the separation of Hugh Gebby and his wife. When he was sent abroad in 1805, she refused to join him and the couple did not see one another again until 1817. In the meantime, Gebby claimed that he had believed his wife was dead and had remarried. In 1823, he appealed to the Down Presbytery to recognize his second marriage despite the fact that his first wife was still living. The Presbytery believed that he had acted in good faith and conceded to his request.[69]

---

65 C O'Dwyer (1975) (ed), 'Archbishop Butler's Visitation Book', *Archivium Hibernicum*, XXXIII, pp 1–90; XXXIV, pp 1–49.

66 GDA, Box C/8.

67 J O'Sullivan (1850–1852), 'Praxis Parochi' (2 vols, unpublished manuscript, Kerry Diocesan Archive), vol 2, p 700.

68 JM Barkley (1952) *History of the Ruling Eldership in Irish Presbyterianism* (unpublished MA thesis, Queen's University Belfast), p 168.

69 Minutes of the Presbytery of Down, 18 Feb 1823 (Presbyterian Historical Society, Belfast).

In the 1750s, Richard Butler, the Catholic bishop of Ossory, had tried to encourage local priests to report on 'public sinners' on a regular basis. It was not, however, until the middle decades of the nineteenth century that the Catholic hierarchy can be documented as making a systematic attempt to police the observation of canon law on marriage. Prior to that time, it is clear that many of the men and women who deserted their spouses simply cohabited with new partners. Again, it is difficult to get a sense of how many such couples there were in a locality or parish. Reports of Catholic clergy provide at least an impressionistic view. In 1826, George Plunkett claimed that when he was first appointed bishop of Elphin in 1814, there were in Athlone and its hinterland 'innumerable couples [who] had lived as man and wife who had never been married and many others in flagrant and notorious adultery'.[70] In 1842, John Murphy, the bishop of Cork and Ross, described how he had been dealing with couples who had been living in 'fornication, adultery, incest'. Murphy wrote that he had a list of 64 couples who 'in obedience to my command, have separated *a thoro*; for where there is abject poverty, with a numerous brood we cannot insist on separation *a mensa*'.[71] In 'Praxis Parochi', John O'Sullivan recalled a parish priest who had found 'six to seven couples living in open public concubinage'. O'Sullivan also acknowledged the continuous problem in the Catholic church of couples who had been refused a dispensation to marry, deciding to cohabit.[72]

O'Sullivan would have undoubtedly agreed with the policy of Bishop John Murphy that cohabiting couples should be compelled to separate. As both he and Murphy acknowledged, it was difficult to separate couples once they began to have children. For this reason, O'Sullivan urged his fellow priests to keep at cohabiting couples 'hammer and tongs', if only as a means of deterring others from following suit: '[i]f the parishioners see a couple giving public scandal without being reproved and corrected by the priest, it will clearly be an incentive to some of them to follow their bad example.'[73]

Throughout the eighteenth and early nineteenth centuries, therefore, Irish men and women arranged for separations from their spouses. Some did it with the aid of their respective churches or the State but many did it without consulting a priest, minister or lawyer. The evidence is scattered and not conducive to quantitative analysis but it is sufficient to argue that the image of a society bound by a puritan code of sexual morality is not an accurate depiction of Irish society before the mid-nineteenth century.

---

70 Cited in E Larkin (1962) 'Church and State in Ireland in the Nineteenth Century', *Church History* 31(3), 294–306, p 300.

71 E Larkin, (1972), 'The devotional revolution in Ireland 1850–1875', *American Historical Review*, 77, 625–652, p 637.

72 O'Sullivan (1850–1852) 'Praxis Parochi', vol 1, p 542.

73 O'Sullivan (1850–1852) 'Praxis Parochi', vol 2, pp 697–698.

3
The Comeback of the Medieval Marriage *Per Verba de Praesenti* in Nineteenth-Century Bigamy Cases

*Maebh Harding**

Introduction

In 1844, the House of Lords was asked to consider the requisite legal steps to marriage formation in Ireland.[1] The case concerned the bigamy conviction of George Millis, a member of the Established Church, who had married his first wife in a Presbyterian ceremony in Ireland before going through a second ceremony of marriage with another woman in a parish church in England. Two questions were raised: the first was whether a Presbyterian clergyman could validly carry out a marriage between a Dissenter and a member of the Established Church. The second was whether the presence of a clergyman was required at all or whether a simple exchange of consent by the parties to be married to each other – the medieval contract *per verba de praesenti*[2] – was enough to form a valid marriage in Irish law.

The case raised greater questions about the competing roles of religious bodies and different court jurisdictions in regulating marriage in Ireland in the early nineteenth century. The ecclesiastical courts of the Established Church had sole jurisdiction to determine the validity of a marriage, and to award matrimonial relief. The temporal courts which applied the civil and criminal law of the State had no jurisdiction to interrogate the legal validity of marriage, as this was determined by ecclesiastical law, but were often required to decide whether a marriage existed as a matter of fact. The chapter will explain the context of the ruling in *Millis* before going on to examine the importance of the religious identity of both the participants and the

* The author wishes to thank Professor Rebecca Probert who commented on an earlier draft of this article.

1 *R v Millis* (1844) 10 Cl & F 534 (HL).

2 Literally meaning a contract by 'words of present tense', this refers to a situation where both parties declare to each other that they are man and wife.

officiating clergyman in the marriage legislation then in force in Ireland. The way in which this marriage legislation was interpreted by the ecclesiastical courts and the temporal courts will then be compared.

Legal arguments that a clergyman was unnecessary to form a legal marriage were increasingly raised in the reported Irish bigamy cases of the early nineteenth century, culminating in the need to refer the ruling in *Millis* to the House of Lords. This chapter argues that the legal force of the contract *per verba de praesenti* was much the same in Irish law in the nineteenth century as it had been in England in the eighteenth century. Such an exchange of promises did not form a marriage recognizable by the temporal courts or ecclesiastical court. Instead, the law required parties to comply with different religious formalities depending on their religion to obtain marital status, with specific restrictions on marriages between Catholics and Protestants. While many marriage ceremonies were performed in irregular circumstances, there is no indication from legal sources that spouses regularly attempted to enter into marriage without the presence of a clergyman or sought any recognition of such an attempt.

Three different factors rendered the argument increasingly desirable to the Crown. First, the existing legislative framework, which had been based on a dichotomy of religious identity as either Established Church or Roman Catholic was challenged by a rise in the number of Dissenter marriages. Second, evidential problems in cases of irregular marriages carried out by the 'degraded clergy' led to greater scrutiny of the formalities of marriages in both ecclesiastical cases and criminal bigamy cases. Finally, it is argued that the legal understanding of the role of the State in regulating marriage formalities was changing. Marriage formalities could no longer be left entirely to the religious tenets of the Established Church and Roman Catholicism, but became a matter of decisive importance for the State.

The ruling in *Millis* was far removed from the reality of marriage practices in Ireland. It did little to clarify the place of Dissenter marriages within the existing Irish legal framework but instead precipitated a legislative change which was now necessary in a (slightly) more religiously diverse society.

The controversy of *R v Millis*

The regulation of the formalities of marriage in Ireland was very different from that in England and Wales. In England, Lord Hardwicke's Marriage Act of 1753[3] required marriages (excepting those of Jews and Quakers) to take place in a recognized church after banns or licence. Marriages which did not comply with this Act were void *ab initio*.[4] In Ireland, there was no such declaratory legislation; instead, the requisite steps for the formation of

3 26 Geo II c 33.

4 This means that such marriages had no legal effect whatsoever.

marriage were left up to the individual religions. The majority of the Irish population was Roman Catholic.

Initially it seems surprising that the judges of the Irish Queen's Bench, who had presided over bigamy trials at assizes around the country for many years, as well as having first-hand knowledge of marriage practices in Ireland, would require a ruling by the English House of Lords on such a basic question of whether or not a Presbyterian marriage ceremony could form the basis of a bigamy charge in Ireland. The very same issue had been considered by the Twelve Judges less than a year previously as inadequate proof of a marriage for securing a bigamy conviction.[5] When hearing *R v Millis* itself, the Queen's Bench had heard the opinion of Dr Radcliffe, presiding judge of the Dublin Consistory Court, on the issue. The fact that the opinion was not taken as binding suggests that the question of the requisite formalities to form a marriage in Ireland was causing controversy not only in the temporal courts but also in the ecclesiastical courts of Ireland and that an authoritative ruling was required.

Irish case law was not relied on as authority in *R v Millis* itself nor was any general awareness of contemporary marriage practices in Ireland shown.[6] Instead, the House of Lords embarked upon a historic review of medieval canon law as it applied in England before the Marriage Act 1753 and assumed Irish law to be largely similar. Whether they were any better equipped to comment on the laws of earlier generations in England than on contemporary laws in Ireland was, however, questioned in Tindal LCJ's judgment:

> it may well become us, the Judges of England of the present day, when for nearly a century the whole doctrine relating to contracts of marriage, as contradistinguished from marriage itself, has become nearly a dead letter in our Courts, to confess that the subject is involved in still deeper obscurity than in the time of our predecessors, and to acknowledge ourselves unable to trace out and define the boundary between the contract and marriage itself, with absolute certainty.

The Lords struggled to put together an opinion to put to the House. Nine judges met and agreed that the offence of bigamy had not been committed (the position taken by the majority of Irish Queen's Bench). That opinion was laid before the Peers on 7 July 1843. Three judges spoke in favour of the opinion: Lords Abinger, Cottenham and the Lord Chancellor Lyndhurst. They all agreed that Millis was not guilty of bigamy but differed in their reasoning. Lord Brougham, Lord Denham and Lord Campbell spoke against the opinion, holding that the first marriage was valid to support a bigamy charge. The

5 *R v Smith* (1843) Cr & Dix 318 and *R v Smith* (1842) Jebb & Bourke, App i.

6 Although reference was made to the purpose of the penal laws: *R v Millis* (1844) 10 Cl & F 534, p 676.

Lords differed in their view of the legal effect of a verbal exchange of consents in English marriage law prior to the Marriage Act 1753. Some argued that it operated in almost the same way as a marriage celebrated in a church, others argued that it had no legal effect whatsoever. As the Lords were equally divided, the ancient rule *semper praesumitur pro negante*[7] was invoked and the appeal was dismissed. George Millis was acquitted and returned to whatever domestic justice his two 'wives' saw fit.

Probert suggests that neither side in the *Millis* case was correct in its understanding of English law.[8] The marriage *per verba de praesenti* was an inchoate status, in effect a betrothal or a contract to marry which had limited legal effect.[9] It created a binding contract which could be enforced in the ecclesiastical courts to compel the celebration of marriage in the Established Church. It also operated as an impediment which could render a later marriage to another voidable, but it was not recognized as conferring the status of 'married' upon the parties. It did not bring with it the right to dower, or the right to administration of the estate of the deceased 'spouse' or render legitimate the children of the union. Marriages *per verba de praesenti* were neither accepted by the common law courts as an equivalent to marriage celebrated in a church nor totally devoid of legal effect. Instead different types of marriage agreement were valid for different purposes.[10] Probert convincingly uses case study methods to show that couples in England in the eighteenth century nearly invariably married in an Anglican Church in full compliance with church formalities.[11] Gordon suggests that reports of marriages carried out without the presence of a clergyman in Scotland in the eighteenth century have been overstated but warns that the inconsistent definitions of irregular marriage by historians and the absence of reliable statistics make it impossible to establish accurate numbers.[12]

For Irish legal historians the ruling in *Millis* raised a number of questions about marriage practice in Ireland in the early nineteenth century. The idea that a valid marriage could be formed *per verba de praesenti* was a medieval Catholic doctrine which had been abolished at the Council of Trent in 1563.[13] However, the *Tametsi* decree, which abolished the marriage *per verba*

---

7 This rule places the obligation on the Crown to positively prove their case, which they failed to do in *Millis*.

8 R Probert (2008) '*R v Millis* Reconsidered: Binding Contracts and Bigamous Marriages', *Legal Studies* 28, 337–355.

9 This should not be confused with the action for breach of promise in the temporal courts, discussed in Chapter 4.

10 Probert (2008) '*R v Millis* Reconsidered', p 351.

11 R Probert (2009) *Marriage Law and Practice in the Long Eighteenth Century: A Reassessment* (Cambridge: Cambridge University Press), ch 2.

12 E Gordon (2013) 'Irregular Marriage: Myth and Reality', *Journal of Social History*, 47(2), 507–525.

13 Council of Trent, Decree *Tametsi* Concerning the Reform of Matrimony (1563).

de praesenti as part of canon law and expressly required Catholic marriages to be solemnized by a priest, did not reach all parts of Ireland until 1827[14] due to the effect of the penal laws. Perhaps the much romanticized image of the DIY marriage *per verba de praesenti* was in fact a common reality in Ireland in the eighteenth and nineteenth centuries, but if that was the case why were the Irish courts unfamiliar with the rules of evidence to determine whether such a marriage had indeed taken place?

Marriage legislation in Ireland in the early nineteenth century

In the early nineteenth century, an incoherent patchwork of legislation formed the legal context for the decision in *Millis*. A very small number of statutes provided for legal impediments to marriage which applied regardless of the religious identity of the celebrant or the parties. For example, statutes dating from Tudor times provided that marriages would be invalid if parties married within the prohibited degrees of relationship[15] and an Act passed in 1811 invalidated marriages with lunatics.[16]

Irish legislation also contained several provisions specifically to combat the problem of clandestine marriages of wealthy heirs under the age of majority who married without parental consent. These ranged from penalties for the celebrant,[17] imprisonment and disentitlement to the heir's fortune for the person attempting to marry the minor without parental consent,[18] to an option for the parent or guardian of the heir to annul any marriage or marriage contract in the ecclesiastical courts within one year.[19]

---

14 The dioceses of Dublin, Kildare, Leighlin, Ossory, Ferns and Meath were the last to receive the decree in December 1827. See Dublin Diocesan Archives, papers of Daniel Murray, 1823–1852 (DDA, AB3 30/10).

15 Marriage Act (No 1) 1537 (28 Hen VIII c 2 [Ire]); Marriage Act (No 2) 1537 (28 & 29 Hen VIII c 17 [Ire]); the Marriage Act 1542 (33 Hen VIII c 6 [Ire]) and the Marriage Act 1835 (5 & 6 Will IV c 54) enacted that 'marriages celebrated before the passing of the Act, of persons within the prohibited degrees of consanguinity or affinity should be absolutely void'. See further M Harding (2012) 'The Curious Incident of the Marriage Act No 2 1537 and the Irish Statute Book', *Legal Studies,* 32(1), 78–108.

16 Marriage of Lunatics Act 1811 (51 Geo III c 37).

17 An Act for the More Effectual Preventing the Taking Away and Marrying Children Against the Wills of their Parents or Guardians 1707 (6 Ann c 16 [Ire]) provided for up to three years' imprisonment for aiding or abetting the marriage as well as ecclesiastical censure for beneficed clergy from the Established Church and punishment as a felony if carried out by a Popish priest.

18 An Act for the Punishment of Such as Shall Take Away Maidens that be Inheritors Being Within the Age of 16 Years or Marry them Without Consent of Their Parents 1635 (10 Cha I c 17 [Ire]); An Act for the More Effectual Preventing the Taking Away and Marrying Children Against the Wills of their Parents or Guardians 1707 (6 Ann c 16 [Ire]).

19 An Act for the More Effectual Preventing of Clandestine Marriages 1735 (9 Geo II c 11 [Ire]), as amended by An Act for the More Effective Preventing of Clandestine Marriages 1749 (23 Geo II c 10 [Ire]) which was designed to target cases where the parties to the clandestine marriage left the court to avoid the nullity suit. For a successful declaration see *Mitchell v Spread* (1799), Rowe's Popery Cases 208 (High Court of Delegates). However it was possible to avoid the statute by marrying abroad *Steele v Braddell* (1838) Milward Rep 1 (Dublin Consistory Court).

Bigamy had been prohibited in Ireland since the seventeenth century.[20] The Bigamy Acts rendered it a felony to marry a second spouse while the first spouse was still alive. Bigamy was punishable by death or transportation to the plantations in America[21] until 1829, when the sentence was reduced to transportation for seven years or imprisonment with or without hard labour.[22] First marriages declared void by a sentence of the court could not sustain a bigamy conviction under the terms of these Acts.

Most of the statutes regulating the celebration of marriage itself and the legal validity of such marriage had their basis in the penal laws dating from the seventeenth century. These rules created a regulatory framework in which marriages were placed into religious categories. The emphasis in statute on the religious identity of the parties to the marriage and that of the celebrant renders it highly unlikely that marriage by simple exchange of promises was a common practice in Ireland in either the eighteenth or early nineteenth centuries. The general effect of the penal laws on Catholic marriage practices is first considered before an outline is given of the specific scope of invalidating prohibitions against mixed marriages.

The effect of the penal laws on Catholic marriage formalities

The penal laws curtailed the practice of Roman Catholicism by imposing penalties on the Roman Catholic clergy.[23] The penal laws were eventually repealed by a series of Catholic Relief Acts passed between 1777 and 1829.[24] However, the cumulative effect of these general prohibitions hampered the ability of the Catholic Church in Ireland to carry out marriages in compliance with the contemporary canon law of the Church of Rome. Some dioceses in Ireland failed to promulgate the *Tametsi* decree until 1827 (as noted above), but there is no evidence in diocesan sources to suggest that marriages conducted in the absence of a priest were common. Two different consultations carried out in the 1780s and in 1824 suggest that, instead, irregular marriages carried out by the 'degraded clergy', also known as 'couple beggars', were the problem of greatest concern.[25]

---

20 An Act to Restrain all Persons from Marriage until their Former Wives and Former Husbands be Dead 1603 (1 Jac I c 11); An Act for the Restraining of all Persons from Marriage till their Former Wives and Former Husbands be Dead 1635 (10 Chas I c 21 [Ire]).

21 The Marriage Act 1725 (12 Geo I c 3 [Ire]) mentions transportation as a punishment.

22 Offences Against the Person (Ireland) Act 1829 (10 Geo IV c 34), s 26.

23 For example, An Act for Banishing all Papists Exercising any Ecclesiastical Jurisdiction, and all Regulars of the Popish Clergy out of the Kingdom 1698 (9 Will III c 1 [Ire]); An Act for Registering the Popish Clergy 1703 (2 Ann c 7 [Ire]), as amended by An Act to Explain and Amend an Act, Intituled An Act for Registering the Popish Clergy 1704 (4 Ann c 2 [Ire]); An Act for Explaining an Act to Prevent the Further Growth of Popery 1709 (8 Ann c 3 [Ire]).

24 See J Kelly 'The historiography of the Penal Laws' in J Bergin et al. (eds) *New Perspectives on the Penal Laws* (Eighteenth Century Ireland Special Issue, Dublin 2011), 27–52, pp 47–48.

25 Archbishop of Dublin (1786–1823) (DDA, AB2 30/8); Archbishop of Dublin (1823–1852) (DDA, AB3 29/1).

The degraded clergy or couple beggars were generally members of the Established Church or Roman Catholic priests who had lost their parish or benefice as a result of disciplinary measures taken by the ecclesiastical courts for breaking canonical rules. Many of the degraded clergy had initially been stripped of their benefice for celebrating irregular or clandestine marriages. For example, Reverend Matthew Harris, the Catholic parish priest of Navan, was degraded for 'irregular celebration of marriage'; Reverend Joseph Wood, a Church of Ireland minister, was degraded for celebrating a marriage outside of the canonical hours and Reverend Jason William, a Church of Ireland minister, was degraded for celebrating the marriage of a ward of court in Chancery.[26] Without a benefice these degraded individuals had no stable source of income and so were financially incentivized to continue carrying out irregular marriages, providing eloping couples with an inexpensive, no-questions-asked, marriage service. Many of the degraded clergy maintained records of the weddings they had celebrated in Marriage Books. Records suggest that 37,648 such marriages were carried out in Cullenswood and Strawmarket in Dublin between 1802 and 1844.[27] While the services of the degraded clergy were clearly in demand in the early nineteenth century, the whole industry was considered very disreputable. Books from 9 Haymarket, Dublin recalled that brides absconded without paying and on occasion stole various items from the house and 'behaved in a very unsuitable manner'.[28] However, such marriages were generally viewed as valid in the eyes of the Catholic Church and in the temporal and ecclesiastical courts if there was sufficient evidence to show that such a ceremony had in fact taken place.

The papers of Archbishop Troy[29] suggest that the decision of whether or not to promulgate the *Tametsi* decree in the diocese in the 1780s was based on practical concerns of how best to combat the problem of irregular marriage celebrations. Dr Troy sent a questionnaire to parish priests in his diocese in 1788. Of the 39 replies, 32 advised against promulgating the decree and only seven were in favour.[30] All replies cited the problem of irregular clandestine marriages by the degraded clergy or 'couple beggars' as the main issue affected by the decree. In January 1824, the Holy See sent a letter to Troy's

---

26 'Report by Mr Herbert Wood on certain registers of irregular marriage celebrated by unlicensed clergymen known as couple-beggars' in *Thirty-Fourth Report of the Deputy Keeper of the Public Records and Keeper of the State Papers in Ireland* HC 1902 [C-1176] xlix, 779, 22–29.

27 According to a schedule furnished by Messrs Samuels, Registrars of the United Diocese of Dublin, Glendalough and Kildare, Record Buildings, Henrietta Street Dublin, reproduced in Robert Matheson (1888) *A Digest of the Irish Marriage Law* (Dublin: HMSO), p 49.

28 *Thirty-Third Report of the Deputy Keeper of the Public Records and Keeper of the State Papers in Ireland*, HC 1901 [C-729] xxxiii, 763, para 5.

29 Archbishop of Dublin (1786–1823) (DDA, AB2).

30 Troy Papers: Marriage and Reserved Cases, Undated (DDA, AB2 29/1).

successor, Archbishop Murray,[31] asking him to explain why the Tridentine Decrees regarding clandestine marriage had not yet been promulgated in Dublin and enquiring if the lack of promulgation had caused any problems. Murray again wrote to the priests in the dioceses where the decree had not been promulgated, seeking their opinions.

Both consultations highlight the limits of excommunication in deterring irregular marriages carried out by the degraded clergy. While spouses were excommunicated for such a practice, in the 1780s some priests reported that they relied on later being absolved.[32] In 1824, Dr Marum of Ossory stated that excommunication scarcely operated as a check on the practice.[33]

The correspondence also shows the desire of the Roman Catholic clergy to maintain the religious identity of their flock. Any measure that might encourage individuals to convert to Protestantism or seek adjudication from the temporal or ecclesiastical courts was seen as highly undesirable. The replies of the 1780s argued that rendering marriages carried out by the degraded clergy invalid in the eyes of the Catholic Church would merely increase the number of lawsuits.[34] It was also suggested that this might encourage Catholics to turn to Protestantism in order to validate their marriages by couple beggars.[35] In 1824, Dr Keating of Ferns expressed his concern that the publication of the *Tametsi* decree in his province would only increase the difficulties of the Catholic community, encouraging them to come into contact with the civil and ecclesiastical laws of Ireland.[36]

This correspondence suggests that marriage *per verba de praesenti* was not seen as a common practice amongst the Roman Catholic community, nor theologically desirable. Instead, individuals who wished to marry irregularly would risk excommunication by undertaking a clandestine marriage carried out by a member of the degraded clergy and then seek absolution. This would have been an entirely unnecessary practice if a simple exchange of vows had created a marriage in the eyes of the Roman Catholic Church.

Statutes to regulate the marriage of Protestants and limit the celebration of 'mixed marriages'

Three different types of deterrent were imposed by statute to prevent mixed marriages between Protestants and Catholics. Penalties were initially imposed

31 Letter from Propaganda commanding Murray to state the reasons why the Tridentine decrees regarding clandestine marriage were not promulgated in Dublin. 20 Mar 1824, Archbishop of Dublin (1823–1852) (DDA, AB3 30/8).

32 Response from John Murphy Parish Priest of St Michael's Dublin, 30 Oct 1788 (DDA, MS AB2 29/1/3).

33 Response from Dr Marum of Ossory, 3 Mar 1824 (DDA, AB3 30/8:1824).

34 Response from Father Clinch of Irishtown, undated (DDA, AB2 29/1/4).

35 Response from Fr Talbot and six priests of St Paul's, Arran Quay, undated (DDA, AB2 29/1/29 (1)); Response from Fr Mullen and six priests, undated (DDA, AB2 29/1/31).

36 Response from Dr Keating of Ferns, 1 Mar 1824 (DDA, AB3. 30/8).

on the parties to the marriage, ranging from automatic disentitlement to estates to being deemed a Catholic.[37] These penalties were lifted in 1792[38] when it was enacted that it would be lawful for Protestants and Roman Catholics to intermarry but only by licence or following banns called in the Established Church.[39]

Severe penalties were imposed against the celebrant of such marriages. Many Acts rendered it a felony punishable by death for a Catholic priest to celebrate a marriage where one of the spouses was a Protestant.[40] Under section 26 of the Popery Act 1709[41] it was presumed that a Popish priest who had celebrated such a marriage had knowingly committed the offence unless he could produce a certificate from the local Established Church certifying that such individuals were not considered to be Protestants.

Members of the degraded clergy also risked serious criminal penalties where they carried out a marriage between two Protestants or a Protestant and a Catholic. Section 1 of the 1725 Act stated that when carried out by a reputed Popish priest, a person pretending to be a Popish priest or a clergyman of the Church of Ireland or any degraded clergyman, such marriages were felonies and the celebrant was punishable by death.[42] It is not surprising that degraded clergymen were included in this statutory deterrent, as, being degraded, they were beyond the control of religious authorities. The statute combatted both the problem of mixed marriages and that of irregular clandestine marriage. Case law suggests that the clergyman's status as 'degraded' could be ascertained from the testimony of registrars of the diocese[43] or on production of the sentence of degradation.[44]

37 An Act to Prevent Protestants from Intermarrying with Papists 1697 (9 William III c 3 [Ire]); An Act to Prevent the Further Growth of Popery 1707 (2 Ann c 6) [Ire]).

38 An Act to Remove Certain Restraints and Disabilities Therein Mentioned, to which His Majesty's Subjects Professing the Popish Religion are now Subject 1792 (32 Geo III c 21 [Ire]), ss 9, 10.

39 32 Geo III c 21 [Ire], s 12. Previously Church of Ireland ministers who published the banns for mixed marriages had been subject to the less serious penalty of ecclesiastical censure under An Act for the More Effectual Preventing of Clandestine Marriages 1735 (9 Geo II c 11), s 6.

40 6 Ann c 16 [Ire] made it a felony for a Catholic priest to celebrate a marriage involving a Protestant heir. This prohibition was reiterated by An Act for Explaining ... an Act to Prevent the Further Growth of Popery 1709 (8 Ann c 3) [Ire], s 2. The Marriage Act 1725 (12 Geo I c 3 [Ire]) decreed that a priest performing such a ceremony after April 1726 would be guilty of a felony and suffer death. Father Timothy Ryan was executed in Limerick in 1727 under this Act. M Wall (1967) *The Penal Laws 1691–1760* (Dundalk: Dundalgan Press), p 21; An Act to repeal certain penal enactments made in the Parliament of Ireland against Roman Catholic clergymen for celebrating marriages contrary to the provisions of certain Acts made in the Parliament of Ireland 1793 (33 Geo III c 21), s 12. Marriages by Roman Catholics (Ireland) Act 1833 (3 & 4 Will IV c 102) finally repealed all provisions, making it a felony for Roman Catholic clergymen to celebrate marriages between Protestants.

41 8 Ann c 3, s 26 [Ire].

42 The Marriage Act 1725 (12 Geo I c 3 [Ire]).

43 *R v Stonage* (1832) Jebb CCR 121.

44 *R v Sandys* (1835) Jebb CCR 166.

It was not until 1745 that legislation specifically addressed the validity of the mixed marriages themselves. Marriages between two Protestants, or a Protestant and a Catholic, which were celebrated by Catholic priests were starkly declared to be null and void at common law without any need for a sentence by the ecclesiastical courts.[45] This Act applied to marriages that were celebrated after 1746 between two Protestants or, where one of the parties was a Papist and the other had merely professed to being a Protestant, within 12 months prior to the wedding.

Establishing religious identity in court

At the time of the *Millis* case the legal validity of mixed marriages depended on both the religion of the parties and that of the celebrant. Whether or not such a celebrant happened to be degraded made no difference to the legal validity of the marriage itself (see Table 3.1).

There were no detailed provisions in the statutes about how the religious identity of the priest celebrating the marriage, or the parties to the marriage, should be ascertained for the purpose of deciding if a mixed marriage had in fact taken place or was legally valid.

Table 3.1 The Catholic versus Established Church dichotomy within the statutory rules relating to the validity of marriage prior to the Marriages (Ireland) Act 1844

	Celebrated in the Established Church	*Celebrated by a Roman Catholic priest*	*Celebrated by a degraded Protestant clergyman*	*Celebrated by a degraded Popish priest*
Two parties are members of the Established Church	Valid	Void *ab initio*	Valid	Void *ab initio*
Two parties are Catholics	Valid	Valid	Valid	Valid
One party is a Catholic; the other is or professes to be a member of the Established Church	Valid	Void *ab initio*	Valid	Void *ab initio*

45 An Act for Annulling all Marriages to be Celebrated by any Popish Priest Between Protestant and Protestant, or between Protestant and Papist 1745 (19 Geo II c 13 [Ire]).

The issue of religious identity was considered by the Galway Assizes and appealed to the King's Bench in *Lessee of Kirwan v Kirwan*[46] in 1826. The case related to the validity of a will by Edmond Kirwan to his heirs in tail, but there was an additional question as to whether Edmond's grandson[47] was entitled to inherit. It was alleged that Edmond's son was a bigamist who had married Celia Hopkins in 1811 in a ceremony carried out by a Roman Catholic priest and then, in 1817, had married Anne Lambert according to the rites of the Established Church. The grandson claiming inheritance was a product of the marriage to Anne Lambert. The case hinged on the validity of the marriage of Edmond's son to Celia Hopkins, which if considered a mixed marriage was void *ab initio*. This would render the grandson legitimate and entitled to inherit.

It was clear that Celia Hopkins had always been a Roman Catholic but the religious identity of Edmond's son was less clear. He had been baptized by a Roman Catholic priest and had attended Roman Catholic places of worship until about 1814. A witness testified that Celia Hopkins and her new husband had been seen receiving the sacrament from a Roman Catholic priest on the day of the marriage. On the other hand, there was evidence that Edmond's son had regularly attended Protestant churches between 1805 and 1811, and two Roman Catholic priests testified that they considered him to be a Protestant and had denounced the couple from the altar for living in a state of prostitution.

The judge directed the jury that if they believed that Edmond's son had professed to being a Protestant in the 12 months previous to the marriage they should find that the grandson inherited under the will. He described profession to the Protestant faith as something unequivocal 'such as a Roman Catholic would not do'. The jury found for the grandson and this ruling was upheld by the King's Bench.

This case set up the identities of Catholicism and Protestantism in opposition to each order, reinforcing the dichotomy of the legislative system. Marriages involving Dissenters caused particular difficulties for a legal system used to viewing religious identity in these terms.

Marriages of and by Dissenters

Marriages of Dissenters had been carried out by the Presbyterian Church since the seventeenth century but their place within the existing legislative framework was fraught with difficulty. They were not considered by the ecclesiastical courts to be full and complete marriages; instead, Presbyterian marriage ceremonies were characterized as marriage contracts *per verba de*

46 (1826) Batty 712.

47 All generations of this highly original family were known as Edmond Kirwan: *Lessee of Kirwan v Kirwan* (1826) Batty 712.

praesenti which could be enforced in the ecclesiastical courts and the parties would be obliged to undergo a marriage ceremony in the Church of Ireland.

In 1737 a remedial Act was passed stating that such couples could no longer be prosecuted in the ecclesiastical courts for not undergoing a ceremony in the Established Church.[48] Whether or not such Presbyterian ceremonies were considered in law to create marriages was finally addressed by statute in 1782. The Dissenters Relief Act 1782[49] established that all marriages between two Protestant Dissenters solemnized by Protestant Dissenting ministers would be good and valid as if they had been solemnized by clergyman of the Church of Ireland. This piece of legislation emphasizes that compliance with a religious system was the touchstone for validity rather than the simple exchange of promises. The Act left several crucial questions unresolved, such as the status of mixed marriage involving a Dissenter if it was not celebrated in the Established Church, and the definition of a Dissenter for the purposes of marriage.

The Dissenters Relief Act 1782 caused a protest in Parliament.[50] Protesters argued that the Act would encourage every species of clandestine and improvident marriage not only between Dissenters but also between Protestants of the Established Church. It was suggested that persons who had only once or twice attended a meeting house could claim to be a Dissenter in order to escape religious formalities, or alternatively to get out of their marriage to a member of the Established Church. Moreover, protesters argued that the effect of the Act would be to allow Dissenter clergymen to celebrate clandestine marriages with impunity as they would escape both ecclesiastical censure and existing criminal penalties. Nearly 50 years later in *Lemon v Lemon*,[51] the Armagh Consistory Court claimed that Presbyterian ministers had indeed taken up the clandestine marriage trade, agreeing to marry any person who paid the sums required for seats in their meeting house but not requiring them to attend.[52]

The 1792 Act, which lifted the criminal penalties for mixed marriages carried out by Catholic clergyman, gave no greater clarity to the situation, merely stating that it authorized Dissenters to celebrate marriages involving Protestants of the Established Church.[53]

---

48 An Act for Allowing Further Time to Persons in Offices to Qualify Themselves Pursuant to an Act Entitled 'An Act to Prevent the Further Growth of Popery; and for Giving Further Ease to Protestant Dissenters with Respect to Matrimonial Contracts' 1737 (11 Geo II c 10 [Ire]).

49 An Act for the Relief of Protestant Dissenters in Certain Matters Therein Contained 1782 (21 & 22 Geo III c 25 [Ire]).

50 Reproduced in A Browne (1803) *A Compendious View of the Ecclesiastical Law of Ireland*, 2nd edn (Dublin: Mercier) App, p 34.

51 (1841) Crawford & Dix 498.

52 (1841) Crawford & Dix 498, p 516. The 'Report by Mr Herbert Wood' (1902) supports this assessment citing Rev Shulze of the German Lutheran Church and Reverend Caldwell of the Presbyterian Church as prolific couple beggars.

53 32 Geo III c 21 [Ire], s 13.

The incomplete regulation of Dissenter marriage created a grey area in the existing legislative framework and it is no surprise that the validity of such marriages was the central issue in *R v Millis* (Table 3.2).

Court adjudication of marital status

In the nineteenth century, the primary jurisdiction for adjudicating marital status lay with the ecclesiastical courts. However, the temporal courts were also required to rule on whether or not a marriage existed in a number of different circumstances.[54] The different courts determined the validity of marriage using different levels of proof for different purposes and the relationship between the two jurisdictions was constantly evolving.

The ecclesiastical courts

The ecclesiastical courts applied ecclesiastical law but were also required to take account of secular legislation relating to the validity of marriage.[55]

Table 3.2 The unclear position of Dissenter marriages prior to the Marriages (Ireland) Act 1844

	Celebrated in the Established Church	*Celebrated by a Roman Catholic priest*	*Celebrated by a Dissenter*
Two parties are members of the Established Church	Valid	Void *ab initio*	Unclear
Two parties are Catholics	Valid	Valid	Unclear
Two parties are Dissenters	Valid	Unclear	Valid
One party is a Protestant or professes to be a Protestant the other a Catholic	Valid	Void *ab initio*	Unclear
One party is a Protestant or professes to be a Protestant and the other is a Dissenter	Valid	Unclear	Unclear

54 The rulings of the Irish Court of Chancery are outside the scope of this piece which instead relies on the reported bigamy cases.

55 For example 'A Jactitation Case', Browne (1803) *A Compendious View*, App, p 5. A suit of jactitation was taken where a Popish priest had carried out a marriage between two Protestants. The court held that because the marriage was void *ab initio* under Irish legislation no sentence of the court to that effect was required. The jactitation suit itself failed as the parties had lived together as man and wife (a defence to a suit of jactitation).

Where a dispute over the validity of irregular marriage existed between the parties, two possible suits could be taken to establish the existence or non-existence of the marriage: jactitation, if the party wished to establish that no valid marriage existed, or a suit to compel the celebration of marriage in *facie ecclesiae*.[56] Where a valid marriage existed in the eyes of the ecclesiastical courts, the parties could seek matrimonial remedies such as separation *a mensa et thoro*,[57] alimony and restitution of conjugal rights. The ecclesiastical courts also considered the status of marriages as an incidental question when granting probate or rights of administration over an estate.

Browne's work on ecclesiastical law, published in 1803, notes that none of the formal requirements in Church canon law were essential to the validity of a marriage under the ecclesiastical law of Ireland except a judge-made rule that marriage must be performed by a person in holy orders.[58] This included ministers of the Established Church and Roman Catholic priests,[59] both of whom were episcopally ordained by a consecrated bishop.

In Ireland, all such suits relating to marriage were heard in the Consistory Court belonging to the local diocese with appeal to the Metropolitan Court of the Archbishop and from there to the Irish Court of Delegates.[60] Wills and rights of administration were determined in the local Consistory Court or in the Court of Prerogatives in Dublin.[61] Dr Radcliffe,[62] who gave evidence to the Queen's Bench in *R v Millis,* presided in all of the superior ecclesiastical courts in Ireland. He had considered the ecclesiastical validity of irregular marriages on a number of different occasions in different contexts in the

56 This would compel the marriage to take place in the Established Church. This cause of action was abolished in 1818 by the Infant Executors (Ireland) Act 1818 (58 Geo III c 81) which enacted, amongst other things, that 'no proceeding should be thereafter had to compel a marriage by reason of the contract of matrimony whatsoever whether *per verba de praesenti* or *per verba de futuro* which should be entered into after the end and expiration of ten days from the passing of the Act'.

57 This ended the spouses' obligation to live together but did not allow them to marry again.

58 Browne (1803) *A Compendious View* p 269.

59 For example *Moriarty v Moriarty* cited in Browne (1803) *A Compendious View*, app, p 19 where the validity of marriage between two Catholics, carried out by a Catholic priest in France, was considered; see also comments in *Lemon v Lemon* (1841) Cr & Dix 514.

60 See Browne (1803) *A Compendious View*, pp 223–224.

61 Jurisdiction lay in the Court of Prerogative if the deceased had assets in more than one diocese.

62 Radcliffe was a rather interesting character who attained a great deal of financial reward from his multiple roles. By special arrangement with the Archbishop of Armagh he also continued his chamber practice in the Courts of Equity. Witnesses to the 19th report of the commissioners appointed to inquire into the duties, salaries and emoluments in all temporal and ecclesiastical courts in Ireland in 1830 alleged that Dr Radcliffe presided over an unfair monopoly of ecclesiastical causes, deliberately limited access to apprenticeships to the court and charged extremely high fees for such apprenticeships. Radcliffe was succeeded as Vicar-General of Dublin by his son. CR Milward (1847) *Reports of Cases Argued and Determined in The Court of Prerogative in Ireland and in the Consistory Court of Dublin during the time of the Late Hon. John Radcliffe, LLD* (Dublin: Hodges and Smith) pp v–x.

years predating *R v Millis*. In all of the judgments the necessity of a clergyman is the underpinning assumption. It is clear, however, that the Dublin Consistory Court was generally reluctant to invalidate marriages. Even the most meagre amount of evidence that a ceremony, with some kind of presiding clergyman, had taken place would give rise to a presumption that a valid marriage had been carried out. This presumption would then have to be displaced. For example, in *Smith v Smith*[63] the evidence of the marriage consisted of a statement by a couple beggar, the Reverend Connel, and character references about whether or not Joanna Smith was the type of woman who would take up with a man without a marriage ceremony. Although the direct evidence of Connel, who was an infamous character and a low couple beggar, was given little weight, the supporting evidence was such that the court held that a clandestine ceremony had indeed taken place and upheld the marriage.

In *Maxwell v Maxwell*,[64] a suit for the restitution of conjugal rights, the couple had been married by the Reverend Joseph Wood, a couple beggar of Haymarket Dublin, in 1826 in a house at Mount Pleasant. The parties and the minister were of the Established Church. There was very little evidence in the case that the marriage ceremony had actually taken place, as Joseph Wood had since died. Radcliffe emphasized that, in Ireland, all that was required to enter into a marriage was an exchange of vows with the intervention of a priest in holy orders. Circumstantial evidence was sufficient to prove a marriage and strict proof by certificate could not be expected in a country where marriage registers were generally disregarded and the law was very loose. The evidence for the marriage consisted of statements by both parties and evidence about the wife's situation, upbringing, previous conduct and character and evidence about the extended family's recognition of the wife and child. The marriage was upheld.

The court also avoided pronouncing a sentence of invalidity of marriage if the case could be resolved another way. For example, in *Cobbe v Garaton*,[65] Radcliffe did not rule on the validity of either marriage in the dispute and instead dismissed the suit for lack of evidence.

In mixed marriage cases where the religious identity of the spouses or the clergyman could render the marriage void on a statutory basis, a more careful consideration of the evidence is seen, yet even here the evidence rules of the Dublin court tend to uphold irregular marriage if at all possible.

In *Legeyt v O'Brien*,[66] the court considered the evidence needed to establish the religious identity of the celebrant. This case involved a marriage carried out by Reverend Joseph Wood in 1827 during the Donnybrook Fair between

63 (1821) Milward 120 (Prerogative Court).

64 (1832) Milward 290 (Dublin Consistory Court).

65 (1841) Milward 529 (Dublin Consistory Court).

66 (1834) Milward 325 (Prerogative Court).

Robert Poole and Mary O'Brien. There was only one witness who testified that Wood was a member of the Established Church. Robert Poole was a Protestant and Mary O'Brien a Catholic. A local Roman Catholic clergyman gave evidence that he had been approached by the couple and had refused to marry them and encouraged the couple to find a Protestant clergyman. Several depositions established that Wood was reputed to be a clergyman and authorized to celebrate marriage. Radcliffe held that once the fact of the ceremony had been proved it fell to the party impugning it to show it void at law. The marriage was upheld.

In *O'Connor v M'Cann*,[67] a case in the Prerogative Court relating to letters of administration, the legitimacy of the deceased's daughter was in question. In this case, a marriage between Margaret Forbes and Ross McCann had been celebrated by a Roman Catholic priest in 1791. While it was clear that McCann was a Catholic it was alleged that the marriage was invalid because Margaret was a Protestant, or had at least professed to being a Protestant in the 12 months before the wedding. Margaret's first marriage had been to a Protestant clergyman who had died in 1783. Margaret was appointed guardian of her children with her first husband on 17 July 1790. In these guardianship proceedings she had asserted, in an affidavit, that she was a Protestant. Margaret's second marriage had taken place very quietly less than a year after guardianship proceedings on 21 June 1791. Margaret had never attended a service in a Protestant Church or carried out any devotional acts. The court held that a public and unequivocal act showing adherence to the Protestant religion was required to avoid a marriage.[68] The court upheld the marriage, noting that the affidavit had been made on 13 March 1790, over 12 *lunar months* before the second marriage, and that Margaret had at all times believed herself to be a Catholic.

However, in spite of an evidential system that tended to uphold marriages, it is clear from the 1840 case of *Lemon v Lemon*[69] that marriages carried out by Presbyterians were not considered lawful in the ecclesiastical court. This case related to rights of administration over the estate of Thomas Lemon. Two women had come forward as his 'widow': Jane Lemon and Eleanor Lemon. Eleanor, a Roman Catholic, had married Thomas, a member of the Established Church, in a ceremony carried out by Rev William Charleton, a minister of the Presbyterian congregation. Two written documents were produced in evidence, the certificate of marriage from Charleton which was not formally received in evidence and the last will of Thomas in which he bequeathed Jane a legacy but described her as Jane McQuatty the mother of his sons.

---

67 (1829) Milward 204 (Prerogative Court).

68 The court referred to the ruling of the temporal courts in *Lessee of Kirwan v Kirwan* (1826) Batty 712.

69 (1841) Crawford & Dix 498 (Armagh Consistory Court).

The court noted that differences of religion in Ireland afforded frequent opportunities for clandestine and irregular marriages. All the legislation assumed that a lawful marriage must be carried out by a clergyman episcopally ordained. The only exception was the Dissenter Relief Act 1782,[70] but as neither Eleanor nor Thomas was a Protestant Dissenter, the marriage could not be upheld as valid.

The temporal courts

The temporal courts did not have jurisdiction to consider the ecclesiastical validity of a marriage. However, in certain circumstances they had to consider whether a marriage existed as an incidental fact to a dispute. The rulings of the ecclesiastical court could be used as evidence of the status of a marriage in the temporal courts, but were not necessarily conclusive.[71] One reason for this apparent inconsistency was that rules of evidence were different in ecclesiastical and temporal courts and could differ even within a court system depending on the cause of action. A finding by the ecclesiastical courts about the status of a marriage might not be admissible in evidence in later proceedings if it did not take the correct form of a declaration or judgment, particularly if the court had avoided declaring a marriage to be invalid and determined the issue in a different way.[72]

Bigamy convictions by jury trial were common at assizes around the country in the early nineteenth century.[73] Most cases were straightforward and hinged on the level of evidence available to show that two marriage ceremonies had in fact taken place. However, by the 1830s, reported cases showed that circuit judges were increasingly asked to direct the jury as to the legal validity of irregular marriage ceremonies presented in evidence.

In *R v McLaughlin*[74] the validity of marriages celebrated by Dissenting ministers was first raised in connection with bigamy. In this case the prisoner was a member of the Established Church and his first wife was a Presbyterian.

70 An Act for the Relief of Protestant Dissenters in Certain Matters Therein Contained 1782 (21 & 22 Geo III c 25 [Ire]).

71 For example, Browne cites the Duchess of Kingston case from 1776 where a sentence in a suit for jactitation was not successful in barring a prosecution for bigamy. Browne (1803) *A Compendious View*, p 259.

72 For example in *Ryan v Ryan*, cited in Browne (1803) *A Compendious View*, app, p 21, the Ossory Consistory Court determined that Captain Ryan's first marriage was invalid on confessional evidence from the woman who was reputed to be his first 'wife'. When Captain Ryan died both his first 'wife' and his second 'wife' applied for rights of administration in his estate. The court allowed the claim of the first wife as an appropriate sentence of nullity was not possible on the sole confession of the parties. See also *Goodin v Smith* (1831) Milward 236 (Prerogative Court).

73 An examination of the remaining Crown books from assizes prior to 1844 suggests that many men were routinely convicted by juries of bigamy. See for example, County of Westmeath Lent Assizes 1833 (NLI MS 807); County of Carlow Lent Assizes 1837 (NLI MS 807); Kings County Lent Assizes 1838 (NLI, MS 807); County of Donegal Lent Assizes 1838 (NLI, MS 12,911); Lifford Spring Assizes 1841 (NLI, MS n3913, p 3584).

74 (1841) Crawford & Dix 315.

His first marriage was celebrated by a Presbyterian clergyman. The second marriage was also celebrated by a Presbyterian clergyman. Although counsel for the prisoner objected that neither marriage was legally valid, the conviction was upheld. The report noted that it was the 'general opinion of the judiciary' that marriages between persons of the Established Church could be lawfully celebrated by Dissenting ministers. As we have seen, there was no legislative authority for this point and so it was revisited in subsequent cases.

The level of evidence needed to show that a valid Presbyterian marriage had been formed in Scotland was given great scrutiny in *R v Charleton.*[75] Alexander Charleton was tried at the Monaghan spring assizes for bigamy and found guilty. His first marriage took place in Dumferline in Scotland in 1824 where he was married in a house by a Presbyterian minister to Mary Phelps. His second marriage took place in Monaghan in 1838 in Glaslough and this was carried out by the rector of the parish in Donogh Church. The issue at trial was whether a clergyman, who had given evidence of what was required to enter into a valid marriage for the purposes of Scotch marriage law, had been suitably qualified as a witness. The case was reserved for the consideration of the Twelve Judges. The judges upheld the conviction and the prisoner was given a sentence of six months' imprisonment.

In *R v Smith,*[76] Samuel Smith, a member of the Established Church, had married Margaret Smith, a Presbyterian, in 1831. The marriage was carried out by a Presbyterian minister according to Presbyterian forms. In 1839, Smith was married in St Anne's Church by the parish minister to Jane Gordon. It was argued by the defence that the first marriage was not a legal marriage according to the laws of Ireland. Crampton J refused to direct a verdict of acquittal and the prisoner was sentenced to seven years' transportation. However, Crampton J referred the question to the consideration of the Twelve Judges. The Crown argued that the presence of a clergyman was not necessary under the common law in Ireland and the Twelve Judges considered the judgment of Lord Stowell in *Dalrymple.*[77] The court was divided on the question and seemed reluctant to invalidate marriages carried out by Presbyterian ministers, lest it should bastardize a great number of children and cause problems in Ulster. The majority of the judges found the marriage to be invalid.[78] Only Foster J and Perrin J upheld the marriage. The prisoner was recommended a free pardon.

R v Millis and *R v Carroll* were argued separately in the Queen's Bench in 1842.[79] Millis had been tried by Perrin J at the Carrickfergus Spring Assizes in

75 (1839) Crawford & Dix 315; (1839) Jebb CCR 267; (1839) 2 Jebb & Symes 54.

76 (1843) Crawford & Dix 318 and (1842) Jebb & Bourke, App i.

77 *Dalrymple v Dalrymple* (1811) 2 Hag Con 54; 161 ER 665.

78 Pennefather CJ, Doherty CJ, Brady CB, Burton J, Pennefather B, Torrens J, Crampton J and Ball J.

79 (1842) Hamilton Smyth & Bourke, p 3 (*Millis*); p 215 (*Carroll*).

1842. Carroll had been tried at the Armagh Spring Assizes in 1842 by Crampton J. Both cases involved marriages conducted by a Presbyterian minister. The judges could not agree and it was clear that the idea of marriages *per verba de praesenti* had now taken root. Perrin J found the marriages as contracts *per verba de praesenti* to be valid *de facto* and *de jure* and upheld the conviction. Burton J found that the marriages were contracts *per verba de praesenti* but as such did not support a bigamy conviction. Pennefather CJ agreed with Burton J that the marriages were not validly celebrated *in facie ecclesiae* and that mere contract *per verba de praesenti* did not support a bigamy conviction.

Why did the temporal courts come to this impasse?

An important factor in the disagreement was a statement by Lord Stowell in the Scottish case of *Dalrymple v Dalrymple*[80] that prior to the Marriage Act 1753, a marriage in England could be formed by the simple exchange of consent between the parties. This judgment ruled that a valid marriage had been created in this manner in the Scottish case before the court. The judgment thus elided the issues of the force of a marriage contract entered into by the parties alone and the validity of a clandestine marriage entered into in the presence of a priest or clergyman of dubious credentials. If no clergyman was considered necessary, their religious identity was no longer a factor. The argument had greater force in the Irish temporal courts than in the ecclesiastical courts.

In *Lemon v Lemon,*[81] Miller DD accepted the judgment in *Dalrymple* as far as it related to the law of Scotland but queried its larger scope. Miller attributed the confusion in *Dalrymple* to an incorrect understanding of the role of the temporal and ecclesiastical courts. The temporal courts often assumed that the religious part of any marriage was compliant, when considering marriage as a fact to be proven. However, ecclesiastical courts could investigate the validity of the marriage under ecclesiastical law. Retrospective analysis of the practice of the temporal courts in accepting an apparently ecclesiastically invalid marriage, at face value, for certain purposes, did not mean that ecclesiastically invalid marriages were valid marriages in all courts for all purposes.[82]

In the temporal courts the reliance of the Crown on the idea of a valid marriage *per verba de praesenti* to secure a conviction in cases where marriages were carried out by Presbyterians is understandable. The evidential difficulties that arose when it came to assessing the validity of Dissenter marriages within a legislative framework based on the distinction between Catholic and Protestant, and the inconsistent approach of the assizes judges to the question, must have made it very tempting to avoid all questions of

80 *Dalrymple v Dalrymple* (1811) 2 Hag Con 54; 161 ER 665.

81 (1841) Crawford & Dix 508.

82 (1841) Crawford & Dix 508, p 520.

religious identity and suggest that the consent of the parties was the only relevant factor.

The aftermath of *Millis*

The Marriages (Ireland) Act 1844[83] was passed shortly after the unsatisfactory ruling in *Millis*. It provided that all marriages carried out by members of the Established Church or Presbyterians after 31 March 1845 must be preceded by the calling of the banns or a licence or by giving notice to the Registrar. Section 4 of the Act made it clear that marriages between a Presbyterian and a non-Presbyterian were valid if carried out in a Presbyterian meeting house.[84] Section 12 set out that marriages carried out by Quakers and Jews according to their usages were good in law as long as both parties belonged to the same religion and notice had been given to the Registrar.

The Act went a long way to establishing the legal validity of Presbyterian, Quaker and Jewish marriage and abolishing the practice of clandestine marriages. The Act is a watershed in secular regulation of marriage. For the first time in Ireland, the State prescribed the steps necessary to legally form a marriage, rather than the previous regulatory approach of forbidding particularly disliked practices and leaving the rest up to the individual religions. However, marriages between two Roman Catholics were exempted from this Act and left to the operation of the common law without any requisite State formalities until the Registration of Marriages (Ireland) Act 1863[85] which merely imposed an obligation on the husband to register such marriages.[86]

It is argued that the idea of a legal marriage *per verba de praesenti* was desirable to the Lords in *Millis* when reviewing Irish law as an unfamiliar archaic system. Existing Irish legislation regulated marriages according to strictly defined religious categories which did not properly encompass Dissenter marriage. By eliding the issue of irregular marriage formalities with the question of the legal force of a contract *per verba de praesenti* the Lords avoided the need to sift through the penal laws and reason by analogy for Presbyterians. The revival of the medieval contract *per verba de praesenti* as the essence of marriage in an operational sense, rather than a theological context, also reflected a more modern English approach to regulating marriage through uniform rules applicable to all religions.

83 7 & 8 Vic c 81 as amended by the Marriages (Ireland) Act 1846 (9 & 10 Vic c 72), which provided for marriage in cases where one of the parties intending the marriage resided in England or Scotland.

84 The only bases for annulling marriage under the 1844 Act were where the parties had knowingly and wilfully married without banns, licence or certificate or knowingly and wilfully married in a place other than that stated in the banns, licence or certificate. The Marriages (Ireland) Act 1844 (7 & 8 Vic c 81), s 49.

85 26 & 27 Vic c 90.

86 Non-registration did not affect the legal validity of the marriages. Under s 11 of the Act a £10 fine was imposed on the husband for non-compliance.

4

The Action for Breach of Promise of Marriage in Nineteenth-Century Ireland

*Michael Sinnott**

Introduction

In December 1820, Lord Norbury presided over the three-day *Caila v McNamara*[1] trial in the Irish Court of Common Pleas. Before a 'court crowded to excess', Thomas Wallace KC (one of five barristers for the plaintiff) alleged that the 'fortune hunter' defendant had, 'without any sense of religion or morality', 'deeply disgraced his country' by breaching his promise to marry the plaintiff, who had been once 'beautiful', but 'misery withered those charms that were then in all the bloom of loveliness'. Wallace closed the plaintiff's case with an 'appeal to the feelings of the jury, who, by their verdict, would protect the injured from being a prey to such baseness and ingratitude', before sitting 'amid great applause'. Henry Deane Grady KC, one of six barristers for the defence, replied in a similarly theatrical fashion, warning the jury 'not to be seduced by the artificial tears of [the plaintiff's] counsel'. He called the plaintiff a 'kept mistress' and demanded the jury not 'reward immorality, impurity, and prostitution' by ruling for the defendant. The drama was not confined to the Four Courts. After the jury awarded the plaintiff £2,000 damages for the defendant's breach of his promise to marry her, the defendant and three or four 'athletic young men' set upon the plaintiff's leading barrister in Sackville Street and beat him with a whip.[2] The

* I wish to thank Kevin Costello and Niamh Howlin for their invaluable comments on earlier drafts of this paper, as well as all who attended the Law and the Family 1750–1950 Round Table at University College Dublin for the discussion and suggestions.

1 *Freeman's Journal*, 11, 12, 13 Dec 1820.

2 *Freeman's Journal*, 15 Dec 1820. M Luddy (2011) *Matters of Deceit: Breach of Promise to Marry Cases in Nineteenth- and Twentieth-Century Limerick* (Dublin: Four Courts Press), p 34.

defendant subsequently 'fled justice' and a reward of 200 guineas was offered by concerned citizens of Dublin for his capture.[3]

Before the Family Law Act 1981, an engagement between two parties could constitute a binding contract at common law. If a party to a marriage contract broke their promise, they could have damages awarded against them by the courts. These trials were often founded upon evidence of intimate letters and salacious witness testimony, frequently drawing widespread media attention. This chapter examines nineteenth-century Irish breach of promise of marriage trials, exploring the legal and evidential elements of the action, as well as the tactics employed before the courts. Four aspects of the action will be examined: gender; the contract; the breach; and finally, the damages.

Gender and the nature of the action

The vast majority of the Irish breach of promise claims were initiated by women.[4] In Lettmaier's study of 242 English trials from 1800 to 1940, she found that only 3.7 per cent of actions involved male plaintiffs.[5] The reason for this gender discrepancy goes to the heart of the action. In *Blake v Wilkins*,[6] a male plaintiff, Lieutenant Blake, brought an action against Mary Wilkins, an elderly widow. The defendant's barrister, Charles Phillips, admitted that the action did not 'belong exclusively to a female', but considered the proceedings to suit a woman better because

> every female object being more exclusively domestic, such a disappointment is more severe in its visitation because the very circumstance concentrating their feelings renders them naturally more sensitive of a wound – because their best treasure, their reputation, may have suffered from the intercourse because their chances of reparation are less, and their habitual seclusion makes them feel it more; because there is something in the desertion of their helplessness which almost merges the illegality in the unmanliness of the abandonment.

Phillips continued by mocking Blake, commenting '[w]hat a loss the navy had of him, and what a loss had he of the navy! Alas, Gentlemen – he could not resist his affection ... Almighty love eclipsed the glories of ambition – Trafalgar and St Vincent flitted from his memory'.[7] Blake subsequently

3 *Freeman's Journal*, 28 Dec 1820.

4 See Luddy (2011) *Matters of Deceit*, p 11.

5 S Lettmaier (2010) *Broken Engagements: The Action for Breach of Promise of Marriage and the Feminine Ideal, 1800–1940* (Oxford: Oxford University Press), p 27.

6 *Freeman's Journal*, 31 Mar 1817; *Belfast Newsletter*, 8 Apr 1817; P Pindar (1817) *The Humorous Speech of Charles Phillips, Esq. in Blake v Wilkins* (London: William Hone London).

7 Pindar (1817) *The Humorous Speech of Charles Phillips*.

withdrew his claim. In *G v H*,[8] the *Belfast Newsletter* produced a scathingly sarcastic piece, commenting that the male plaintiff 'Captain G', 'the gallant son of Mars', had 'accepted of compensation for the wounds inflicted on his heart by the obdurate fair one'. While Captain G settled the matter for an impressive £550, the article hints at popular scorn for the male plaintiff.

Although, as the Law Reform Commission commented in its pre-abolition review of the law, '[a]n action for breach of promise to marry may be taken by a man as well as a woman',[9] during the nineteenth century the Irish action was like the English, 'theoretically gender-neutral', but 'in practice gender-specific'.[10] As Lettmaier explains, '[m]arriage was [a woman's] mission, her one and only purpose in life ... [w]hen a woman failed ... to get married, she was perceived as having suffered a genuine injury'.[11] In a more typical female-plaintiff, male-defendant suit, Daniel O'Connell argued that, 'although man had a thousand chances and a thousand occupations, woman had only one prize in the lottery of life – the chance of a husband'.[12] In the same vein, Edward Litton KC argued before the Court of Exchequer in 1831:

> [i]f a man be affected [by a breach of promise], he can go abroad and mix in the pleasures of the world, he can go to plays, balls and public assemblies and forget his grief in the amusements afforded by society; but wound a woman's heart once – take her happy home from her, and you send her an outcast on the world. Win her heart and betray it, and you send her a bankrupt on society, without a hope except that death may relieve her from the canker, which consumes her heart. She is left to the contempt of her own sex and rendered an incubus on the happiness of her friends and relatives.[13]

Men were considered immune to such wounds and therefore could not succeed in court.

8 *Belfast Newsletter*, 28 Apr 1843.

9 Law Reform Commission, *Working Paper on the Law Relating to Breach of Promise of Marriage* (LRC 4-1978), p 1.

10 Lettmaier (2010) *Broken Engagements*, p 30. See Chapter 6 of this volume for a discussion of the tort of criminal conversation, a gender-specific action open only to husbands.

11 Lettmaier (2010) *Broken Engagements*, p 64.

12 *Wynn v Warner*, *Freeman's Journal*, 19, 20, 22 Aug 1823; *Belfast Newsletter*, 22 Aug 1823.

13 *Little v Lynch*, *Freeman's Journal*, 26 Oct 1831; *Belfast Newsletter*, 1 Nov 1831. See also Thomas O'Hagan's closing speech in *Nowlan v Sullivan*, *Freeman's Journal*, 23, 24 June 1851.

The components of the action

The claim for breach of promise began as an action of assumpsit, brought before civil courts for breach of contract.[14] However, attempts to place the action neatly within any modern taxonomy of private law have proven problematic.[15] The action needs to be approached as a meeting point between legal and social institutions of nineteenth-century Ireland and as both a reaction to, and an encouragement of, societal conceptions of femininity, masculinity, relationships and family. However, as a matter of law the basic ingredients of a breach of promise action were clear. As explained by O'Grady LCB in *Madden v McEgan*,[16] there were three aspects for a jury to consider: firstly, whether the plaintiff had proved the existence of a contract for marriage; secondly, whether that contract was breached; and thirdly, if the prior two conditions were met, the appropriate amount of damages needed to remedy the breach. Each of these elements shall be examined.

Forming the contract to marry

The promise

As outlined in the second edition of Chitty's *Contracts*, '[i]n order to constitute a binding contract, there must be a definitive promise by the party charged, accepted by the person claiming the benefit of such promise'.[17] Until 1869, the parties to a breach of promise action were not competent witnesses,[18] and so other forms of evidence were needed to make out the claim. As Ball J explained in *Forrest v O'Brien*,[19] a promise could be established by 'direct unequivocal testimony', such as oral and written evidence, and also from 'collateral subjects'. In some cases, there was plenty of direct evidence. In *Sutter v Courtney*,[20] the plaintiff produced a written contract to marry, signed by the defendant. Similarly, promises to marry were evidenced by written

14 *Little v Lynch, Freeman's Journal*, 26 Oct 1831; *Belfast Newsletter*, 1 Nov 1831. See Lettmaier (2010) *Broken Engagements*, p 18.

15 Lettmaier (2010) *Broken Engagements*, p 21.

16 *Freeman's Journal*, 15 Dec 1809.

17 J Chitty (1834) *A Practical Treatise on the Law of Contracts* (London: Milliken and Son), p 8. See Warren Swain (2015) *The Law of Contract 1670–1870* (Cambridge: Cambridge University Press), pp 182–184. It is important to note that the concepts of 'offer and acceptance' were only coming into widespread use during the early nineteenth century with the development of the will theory, following the English translation of Robert-Joseph Pothier's *Traité des Obligations* in 1806. See David Ibbetson (1999) *A Historical Introduction to the Law of Obligations* (Oxford: Oxford University Press) pp 220–223.

18 Evidence Further Amendment Act 1869 (32 & 33 Vic c 68), s 2; Law Reform Commission (1978) *Breach of Promise of Marriage*, p 2.

19 *Freeman's Journal*, 21, 22 Mar 1845.

20 *Freeman's Journal*, 20 Mar 1841. See also *Caila v McNamara, Freeman's Journal*, 11, 12, 13 Dec 1820; *Murray v Redmond, Belfast Newsletter*, 10 Aug 1847; *Harding's Case, Nation*, 25 Mar 1865.

marriage settlements.[21] The issue of oral contracts[22] arose before the Court of King's Bench in 1815, when Downes LCJ rejected Peter Burrowes QC's argument that engagements not evidenced in writing were unenforceable.[23]

Irish engagements usually involved several additional parties to the two betrothed who could testify as to the existence of the promise. As courtships were often carefully supervised by the woman's family, marriage proposals were rarely private; friends and relatives were consulted and parental consent was important when dowries and inheritance were involved.[24] In cases involving the upper classes, solicitors were retained for the financial arrangements involved, such as arranging for money to be settled in trust on the bride-to-be.[25] Similarly, a clergyman would need to be contacted to arrange the marriage licence and ceremony. In the Court of Queen's Bench in 1852, the parish priest for Blanchardstown Reverend Michael Dungan deposed that the defendant came to him seeking a marriage certificate and publication of the banns.[26]

If family members were unaware of an engagement, for example in the case of a secret relationship, there would frequently be evidence of written correspondence between the parties. Newspapers relished printing these intimate letters in detail. In *Wynn v Warner*,[27] 15 letters from the defendant were read aloud by the plaintiff's barrister, Daniel O'Connell. Henry Deane Grady admitted that 'no man could deny to [his client] the title of *a man of letters*'. Over 80 letters between the parties were read to the Court of Common Pleas in one 1872 case.[28] In an early case reported in the *Belfast Newsletter*, a letter was read containing the following 'curious scrap of amorous poetry': 'When I behold your sparkling eyes, I rave, I burn, I dote, I *dies*'.[29]

The courts were also willing to imply the existence of a contract to marry from the circumstances.[30] As explained by Chitty, it was not 'necessary to prove an express promise to marry in *totidem verbis*. The contract may be evidenced by the unequivocal conduct of the parties'.[31] Ball J told one jury in 1845 that, in the absence of direct evidence, they could find a contract

21 *Kavanagh v McGarry*, *Belfast Newsletter*, 12 Nov 1820; *Bowers v Morris*, *Freeman's Journal*, 13 Mar 1840; *Campion v Drew*, *Freeman's Journal*, 14, 16 Aug 1841.

22 See Chitty (1834) *A Practical Treatise*, pp 425–426 for treatment of the promise to marry in the context of the Statute of Frauds 1677 (29 Car II c 3).

23 *Smith v Dillon*, *Freeman's Journal*, 1 Jul 1815.

24 See *Bowers v Morris*, *Freeman's Journal*, 13 Mar 1840.

25 See Chapter 5 in this volume.

26 *Walsh v Lacken*, *Freeman's Journal*, 4 Feb 1852.

27 *Freeman's Journal*, 19, 20, 22 Aug 1823; *Belfast Newsletter*, 22 Aug 1823.

28 *Garvey v Lindsay*, *Freeman's Journal*, 21, 22, 24, 25 June 1872.

29 *Anonymous case*, *Belfast Newsletter*, 18 Aug 1789.

30 Lettmaier (2010) *Broken Engagements*, pp 34–36.

31 Chitty (1834) *A Practical Treatise*, p 425.

to marry from 'the demeanour of the parties towards each other, from the conduct of their relations or friends mutually, and in fact from the general aspect of the case'. [32] There, the defendant alleged that he had never made an explicit promise to marry the plaintiff, but the evidence suggested that he had 'acted in every respect as the accepted suitor'. The jury decided there was a contract, awarding £250 damages. In *Berbick v Byrne,*[33] there was no evidence of any actual promise proffered. Instead, one witness testified that the plaintiff and defendant had travelled to chapel and prayed together. Another witness stated that they had observed the defendant 'mending the bolt of the winder shutter of the plaintiff's parlour'. Lord Norbury charged the jury and commented that there was 'strong presumptive evidence of a promise', as 'it was seldom the case that other evidence could be produced as these things were seldom transacted in the presence of a third person'. The jury agreed, returning a verdict for the plaintiff and damages of £40. Similarly, in 1839 in the Court of Common Pleas, one jury awarded £100 damages despite Doherty CJ commenting that he 'never knew a case where the evidence was so vague and unsatisfactory'.[34] The jury thought otherwise. It is questionable whether juries were inferring the meeting of minds or agreement necessary for the existence of a contract on the evidence or finding 'a promise where, under the circumstances, the defendant *should* have promised'.[35]

Following the Evidence Further Amendment Act 1869 ('the 1869 Act'), parties to a breach of promise suit could give evidence personally in court. As a precaution against invented claims, a plaintiff could not recover unless her evidence was corroborated 'by some other material evidence'.[36] It appears that courts were relatively relaxed in the collaboration requirement. For example, in *Garvey v Lindsay,*[37] the only corroborating evidence was a letter which the plaintiff herself had written after the alleged promise had been made. Monahan CJ refused the defendant's application for a direction that the 1869 Act had not been complied with, preferring to leave the matter to the jury.

The counter-promise

The other side of any contact is the acceptance, as 'assent or consent must be mutual'.[38] While a defendant's offer to marry was a vital issue in proceedings, far less attention was paid to the plaintiff's counter-promise, which acted as both the acceptance of the plaintiff's offer and as the necessary

32 *Forrest v O'Brien, Freeman's Journal,* 21, 22 Mar 1845.

33 *Freeman's Journal,* 23 Jul 1814.

34 *Herbert v Nalty, Freeman's Journal,* 8 Nov 1839.

35 Lettmaier (2010) *Broken Engagements,* p 36.

36 Evidence Further Amendment Act 1869 (32 & 33 Vic c 68), s 2.

37 *Freeman's Journal,* 21, 22, 24, 25 June 1872.

38 Chitty (1834) *A Practical Treatise,* p 18.

consideration.[39] Although Chitty suggested that 'the plaintiff must give some evidence that she had, by word or action, accepted the defendant's proposal',[40] in 1820, Lord Norbury instructed one jury, 'where there was a solemn promise on the part of the man, and the lady received this promise in silence, the law says there is reciprocity ... her silence is construed into consent'.[41] Lord Norbury stated his authority for this principle of law came from the early eighteenth-century jurist, Holt LCJ, who was, Lord Norbury rather bizarrely felt, 'as good a judge of women, as I or any other judge'. As Lettmaier observes, 'anything short of outright rejection of the defendant would be taken as an implied promise to marry'.[42]

Attacking the nature of the promise

Proving the existence of a contract was not always without obstacles. Occasionally, defendants attacked the nature of the promise. Chitty commented that generally, '[n]o contract is raised by a mere *ex parte* affirmation in discourse; a mere overture or offer to enter into agreement, not definitively and expressly assented to by both parties'.[43] In *Smith v Dillon*,[44] which involved a rare victory for a male defendant, his barrister argued that a promise to marry should be 'solemn and deliberate, and not a light, flimsy, and complimentary one'. The judge instructed the jury that if they 'considered it a[n] ... engagement made in a moment of levity ... they must find for the defendant'. The promise had been made at a ball, and the jury evidently thought the evidence of flippancy negated the suggestion of a solemn promise, finding for the defendant. In 1833 at the Cork Assizes, another defendant attacked the nature of the promise and argued that the promise was not a general one, but a promise to marry on condition of receiving a dowry of £800.[45] As this dowry was not forthcoming, the defendant suggested that there was no contract. Unlike in *Smith v Dillon*, the jury awarded £200 damages against him.

The breach

After establishing the existence of the promise to marry, the plaintiff had to show the defendant had breached that promise. This was straightforward in cases where the male defendant had subsequently married another

39 Lettmaier (2010) *Broken Engagements*, p 36.

40 Chitty (1834) *A Practical Treatise*, p 14.

41 *Caila v McNamara, Freeman's Journal*, 11, 12, 13 Dec 1820. See also DR Pigott in *Forrest v O'Brien, Freeman's Journal*, 21, 22 Mar 1845.

42 Lettmaier (2010) *Broken Engagements*, p 37. See Chitty (1834) *A Practical Treatise*, p 25.

43 Chitty (1834) *A Practical Treatise*, pp 8–9.

44 *Freeman's Journal*, 1 Jul 1815.

45 *Dunlevie v Barry, Belfast Newsletter*, 29 Mar 1833.

woman.[46] In other cases the defendant would simply cease communication, and when a family member or friend of the plaintiff enquired, the defendant would refuse outright to proceed with the engagement.[47] Occasionally the defendant would refuse to marry the plaintiff and attempt to justify his refusal. Refusals could be absolute, or a refusal to marry within a reasonable time. Defendants occasionally admitted that they had promised to marry, but that the completion was conditional on some future event, and if the event had not yet occurred there was no breach. These denials do not appear to have convinced juries. In 1870, a widower defendant argued before the Court of Exchequer that he was always willing to marry the plaintiff but that he had made clear he could not do so until his adult daughters found suitable husbands of their own.[48] He maintained that he was still willing to marry the plaintiff if the court would adjourn. The jury, however, felt that the defendant had failed to marry the plaintiff within a reasonable period, awarding £100 damages. In *Fortune v Conolly*,[49] the defendant suggested that the marriage was conditional on the proposed dowry being raised to £2,000, but instead had £1,500 damages awarded against him. Arguing a future condition had not yet been met was, however, successful in an 1872 case before Monahan CJ in the Court of Common Pleas; the female defendant successfully argued that her promise had been conditional on the male plaintiff converting from Catholicism to Protestantism.[50]

Damages and mitigating factors

Once a solemn binding promise had been established and a breach proven, the jury was bound to award damages to the plaintiff but retained great discretion as to amount. The award of damages provides one of the action's greatest deviations from traditional nineteenth-century contract law, as juries were asked to go beyond the 'well-established principle that plaintiffs' losses should normally be calculated by reference to their lost expectations'.[51] As

46 *Rubie v Foley*, *Belfast Newsletter*, 7 Aug 1838; *Freeman's Journal*, 7 Aug 1838.

47 *Dunlevie v Barry*, *Belfast Newsletter*, 29 Mar 1833.

48 *St Lawrence v Skehan*, *Cork Examiner*, 27 June 1870; *Freeman's Journal*, 27 June 1870.

49 *Freeman's Journal*, 1 Mar 1806.

50 *Knox v Arnold*, *Dundalk Democrat*, 30 Nov 1872.

51 Ibbetson (1999) *Law of Obligations*, p 229. See also: Swain (2015) *The Law of Contract*, pp 196–197; W Swain (2010) 'The Classical Model of Contract: The Product of a Revolution in Legal Thought?', *Legal Studies*, 30(4), 513–532, 524–525. Swain argues that the expectation model became 'axiomatic' and 'unambiguously established' in the early nineteenth century, but had been in practice employed by juries for much longer. The status of consequential losses, however, argues Swain, remained uncertain until *Hadley v Baxendale* (1854) 1 Ex 410 and its aftermath. See P Atiyah (2003) *The Rise and Fall of Freedom of Contract* (Oxford: Oxford University Press), p 142, ch 6. It is suggested that Atiyah's characterization of the contract to marry as 'wholly executory' fails to take account of the inherent reliance or change of societal position of the plaintiff in these cases.

Lettmaier argues, '[t]he nineteenth-century action for breach of promise lost its moorings both to specific material losses and to conventional contract-based limitations and reinvented itself as a hybrid action'.[52]

An award of damages could serve a number of functions. Firstly, damages could serve a punitive role, punishing the defendant for his alleged social or moral misconduct. Secondly, damages could provide 'emotional damages', compensating 'injured feelings, wounded affections, or loss of honour ... psychological (and resultant physical) distress ... [and] humiliation and public disgrace'.[53] Thirdly, damages might remedy the lost expectations of financial security associated with marriage or, as suggested by defence counsel in *Fitzgerald v Hawkesworth*,[54] constitute an enlarged dowry and help secure a replacement husband. Fourthly, plaintiffs' counsel often called on juries to award exemplary damages to deter other men from breaching promises to marry. Finally, an award of damages could serve as a declaration of a plaintiff's propriety and good conduct through the alleged affair, 'vindicat[ing] the [plaintiff's] fair fame'.[55]

The variety of roles which damages could play allowed barristers to call on a diverse range of factors when attempting to influence the jury's assessment. Jurors' attentions were generally drawn to four considerations: the defendant's wealth; the plaintiff's character and conduct; the defendant's behaviour; and the injury suffered.

The defendant's personal wealth

The most straightforward consideration was the defendant's ability to pay.[56] In 1809, O'Grady LCB expressly instructed one jury to have regard to the defendant's property, commenting that damages 'should make reparation to the one party, without doing irreparable injury to the other'.[57] In almost every case examined, the plaintiff adduced evidence of the defendant's wealth and income. Usually a plaintiff's family member or friend would offer an estimate, but in *Chute v Blennerhassett*[58] a professional 'valuator of land' was called. Defendants would often dispute such evidence by denying the extent of their holdings or drawing the jury's attention

52 Lettmaier (2010) *Broken Engagements*, p 26.

53 Lettmaier (2010) *Broken Engagements*, pp 48–49. See *Addis v Gramophone* [1909] AC 488, the leading case on damages in contract for hurt feelings, where the breach of promise of marriage action was expressed as an exception to the ordinary rule that damages cannot be given for hurt feelings in actions for breach of contract.

54 (1811) *Speeches of John Philpot Curran, Esq*. Vol. II (I Riley: New York), p 148.

55 *Garvey v Lindsay, Freeman's Journal*, 21, 22, 24, 25 June 1872.

56 See Chapter 6 of this volume for a discussion of the changing relevance of a defendant's wealth over time in an action for criminal conversation.

57 *Madden v McEgan, Freeman's Journal*, 15 Dec 1809. See also *Head v Purdon, Belfast Newsletter*, 20 June 1837; *Freeman's Journal*, 24 June 1837; *Sargent v Spring, Freeman's Journal*, 24 Aug 1810.

58 *Freeman's Journal*, 12, 13 Dec 1865.

to mortgages and outgoings. In *Harrison v Hooks*,[59] the plaintiff's counsel announced that the defendant

> appeared in court ridiculously and fantastically dressed in wretched, poor clothes, with his face dirty, and his appearance very squalid in order that the judge might be led to believe that he was in extreme poverty. So strange was his appearance that the bag-boys and idle loungers about the hall of the Four Courts mobbed him when he was walking about the precincts of the court, and hunted him with cries of 'Hooks, Hooks' down the Quay.

The correspondent for the *Belfast Newsletter* reported that when Hooks took the stand, 'his appearance was the signal for uproarious laughter'.

The plaintiff's character and conduct

The second consideration which the jury entertained was the 'character of the plaintiff'.[60] In his charge to one jury, Bushe LCJ in *O'Reilly v McCan*[61] commented expressly on the degree of 'fault' in the 'lady's conduct' during the engagement. In *Caila v McNamara*,[62] Lord Norbury asked the jury to consider 'has [the plaintiff's] conduct been such as to entitle her to large damages'? This mention of 'character' must be broadly interpreted, as it allowed an examination into any aspect of the plaintiff's life which the court felt may have a bearing on the case. Lettmaier argues that a

> woman's age and physical appearance as well as her deportment during the affair could ... have a huge impact on the amount of damages deemed necessary to compensate her for her suffering. The principle underpinning the award of damages ... was that if the girl be young, pretty, and properly behaved, she should be handsomely recompensed and that her older, plainer or more unorthodox sisters should receive less.[63]

To win damages, a plaintiff's counsel would need to present her case in a manner which 'fitted a narrative of innate femininity that [the jury] had been exposed to throughout their lives'.[64] The ideal plaintiff for any barrister appears to have been a young, beautiful and well-educated woman,

---

59 *Belfast Newsletter*, 14 Jan, 8, 10 Feb 1862; *Cork Examiner*, 10 Feb 1862.

60 *Madden v McEgan*, *Freeman's Journal*, 15 Dec 1809.

61 *Belfast Newsletter*, 15 Jul 1828.

62 *Freeman's Journal*, 11, 12, 13 Dec 1820.

63 Lettmaier (2010) *Broken Engagements*, p 53. The physical appearance and contended virtues of a wife were also central pillars in a jury's assessment of damages for criminal conversation; see Chapter 6 of this volume.

64 Lettmaier (2010) *Broken Engagements*, p 94.

from a respectable family. Before 1869, neither party were competent witnesses[65] and were often absent from court. Barristers could therefore hide inconsistencies[66] which differentiated their client from typical gender norms. In *Rubie v Foley*,[67] the plaintiff's age and appearance were in dispute so the plaintiff's barrister, George Bennett KC, called the plaintiff's 'pretty looking' teenage cousin to give evidence and then asked a subsequent witness whether the much older plaintiff bore a resemblance to that cousin. The defendant's counsel Sergeant Joseph Devonsher Jackson objected, suggesting that if the plaintiff truly resembled her cousin, the plaintiff's legal team 'would have paraded her blooming and fresh with her bonnets and ribbons ... [T]o get hold of such a pretty little witness as that of the feminine gender, is the very best recipe in the world for getting a verdict'. Although the jury decided for the plaintiff, they may have been influenced by Jackson's suggestion as they awarded £20 damages rather than the £1,000 sought.

The defendant would try to present an opposing image of the plaintiff. Juries had a clear image of the role which women should play during courtship, and any deviations would be highlighted. In an 1841 case before Perrin J at the Down Assizes, counsel for the defendant pointed out that the plaintiff had dated letters received from his client, 'act[ing] with attorney-like precision ... that she might have [the letters] ready for such a future occasion as the present'.[68] Alleging that the plaintiff exhibited 'shrewd business sense'[69] clashed with the ideal of a passive and modest woman. In *Garvey v Lindsay*, the defendant argued that plaintiff invented the action and 'thought she would get a sympathetic, soft gullible jury' to assist her extort damages from the defendant.[70] The relationship between the parties was entirely instigated at the middle-class plaintiff's initiative as she wrote letter after letter to the wealthy defendant asking for money; the jury gave a rare verdict for the defendant. In one case before Monahan CJ, a defendant argued that it had been the *plaintiff* who proposed marriage to him. Mr J. D. Clarke QC argued, '[i]n her letters the plaintiff treated the defendant as if he was a school boy. The usual style in these matters was for the gentleman to court the young lady and she to receive his attentions very shyly and when he comes to "pop" the question he is told to go to "mamma"'.[71]

65 Evidence Further Amendment Act 1869 (32 & 33 Vic c 68), s 2. See Law Reform Commission (1978) *Breach of Promise of Marriage*, p 2.

66 See Lettmaier (2010) *Broken Engagements*, pp 96–98.

67 *Belfast Newsletter*, 7 Aug 1838; *Freeman's Journal*, 7 Aug 1838.

68 *Moore v Thompson*, *Belfast Newsletter*, 3 Aug 1841.

69 Lettmaier (2010) *Broken Engagements*, pp 65–66.

70 *Freeman's Journal*, 21, 22, 24, 25 June 1872.

71 *Chute v Blennerhasset*, *Freeman's Journal*, 12, 13 Dec 1865.

One dramatic technique employed by defendants was to allege the plaintiff was, in Chitty's words, 'a loose and immodest woman'.[72] In *Madden v McEgan*,[73] the defendant argued he was justified in his failure to fulfil his promise because of rumours his betrothed had been found in an 'improper situation' with the son of a family friend at a party. His counsel, Sergeant Moore, argued that 'however beautiful [the plaintiff's] face, or graceful her person might be, and whatever extrinsic accomplishments she might have acquired, the morals had been neglected' and having 'neither precept nor example to direct her in the paths of virtue or decorum' she had committed the alleged 'acts of indecency'. Therefore, submitted the defence, the defendant 'was not bound to take a polluted bride into his arms'. This defence could, however, prove a 'double-edged sword'.[74] Richard Jebb KC responded by asking the jury to punish the defendant with 'exemplary damages' for raising such a 'base and abominable defence'.[75] The Lord Chief Baron told the jury: 'There could be no doubt that it is the duty of every man ... to take care that the object of his choice is pure and unspotted; he ought to be assured of this before he enters into the contract – not after', but such considerations could be taken into account to mitigate damages. However, the defendant had gone too far, having 'investigat[ed] ... the plaintiff's conduct from her infancy, and endeavour[ing] to extract from the whole of her life a sufficient justification' for the breach. The jury were unimpressed with the approach, awarding £500 damages after a few minutes' deliberation.

The defendant argued a comparable defence in *Caila v McNamara*,[76] suggesting that the plaintiff had lived with him as a 'kept mistress', who now sought revenge. Plaintiff's counsel, Thomas Wallace KC, countered these accusations, not by attacking the theoretical legal basis for this defence, but by arguing the defendant was barred from raising it as he had reaffirmed the promise three years into the relationship while on notice of any unchaste behaviour.[77] While Wallace admitted that the plaintiff's behaviour in 'speak[ing] of love so soon', was 'indiscreet on the part of the lady', he argued that if it 'was a fault, then it was one that arose from the credulity of the female heart'. Lord Norbury told the jury that 'it is a matter of consideration for you to say whether this lady's conduct in so quick a surrender of her virtue ... was correct'. Although the jury found for the plaintiff, awarding substantial damages of £2,000, this was lower than the £5,000 penalty which the defendant had pledged to pay in a written contract to marry.

---

72 Chitty (1834) *A Practical Treatise*, p 428. See Luddy (2011) *Matters of Deceit*, p 14.

73 *Freeman's Journal*, 15 Dec 1809. See also *Wetherall v Gamble*, *Belfast Newsletter*, 10 Mar 1815.

74 Lettmaier (2010) *Broken Engagements*, p 42.

75 *Madden v McEgan*, *Freeman's Journal*, 15 Dec 1809.

76 *Freeman's Journal*, 11, 12, 13 Dec 1820.

77 See Chitty (1834) *A Practical Treatise*, p 428.

Barristers also occasionally asked juries to award high damages as a method of declaring to the world that their plaintiff had acted properly throughout the engagement. In *Wynn v Warner*,[78] a young plaintiff was jilted by a Cork-based customs official. Daniel O'Connell told the jury, 'she was stained with no crime, her character untainted, her reputation unaffected, morality had not been outraged; the plaintiff came clothed in the garb of innocence' and appealed 'to the jury as fathers, brothers, and men ... give her such a verdict as would prove their opinion of the propriety of her conduct'. Before the Tyrone Assizes in 1840, one plaintiff's counsel insisted that she 'comes into court no partner to the criminality of the defendant's conduct – whatever disgrace, whatever perfidy, belongs to the transaction, lies on the defendant, and on him alone' and the plaintiff was 'driven' to take the breach of promise action to 'vindicate her character'.[79] In *Little v Newenham*,[80] in 1845, plaintiff's counsel begged for 'such damages as will vindicate this lady's fair fame'. Thomas O'Hagan QC informed another jury in 1851 that the plaintiff's father had arranged for her to take the action, to 'vindicate her character'.[81] A jury of peers were asked to investigate the circumstances surrounding a broken engagement and to certify to the community that the plaintiff was without fault by awarding large damages.

Actions of the defendant

The third factor in assessing damages centred on the defendant. Crampton J told one jury in 1852 '[o]n the whole, he would leave it to [them] to estimate what would be the fair amount of damages which the defendant ought to pay for his conduct in the transaction'. [82] Damages could serve as both a punishment and a deterrent.

Irish juries were frequently asked to award damages which would punish; as Edward Litton KC informed the jury in *Little v Lynch*,[83] 'though this crime is not punishable by the criminal law of the realm, yet it is such a crime as deserves greater punishment than many crimes which stand far higher in the catalogue'. An award of damages could also result in a defendant's imprisonment if he was unable to pay; during the nineteenth century imprisonment for debt was a relatively common occurrence.[84] In *Goodwin v Holden*,[85]

78 *Freeman's Journal*, 19, 20, 22 Aug 1823; *Belfast Newsletter*, 22 Aug 1823.

79 *Montray v McCartney*, *Freeman's Journal*, 6 Nov 1840.

80 *Belfast Newsletter*, 19 Aug 1845; *Freeman's Journal*, 19 Aug 1845.

81 *Nowlan v Sullivan*, *Freeman's Journal*, 23, 24 June 1851.

82 *Walsh v Lacken*, *Freeman's Journal*, 4 Feb 1852.

83 *Freeman's Journal*, 26 Oct 1831; *Belfast Newsletter*, 1 Nov 1831.

84 See K Costello (2013) 'Imprisonment for Debt in Early Nineteenth Century Ireland, 1810–1848', *UCD Working Papers in Law, Criminology & Socio-Legal Studies* Research Paper No 9.

85 *Freeman's Journal*, 18 Mar 1847; *Belfast Newsletter*, 19 Mar 1847.

George Tomb QC asked one jury to pause 'before they took the defendant from the bosom of his family and consigned him to a gaol, which would be the result of heavy damages'. In 1827 before the English Court for the Relief of Insolvent Debtors, Yorkshire debtor Richard Harris was imprisoned for four months at the behest of Sarah Bates, following his refusal to pay £150 damages awarded for breach of promise.[86] Ordinarily, a debtor who was prepared to hand over his remaining assets was entitled to automatic release by the Insolvent Debtors Court. Debtors imprisoned for inability to pay damages awarded for a breach of promise could, at the plaintiff's request, be denied release.[87] In 1838, John Johnston appeared before the Irish Insolvent Debtors Court for his failure to pay £70 damages for breach of promise.[88] The detaining creditor, Hamilton Perry, told Johnston he would forego execution of the judgment if Johnston would follow through and marry his daughter. Johnston, however, told the court he would prefer going to prison.

Plaintiffs' barristers also frequently requested juries to award exemplary damages to deter future would-be jilters. In *Blake v Daly*,[89] the jury were called on as 'fathers and brothers' to give a 'wholesome verdict' which would discourage others from repeating the 'dishonourable conduct' of the defendant. However, the jury's role in deterring other men was expressly rejected in *Forrest v O'Brien*,[90] when Ball J told one jury '[t]here has been something said about your verdict holding out a great moral lesson to young officers in the army and others – You must be aware that this is no part of your duty; you have nothing to do with setting up a moral lesson'.[91]

In calling on the jury to consider the defendant's behaviour, the plaintiff's barrister would often allege the defendant's promise was 'basely and dishonourably broken',[92] making out that the defendant was the 'vilest and meanest knave in creation'[93] and pointing to specific aggravating factors. In one 1812 trial before the Cork Assizes, the defendant, who had recently returned from college, was accused of seducing his father's maid under promise of marriage. She subsequently birthed a 'lovely baby'. The jury awarded 100 guineas damages, or the equivalent of 50 times the plaintiff's yearly income.[94] Any defendant's compatibility with prevailing standards of masculinity could also

86 E Cooke (1839) *A Treatise Upon the Law and Practice of the Court for Relief of Insolvent Debtors* (London: Henry Butterworth, Bookseller and Publisher), p 223.

87 Insolvent Debtors (Ireland) Act 1840 (3 & 4 Vic c 105), s 68.

88 *Re John Johnston*, *Freeman's Journal*, 7 May 1838.

89 *Belfast Newsletter*, 13 Apr 1821.

90 *Freeman's Journal*, 21, 22 Mar 1845. See also *Nowlan v Sullivan*, *Freeman's Journal*, 23, 24 June 1851.

91 *Freeman's Journal*, 21, 22 Mar 1845.

92 *Birket v Bates*, *Freeman's Journal*, 6 Mar 1838; *Belfast Newsletter*, 9 Mar 1838.

93 *Sheehan v Stack*, *Cork Examiner*, 19 Jul 1870.

94 *Sullivan v Lackney*, *Freeman's Journal*, 2 Apr 1812.

be averted to in court; juries had a distinct understanding of the way men should act when paying addresses to a woman. In *Morrow v Menzies*,[95] Crampton J commented on the 'sordid motives' of the defendant, in abandoning the plaintiff for another woman. In *Blake v Daly*,[96] the plaintiff's brother-in-law testified at the Galway Assizes that when he had pressed the defendant about the proposed marriage, the defendant was unable to give a coherent answer and broke down weeping. Burton J was rather critical of the 'degree of inconsistency' in the behaviour of the defendant in failing to act decisively, commenting that he was a man of 'despicable understanding'. In *Harrison v Hooks*,[97] the defendant complained during his examination that he was being persecuted by the plaintiff and began to weep, eliciting 'shouts of laughter' from the audience. In *Nowlan v Sullivan*,[98] the defendant declined to marry the plaintiff because he believed she had developed tuberculosis. Her barrister told the court the defendant had 'bravely and chivalrously' accepted his fiancé's life was in danger, but was not going to risk his own health by being associated with her. One male plaintiff in 1849 alleged that the defendant had breached her promise to marry him when she married another on the appointed wedding day. The defendant argued that she was willing to marry the plaintiff, but when he did not arrive, she called for another suitor to approach and marry her 'like a man'.[99]

In *Caila v McNamara*,[100] the plaintiff's barrister Thomas Wallace KC ridiculed Lieutenant McNamara, suggesting that he was an unpleasant character and had only brokered the relationship with the widowed Caila because he was in debt. Humorous reference was made to the fact he had pawned his regimental breeches and requested money from Caila to redeem them. Wallace further alleged that the defendant had then pawned property taken from her home. The relationship finally came to an end when the defendant married another woman with a larger fortune, and the defendant was labelled a 'seducer' whose plans to entrap the defendant were met with 'success and mischievous execution'.

In reaction to these accusations, defence counsel would often try and excuse the breach on more compelling grounds than those of 'unmanl[y] ... abandonment'.[101] Such excuses were far from flattering to defendants, often suggesting that they were 'young fools or old dotards who are objects of pity rather than derision'.[102] Such an approach could reduce damages in

95 *Freeman's Journal*, 16 Jul 1846.

96 *Belfast Newsletter*, 13 Apr 1821.

97 *Belfast Newsletter*, 14 Jan, 8, 10 Feb 1862; *Cork Examiner*, 10 Feb 1862.

98 *Freeman's Journal*, 23, 24 June 1851.

99 *Dunlop v Wallace*, *Anglo-Celt*, 6 Jul 1849.

100 *Freeman's Journal*, 11, 12, 13 Dec 1820.

101 *Blake v Wilkins*, *Freeman's Journal*, 31 Mar 1817; *Belfast Newsletter*, 8 Apr 1817.

102 *Sheehan v Stack*, *Cork Examiner*, 19 Jul 1870.

two ways: firstly, a jury might be more accommodating where there was a genuine reason for the breach; secondly, making the defendant out to be a ridiculous or absurd figure could suggest that the plaintiff had not missed out on much by losing the possibility of marrying him.

One such excuse was that of old age or illness. In *Kelly v Gannon,*[103] the defence examined the 65-year-old defendant's doctor to show he was 'labouring under a dropsical complaint, and ... was ... weighed down with infirmity, imbecility and age' and therefore marriage was undesirable for both parties. One defendant argued before the Court of Exchequer in 1806 that he was suffering from 'insanity and temporary derangement' at the time of making the promise.[104] He pointed to a period spent in the 'house of a medical gentleman ... celebrated for the care and management of patients of that description'. However, under cross-examination it was revealed that his stay was actually due to 'an improper and incautious use of a medicine too frequently resorted to'. In *Leonard v Hartford,*[105] the plaintiff's counsel anticipated an old-age/infirmity defence, calling the defendant a 'Romeo of sixty' and describing an occasion where he leapt over a wall to meet the plaintiff, telling the jury 'I doubt you would have recognised your fellow citizen if you had met him that morning'. On cue, the defence responded, arguing that the defendant's 'feebleness of ... body, and weakness of ... mind' had been taken advantage of by the plaintiff and her family. It seems that an age discrepancy between the parties, though frequently commented on in the proceedings, was not considered a real barrier to a potential marriage. In each of these three cases the jury apparently rejected the defence, awarding £150, £1,500 and £325 damages respectively. Luddy notes,

> [y]ounger women courting older men was a common enough occurrence in these court cases but one always noted by lawyers as laughable and somehow unnatural. Juries recognized that older men often had considerable wealth and this was understood and accepted as a pragmatic transaction.[106]

A second attempt to excuse the defendant's behaviour could be founded on his capacity to contract, alleging that he was too young or too drunk to promise anything. In *Fitzgerald v Hawkesworth,* Downes LCJ observed that 'any matrimonial contract, perfected while either of the contracting parties are minors, is to all intents and purposes illegal, and should be dissolved'.[107] He agreed with the defendant's barrister, John Philpot Curran, that it was necessary to draw 'a striking contrast between inconsiderate engagements

103 *Freeman's Journal,* 18 Dec 1812.

104 *Fortune v Conolly, Freeman's Journal,* 1 Mar 1806.

105 *Freeman's Journal,* 6, 12 Aug 1823; *Belfast Newsletter,* 19 Aug 1823.

106 Luddy (2011) *Matters of Deceit,* p 17.

107 (1811) *Speeches of John Philpot Curran,* p 177.

in nonage, the mere ebullitions of romantic spirits, and those solemn contracts entered into in mature years, which to violate is considered criminal by the laws of God and man'.[108] Unfortunately for the defendant, the jury decided that he had subsequently reaffirmed his promise on reaching majority, awarding £2,500 damages.[109] In *McLaren v Osborne*,[110] on examination of the female defendant's mother, it was revealed that the defendant was a minor and Whiteside LCJ immediately directed a verdict in her favour. In *Head v Purdon*,[111] defence counsel focused on the defendant's apparent youth, remarking to the jury, 'God help them all if the letters of their youth were brought up in judgment against them'. However, plaintiff's counsel countered this suggestion of immaturity by pointing to the defendant's education at Oxford and his time spent in the diplomatic service as an 'attaché of an embassy to Sweden' under Lord Vesey Fitzgerald. It was alleged that he had 'seen much of the world' and his actions were 'calculated to make an impression on the female heart'; the jury awarded £3,000 damages.

A number of defendants also argued that they lacked the capacity to promise because they were intoxicated. In 1865 before the Cork Assizes, the defendant argued that he was 'so drunk as to be unable to understand what he was doing' when he signed a written promise to marry, pointing to his unsteady signature.[112] In *Walsh v Lacken*,[113] defence counsel argued that his client had been 'put to bed drunk every night he was in the Walsh's house' and that he had been 'befooling himself while under the influence of a drunken fit'. Despite Chitty's suggestion in 1834 that 'such an intoxication as entirely deprives a party of the use of his reason, seems to avoid [a contract] entered into by him during this mental incapacity',[114] neither defendant appears to have convinced the jury, and both had £50 awarded against them.

A third method employed by defendants to excuse their behaviour was to allege that they lacked the finances to support a married household. Because of the doctrine of coverture,[115] a nineteenth-century marriage was also an important economic alliance. Given the importance of property and income one might suspect that poverty could provide a successful defence. However, it does not appear to have convinced juries who seem to have thought that if you cannot afford to marry a young lady, you should not court her in the first place. In 1844, Captain O'Brien of the 72nd Highlanders regiment began paying his addresses to Miss Forrest while stationed near her home in

108 Curran (1811) *Speeches*, p 173.

109 Curran (1811) *Speeches*, p 178.

110 *Freeman's Journal*, 29 July 1868.

111 *Belfast Newsletter*, 20 June 1837; *Freeman's Journal*, 24 June 1837.

112 *Harding's Case, Nation*, 25 Mar 1865.

113 *Freeman's Journal*, 4 Feb 1852.

114 Chitty (1834) *A Practical Treatise*, p 113.

115 See Chapter 5 in this volume.

Mitchelstown. Despite being publicly accepted as her suitor, O'Brien subsequently refused to marry Forrest because his sole source of income, his daily pay of 11 shillings plus candle and coal allowance, would not be sufficient to support her in as affluent a lifestyle as she had enjoyed with her parents. The jury awarded £250 damages and the foreman indicated that they would have awarded more if the defendant had any wealth beyond his pay.[116] In *Little v Newenham*,[117] the defendant met his alleged fiancé at the home of a mutual acquaintance in Cork and was so enraptured that he proposed immediately. The proposal was accepted and an appointment was made for the defendant to meet the plaintiff's family solicitor. The day before the meeting, the defendant looked into his own financial affairs and realized he was not nearly as wealthy as he had assumed. He then refused to marry the plaintiff as they would have to do without the 'comforts and station' to which they were accustomed. The jury was again not impressed, awarding £700 damages.

Fourthly, a defendant might suggest that he refused to marry the plaintiff because he had entered the contract under a misrepresentation or fraud.[118] In one early case, the defendant successfully excused his refusal to marry the plaintiff on the basis that she

> had concealed from the defendant her natural temper and disposition, the vices to which she was addicted, and had fallaciously represented herself to have great expectations from a relation: that, in the company of the defendant, she appeared to be the model of prudence, of gentleness of manners, and sensibility of soul; but that her true character was that of a common scold, a virago, and a slattern; that she was much addicted to liquor, and had no pecuniary expectations; that the Defendant having accidentally paid her a visit at a time he was not expected; her clothes and linen were stained with liquor and snuff, her cap on one side, and half off her head; her face pale and livid; her lips black and parched; her eyes red and staring; her voice hoarse and faltering.[119]

In *Kingsley v Peile*,[120] the jury allowed a female defendant to resile from her promise to marry the plaintiff, on the grounds that he had misrepresented his income.

The final excuse considered here is that the defendant had withdrawn from the engagement on the advice of his family and friends. In *Moore v*

116 *Forrest v O'Brien*, *Freeman's Journal*, 21, 22 Mar 1845.

117 *Belfast Newsletter*, 19 Aug 1845; *Freeman's Journal*, 19 Aug 1845.

118 See Chitty (1834) *A Practical Treatise*, p 489.

119 *Anonymous case*, *Belfast Newsletter*, 18 Aug 1789

120 *Weekly Irish Times*, 20 Jan 1883.

Thompson,[121] Perrin J held that evidence suggesting the defendant's mother was unaware of the engagement was admissible, but only in mitigation of damages as '[i]f the defendant acts a wanton and reckless part, a jury will give heavier damages than if he is persuaded by his parents'. The jury awarded £35 to the plaintiff, substantially less than the £500 claimed. In *Head v Purdon*,[122] the plaintiff was awarded £3,000 despite the defendant claiming that his father's dying wish was for him to cancel the engagement. Defendants occasionally broke off engagements for fear of being disinherited; in *Chute v Blennerhassett*,[123] it was suggested that the breach occurred because of the disapproval of the defendant's elderly bachelor uncle worth £6,000 a year.

Injury to the plaintiff

The final factor that a jury would consider was the injury suffered by the plaintiff. In a case before Jebb J at the Kilkenny Assizes, plaintiff's counsel asked the jury to pay attention to 'the specific detriment which the plaintiff had sustained ... how materially her prospects in life had been impaired by the defendant'.[124] The defendant's breach could cause three injuries: emotional and physical damage; reputational damage; and lost opportunity. Firstly, it was often alleged that being abandoned by her suitor caused the emotional pain of a broken heart. Hurt feelings would, it was argued, also lead to physical illness, but little evidence was ever produced on the subject. In *Little v Lynch*,[125] the plaintiff's barrister alleged that his client had suffered 'as grievous and as deep an injury as could be inflicted on a female – an injury which, accompanied as it is with insult, has destroyed her happiness and peace of mind, and is likely to destroy her life'. The plaintiff's sister testified that she was in bad health, 'as if in decline'. The defendant complained that no evidence of a 'medical gentleman' was produced to prove the injury, but the jury seemingly felt this was unnecessary, awarding £100 damages. Lettmaier argues the fact that 'a broken engagement would break a woman's heart and physically prostrate her was, in the nineteenth century, regarded as a truth too universally acknowledged to call for especial mention'.[126] As plaintiff's counsel in *Leonard v Hartford*[127] explained,

> [t]here is something in the bare mention of a young lady having to seek reparation in damages, through the medium of a court

121 *Belfast Newsletter*, 3 Aug 1841.

122 *Belfast Newsletter*, 20 June 1837; *Freeman's Journal*, 24 June 1837.

123 *Freeman's Journal*, 12, 13 Dec 1865.

124 *Leonard v Hartford*, *Freeman's Journal*, 6, 12 Aug 1823; *Belfast Newsletter*, 19 Aug 1823. See also O'Grady LCB's charge in *Sargent v Spring*, *Freeman's Journal*, 24 Aug 1810.

125 *Freeman's Journal*, 26 Oct 1831; *Belfast Newsletter*, 1 Nov 1831.

126 Lettmaier (2010) *Broken Engagements*, p 49.

127 *Freeman's Journal*, 6, 12 Aug 1823; *Belfast Newsletter*, 19 Aug 1823.

> of justice ... which suggests to the mind and imagination more of pain, humiliation, and suffering, than any description of mine could convey, and precludes therefore, the necessity of stating more than this.

Defence counsel occasionally attempted to undermine suggestions of injury by pointing to the short length of the engagement or the unsuitability of the match implying that no deep injury could be felt by the plaintiff. One defendant attempted to have his potential damages reduced before the Court of Exchequer in 1830 by arguing that he was too old for any real affection to have developed between them and the plaintiff therefore came before the jury 'without the least substantial wrong to complain of'.[128] The jury seemingly disagreed, awarding £700 damages.

The scope for the plaintiff's barrister to allege emotional anguish and physical illness was dramatically wider when, prior to 1869, the plaintiff could not give evidence in court.[129] After the 1869 Act was passed, the plaintiff could take the stand and be examined on the extent of her hurt feelings. In *Wallace v Mulvey*,[130] the plaintiff refused to answer the defence counsel's questions about when she fell in love. In 1862, in the unusual case of *Harrison v Hooks*, the parties were allowed to give evidence by mutually consenting to forego the statutory prohibition. When the plaintiff was questioned in the witness box about her love for the defendant, she replied: 'I do not know anything about love'.[131] These questions were calculated to demonstrate there was no affection between the parties, and therefore the plaintiff could not suffer from heartbreak. However, as suggested by Luddy, although 'Irish marriages were expected ... to include some level of affection they were primarily enterprises that were shaped by social and economic compatibility'.[132] The absence of love did not dissuade a jury from awarding damages, and Catherine Wallace and Agnes Jane Harrison received judgment for £10 and £50 respectively.

Secondly, the defendant's breach of promise could subject the plaintiff to reputational damage and public humiliation. In one 1870 action, the plaintiff was concerned with being talked about among the Killaloe community when it became 'generally reported through town that you [the defendant] are going to be married to some widow and that you have broken off your engagement with me'.[133] It seems to have been accepted that reputational

128 *Kavanagh v McGarry*, *Belfast Newsletter*, 12 Nov 1820.

129 See Lettmaier (2010) *Broken Engagements*, pp 95–103.

130 *Cork Examiner*, 29 June 1870.

131 *Harrison v Hooks*, *Belfast Newsletter*, 14 Jan, 8, 10 Feb 1862; *Cork Examiner*, 10 Feb 1862.

132 Luddy (2011) *Matters of Deceit*, p 10.

133 *St Lawrence v Skehan*, *Cork Examiner*, 27 June 1870; *Freeman's Journal*, 27 June 1870.

damage would be most keenly felt among those of a higher social status. In *Savage v Carse*,[134] the plaintiff's barrister told the jury that although

> he would not ask the same amount of damages as he would seek for, supposing she ranked in higher life, still she had her feelings equally with a female of higher rank, better education, and more delicate sentiment. The poor have their feelings as well as the rich... [u]nder wrong impressions their honour should not be sullied, and themselves thrown as outcasts on the world.

Finally, breach of promise meant the loss of financial security associated with a husband. Employment opportunities were limited for women and the economic stability in marrying an income-generating man was a tangible benefit.[135] There may also have been an opportunity cost where the plaintiff had turned down other suitors[136] or employment opportunities,[137] in addition to her impaired prospects of finding replacements. As argued by Thomas O'Hagan QC in 1851, '[f]ew men would readily take to their bosom a woman who had been rejected by another'.[138] In 1883, O'Brien J observed, 'one of the chief reasons' why a breach of promise by a man 'was of more consequence' than that of a woman was because a woman could find herself 'unable to form a new engagement of the same character' as '[w]omen possessed much less freedom of action than men, who had much greater facilities for forming new engagements to marry'.[139]

Conclusion

Towards the end of the nineteenth century, public sentiment towards the action for breach of promise seemingly shifted. As Luddy notes, newspaper reports which had been so sensational at the beginning of the nineteenth century became 'matter-of-fact'.[140] The *Cork Examiner* complained in 1870 that

> scarcely an assize elapses without at least a dozen spinsters bringing up their neglected attractions to be appraised by chivalrous juries of their fellow countrymen and making considerably more of damaged hearts, in a pecuniary way, than they could ever have hoped to derive from the sale of the same organs in a sound condition in the fair and open market.[141]

134 *Belfast Newsletter*, 9, 12 Mar 1847.

135 Luddy (2011) *Matters of Deceit*, p 7.

136 *St Lawrence v Skehan, Cork Examiner*, 27 June 1870; *Freeman's Journal*, 27 June 1870; *Harrison v Hooks, Belfast Newsletter*, 14 Jan, 8, 10 Feb 1862; *Cork Examiner*, 10 Feb 1862.

137 *Bardon v Douglas, Irish Times*, 21 Nov 1888.

138 *Nowlan v Sullivan, Freeman's Journal*, 23, 24 June 1851.

139 *Kingsley v Peile, Weekly Irish Times*, 20 Jan 1883.

140 Luddy (2011) *Matters of Deceit*, p 20.

141 *Sheehan v Stack, Cork Examiner*, 19 July 1870.

Lettmaier argues that in England the action reached its peak popularity towards the end of the nineteenth century, with the proliferation of lower-class actions leading to the 'vulgarization' of the suit[142] and its decline.[143] However, Luddy reports that in Ireland the number of cases never reached the 'epidemic' proportions considered in England.[144] Any vulgarization which did occur was exacerbated by a suggestion that the action was becoming a method of extorting money from innocent men. *Garvey v Lindsay*, in 1872, can be considered a turning point as one barrister successfully defended his client by arguing that awarding damages was making 'the court an engine for legalised plunder'.[145] Despite suggestions in the 1880s, by those such as O'Brien J, that a 'strong opinion prevailed that breach of promise of marriage should no longer constitute grounds for an action for damages',[146] the action continued to be employed until as late as the 1970s. For example, in 1977 school teacher Maura Hartnett of Banteer was awarded £11,000 by Finlay J in the High Court when Tony O'Neill, a farmer from Ennis, refused to carry out his promise of marriage.[147]

It was not until the Family Law Act 1981 that engagements to marry were emptied of their legal content.[148] The Law Reform Commission noted that '[w]hilst the stigma of a broken engagement may have lessened in recent years, the fact remains that the experience of being jilted by a person who has perhaps behaved with deceit or callousness is often a very painful and humiliating one'.[149] However, '[t]he risk that a girl whose engagement has been broken will thereafter be shunned by potential marriage partners may well have lessened greatly in recent years'.[150]

The action for breach of promise was one which, like other legal actions such as criminal conversation[151] and seduction, became an enforcement mechanism of social structures of nineteenth-century Ireland. Victorian conceptions of family, courtship and gender became wrapped up before the courts in a sensational web of love letters and intimate gossip and a series of rules of social etiquette, as explained by barristers before a jury, were printed in daily newspapers and spread around the country. Despite growing pressure, the action continued well beyond the nineteenth century. In as late as 1996, one plaintiff attempted to reignite the action before the High Court.[152] Kelly J, however, confirmed that the action for breach of promise had been relegated to legal history.

---

142 Lettmaier (2010) *Broken Engagements*, p 128.

143 Lettmaier (2010) *Broken Engagements*, p 171.

144 Luddy (2011) *Matters of Deceit*, p 11.

145 *Freeman's Journal*, 21, 22, 24, 25 June 1872.

146 *Kingsley v Peile*, *Weekly Irish Times*, 20 Jan 1883.

147 *Hartnett v O'Neill*, *Irish Press*, 15 Nov 1977.

148 s 2.

149 Law Reform Commission (1978) *Breach of Promise of Marriage*, p 38.

150 Law Reform Commission (1978) *Breach of Promise of Marriage*, p 39.

151 See Chapter 6 in this volume.

152 *Ennis v Butterly* [1996] 1 IR 426, 436 (IEHC).

5
Married Women's Property in Ireland, 1800–1900

Kevin Costello

Before 1870 a married woman was denied the right to enjoy her own property. The classical common law rule of married women's property provided that, throughout her marriage, her personal property vested entirely in her husband. The property she held on entering marriage became her husband's property; the property she earned during marriage also became her husband's property. The Dublin barrister, James Clancy, author of one of the leading early nineteenth-century studies on the topic – the book was reprinted both in England and America – formulated the principle as a

> general rule of the common law of England that a married woman cannot possess personal property, and that everything of this nature to which she is entitled at the time of her marriage, and which accrues in her right during its continuance is vested solely in her husband.[1]

The rules of married women's property also deprived the married woman of access to credit. In common law theory man and wife became one person; the wife was 'scarcely considered to have a separate existence'.[2] A consequence of the dissolution of the independent legal identity of a wife upon marriage was the wife's inability to sue or to be sued. 'By the common law of England, a married woman is incapable of entering into any engagement, as a feme sole or suing or being sued as such'.[3] This rule locked married women out of activities, like shopping or shopkeeping, in which goods were provided on credit. Suppliers or retailers were, after all, unlikely to advance goods on credit to a customer from whom the debt could not be recovered.

1 J Clancy (1827) *A Treatise of the Rights, Duties and Liabilities of Husband and Wife at Law and in Equity*, 3rd edn (London: J. Butterworth), p 1.

2 Clancy (1827) *A Treatise*, p 22.

3 Clancy (1827) *A Treatise*, p 54.

This account of married women's property in Ireland examines three issues in particular. The first is the extent to which use was made in Ireland of the marriage settlement as a means of protecting married women from the property claims of their husbands. A second is the story of the social campaign in Ireland to reform the laws of married women's property. A third is an assessment of the effect of the Married Women's Property Acts 1870–1882 in removing restrictions on the capacity of married women to act as consumers and to engage in trade by themselves.

Married women's property in Ireland 1800–1870

There were two principal techniques for avoiding the total loss of property rights which a married woman suffered on marriage: the marriage settlement and the gift by will. The term marriage settlement can be used broadly to include any pre-marital financial arrangement (such as the provision of a dowry, which was so common in nineteenth- and early twentieth-century Ireland).[4] But the term also includes the more specialist arrangement in which assets were given to trustees to manage on behalf of a couple which was to become married. This was the technique used by families to protect their daughters as they entered marriage from husbands abusing their control over the marriage property.

Since the sixteenth century the trust had been recognized as a device into which money could be channelled to a wife, free from her husband's claims.[5] Fathers anxious to protect their daughters from inconsiderate or grasping husbands could convey land or money to trustees. The function of these trustees was to manage this trust and to distribute its profits to the wife. The wife was entitled to hold the income – pin money – generated by these trusts completely independent of the husband. The wife's independent right to use the money generated by these trusts, while not recognized by the common law courts, was enforceable in the Court of Chancery.

Bequests provided a second means of conveying property to wives free from the ordinary claims of the husband. A provision in a will which left money to a wife to her 'sole and separate use' could exclude her husband from that property: where it was manifestly intended that the wife should take the property, equity would consider the husband a mere trustee of the property.

---

4 KH Connell (1962) 'Peasant Marriage in Ireland: Its Structure and Development Since the Famine', *Economic History Review*, 14(3) 502–523; SJ Connolly (1985) 'Marriage in Pre-Famine Ireland' and D Fitzpatrick (1985) 'Marriage in Post-famine Ireland' in A Cosgrove (ed) *Marriage in Ireland* (Dublin: College Press) 78–98; C Curtin, E Devereux and D Shields (1992) 'Replaying "The Match": Marriage Settlements in North Galway', *Irish Journal of Sociology*, 2, 85–92.

5 *Wytham v Waterhouse* (1596) Tothill 91. JH Baker (2002) *An Introduction to English Legal History*, 4th edn (London: Sweet and Maxwell), p 486.

The court could enforce compliance by the husband with the donor's intention that the property be the wife's alone.[6]

At the start of the twentieth century, AV Dicey recollected the practice of the wealthy, prior to the reforms of the 1870s, in using marriage settlement trusts as means of protecting their daughters from the law of married property. 'The daughters of the rich', he said, 'enjoyed for the most part the considerable protection of equity, while the daughters of the poor suffered under the severity and injustice of the common law'.[7] This argument – that the daughters of the rich were protected by separate property trusts – was regularly made.[8] In 1869 Lord Cairns observed, during the House of Lords debate on the Married Women's Property Bill, that securing the wife's property by the use of trustees was the 'usual practice among the upper classes'.[9]

A closer examination of those pre-nuptial trusts amongst the landed upper class in Ireland suggests something more varied: that while pre-nuptial trusts were common, the object of the trust was not always directed to protecting the wife's property during marriage. The underlying planning objectives varied. The most common object was to establish a pension (a jointure) for the wife in the event that her husband died. The concern underlying many of these settlements, therefore, was not with property relations within marriage, but with property relations after marriage. These settlements were drawn up on the instruction of fathers who were more anxious about ensuring that their daughters would be pensioned if widowed, not with pensioning them during marriage. The planning was usually directed to the later stage of their daughters' lives, not to the early or middle stages.

The class which probably most often negotiated marriage settlements was wealthy landed families. The Belfast social activist, Isabella Tod, in her evidence to the Parliamentary Select Committee on Married Women's Property, mentioned the difficulty of obtaining suitable persons to act as trustees as a common disincentive to families at the lower ends of the middle class being able to establish protective settlements.[10] Funding a trust required reserves of cash or land sufficient to yield an annual income. The trustees in settlements negotiated amongst wealthy landed families tended to be made up of members from each of the two families. Henry Bolton and Charles Deane were trustees to the marriage settlement of Emily Bolton and the son of the

6 Clancy (1827) *A Treatise*, p 54.

7 AV Dicey (1905) *Lectures on Relations between Law and Public Opinion* (London: Macmillan), p 381.

8 *Special Report from the Select Committee on Married Women's Property Bill* (HC) 1867–1868 (441), p 74 ('as a rule among the upper classes, they always do protect themselves by marriage settlements').

9 *Hansard 3 (Lords)* cxcviii 379 (30 Jul 1869).

10 *Special Report from the Select Committee on Married Women's Property Bill, Together with the Proceedings of the Committee, Minutes of Evidence, Appendix and Index*. HC 1867–1868 (441), cccxxxix, 76.

architect Sir Thomas Deane.[11] Family solicitors sometimes agreed to serve as trustee.[12] Trusted members of the community – bank managers, clergymen,[13] and the manager of a lunatic asylum[14] – can also be found acting as trustees in nineteenth-century Irish marriage settlements. These settlements might protect a daughter in four ways: by providing for a jointure; by ensuring her security in case her husband became insolvent; by protecting her existing property; or by providing the wife with a dedicated income stream legally protected from her husband.

Marriage settlements and the protection of widows

In most nineteenth-century landed Irish marriage settlements the real concern was not with the plight of the wife during the marriage, but with what would happen after the marriage when her husband had died. The family's far-sighted object was to create a pension for the daughter during her widowhood. At common law, a woman holding freehold land was protected by the right of dower (the right to a life estate in one-third of the real property held by her deceased husband). The right of dower was, however, fragile and could be defeated. The first erosion came under the Statute of Uses 1634[15] which enabled the right of dower to be extinguished by substituting a jointure – a 'competent livelihood' (though not necessarily, as at common law, one-third of her late husband's lands) for the widow's dower. Then the Dower Act of 1833[16] even more seriously weakened the wife's automatic right to dower by allowing a husband to extinguish his wife's dower entitlements by a simple deed. Under the 1833 Act, a woman who married into a landed family would lose her right to dower where 'by any deed executed by him, it shall be declared that his widow shall not be entitled to dower'. There was no duty on the husband to settle a jointure on the wife in place of the loss of dower.

The dilution, by the 1634 and 1833 Acts, of the widow's default right to dower, required the families of daughters entering marriage to take the initiative and to ensure that the daughter was provided for during widowhood. The marriage settlement with provision for a jointure continued, into the nineteenth century, to provide the usual substitute for dower. For instance, the Palmer and Ellis marriage settlement of 1869 involved the father of the bride, Thomas Ellis, conveying a sum of £1,500 as the marriage portion, while the father of the groom conveyed land to trustees to provide a jointure for his future daughter-in-law, Sarah. This jointure took the form of an

11 Registry of Deeds 1869, Book 16, No 82.

12 O'Sullivan marriage settlement, 20 Mar 1884 (NLI, D 6629).

13 Registry of Deeds 1869, Book 4, No 6.

14 Registry of Deeds 1869, Book 13, No 14.

15 10 Chas I, sess 2, c 1.

16 3 & 4 Will IV c 105.

annuity of £100 'in bar of dower and free bench payable quarterly'.[17] These settlements indicate little interest in protecting the wife during the marriage. On the contrary, their usual object – during the marriage – was to create a private income for the husband (and not the wife). The marriage settlement agreed before the marriage of Patrick Kennedy and Sarah Sherlock provided that Patrick Kennedy, in consideration of the portion provided by Sarah's family, should grant 67 acres to two trustees 'for the use of Patrick during his life'. The wife's interest only came into being on the death of her husband when she was to be provided with a rent charge of £50.[18] In a deed of 1879, it was settled that the father of the groom should contribute £4,000 and that the father of the bride settle £3,000 to be invested in Great Northern Railway stock upon trust to pay an annual income to the husband. The wife only became entitled to income if she survived him.[19] Again, no provision was made to secure an income for the wife during coverture. The purpose was to set up the husband and then to provide for the wife, but only if her husband pre-deceased her.

Marriage settlements as insolvency protection devices

The object underlying another – far smaller – category of marriage trust was to function as a husband's insolvency protection device. Here the object was to provide some basic family support to the wife in the event of the husband's insolvency. These settlements would usually provide an income for the husband during marriage, but with a proviso that the money would be diverted to his wife in the event of the insolvency of the husband. The settlement drawn up on the marriage of Frances Catherine Luby provided that her future husband, Lancelot, should put his Dublin Wicklow Wexford Railway Company shares in trust, and that the trustees should pay him the income and dividends of such funds 'during his life or until he should become a bankrupt or insolvent'. If Lancelot became insolvent or bankrupt it was provided that the trustees should pay the dividends to Frances during her life 'to her separate use'.[20] Another version of the bankruptcy protection settlement can be found in the arrangement made by a father named William Farrell in which he put two houses in Queen Street in Dublin in trust for the groom, on the condition that the houses should be sold in the event of the husband's 'bankruptcy or insolvency or entering into a composition with his creditors'.[21]

There was a legally recognized distinction between settlements designed to provide security for wives in the event of bankruptcy, and settlements

17 Registry of Deeds 1869, Book 1, No 165.

18 Registry of Deeds 1869, Book 11, No 67.

19 Registry of Deeds 1878, Book 9, No 141.

20 Registry of Deeds 1869, Book 10, No 185.

21 Registry of Deeds 1851, Book 1, No 9.

designed to defraud creditors. The distinction lay in the intention with which the arrangement was made. The difference between the fraudulent case and the non-fraudulent case was that in the non-fraudulent case the arrangement had been made before marriage; the wife had provided a dowry. The insolvency protection provision was made by the husband 'in consideration of the wife's fortune' (and not with the intention of defeating his creditors).[22] In the fraudulent case, on the other hand, there had been no receipt of a dowry, and the husband's property was being settled on his wife, not in consideration of a dowry but purely to evade his creditors in a post-nuptial crisis. In *Re Hunt*, a case heard by the Insolvent Debtors Court sitting on circuit in Wicklow in 1850, a Mr Vere Dawson Hunt, who had a chronic gambling habit, had obtained credit of over £5,000 from shopkeepers and moneylenders in Cork. To evade his creditors, he had made a marriage settlement in which he settled all of his property on his wife. The device was condemned as an attempt to 'completely plunder his creditors and in fraud of his creditors'.[23] In 1868 the American eccentric, George Francis Train, was arrested in Dublin for debts owed to the Ebbw Railway Company. Train told the Court of Bankruptcy in Dublin that the entire of his American and Australian assets had been settled on his wife. When Judge Miller condemned the device as a fraud on creditors, Train threatened to 'appeal to the army and navy of the United States' and warned the judge that 'I will yet have the power to remove you from the bench'.[24]

Settlements to protect the wife's previously acquired assets

In another small category of marriage trusts the purpose was to preserve for the wife, free from the common law claims of her husband, assets which the wife-to-be had previously accumulated as a single woman. For instance, women who, before their marriage, had acquired money under a will would use the trust to protect it from their future husband. In 1811, Anne Metcalfe, from Ballybrittas in Queen's County, made over an inheritance of £150 to a trustee called William Kehoe 'to be placed out by him in government and other good and sufficient securities in trust that he, the said William, would receive the interest and profits of the same and apply same trusts to the hands of the said Anne, notwithstanding her coverture'.[25] When, in 1821 Anastasia Fairthlough married – possibly beneath her – Fenton Fitzpatrick, a carpenter from Rathmines, her concerned family ensured that lands which she owned in Dolphin's Barn, as well as her 'household furniture, household

22 EE Deacon (1847) *The Law and Practice of Bankruptcy* (London: Shaw and Sons), p 242.

23 *Freeman's Journal*, 23 Oct 1850. J Levy (1859) *The Law and Practice of Bankruptcy and Insolvency: Embracing the Irish Bankrupt and Insolvent Act 1857*, 3rd edn (Dublin: Hodges, Smith), pp 301–302.

24 *Freeman's Journal*, 24 June 1868.

25 Registry of Deeds 1811, No 443287.

stuff, plate, china' were handed over to trustees 'for the sole and separate use and benefit of the said Anastasia ... notwithstanding her coverture'.[26]

Private moneylending for profit by single women with capital was common in nineteenth-century Ireland. Single women who had lent money might, before marriage, use a settlement to prevent repayments due to them from their borrowers, falling into the hands of the new husband.[27] Women who had made money as shopkeepers before marriage also used the trust as a means of keeping the shop and its stock from her husband. For instance, Elizabeth McDermott, 'seized of furniture and saleable goods in her shop to the amount of fifty pounds' transferred the premises and stock to trustees to be 'held for fifty years ... free from all debts or engagements of [her] said intended husband, notwithstanding her coverture, as if she were a feme sole ... and unmarried'.[28] Trusts could be used to enable a shopkeeper to continue trading despite marriage and coverture; this freed her from the threat that an overbearing husband might decide to appropriate the business. Ellen Joyce, who carried on a successful business as an egg and poultry merchant, settled all of her stock, capital, merchandise, money and securities for money ... notwithstanding coverture' for her 'own sole and separate benefit, free from all marital control and interference'.[29]

Settlements providing for a wife's separate property

Of course, some of these marriage settlements – but probably not more than one-quarter – involved provision for a separate income for the wife in order to safeguard her from an irresponsible or stingy husband. In 1821 on the marriage of a shopkeeper, called Henry Cortell, to Susan Hughes, Henry agreed, in return for the dowry provided by Susan, to hand over £2,000 to the trustees to create an income for Susan's 'own sole and separate use notwithstanding her coverture'.[30] In 1833, on the marriage of Thomas Arthur and Margret Curtis, the groom agreed to pay £100 to three trustees for the 'full and sole use and benefit of the said Margret Curtis during her life'.[31] Often the income was secured by the groom's family making an assignment of lands to trustees, with the trustees having the entitlement to collect rent from those lands. When, in 1869, Emily Bolton of Middlesex Square married John Deane, lands in Tipperary were assigned to the trustees 'to [Emily's] own use independent

---

26 Registry of Deeds 1821, No 516831.

27 In 1869, Mary Anne Banks who had lent money to Frances Solthen of Leeson Street, set up a trust to protect the security which her debtor had given her – an insurance policy worth £750 – from falling into the hands of her future husband (Registry of Deeds 1869, Book 4, No 143).

28 Registry of Deeds 1851, Book 1, No 9.

29 Registry of Deeds 1869, Book 3, No 253.

30 Registry of Deeds 1821, No 517062.

31 *Arthur v Arthur* [1848] 11 Ir Eq Rep 511.

[of her husband]'.[32] But such clauses (found in less than one-quarter of settlements) were not standard in the same way that jointures were. Susan Staves' finding for eighteenth-century England, that separate property provisions, while 'less frequent' than jointures were still 'quite often' settled on wives, is true also for nineteenth-century Ireland – with an emphasis on 'quite'.[33]

The restraint on anticipation

Even wives with settlements providing for separate property protected by careful trustees were vulnerable. The problem was that the wife's separate property could easily be defeated by husbands pressurizing wives to hand over their separate property once they had received it from the trustees. This was confirmed in two late eighteenth-century decisions of the English Court of Chancery: *Hulme v Tenant*[34] and *Pybus v Smith*.[35] In both cases, wives entitled to receive separate property had signed bonds assigning the benefit of that separate property to their husband's creditors. These agreements to waive their separate property were held enforceable. The effect of the recognition of the liberty of a married woman to give away her separate property was, of course, to defeat the object for which the 'equitable doctrine of the separate estate of a married woman had originally been invented'.[36]

In order to defeat the power of a wife to alienate her own property a clause was invented which had the effect of preventing a married woman from alienating her separate estate: the restraint upon anticipation. The clause restraining anticipation was usually expressed in the words 'not to have power to deprive herself by anticipation'. Lord Thurlow is generally credited with inventing the restraint upon alienation in the so far unidentified 'Miss Watson's case' at some point in the period between 1791 and 1804.[37] There is some evidence that, even before Lord Thurlow's invention, conveyancers were experimenting with a similar formula intended to act as a restraint upon alienation. In 1777 Samuel Horner, a sugar boiler from Finglas, made provision in his will for an annuity for his wife, adding that she should 'not have it in her power, nor any husband she may marry hereafter to set alienate or otherwise dispose of said annuity'.[38]

The restraint upon alienation does not appear to have become a routine feature in marriage settlements in Ireland until the middle of the nineteenth

32 Registry of Deeds 1869, Book 16, No 82.

33 S Staves (1990) *Married Women's Separate Property in England, 1660–1833* (Cambridge, Massachusetts: Harvard University Press), p 132.

34 (1778) 1 Bro CC 16.

35 (1791) 3 Bro CC 329.

36 WG Hart (1924) 'The Origin of the Restraint upon Anticipation', *Law Quarterly Review*, xl, 221–226, p 221.

37 Hart (1924) 'The Origin of the Restraint'; *Brandon v Robinson* (1811) Ves Jun Rep 429, 34 ER 379.

38 Prerogative Wills Ireland 1777 A–L f. 29 (NAI, MF GS 41/5).

century. Mid-nineteenth-century examples include the 1869 marriage settlement of Emily Bolton, which provided her with the rent charge of lands in Tipperary for her own use and provided that she was 'not to have power to deprive herself by anticipation'.[39] The family of a Galway city woman, Anne Tighe, settled £150 'upon trust to pay the dividends and interest to 'the said Anne Tighe for her sole and separate use but without power of anticipation'.[40] In 1878 a shirt manufacturer called George Walker undertook to liquidate a policy of assurance which he held with the Scottish Provident Institution, the profits of sale of which were to be invested for his future wife's 'separate use' and subject to the condition that she was not to have 'power to deprive herself thereof in anticipation'.[41]

Separate property and wills

Separate property might be conveyed to a married woman at two points. First, a daughter might obtain separate property from her father, on her marriage, conveyed through a marriage settlement. Later in the marriage, a married woman might obtain separate property, conveyed by a will after her father had died.

The will was an easier method of creating separate property than the marriage settlement. It was not necessary that a trustee be put in place to receive and dispose of the bequest. All that was required was language clearly expressing the intention that the wife was to have the gift, to the exclusion of her husband.[42] It was not necessary that a trustee be appointed; the husband was regarded, instead, as his wife's trustee of this separate property. Because of its simplicity, the will may have been a more common method of creating separate property than the marriage settlement. Bequests by fathers to their married daughters for 'their sole and separate use' regularly appear in eighteenth- and nineteenth-century Irish wills. In 1811 Elizabeth Sherrard, wife of David Sherrard, 'of Great Britain Street in the north suburbs of the city of Cork' received from her father

> one annuity of five hundred pounds to be payable to her during her natural life on her own sole and separate receipt ... notwithstanding her coverture, the same as if she was sole and unmarried without any control dominion or intermeddling of her husband.[43]

39 Registry of Deeds 1869, Book 16, No 82.

40 Registry of Deeds 1869, Book 3, No 240.

41 Registry of Deeds 1878, Book 2, No 83.

42 *Rollfe v Budder* (1724) Bunb 187, 134 ER 642; Clancy (1827) *A Treatise*, pp 256–260; FA Inderwick (1866) *The Law of Wills as Administered in the Court of Probate in England* (London: William Maxwell), pp 4–14.

43 Will of Kennedy Lynass, 21 Apr 1813, Court of Prerogative Will Book (NAI, MS MFGS 41/6).

In 1850 William Scott from County Down bequeathed 'to my daughter Mary Martin, twenty pounds to be paid six years after my decease and she to have the full power of receiving the same without the control of her husband'.[44] Fathers were not the only source of separate property. In 1861 Mary McCarthy from Great Britain Street in Cork City bequeathed £50 to her mother 'free from the control, debts, and engagements of her husband' (Mary's father).[45]

Marriage settlements and separate property in nineteenth-century Ireland

It is impossible to estimate the number of married women in nineteenth-century Ireland with their own spending money. Some of these trust-type settlements were registered. Registration of instruments 'affecting land' under the Registration of Deeds Act 1707,[46] while strictly not compulsory, was, in effect, essential to the security of transactions, and registrations provide some guide to the number of marriage settlements in which land was put into trust. The figure is small, relative to the number of marriages. In 1869 there were less than 200 marriage settlements enrolled at the Registry of Deeds.[47] But this figure both understates and overstates the number of marriage settlements. It overstates the number of marriage settlements providing wives with separate incomes because the majority of marriage settlement trusts were more concerned with providing a widow's pension, rather than with providing a separate income during marriage. On the other hand, figures from the Registry of Deeds understate the number of settlements creating independent property for wives. This is because, in addition to those marriage settlements in which land was put into trust, there was a second category which involved the transfer to trustees of money or shares alone, and which did not involve land.[48] Since these did not affect land they would not have been registered. There is no way of knowing the number of these arrangements.

Another way of measuring the extent of the possession of separate property by married women is to count the number of wills made by married women. Spinsters and widows made wills; but married women usually did not have the property – all family property was their husband's – with which to make wills. The only exception was where they had separate property.[49] The number of wills made by married women is, therefore, a measure of the extent of separate property. The wider the distribution of separate property, the greater

44 Will of William Scott, 15 Aug 1850, Down and Conor Will Book (NAI, MFGS 41/8).

45 Will of Margaret McCarthy, 14 Oct 1861, Cork District Registry Will Book Apr 1862–Feb 1864, f 8 (NAI, MFGS 41/19).

46 6 Anne, c 2 [Ire].

47 Registry of Deeds 1869 Books 1–39.

48 Examples include *Ex p Hodgens* (1847) 11 Ir Eq Rep 99; *Arthur v Arthur* [1848] 11 Ir Eq Rep 511.

49 FA Inderwick (1866) *The Law of Wills as Administered in the Court of Probate in England* (London), pp 4–14.

the number of wills that would have been made by married women. In fact, the number of grants of probate issued in Ireland for wills made by married women was tiny. In 1859 only one out of 1,602 wills proven was made by a married woman. In 1869 just 19 out of the 3,222 wills granted probate had been made by married women.[50]

Coverture and the economic and consumer activity of married women in nineteenth-century Ireland

Married women as traders 1800–1870

Married women, before the married women's property law reforms of the late nineteenth century, could not be made amenable to an action in debt. This, in turn, affected the ability of a married woman to be economically active. Entering business depended on the ability to obtain credit. Since married women could not be sued for not repaying credit, they were unlikely to be given credit in the first place.

The only case in which a married woman might be sued in debt (and might, as a result, be granted credit) was where she had separate property and had expressly promised to pay out of this separate property. In legal theory a married woman dealing with her separate property became a single woman, and could be sued in the same way that a single woman could be sued; a married woman with separate property 'could dispose of it as a feme sole'.[51] But the recovery of debts incurred by married women pledging their separate property was technically awkward. The usual form of married woman's separate property was rental income. Since a married woman's independent right to such a separate estate was recognized only at equity, the creditor's remedy was by attachment of that rental income in the court of chancery. A creditor who tried to recover in a court other than chancery would have its case dismissed. In *Pepper v Kelly*[52] a separated married woman, who, under a separation agreement, was in receipt of a maintenance payment to her separate use, promised her creditor that that separate income would be available to him in case she defaulted. She did default and the creditor misadvisedly sued in the common law side of the Court of Exchequer. The Court of Exchequer sent the creditor away telling him that while he 'may not be without his remedy in a court of equity' he had been mistaken in suing in a court of common law. In a rare Irish example of a married woman's creditor going to chancery, *Copperthwaite v Tuite*,[53] the creditor instituted a suit in Chancery in order to attach a rent charge on lands which had been settled on her marriage to her

50 *Calendar of Grants of Probate and Letters of Administration from 1 Jan 1868 to 31 Dec 1868* (Dublin: Alex Thom).

51 *Francis v Wigzell* (1816) 1 Madd 258, 261; 56 ER 96, 97.

52 [1843] 6 Ir Law Rep 530.

53 (1848) 13 Ir Eq Rep 68.

separate use. But the Court of Chancery was expensive. The most convenient, and usual, court for the recovery by suppliers of mid-level debt was the civil bill court. The civil bill court was not a court of equity and was not available to the creditors of married women who had pledged their separate property.

This immunity from suit in debt and its unattractiveness to creditors must, in part at least, account for the relatively small number of women who carried on self-employment after marriage. Coverture did not, however, totally suppress all economic activity by married women. Some married women did manage to carry out retail business in their own account. The 1871 Irish census records the existence of 9,428 women acting as 'general dealers' of various kinds.[54] Shopkeeping was the most common form of self-employment carried on by married women: there were 3,174 married women shopkeepers in Ireland in 1871, and 454 grocers.[55] Shopkeeping was an occupation which depended on credit and the law of married women's property meant that wholesaler creditors risked incurring financial losses when they extended credit to these married women traders. These married women may have been able to trade because there were suppliers willing to take the risk of not being able to sue if the married woman defaulted. Or it may have been because the suppliers may have obtained guarantees from the shopkeeper's husband. A few married women shopkeepers even managed their business through trusts. Ellen Bernie from Wexford put her shop into the hands of trustees for her 'own sole use and benefit'.[56] The trustees were given the premises and stock and were directed to collect the profits. The legal effect of the arrangement was that the shop and its profits were hers, and were 'freed and absolutely discharged from the engagements of her husband'.

Married women and consumer credit before 1870

The laws of coverture also affected the ability of married women to obtain consumer credit. A shop had no means of recovery if she defaulted. Still, some shopkeepers would provide goods on credit to married women in reliance on the common law doctrine of necessaries: the doctrine under which a wife was regarded as her husband's agent when she purchased necessaries. As she was her husband's agent, the husband could be sued for her debt, and this encouraged shopkeepers to extend credit to married women for basics, like food. On the other hand, shops could not rely on the doctrine where a married woman ordered luxuries that could not be classified as absolute necessaries. In *Allen v Field*[57] a jury sitting in the Irish Court of Exchequer in 1872 held that nightdresses, a dressing gown, and underclothes, purchased by a wife from a drapers in Grafton Street, were 'luxuries'. The result was that her

54 *Census of Ireland, 1871. Part III. General Report* (HC 1876 [C-1377]), p 224.

55 *Census of Ireland, 1871*, p 243.

56 Registry of Deeds 1869, Vol 13, No 14.

57 *Freeman's Journal*, 10 & 16 Dec 1872.

miserly and vindictive husband (who had not allowed her any new clothes in six years) was not liable. Cases like these made Irish shops reluctant to risk providing goods on credit to married women for anything other than absolute essentials. Isabella Tod explained that the supply of consumer credit to married women depended upon '[tradesmen choosing] to run the risk of having to fight for payment of his account in a court of law, and to wait the sentence of a chance jury as to what may be considered necessaries for a lady'.[58]

Husbands and their wives' earnings

The incident of the coverture rule to which late nineteenth-century public opinion most objected was the right which it gave to an abusive husband to simply help himself to all of his wife's assets. The Irish suffragist, N. J. Gossan, dramatically denounced the common law for allowing 'drunken ruffians [to swoop] down upon the little property accumulated by their wife's industry and self-denial and then rushing off to gorge their brutal appetites with the proceeds'.[59]

Exploitation by husbands was increasingly brought to prominence as urban working class women entered employment in factories. Property acquired through the wages earned by these working women was being taken by their husbands or their creditors. Parliament was told of incidents involving working married women in which a husband was caught 'forcibly taking away the furniture while his wife was working at the mill'.[60] There were also cases where husband's creditors, usually publicans, recovered debts by seizing household goods which had been acquired by the working wife: 'they run up debts at the public houses which the women must discharge ... under the threat of having their furniture or other property taken to pay it'.[61]

The first, limited, statutory relief against the doctrine of coverture came in the form of the Married Women's Property (Ireland) Act 1865. The 1865 Act operated in the most extreme case: the woman who, having been deserted by her husband, had been forced to work, and whose husband then returned to seize the property earned through that work. The 1865 Act allowed deserted wives to petition justices for an order protecting their property. The Act only applied in very restricted cases. Desertion was a pre-condition to the operation of the Act. Expulsion would not do. This was confirmed in an 1879 ruling by the Irish High Court which received very negative attention in the English feminist press.[62] The applicant in *Re Hogg* was a middle-class wife,

58 *Northern Whig*, 1 Oct 1873.

59 NJ Gossan (1876) *A Plea for the Ladies* (Dublin: William J Dunbar), p 6.

60 *Special Report from the Select Committee on Married Women's Property Bill, Together with the Proceedings of the Committee, Minutes of Evidence, Appendix and Index*. HC 1867–1868 (441), cccxxxix, 75.

61 *Special Report from the Select Committee on Married Women's Property Bill* 75.

62 *Re Hogg*. *Women's Suffrage Journal*, 1 Oct 1879, p. 170

who had been forced to flee her home by reason of abuse by her husband, who had never supported her and who been charged with indecent assault. She subsequently made a success of a laundry business, and petitioned for protection under the 1865 Act. The application was refused; her husband had not actually physically deserted her; it was irrelevant that he had effectively abandoned her. Judge Harrison said that he was informed that Lord [Thomas] O'Hagan 'who drew the Act' was 'particular that it should be shown upon the order that desertion had taken place'.

Alcohol-related violence almost always formed the background to these property protection applications. Catherine Kennedy from Killiney petitioned for a protection order in 1897 alleging that her husband was 'always drunk, and since his desertion he had twice forcibly broken into my place and took away my bedclothes and other property I [was] able to earn for myself'.[63] Anne Murphy, who was supporting herself by carrying on the business of a green grocer in Ranelagh, deposed that her husband was of 'very intemperate habits ... continually beating and ill-treating me'.[64] The husband of Teresa Murphy of Nicholas Street had stabbed her and

> on one occasion he had cut my head with a shovel, and on another occasion with a bellows. He broke my ribs on another occasion and he also broke my finger. At present he is suffering imprisonment for scalding me with a kettle of water ... He is in the habit of throwing knives.[65]

The campaign for reform of married women's property in Ireland

Arguments for reform of the law of coverture were being rehearsed in progressive circles in Ireland even before organized campaigning began in the 1860s. In 1849, the Trinity College political economist, Mountiford Longfield, recommended to the Select Committee on the Poor Law in Ireland that, in place of the married settlement, married women would be better protected by the abolition of the husband's rights to his wife's property. He suggested law reform along the lines of 'such laws as those in other countries making the property of married women their own property, not subject to control by their husbands'.[66]

The immediate origins of the reform campaign in England had an Irish dimension. In 1867, Belfast hosted the annual congress of the National Association for the Promotion of Social Science. The venue was Queen's University

63 Affidavit of Catherine Kennedy, 7 June 1897 (NAI 1C/72/860).

64 Affidavit of Anne Murphy, 17 May 1892 (NAI 1C/72/860).

65 Affidavit of Teresa Murphy, 20 Mar 1900 (NAI 1C/72/860).

66 *Tenth Report from the Select Committee on the Poor Laws (Ireland)* (HC 1849 (301) xv, 647, pp 12, 13).

and sessions on issues like law reform, economic development and criminology were reported in great detail in the Irish press. One of the more popular papers, on the reform of married women's property, was delivered by George Hastings, the secretary of the National Association (and a future Liberal MP).[67] The room was packed for this lecture. Lord O'Hagan joked that while

> questions of law reform in general seemed to excite little interest among ordinary members of the Congress, there was one subject [married women's property] which drew an immense audience. The room was crowded and the ladies especially seemed to take a deep interest in the discussion.[68]

Sitting in the audience was the New York lawyer and law reformer, David Dudley Field, who had travelled from America especially for the conference. New York had abolished the husband's right to his wife's property in 1848,[69] and in the course of his paper George Hastings turned to Field and asked him how the reform of the law of coverture had worked in New York. Field replied that the majority of New Yorkers were so much in favour of the law that 'any changes which had been made to it were towards making it more completely favourable to the women'.[70]

The Belfast meeting was the catalyst for the re-commencement of a national political campaign in England for reform of the law. In the same month, prompted by the proceedings in Belfast, a petition with 300 signatures was presented to the council of the Social Science Association, drawing its attention to the injustice of the law affecting the property of married women. The petition was referred to the Jurisprudence Department of the National Association for the Promotion of Social Science, which, in turn, enlisted the Liberal MP and lawyer, William Shaw Lefevre.[71] In April 1868 Lefevre, along with John Stuart Mill MP and Russell Gurney MP, introduced the Married Women's Property Bill.[72]

When, in May 1868, a pressure group, the Married Women's Property Association, was established in London, activists in Ireland affiliated to the English group. Two committees were established, one in Dublin and the other in Belfast. The driving force behind the Dublin campaign was the gothic novelist Anne Robertson, who had established links with the English feminist

67 GW Hastings (1868) *Transactions of the National Association Belfast Meeting 1867* (London: Longmans), p 292.

68 *Northern Whig*, 13 Oct 1868.

69 L Holcombe (1983) *Wives and Property. Reform of the Married Women's Property Law in Nineteenth Century England* (Toronto: University of Toronto Press), p 158.

70 *Northern Whig*, 18 September 1867.

71 GW Hastings (1868) *Transactions of the National Association Belfast Meeting 1867* (London: Longmans), p 292.

72 HC 1867–1868 (89).

leader Lydia Becker, and who organized the Dublin operation from her home in Blackrock.[73]

Belfast had, at first, been slower to organize; Isabella Tod told a parliamentary hearing in July 1868 that while there were committees in Dublin 'it does not take that form in Belfast'. However, 'the feeling [was] very decided among the body of educated ladies [in Belfast]',[74] and in the autumn of 1868 a Belfast committee led by Mrs Sharman Crawford and Isabella Tod had been established and was seeking endorsement from influential 'ladies and gentlemen of all shades of opinion'.[75] These committees busied themselves collecting signatures for the petitioning campaign organized by the Married Women's Property Association. In 1869, 14 petitions from Ireland were laid before the House of Commons.[76] When, in the spring of 1870, Parliament hesitated before accepting the Married Women's Property Bill, Belfast sympathizers were urged to sign petitions lodged in the 'Library Linen Hall, Mr Atchinson's Castle Place and at the Athenaeum Castle Place'.[77] The *Women's Suffrage Journal* singled out those married women's property rights' campaigners from the 'sister country', who

> amid her own troubles, finds voice to raise on behalf of justice to women. Last year numerous petitions signed by great numbers of persons went up from various cities and counties in Ireland for the franchise for women and the married women's property bill. This year Dublin led the way in the same course.

Anne Robertson told a meeting in Molesworth Hall that 'so far from standing in the background, Dublin, next to London and Manchester, sent more signatures ... to Parliament than any other place in the United Kingdom'.[78]

The second campaign 1870–1882

Parliament in 1870 was unable to complete the full transition from coverture to separate ownership. Instead, the Married Women's Property Act 1870 only half-abolished coverture. The measure, which had originally been proposed by George Hastings MP and John Stuart Mill MP in 1868, had provided that a married woman would be entitled to hold all property 'whether belonging to her before marriage or acquired by her in any way after marriage' free

73 GW Hastings (1869) *Transactions of the National Association 1868* (London: Longmans), p 281; *Freeman's Journal*, 28 June 1870.

74 *Special Report from the Select Committee on Married Women's Property Bill* 76.

75 Isabella Tod to Lord Dufferin, 12 Sept 1868 (PRONI, D/1071/H/B/T/219/1).

76 *Committee for Promoting the Married Women's Property Bill. Annual Report 1869* (Manchester: A Ireland).

77 *Northern Whig*, 10 Mar 1870.

78 *Women's Suffrage Journal*, 1 Apr 1870, 2 May 1870.

from her husband.[79] By contrast, the Act of 1870, as finally enacted, merely enabled a married woman to acquire two types of separate property: (i) wages and earnings acquired *after marriage* in an occupation or trade (section 1); and (ii) a sum less than £200 acquired through a will or deed (section 7). Outside of these exceptions, a husband continued to retain his old legal right to his wife's property.

The 1870 Act made a wife's *post-nuptial* earnings in trade or employment her own. By implication, earnings and property which she had acquired before marriage became her husband's as before. A woman who, before she married, had acquired money through shopkeeping, or by renting property, or who had inherited money or jewellery or paintings, lost all her rights to that property once she married. Unless she took the precaution of putting the money in trust 'all she possesses at her marriage passes to her husband'.[80] The 1870 Act allowed a woman to hold on to small bequests (of sums less than £200). But she had no right to larger inheritances. The Married Woman's Property Association complained that 'if a man gives to a married woman a legacy of two hundred pounds that is her own [;] if he makes it two hundred guineas it is her husband's'.[81] Writing from Leeds, in 1871, where she was attending the Congress of the National Association for the Promotion of Social Science, Isabella Tod described the 1870 Act as 'incomplete and soiled'.[82]

The injustice of continuing to allow, even after the 1870 Act, undeserving husbands to help themselves to their wife's property was vividly illustrated to an English audience by one widely publicized Irish case: *Lynch v Cork and Macroom Railway*.[83] The case arose out of an action for personal injuries taken by a married woman, Ellen Lynch. Ellen Lynch's husband had deserted her, leaving her to fend for herself by working as a dressmaker and by taking in lodgers. Ellen had sued the Cork and Macroom Railway for personal injuries, and when a settlement of £75 was accepted by Mrs Lynch, her husband made an application that the money should be handed over to him. The 1870 Act only made a wife's 'earnings' her own property. But damages were not 'earnings'. 'It could hardly be said that the damages here payable would be personal earnings'.[84] The Court of Exchequer, in light of wording of the 1870 Act, had no choice but to hold that the 1870 Act did not apply, and to hand

79 s 2 of the Married Women's Property Bill 1868 had provided that every woman who marries ... shall, notwithstanding coverture, have and hold all real and personal property whether belonging to her before marriage or acquired by her in any way after marriage' (HC 1868–1869 (20)).

80 *Married Women's Property Association. Annual Report 1880* (Manchester: A Ireland), p 16.

81 *Committee for Promoting the Married Women's Property Bill. Annual Report 1879* (Manchester: A Ireland), p 39.

82 *Northern Whig*, 17 Oct 1871.

83 (1879) *Irish Law Times and Solicitors Journal* 260.

84 Ibid.

the money over to her husband. As the case ended, Baron Dowse, acknowledging the injustice of the 1870 Act, reflected that the outcome provided a strong argument for extending electoral rights for women and 'for those who wish to have women legislating for women'.

The decision in Dublin in the *Lynch* case caused a minor outcry in England. The *Lynch* judgment was raised at the annual general meeting of the Married Woman's Property Association.[85] Lydia Becker's *Women's Suffrage Journal* denounced the judgment of the Irish Exchequer. It was the ruling of the 'High Court of Justice – for men. It would seem to be the High Court of Injustice for women'.[86]

A comprehensive right for married women to hold their own property was eventually secured by the Married Women's Property Act of 1882. Section 2 set aside the right of husbands to take their wives' personal property. It substituted, instead, the right of married women to ownership of all of their property:

> every married woman was to be entitled to have, and to hold, as her separate property ... all real and personal property which shall belong to her at the time or marriage or shall be acquired by, or devolve upon her, after marriage.

The campaign had eventually, on the second attempt, succeeded, and the Married Woman's Property Association dissolved itself.[87]

Married women's property after the Married Women's Property Act 1882

Married women as consumers after the Married Women's Property Acts

The 1882 Act allowed a married woman access to credit, and to the activities associated with having access to credit: access to credit as a customer running an account at a shop, or access to credit as a trader obtaining supplies from wholesalers on credit. Under the 1882 Act all property earned or held by a married woman was hers; not her husband's. Since it was hers, it was amenable to her creditors if she defaulted. The creditor was secured. In theory, this reform should have resulted in an increase in married women engaging in credit-dependant activity.

In fact, the Acts of 1870–1882 did not result in a massive flow of consumer credit to married women. Debt litigation provides one means of measuring the amount of credit obtained by married women. In some districts, court clerks, making entries in civil bill books, would specifically record the fact

85 *Married Women's Property Association. Annual Report 1880* (Manchester: A Ireland), p 16.

86 *Women's Suffrage Journal*, 2 June 1879.

87 *Report of the Married Woman's Property Committee 1882* (Manchester: A, Ireland), p 12.

that a defendant was a married woman. It is plausible that the greater the amount of credit held by married women the higher the number of debt actions that would be taken against married women. In fact, the number of defendants recorded as 'married women' in debt actions in the 1880s was relatively small. In Easter term 1888 there was only one instance of a married woman (out of a total number of 116 defendants) being sued at Kingstown Civil Bill Court – a Mrs Cunningham, sued by the drapers, Robert Shaw and Company.[88] In the summer term of 1904 there were just two actions against married women.[89] Even in 1918 the figure was just two (out of 59 civil bills).[90]

The evidence from the Dublin suburb of Kilmainham is similar. Of the defendants sued by civil bills in the summer term at Kilmainham in 1888 there were just two married woman (out of a total of 309 defendants).[91] In the June sittings of 1899 at Kilmainham, 14 defendants (out of 1070) were recorded as 'married women'.[92] In the same term in 1908 there were just 11 cases (out of 309 cases), and in 1918 10 (out of 240) cases in which the defendants were designated as married women.[93] It was, on the other hand, quite common to find married women and their husbands being sued together, which may be explained by creditors extending credit to married women only where their husbands guaranteed the debt: when, for instance, in 1892, Singer & Co sued in Cork Borough Civil Bill Court for the recovery of money owed for a sewing machine, the defendants were named as Daniel O'Leary and Mary O'Leary.[94] Whatever the cause, in late nineteenth- and early twentieth-century Ireland, it was more commonly the husband who opened credit accounts, and received the bills, and who was sued when those bills were unpaid.

Married women's independent consumerism was predicated on their having independent property in the first place. If they had nothing, there was nothing for the creditor to take. Non-working married women would have had little in the way of independent assets, and shops may have been reluctant to extend credit to married women with little more than clothes or jewellery for the sheriff to seize. Shops were warned to check for the existence of a separate estate where married women were seeking goods on credit. In 1899 an English solicitor observed that goods were being supplied on credit

88 Civil Book, Kingstown 1886–1889 (NAI, IC/ 40/17).

89 Civil Bill Book, Kingstown 1904 (NAI, IC/16/ 48).

90 Civil Bill Book, Balbriggan and Kingstown 1918 (NAI/70/94). In 1919 the figure was one out of 44 civil bills (ibid.).

91 Civil Bill Book, Kilmainham 1888–1889 (NAI, IC/40/18).

92 Civil Bill Book, Kilmainham 1899 (NAI, 1C/16/39).

93 Civil Bill Book, Kilmainham 1908 (NAI, IC/28/36); City of Dublin and Kilmainham Civil Bill Book 1919 (NAI/IC/40/18).

94 Civil Bill Book, Cork Borough, May 1891 to July 1892 (NAI, 1D/37/26).

'on the very faintest of evidence that they [had] separate estate and without any enquiry whether that estate, if it exists at all, can be made available in the case of failure'.[95]

The understanding that married women were risky consumer debtors was compounded by the decision of the English Court of Appeal in 1887 in *Scott v Morley*[96] which held that the remedy of imprisonment for debt under the Debtors Act 1872 still widely used by shopkeepers against their poorer debtor customers – could not be deployed against married women. The unavailability of imprisonment deprived creditors of the most effective last-resort remedy for the most difficult of debtors, and this may have acted as a further disincentive. The creditors' protection journal, *Stubbs Gazette*, set out the difficulties caused by the non-availability of the threat of imprisonment to shops trying to recover debts from married women: 'when she has put her property out of the reach of her creditors there is absolutely no remedy of any kind, as an order of commitment against her under the Debtor's Act [1870] cannot be obtained'.[97]

Married women in business after the Married Women's Property Acts 1870–1882

The ability of married women to hold separate property, which could then be recovered by suppliers if they defaulted, facilitated married women's ability to obtain stock on credit. In theory, it enabled married women to enter into trade. One of the hopes of the social reformers of the 1870s had been that allowing married women to enjoy for themselves any profits which they might make in business (and not to have their earnings plundered by their husbands) would incentivize women to enter trade.[98] Ultimately, the number of married women who availed themselves of the chance to undertake independent business activity was very small. Bankruptcy records provide a source of data on married women who acted as traders. Under the Married Women's Property Act 1882, married women trading separately from their husbands could be adjudicated bankrupt.[99] Only one per cent of bankruptcies in Edwardian Ireland involved married women.[100] Grocery shopkeeping, managing public houses and running draperies, usually in rural areas, were the most common forms of self-employment pursued by that small group of

95 Anon (1889) 'Remedies in Respect of Married Women's Liabilities', *Irish Law Times and Solicitors Journal*, 585, 598.

96 (1887) 20 QBD 120.

97 *Stubbs Gazette*, 15 Mar 1893.

98 *Special Report from the Select Committee on Married Women's Property Bill Together with the Proceedings of the Committee, Minutes of Evidence, Appendix and Index* (HC 1867–1868 (441), cccxxxix).

99 s 1(5) of the Married Women's Property Act 1882.

100 Out of 1517 petitions for bankruptcy between 1899 and 1907, 21 married women were adjudicated bankrupts. *Judicial Statistics Ireland* 1899–1907; *Dublin Gazette* 1899–1907.

Irish married women who, following the married women's property reforms, went into business on their own.[101]

Married women's property in Ireland before and after the Married Women's Property Acts

The marriage settlement may not have been used by the landed upper class in Ireland to the same extent as it is sometimes claimed to have been used in England. In England in the nineteenth century, the marriage settlement was said by contemporaries to have been a common means of mitigating the doctrine of coverture, and providing wives with a protected independent income. In Ireland, at least amongst the landed upper class, the purpose was usually not the protection of wives from selfish or reckless husbands. Instead, the principal purpose of the settlement was to provide an old age pension for wives where they outlived their husbands. Law reform came with the Married Women's Property Acts 1870–1882. These Acts could have liberated married women to enter the market for consumer and commercial credit, to act as independent consumers, and to trade on their own account. But the Married Women's Property Acts 1870–1882 only gave married women the liberty to dispose of property where they had acquired their own earnings or property. Since they did not earn or acquire their own property, they could not enjoy the liberties granted by the Acts. In practice, in the late nineteenth and early twentieth century, consumer credit was still restricted to the economically active husband. And only very few married women took advantage of the removal of the restrictions on their going into business.

101 *Dublin Gazette* 1900–1907: shopkeeping (six cases); drapers (four cases) and publicans (four cases). Of the married women adjudicated bankrupt by the Belfast Court of Bankruptcy between 1890 and 1910, drapers (Elizabeth Exsham (BANK 1/1/63) Maria Carlisle (BANK 1/1/778) Florence Moody (BANK 1/1/1066), Sarah Allison (BANK 1/1/1096) and Sarah McDonnell (BANK 1/2/761)) and publicans (Rachel Gordon BANK 1/1/246), Rachel McIlroy (BANK 1/1/771), Sarah McConnell (BANK 1/1/597) and Mary Mulholland (BANK 1/1/768)) were the largest trading groups.

6
Adultery in the Courts: Damages for Criminal Conversation in Ireland

*Niamh Howlin**

Introduction

In April 1806, the Irish revolutionary Valentine Browne Lawless, the 2nd Baron Cloncurry, noticed his young wife Eliza walking arm-in-arm with Sir John Bennett Piers, a notorious womanizer, spendthrift and gambler. Cloncurry grew suspicious and confronted his wife, who tearfully confessed to having an affair with Piers. A miniature portrait of Piers and a lock of his hair were found among her possessions. To make matters worse, Cloncurry and Piers had been friends since their school days; furthermore, Piers owed Cloncurry a substantial sum of money. While nothing, presumably, could entirely assuage Lord Cloncurry's hurt feelings and wounded pride in such circumstances, the subsequent award of £20,000 in damages by a King's Bench jury may have helped.[1] Represented by John Philpot Curran and Charles Kendal Bushe, he sued Piers for 'criminal conversation'.[2]

---

* I wish to acknowledge with thanks the assistance provided by Ms Clare Cresswell in preparing this chapter.

1 S Wolfram (1985) 'Divorce in England', *Oxford Journal of Legal Studies*, 5, 155–186, notes, p 169, that this was the highest sum awarded for criminal conversation in England or Ireland.

2 Anon (1807) *A Full and Accurate Report of the Trial of Sir John Piers for Criminal Conversation with Lady Cloncurry: Taken in Shorthand by an Eminent Barrister Concerned in the Cause* (Dublin: C La Grange). Piers had meanwhile fled to the Isle of Man and Lady Cloncurry, portrayed as 'artless and weak', also left the country with her reputation in tatters. She later gave birth to a son presumed to be Piers'. The Cloncurrys divorced in 1807 and Lord Cloncurry remarried four years later: PM Geoghegan (2009) 'Lawless, Valentine Browne (Baron Cloncurry)' in J McGuire and J Quinn (eds) *Dictionary of Irish Biography* (Cambridge: Cambridge University Press) (http://dib.cambridge.org/viewReadPage.do?articleId=a4713), 11 April 2017. John Betjeman penned a poem about the seduction and affair in the 1930s: 'The nobility laugh and are free from all worry / Excepting the bride of the Baron Cloncurry. But his lordship is gayer than ever before / He laughs like the ripples that lap the lake shore / Nor thinks that his bride has the slightest of fears / Lest one of the guests be the Baronet Piers.' John Betjeman (under the pseudonym Epsilon), 'Sir John Piers', 1938, republished in J Betjeman (1940) *New Light for Old Chancels* (London: John Murray).

Criminal conversation or 'crim con' was a 'notorious'[3] civil action which allowed a cuckolded husband to recover damages from his wife's lover. It evolved out of de facto blackmail agreements in the late seventeenth century and gained popularity among the English nobility in the eighteenth century. The first point to note in relation to crim con is that adulterous men and women were treated differently by the law.[4] A wife could not bring an action of criminal conversation against her husband's mistress. Although 'adultery by either sex was a serious marital offence',[5] when committed by a wife it was injurious not only to her husband but also to society more generally,[6] particularly given the importance of property, paternity and legitimacy in the eighteenth and nineteenth centuries.[7]

The nature of crim con actions

The nature of crim con in Ireland and the profile of litigants changed over time. As in England, crim con cases were originally the preserve of the wealthy elite, and in the late eighteenth and early nineteenth centuries, actions tended to be brought by wealthy or aristocratic men.[8] The 1816 case of *Binns v Scott* was even described by counsel as 'novel' because the parties were 'not in high life'.[9] However, from the second half of the nineteenth century crim con actions were increasingly taken by men of more modest means such as, for example, a stationmaster,[10] a coal merchant,[11] a mill-worker,[12] a

3 S Staves (1982) 'Money for Honour: Damages for Criminal Conversation', *Studies in Eighteenth-Century Culture*, 2, 279–297.

4 A wife's adultery was sufficient grounds for divorce, whereas a husband's adultery had to be accompanied by some aggravating factor, such as incest, bigamy, unnatural practices or cruelty: see Chapter 7. In Scotland, adultery by either sex constituted grounds for divorce: see L Leneman (1996) '"Disregarding the Matrimonial Vows": Divorce in Eighteenth and Early Nineteenth Century Scotland', *Journal of Social History*, 30(2), 465–482.

5 L Stone (1993) *Broken Lives: Separation and Divorce in England 1660–1857* (Oxford: Oxford University Press), p 303.

6 See A Sumner Holmes (1995) 'The Double Standard in the English Divorce Laws, 1857–1923', *Law and Social Inquiry*, 20(2), 601–620.

7 See Chapter 12.

8 *Cloncurry v Piers* (1807); *Doyle v Brown* (1820), *Crim. Con. A Full, Faithful and Impartial Report of the Trial, wherein Sir John M. Doyle, KCB & KTS was Plaintiff, and George Peter Brown, Esq, Defendant. For Criminal Conversation with the Defendant's Wife* (Dublin: James Charles). However, this was not universal; Wolfram (1985) 'Divorce in England', p 172, cites a number of English examples of crim con damages being awarded to farmers, butchers, drapers and other tradesmen.

9 *Binns v Scott* (1816), *Crim Con William Binns, Plaintiff, John Scott, Defendant, Before the Hon Justice Mayne* (Dublin: Wm Espy), p 4. It was not, however the only such case; in *Patterson v Pullen*, *Freeman's Journal*, 2 Dec 1800, the plaintiff was a publican while the defendant was a cutler.

10 *Echlin v Brady* (1865) 10 *Irish Jurist* (ns) 188 and *Dundalk Democrat*, 18 Feb 1865.

11 *Hewitt v Lyttle*, *Irish Times*, 16 Dec 1886.

12 *Beaken v Dockeray*, *Irish Times*, 22 Feb 1882.

gardener,[13] a farmer,[14] a chemical manufacturer,[15] a clerk,[16] a teacher[17] and a doctor in a lunatic asylum.[18] The damages sought in such cases were generally much lower than would have been the case in the aristocratic cases of a century before.[19]

Their rarity and potential salaciousness combined to generate great public interest in these trials. Newspapers reported the cases in detail,[20] and courtroom attendance was so high[21] that it was sometimes regulated by ticket.[22]

The cases that came before the Irish courts involved Roman Catholics,[23] members of the Church of Ireland[24] and other denominations.[25] It was rare for crim con to be taken in response to an alleged rape or sexual assault.[26] The typical scenario was a wife having an adulterous affair with a close friend or acquaintance of her husband, or sometimes with her employer.[27] Inglis observes that the history of Irish sexuality 'remains a relatively hidden, secretive area';[28] some crim con cases were quite unusual and reveal a hidden world of sexual activity among all elements of Irish society. For example, there was the 'well-reared' daughter of a Presbyterian minister, married to a newspaper publisher, who ended up having repeated drunken liaisons with

---

13 *Devlin v Davy*, *Irish Times*, 7 Jan 1888.

14 *Graham v Pattison*, *Irish Times*, 23 June 1935.

15 *Mallon v Barnwell*, *Irish Times*, 25 Jan 1889.

16 *Lowry v Bustard*, *Irish Times*, 16 Apr 1885.

17 *Morrison v Roberts*, *Irish Times*, 30 Jul 1892.

18 *Atkins v Packford*, *Irish Times*, 27 Jan 1887.

19 Staves (1982) 'Money for Honour', p 289, has examined these earlier awards in detail and writes that the amount of damages in such cases was directly related to the 'honour' of the parties involved: 'the courts tried to adjust damages to an estimate of how much honour the individual plaintiff had lost; how much honour each plaintiff had lost, in turn, depended in part on how much honour he was adjudged to have had initially'.

20 Jurors were often warned to disregard any rumours or speculation that they had heard regarding the case: Anon (1804) *A Report of the Trial on an Action for Damages Brought by the Reverend Charles Massy Against the Most Noble the Marquis of Headfort for Criminal Conversation with Plaintiff's Wife* (Dublin: MN Mahon), and *Cloncurry v Piers* (1807).

21 Anon (1835) *Court of Exchequer, Feb 22nd, 1835. Crim. Con. New Trial before the Chief Baron. Hodgens v Mahon* (Dublin: D Scott).

22 *McCraith v Quinn*, *Belfast Newsletter*, 2 Aug 1872.

23 *Coffey v Magee* (1829); *Hurst v McDonnell* (1891); and *Fay v Barber* (1797); Anon (1797) *The Trial of William Barber, for Criminal Conversation with Jane Fay, Wife of Lawrence Fay, In His Majesty's Court of King's Bench in Ireland; Before the Right Honourable Earl Clonmell, and a Special Jury*, 2nd edn (Dublin: J Whitworth).

24 *Doyle v Brown* (1820).

25 The couple in *Binns v Scott* (1816) were reported to have been members of the Methodist Society.

26 One such case, however, was *Graham v Pattison*, *Irish Times*, 28 June 1935.

27 *Lowry v Bustard*, *Irish Times*, 16 Apr 1885; Kinsella v Wingfield, *Irish Times*, 24 Apr 1883.

28 T Inglis (2005) 'Origins and Legacies of Irish Prudery: Sexuality and Social Control in Modern Ireland' *Eire-Ireland* 40(3 & 4), 9–37, p 9.

numerous bank employees in the lanes and alleys of Ballina.[29] There was the upper-middle-class husband who cheerfully prostituted his wife and boasted about it.[30] There was also the woman admitted to a private asylum where sexual relations freely took place between patients, staff, visitors and prostitutes, and who became pregnant, probably by one of the doctors.[31] These sorts of cases belie the myth that there was no extramarital sexual activity in nineteenth- and early twentieth-century Ireland.

Crim con actions might be taken out of revenge, as part of wider marriage breakdown proceedings,[32] or simply to extort money. An example of attempted extortion was *Devlin v Davy*.[33] The plaintiff, an alcoholic gardener, had been imprisoned several times for assaulting his wife, who had obtained a divorce on grounds of cruelty. He brought a crim con action against Davy, a doctor from Terenure. However, both Devlin's daughter and his daughter-in-law testified that he had offered them money to give false testimony against the defendant. The daughter described her father as a 'villain and a ruffian', and told the court that her mother had financially supported the family for years. The jury, unsurprisingly, returned a verdict for the defendant, and the judge was particularly critical of the plaintiff, making an order that the Crown Solicitor should institute criminal proceedings against him for perjury. *Matthews v Moniali*[34] is another example of attempted extortion. The defendant was a married Church of Ireland clergyman who had recently fired his steward, the plaintiff. There were numerous cases which did not appear to be bona fide,[35] or which may have involved a conspiracy against the defendant.[36] Some plaintiffs viewed crim con as the solution to their dire financial situations, especially where they could target a creditor as a defendant.[37]

29 *Joynt v Jackson* (1880).

30 *Mansergh v Hacket* (1807), p 10.

31 Anon (1816) *Crim Con. Report of a Trial, in the Court of Common Pleas, on Saturday, Dec 14, 1816. John Hinds, Gentleman Attorney, Plaintiff. Philip Perry Price Myddleton, Defendant* (Dublin: R Conolly).

32 By the late eighteenth century, a crim con action was part of the slow, expensive process of obtaining a parliamentary divorce. See D Urquhart (2013) 'Ireland and the Divorce and Matrimonial Causes Act of 1857', *Journal of Family History* 38, 301–320. See WH Kisbey (1871) *The Law and Practice of the Court for Matrimonial Causes and Matters* (Dublin: W M'Gee), pp 1–2. By the turn of the nineteenth century, many crim con cases in England involved some level of collusion between the parties: Stone (1993) *Broken Lives*, p 24; K Binhammer (1996) 'The Sex Panic of the 1790s', *Journal of the History of Sexuality* 6(3), 409–434, p 429.

33 *Irish Times*, 7 Jan 1888.

34 *Freeman's Journal*, 14 Jul 1866.

35 *Todd v Alexander*, *Irish Times*, 20 Jan 1917; *Toner v Bullick*, *Belfast Newsletter*, 9 Jul 1900.

36 *Aylward v Morrisson*, *Belfast Newsletter*, 10 Sept 1813. McClelland B was appalled, and declared a nonsuit.

37 *Brown v Blake* in M Browne (1817) *Irish Gallantry! Fairburn's Edition of the Unprecedented Trial between Mark Browne and Joseph Blake for adultery*, 4th edn (Dublin, 1817); *Binns v Scott* (1816); *Keenan v Pringle*, *Irish* Times, 5 Feb 1891.

In *Murdock v Rynn*,[38] the wife testified that her husband suggested that she ought to be 'found' in some 'awkward places with Mr Rynne', with whom she was on friendly terms, and that he would share with her any money recovered from him.[39]

The mechanics of crim con

As Lobban explains:

> The common law of torts was shaped by the medieval distinction between trespass and the action on the case. By the late eighteenth century, it was accepted that the former was used for direct harms, and the latter for consequential ones. The action on the case was a particularly broad form, and was used for a large variety of wrongs, including slander and libel, trover, nuisance, and negligence.[40]

Crim con could be pleaded either as an action in trespass[41] or on the case.[42] In relation to the former, the trespass was on the husband's rights in relation to his wife.[43] Case was a form of action which developed out of trespass, but allowed for damages for less immediate and direct injuries.[44] Chitty considered it more convenient to plead crim con on the case, because the injury to the plaintiff was generally 'not immediate, but consequential'. Pleading on the case rendered it unnecessary for the plaintiff to specify exactly when and where the incident (or incidents) of adultery had occurred.[45] This avoided not

38 *Belfast Newsletter*, 2 May 1894.

39 Also *Taaffe v Fitzgerald*, *Belfast Newsletter*, 1 Mar 1816.

40 M Lobban (2010) 'Tort' in J Baker (ed), *The Oxford History of the Laws of England* (13 vols) (Oxford: Oxford University Press), vol 12, p 888.

41 *Blachford v Latouche*, *Freeman's Journal*, 13 Jan 1811 and *Hodgens v Mahon* (1835), p 1.

42 According to Chitty, 'in actions of crim con it has always been the practice to bring trespass or case indiscriminately, on the ground that the party aggrieved might waive all damages resulting from the trespass' (J Chitty (1844) (H Greening (ed)), *Chitty's Treatise on Pleading and Parties to Actions: with Second and Third Volumes Containing Modern Precedents of Pleading and Practical Notes*, 3 vols, 7th edn (London: Sweet), vol 2, p 483). Ferguson described crim con as 'an action on the case for the special damage' (WD Ferguson (1841–1842) *A Treatise on the Practice of the Queen's Bench, Common Pleas, and Exchequer of Pleas in Ireland, in Personal Actions and Ejectments* vol 2 (Dublin: A Milliken), p 1192).

43 Chitty (1844) *Treatise on Pleading*, p 483.

44 W Blackstone (1800) *Commentaries on the Laws of England* vol 3, 13th edn (London: A Strahan), p 122, describes trespass on the case as a 'universal remedy' for 'wrongs unaccompanied by force'. It also allowed for compensation in cases where the injury was caused by omission, or where it was not immediately injurious. The actions of seducing a wife away from her husband, and harbouring another man's wife could also be pleaded on the case: *Winsmore v Greenbank* (1745) Willes 577: 125 ER 1330.

45 Chitty (1844) *Treatise on Pleading*, p 483.

only potential evidentiary difficulties, but also the potential unpleasantness of having to delve into the specific details of the extramarital intercourse.

Irish crim con cases were usually tried by special juries,[46] who determined whether adultery had been proven, and if so, the quantum of damages to be awarded. These were cases 'wherein juries are permitted to exercise a degree of discretion not common in other cases, and wherein they are entire judges of facts'.[47] Nevertheless, either party could apply for a verdict to be set aside on the basis that it went against the weight of evidence, and that it was a verdict that no reasonable jury could have reached.[48] Where a defendant conceded that adultery had taken place and allowed judgment against him in default, a jury of six was appointed with the sole purpose of assessing damages.

Proving crim con

A number of facts had to be proven before a trial jury awarded damages for crim con. First, it had to be established that the plaintiff and his wife had in fact been married.[49] Production of a marriage register was unnecessary; usually the testimony of the clergyman who had performed the marriage ceremony sufficed. It was unnecessary to prove that the defendant knew that the woman was married.[50] The plaintiff then had to prove adultery between his wife and the defendant. Given the nature of the act, most cases involved circumstantial evidence, often from servants.[51] This might include details of extended or nocturnal visits, secret letters,[52] whispered conversations,

46 For an explanation of special juries, see N Howlin (2017) *Juries in Ireland: Laypersons and Law in the Long Nineteenth Century* (Dublin: Four Courts Press). Crim con cases which were tried at assizes were more likely to go before a common jury: *Dunlop v Johnson, Belfast Newsletter*, 22 Jul 1886 and *Cronin v Murphy*, *Belfast Newsletter*, 17 May 1897. The latter was subsequently retried by a special jury.

47 *Fay v Barber* (1797), p 22.

48 For example, *Cronin v Murphy* (1897). A motion to set aside the verdict in *Joynt v Jackson* was unsuccessful: *Irish Times*, 18 Jan 1881. Both *Fay v Barber* (1797) and *Hodgens v Mahon* (1835) were tried twice.

49 Chitty (1844) *Treatise on Pleading*, p 484. This could prove difficult. In *Fay v Barber* (1797) the defendant claimed a non-suit on two grounds: Mr and Mrs Fay were allegedly of different religions, and had been married by a Catholic priest: see Chapter 3.

50 In *Worrall v Snow, Belfast Newsletter*, 12 Aug 1874, Mrs Worrall had concealed the fact that she was married, yet her husband still recovered damages. Chitty (1844) *Treatise on Pleading*, p 484, pointed out that it was unnecessary in such cases to allege or prove that the defendant knew that the woman was married, but that such knowledge was necessary in cases of seducing or harbouring a wife or servant.

51 According to Kisbey (1871) *Law and Practice*, p 7, where there was no direct evidence of adultery, 'the circumstances must be such as would lead the guarded discretion of a reasonable and just man to the conclusion'. In *McDonnell v Weddick, Freeman's Journal*, 21 June 1873, unusually, the only evidence proffered was the husband's uncorroborated testimony, and the case failed.

52 *Fay v Barber* (1797).

secretly commissioned portraits or the discovery of keepsakes,[53] closed[54] or locked[55] drawing-room doors, clothing torn, stained or in disarray,[56] beds that appeared to have been slept in by two persons,[57] and so on.[58] Servants might become suspicious if they were sent out of the house on apparently frivolous errands.[59] Sometimes the husband discovered his wife and her lover together. In *McCraith v Quinn*,[60] for example, the suspicious husband had followed his wife when she went out riding, and discovered her on a side-road conversing with the defendant, who had already been barred from their house. The enraged husband 'beat him with a stick, which he broke across his back'.[61] Events were even more dramatic in *Conyers v Westropp*,[62] where Mr Conyers burst into his wife's room with the aid of a few servants, and found the couple in flagrante. Westropp, a magistrate, jumped out of the bed in his shirt and 'a struggle ensued; Mrs Conyers interposed, endeavouring to screen her seducer from the vengeance of her husband; and she too was undressed'. Westropp fired a pistol, and received a severe beating at the hands of Conyers' servants, suffering a fractured skull and numerous lacerations from pitchforks. He was thrown out into the yard, covered with blood, whereupon Mrs Conyers flung herself over him, dressed only in a chemise, so that they would not kill him. One of the more sensational cases involving directly witnessed intercourse was *Joynt v Jackson*,[63] where several witnesses testified to having seen Mrs Joynt engaging in 'immoral acts' with around eight different men in the town of Ballina.

It was not enough simply to show that the plaintiff had been married and that adultery had taken place between his wife and the defendant. An actual loss to the plaintiff had to be proven, especially if crim con was pleaded as an action on the case.[64] This loss had to be shown to be caused by the

53 *Cloncurry v Piers* (1807).

54 *Hodgens v Mahon* (1835).

55 In Anon (1807) *The Trial of J. Hacket, Esquire, for Adultery with Mrs Mansergh. In the Irish Court of Exchequer on Dec the 10th, 1807* (London: J. Day), the maid had grown suspicious because her mistress was in the habit of locking the doors when Mr Hacket called, so she 'spoiled all the locks, so that they could not secure the doors'. She then burst into the drawing-room where they were 'and caught them both upon the carpet', p 6.

56 *Cloncurry v Piers* (1807).

57 *Fay v Barber* (1797); *Hodgens v Mahon* (1835).

58 *Doyle v Brown* (1820) involved testimony from a ship steward, hoteliers, chaise drivers and waiters.

59 In *Hodgens v Mahon* (1835) the maid was sent out for butter at 9 pm.

60 *Belfast Newsletter*, 1 Aug 1872.

61 *Belfast Newsletter*, 1 Aug 1872. In *Smith v Kearon*, *Irish Times*, 13 Feb 1957, the plaintiff apparently spotted the defendant sneaking out of his wife's bedroom.

62 *Belfast Newsletter*, 20 May 1834.

63 *Joynt v Jackson*, *Irish Times*, 11, 12, 13 and 15 May 1880.

64 As will be discussed below, this hinged on demonstrating the wife's high worth, the husband's happiness during the marriage and his misery upon discovering the adultery.

defendant's acts.[65] So for example, in *Joynt v Jackson*, Mrs Joynt had had adulterous affairs with a number of men, including her brother-in-law, but Jackson, as her first seducer, was considered the initial cause of the plaintiff's loss.

The wife's voice was not heard in late eighteenth- and early nineteenth-century crim con cases. The action lay between her husband and her alleged lover; a wife could neither testify nor have witnesses to testify on her behalf. She might have her reputation destroyed in court[66] without being afforded a right of reply. She was 'not regularly before the court, though more deeply involved in the event than either of the others; who has no advocate ... to plead her cause, or to defend her from obloquy, from infamy, from destruction'.[67] Sir George Bowyer, MP for Dundalk, remarked in 1854 that

> although the wife was upon her trial, and its issue might involve her utter ruin and destruction, she had no part in the proceeding. She was not heard at all ... The most abominable charges might be brought against her by witnesses in the action, and enforced by all the eloquence and ingenuity of counsel; she might thus be held up to the world as a being utterly degraded; yet she was neither allowed to produce a single witness, nor to say a single word, either in vindication of her innocence or in mitigation of the imputed guilt.[68]

His proposed bill[69] sought to allow wives in crim con cases to testify,[70] but was defeated. However, the Evidence Further Amendment Act 1869[71] provided that '[t]he parties to any proceeding instituted in consequence of adultery, and the husbands and wives of such parties, shall be competent to give evidence in such proceeding'. As a consequence, by the late nineteenth century it was increasingly common for wives (and indeed husbands[72]) to take

65 JD Mayne (1872) *A Treatise on the Law of Damages: Comprising their Measure, the Mode in which they are Assessed and Reviewed, the Practice of Granting New Trials, and the Law of Set-Off*, 2nd edn (Lumley Smith (ed), London), p 381.

66 For example, in *Fay v Barber* (1797) the judge spoke of the wife's 'baseness' and described the defendant as 'keep[ing] a whore.'

67 *Cloncurry v Piers* (1807), p 91.

68 *Hansard 3*, lxxxii [420–421] 4 Apr 1854.

69 *A Bill to Amend the Law Regarding Actions for Criminal Conversation 1854*, HC 1854 (61) ii, 121.

70 It also proposed the replacement of damages with a court-imposed fine, thus preventing a husband from benefiting materially from his wife's adultery.

71 32 & 33 Vic c 68, s 3. See Chapter 4.

72 *Whittaker v Berry*, *Irish Times*, 12 Feb 1894.

the stand and testify either that adultery had not taken place,[73] or admit that it had taken place but with the husband's full knowledge.[74]

Rationale for crim con damages

What was the rationale for crim con actions? As well as providing compensation to the husband for the infringement of his rights, McCardie J in the English case of *Butterworth v Butterworth* suggested a more 'cogent moral foundation' for the action:

> The law has ever regarded the sanctity of married life as a matter of grave moment. It may be, therefore, that one of the original objects of the action was to maintain the purity of married life, and to defend the honour of husband, wife and children. The risk of damages might well have been deemed a check to the wanton inclinations of an intending adulterer.[75]

Under this interpretation, crim con not only served to vindicate the husband's rights, but could also to deter potential adulterers[76] and uphold the sanctity of marriage. However, this moral rationale for crim con was not fully developed until the Victorian period; earlier crim con cases were more concerned with compensation and loss of honour.

An examination of some 80 Irish cases as well as general statements of the law in England and Ireland indicates that the purpose of crim con damages changed over time. Much of the early focus was on the exemplary or punitive nature of the damages: for example, Blackstone wrote that adultery with another man's wife was the greatest civil injury recognized by law, and 'the damages recovered [were] usually very large and exemplary'.[77] An Irish judge, Smith B, in *Massy v Headfort*, pointed out in 1804 that 'this sort of action partakes of the nature of penal prosecution, and that large and exemplary

---

73 For example, *Beamish v Longley, Belfast Newsletter,* 25 Mar 1875; *Murdock v Rynn, Belfast Newsletter,* 2, 3, 4, 7 May 1894; *McDonnell v Weddick, Freeman's Journal,* 21 June 1873.

74 For example, *Joynt v Jackson* (1880), *Morrow v Morrow* [1914] 2 IR 183 and *Graham v Pattison, Irish Times,* 23 June 1935. In *Morrow,* Cherry LCJ commented, p 188, that it was 'most unusual to examine the wife as a witness to prove her own guilt' and in *Graham,* Dowse CB observed that the wife was probably 'actuated by a wish to make the husband whom she had wronged the only atonement she could make'. *Irish Times,* 18 Jan 1881.

75 *Butterworth v Butterworth* [1920] P 126, p 132.

76 A similar reading of crim con is also provided by DT Andrew (2013) *Aristocratic Vice: The Attack on Duelling, Suicide, Adultery, and Gambling in Eighteenth-Century England* (Yale: Yale University Press), p 230.

77 W Blackstone (1800) *Commentaries on the Laws of England* vol 3, 13th edn (London: A Strahan), p 139.

damages are usually awarded'.[78] He observed that compensation in such cases was difficult to 'calculate with exact precision', and that therefore:

> Juries should not be parsimonious in the damages which they award; but, on the contrary, should be liberal, to a degree bordering on prodigality and profusion, for the benefit of public example, and the protection of public morals.[79]

In early nineteenth-century Ireland, the parties' rank and fortune were held to be relevant considerations in estimating damages.[80] This would appear to be at odds the English courts' approach around this time. In an English case decided in the same year as *Massy*, Lord Ellenborough advised jurors to be dispassionate and to focus on the loss sustained by the plaintiff: '[t]o the extent to which the plaintiff has suffered real injury, he will expect at your hands reparation.'[81] Three months later, he told another jury that the defendant's financial circumstances were irrelevant.[82] In *Campbell v Hook*, another English case, Lord Kenyon pointed out that he knew nothing of the defendant's financial circumstances, implying that they had neither been adduced in evidence nor referred to by counsel.[83] By the 1850s, the English view of crim con damages had gained traction in Ireland, with the court in *Wilson v Leonard*[84] holding that the jury ought to be guided solely by the injury to the plaintiff, and not the punishment of the defendant. The value of the defendant's property in this case was withheld from the jury, because it was deemed

78 *Massy v Headfort* (1804). By contrast, Lord Kenyon in Anon (1793) *The Proceedings Against Major Hook for Criminal Conversation with his Own Niece Mrs Campbell, Wife of Captain Campbell, before Lord Kenyon and a Special Jury. At Westminster, Feb 26th, 1793* (London: np), p 33, expressly stated: 'this is a civil action, and that it is not a proceeding to punish the party as if he had been guilty of a breach of any criminal law of the country.'

79 *Massy v Headfort* (1804), p 86. Similarly, counsel in *Taaffe v Fitzgerald* called for ample and exemplary damages: *Belfast Newsletter*, 1 Mar 1816. By contrast, however, Lord Norbury in *Guthrie v Sterne* said 'there is nothing I would so strongly recommend to jurors, as moderation in damages'. However, it is difficult to know whether he was being sarcastic here, given the jocular tone of his charge and his general reputation; he also commented, somewhat oddly, that 'had the Defendant been in possession of as many "Christian" virtues as he had "Christian" names, he would not have been guilty of the crime of seduction.' Anon (1815) *Crim Con. Court of Common Pleas, Friday, June 9, 1815. John Guthrie, Esq, Plaintiff; WPBD Sterne, Esq, Defendant* (Dublin: W Espy).

80 *Massy v Headfort* (1804), p 89 and *Blachford v Latouche*, *Freeman's Journal*, 13 Jan 1811. See Chapter 4 for a discussion of the relevance of such factors in determining damages for breach of promise of marriage actions.

81 Anon (1804) *The Proceedings on the Trial of Captain J Caulfield for Criminal Conversation with the Wife of Captain George Chambers, Daughter of the late Lord Rodney. Before Lord Ellenborough, in the Court of King's Bench, on the 3rd Dec 1804* (London: np), p 82.

82 Anon (1805) *The Proceedings against Henry Jadis, Esq. for Criminal Conversation with the Wife of the Hon Allan Hyde Gardner, Captain in his Majesty's Navy, and Son to Lord Gardner, Before Lord Ellenborough, In the Court of King's Bench, Guildhall, on Saturday the 2nd of Mar 1805* (London: np), p 71.

83 *Campbell v Hook* (1793), p 35.

84 (1852) 5 *Irish Jurist* (os) 101.

irrelevant to their calculation of damages, bringing Irish jurisprudence into line with a number of English decisions.[85]

Aside from occasional instances where rogue juries appeared to award punitive damages,[86] the focus on compensation remained well into the twentieth century. In 1974 the Supreme Court confirmed that damages ought to be restricted to what could be considered compensatory in respect of the loss suffered,[87] and in 1979 a jury was warned that 'there should not be any element of punishment of either side'.[88]

The assessment of damages

Staves points out that crim con actions raised interesting questions about

> the meaning of money, the relationship between money and class, the expectations of the rights and responsibilities within marriage; of whether or not wives may be considered the property of their husbands; or more generally, of whether there is any such thing as property in persons.[89]

In assessing damages, juries had to take account of several factors, 'the relative weight attached to each of which changed over time'.[90] As discussed, in the late eighteenth century, the emphasis was on the plaintiff's loss of honour, especially if there was the possibility of illegitimate offspring.[91] From around 1750 the primary concern became the plaintiff's loss of his wife's comfort and society. During this period, the size of the damages depended on how happy the couple had been before the alleged affair.[92] This is reflected in a statement from Buller in 1817:

> As to adultery the action lies for the injury done to the husband in alienating his wife's affection, destroying the comfort he had

85 See *Calcraft v Earl of Harborough* (1831) 4 C & P 499: 172 ER 798; *James v Biddingdon* (1834) 6 C & P 589: 172 ER 1377; *Wilton v Webster* (1835) 7 C & P 198: 173 ER 87.

86 In *Fleming v Purcell, Belfast Newsletter*, 23 Feb 1893, a jury awarded £1,000 damages 'to mark their strong condemnation of the defendant's conduct'. The damages in *Joynt v Jackson* may also have been punitive: Anon (1880) *Authentic Report of the Crim Con Trial of Joynt v Jackson in the Exchequer Court, Dublin, Commencing May 10th, 1880* (Dublin: Edward Smith).

87 *Maher v Collins* [1974] 1 IR 232.

88 *Mulvaney v Collins, Irish Times*, 10 Nov 1979.

89 Staves (1982) 'Money for Honour', p 279.

90 Stone (1993) *Broken Lives*, p 303.

91 As Stone writes, 'the principal fear was pollution of blood in a patrilineal primogenitural society': L Stone (1990) 'Honour, Morals, Religion and the Law: The Action for Criminal Conversation in England 1670–1857' in A Grafton and A Blair, *The Transmission of Culture in Early Modern Europe* (Philadelphia: University of Pennsylvania Press), p 292. See Chapter 12.

92 Stone (1990) 'Honour, Morals, Religion', p 293.

> from her company and raising children for him to support and provide for. And as the injury is great so the damages given are commonly very considerable. But they are properly increased or diminished by the particular circumstances of each case; the rank and quality of the plaintiff, the condition of the defendant, his being a friend, relation, or dependent of the plaintiff or being a man of substance, proof of the plaintiff and his wife having lived comfortably together before her acquaintance with the defendant and her having always borne a good character till then, and proof of a settlement or provision for the children of the marriage, are all proper circumstances of aggravation.[93]

A similar description of how to assess crim con damages was given in the English case of *Butterworth*[94] and later approved and summarized by O'Higgins CJ in *Maher v Collins:*

> In awarding compensatory damages, regard should be had to (a) the actual value of the wife to the husband, and (b) the proper compensation to the husband for the injury to his feelings, the blow to his marital honour and the hurt to his matrimonial and family life.[95]

The various aspects of this will be examined in turn.

The assessment of the actual value of the wife to the husband had both consortium and pecuniary aspects. The latter was straightforward, and involved the plaintiff demonstrating the loss of his wife's services; for example, her neglect of him, their children[96] or her household duties.[97] It was claimed in *Patterson v Pullen,*[98] for example, that after the wife had intercourse with the defendant, 'her sobriety no longer remained, her strict attention, her economy and attention to her husband's interests were sacrificed to an indulgence in infidelity, to a waste of his property, and to disgust of his person!'[99] By the nineteenth century, the main premise of the action was founded upon the

93 F Buller (1817) *An Introduction to the Law, Relative to Trials at Nisi Prius*, 7th edn (London: Bridgman), pp 26a–b.

94 *Butterworth v Butterworth and Englefield* [1920] P 126

95 [1975] 1 IR 232, at 237.

96 See *Hodgens v Mahon* (1835), p 9.

97 In *Binns v Scott* (1816), p 4, Mrs Binns was described as 'a discreet woman whom [Mr Binns] looked upon as a faithful ally in his business, and a governess of his children'. In *O'Reilly v McKay,* the wife was described as 'a good mother and a good housekeeper'.

98 *Freeman's Journal*, 2 Dec 1800.

99 In *Maher v Collins*, O'Higgins CJ was at pains to emphasize that the husband had suffered no loss of his wife's services 'or other tangible hurt' – there had been no break-up of the family home, and she continued to run his businesses – but that 'the wrong done to him was largely concerned with the invasion of the privacy caused to his honour as a husband'. *Irish Times*, 5 Dec 1974.

husband's loss of his wife's society; so he generally had no standing if he had been separated from his wife at the time of the alleged adultery.[100]

The plaintiff also had to establish his wife's high worth in terms of her physical attributes, sweet temperament, helpfulness and so on. Thus the wives in these cases were almost invariably portrayed by their husbands' lawyers as beautiful, charming and engaging. Mrs Brown was 'a person of considerable personal beauty';[101] Mrs Conyers was 'a lady of extraordinary beauty';[102] Mrs Hurst was 'young and good-looking';[103] while Mrs Taaffe was 'the charm of every circle – gay, young, playful, lovely and innocent'.[104] As the solicitor general explained in *Mansergh v Hacket,* '[i]n cases of this nature, the lady is ... represented, in order to engage your sympathy, as a paragon of virtue, an angel of light before your fall'.[105] This fitted with the wider Victorian narrative of married women as passive, virtuous, dedicated 'household angels'.[106] Some wives were also portrayed as passive victims, falling prey to predatory men, who pursued them relentlessly until finally the wife succumbed.[107] As Binhammer observes, '[t]he question of the wife's passive or active sexual nature [became] the pivotal issue' in these trials.[108]

As for the husband's loss of consortium, crim con damages are one of the earliest examples of damages being awarded for emotional pain and suffering.[109] Staves describes the eighteenth-century law as 'reflecting the more general cultural awareness of such psychological intangibles'.[110] The plaintiff sought to maximize his damages by proving that he and his wife had lived in

---

100 J Clancy (1819) *An Essay on the Equitable Rights of Married Women: With Respect to their Separate Property and also on their Claim to a Provision Called the Wife's Equity: To Which is Added the Law of Pin-Money, Separate Maintenance, and of the other Separate Provisions of Married Women*, 2nd edn (Dublin: C Hunter), p 451. Unusually, however, in *Lismore v Bingham, Freeman's Journal*, 21 Apr 1825, this served merely to mitigate damages to one shilling.

101 *Brown v Ibbetson, Freeman's Journal*, 13 Nov 1845.

102 *Conyers v Westropp, Belfast Newsletter*, 20 May 1834.

103 *Hurst v McDonnell, Belfast Newsletter*, 16 June 1891.

104 *Taaffe v Fitzgerald, Belfast Newsletter*, 1 Mar 1816. There are many further examples of positive descriptions of wives by plaintiffs: *Beamish v Longley, Belfast Newsletter*, 23 Mar 1875; *Vanston v Whitecroft, Belfast Newsletter*, 11 June 1897.

105 *Mansergh v Hacket* (1807), p 8.

106 J Rowbotham (1989) *Good Girls Make Good Wives: Guidance for Girls in Victorian Fiction* (London: Blackwell), p 52.

107 In *Cloncurry v Piers* (1807), counsel argued, p 11, that '[a]lmost from the first moment in which Sir John Piers beheld this unfortunate lady, he had formed unwarranted and unjustifiable designs against her'. The plaintiff in *O'Reilly v McKay, Irish Times*, 22 Oct 1954, described his wife as 'weak', and having been 'led astray'.

108 Binhammer (1996) 'The Sex Panic of the 1790s', p 427.

109 Along with damages for breach of promise for marriage: see Chapter 4. It was around this period that damages for 'nervous shock' began to be awarded: Lobban points out that 'in the mid-nineteenth century, plaintiffs increasingly claimed for non-visible injuries'. Lobban (2010) 'Tort', p 992.

110 Staves (1982) 'Money for Honour', p 293.

matrimonial harmony and domestic bliss before the defendant intervened. As Lord Norbury said in *Nugent v Norie*,[111] if the husband could not show that he had lost 'connubial happiness', his claim must fail.[112] Friends and acquaintances would describe the marriage as happy and mutually satisfactory.[113]

Regarding the husband's injured feelings and damaged honour, he was almost invariably presented as heartbroken, outraged and humiliated. Evidence would be adduced as to his despair, and his signalling disapproval of the adultery by refusing to live with his wife thereafter.[114] In determining the extent of this injury to the plaintiff, jurors took account of various aggravating and mitigating factors. Blackstone wrote in 1797 that damages were

> properly increased and diminished by circumstances; as the rank and fortune of the plaintiff and defendant; the relation or connection between them; the seduction or otherwise of the wife, founded on her previous behavior and character; and the husband's obligation by settlement or otherwise to provide for those children, which he cannot but suspect to be spurious.[115]

First, the husband's injury could be exacerbated by the defendant's conduct or situation. Enticing the wife away or harbouring her after the adultery[116] could aggravate damages, as could his close friendship with the plaintiff: in *McCraith v Quinn*,[117] damages of £5,000 were awarded where the defendant was the plaintiff's close friend, first cousin and best man.[118] Other circumstances could further aggravate the injury to the plaintiff and, consequentially, the damages to which he was entitled. In *Massy v Headford*, for example, the plaintiff was a Church of Ireland minister, and his counsel placed much emphasis on the timing of the act of adultery:

> The day was Sunday, the hour the time of Divine Service; yes gentlemen, on that day, and on that hour, set apart for the service of our Creator, whilst the Reverend Rector was bending before the altar of his God ... upon such an occasion did the noble lord think proper to commit this honourable breach of hospitable faith.[119]

111 *Freeman's Journal*, 26 Feb 1818.

112 See Staves (1982) 'Money for Honour', p 282.

113 *Fay v Barber* (1797); *Guthrie v Sterne* (1811).

114 In *Cloncurry v Piers* (1807), p 20, Lord Cloncurry wrote to his father-in-law upon discovering his wife's affair, and her brother removed her from the house and from the country.

115 W Blackstone (1796) *Commentaries on the Laws of England* vol 3, 13th edn (Dublin: White, Bryne and Rice), pp 333–334.

116 McCardie J in *Butterworth v Butterworth* [1920] P 126, p 131.

117 *Belfast Newsletter*, 1 Aug 1872.

118 Similar damages were awarded in *Doyle v Brown* (1820), and *Taaffe v Fitzgerald, Belfast Newsletter*, 1 Mar 1816.

119 *Massy v Headfort* (1804), pp 7–8.

In *Fay v Barber* the judge spoke of the 'wanton lewdness' of the defendant, 'to keep a whore at the husband's expense, and make him pay for that which he does not enjoy'.[120] On the other hand, the defendant's age and marital status were both relevant factors;[121] a mitigating factor might be, for example, 'evidence that the Defendant was a giddy boy, unsettled in his principles, and seduced to gratify the lewdness of a wanton woman'.[122]

Second, the general conduct and character of the wife almost invariably came under scrutiny in crim con actions. Binhammer argues that 'what is on trial in crim con actions is not the individual guilt or innocence of the men involved but the sexuality of the new domestic woman'.[123] In 1854, Bowyer observed that if the wife's 'previous character were bad, the injury to the husband would be less. Thus, it was the interest of the defendant to run down the character of the woman in order to diminish the amount of damages'.[124] There are many examples of defendants portraying their lovers as wanton, lascivious, of defective character and loose morals.[125] In *Cloncurry v Piers*, for example, much was made of the fact that Lady Cloncurry had allegedly committed adultery with Piers the first time they had found themselves alone. The implication was that she was not 'a modest woman, bred up in religious habit, of a retired disposition', and this greatly reduced her value.[126] The Chief Justice described it as 'a conquest of no great difficulty ... The conquest was so easy... That her value could not be highly estimated'.[127] The jury found for the plaintiff, and while the damages awarded were high, at £20,000, this was only one-fifth of the £100,000 sought, suggesting that while they were convinced that the adultery had taken place, they considered Lady Cloncurry to be devalued for the reasons outlined. In *Blachford v Latouche*[128] the wife was in her thirties, had been married some 14 years, and was portrayed as having flung herself upon the relatively young, innocent defendant. Counsel for Latouche asked the jury,

> what loss has the plaintiff sustained in being deprived of the society of a woman who, herself advanced in years, with a perfect knowledge of the world, after a few weeks acquaintance with a

---

120 *Fay v Barber* (1797), pp 24–25.

121 *Massy v Headfort* (1804), p 98.

122 *Fay v Barber* (1797), p 25. Also *Townley v Lyle*, *Irish Times*, 6 Feb 1886.

123 Binhammer (1996) 'The Sex Panic of the 1790s', p 422.

124 *Hansard 3*, cxxxii [421] 4 Apr 1854.

125 According to Buller, the defendant could 'call witnesses to her general character': F Buller (1806) *An Introduction to the Law Relative to Trials at Nisi Prius: Containing Additions to the Present Time* (New York: Riley & Co), p 296.

126 *Cloncurry v Piers* (1807), p 101.

127 *Cloncurry v Piers* (1807), p 144. It was also argued, p 102, that the speed of Lord and Lady Cloncurry's courtship and engagement suggested that her family had been anxious, because of her defective character, to marry her off.

128 *Freeman's Journal*, 13 Jan 1811.

> mere boy, would, in defiance of the honour of her sex, and of her sacred duty as a wife, have been guilty of such a crime?

Again, the jury awarded just one-fifth of the damages sought.

A defendant might also disparage his lover's physical attributes; Mrs Binns, for example, was variously described by the defendant's witnesses as 'middle aged ... lusty' 'not very handsome ... a large corpulent woman'.[129] Even up to the late twentieth century, a defence strategy appeared to be to portray the wife as being of low worth. Counsel for the plaintiff, in cross-examining the defendant in *Mulvaney v Collins*, asked 'are you asking the jury to say she is a worthless slut who is worth nothing to a decent married man?'[130] The defendant did not answer, but later agreed that she was a completely worthless woman.

Third, the husband's conduct was also scrutinized, and he could expect to have his damages reduced[131] if he was abusive.[132] In *Patterson v Pullen*,[133] Lord Kilwarden observed that that although the plaintiff's abuse of Mrs Patterson did not disentitle him to damages, it would 'disqualify him from heavy damages', and he was awarded just sixpence. If the husband were known to have had adulterous affairs of his own, this might also reduce his damages, for two reasons: first, because evidence of his unfaithfulness negated arguments of matrimonial happiness before the wife's seduction, and second, 'because such dissipation and neglect is likely to set a bad example to the woman: it tends to sap her morals, to estrange her affections, and facilitate her seduction'.[134] In *Glerawley v Burn*,[135] defence counsel argued that Glerawley's extended absences from home had left his wife 'exposed to the shoals of seduction', and relatively low damages were awarded. If connivance by the husband could be proven, this defeated the action altogether. In many cases, however, connivance was difficult to prove, and juries merely awarded low damages if they were suspicious. For example, in *Geoghegan Nowlan v Glentworth*,[136] both parties were imprisoned in the Dublin Marshalsea for debt. They became friends and Mrs Nowlan became Viscount Glentworth's mistress, with her

---

129 *Binns v Scott* (1816), pp 10, 16.

130 *Irish Times*, 10 Nov 1979.

131 Kisbey (1871) *Law and Practice*, p 17.

132 In *Fay v Barber* (1797) there was evidence that the husband was abusive towards his wife, and on one occasion he had locked her in a closet for 19 days without a fire or adequate food. He recovered £1,000 damages. The jury may have been of the view that his treatment of his wife on that occasion was somewhat justified, as he had acted out of jealousy and suspicion of the defendant.

133 *Freeman's Journal*, 2 Dec 1800.

134 *Massy v Headfort* (1804), p 91.

135 *Belfast Newsletter*, 4 June 1820. Note that this was an action involving the Irish peer, Viscount Glerawley, which was tried in the English Court of King's Bench.

136 *Freeman's Journal*, 10 Jul 1822.

husband's knowledge. Although connivance was not definitively proven, the jury, no doubt suspicious, awarded only 40 shillings in damages.[137]

The plaintiff's conduct in relation to his wife came under close scrutiny in the case *Hodgens v Mahon.*[138] Miss Walker had been made a ward of Chancery as a child, and was abducted from her boarding school by Hodgens at the age of 13. He was arrested and imprisoned, but after petitioning the Lord Chancellor he was released on recognizances of £20,000 that he would not go near Miss Walker again. However, he could not resist; he kidnapped her a second time, fleeing to the continent where they lived as man and wife for several years, having been married by a 'degraded clergyman'.[139] When she came of age they returned to Ireland and Hodgens presented her to the Lord Chancellor, asking whether or not it would be in her best interests to be officially married to him now that she was free to choose. The inevitable conclusion was that because she had been living with Hodgens as his wife for the past six years, it was unlikely that anyone else would now want her, and her reputation would be ruined if they were not married. This, according to the Chief Baron, was to be considered by the jury as a factor likely to diminish any award of damages: 'If a man comes to seek damages for a lost property it is fair for the jury to say to him "did you come honestly by that property."' Similarly, he should be able to show 'how he became possessed of that wife'.[140] The judge (and, unsurprisingly, counsel for the defendant) was very critical of Hodgens' actions, asking, 'if he did use the privilege of a husband upon the person of that infant, how dare he come into this court seeking for the compensation of your verdict'.[141] The jury awarded the plaintiff a paltry £200 in damages; a small fraction of the £10,000 sought.

Finally, the existence of children often presented itself as an aggravating factor. The adulterous wife had not only betrayed her husband but had also abandoned her children, who would have to live with their mother's infamy. In one case it was said that adultery 'makes the children hated of the parent, and daughters travel through life, reproached with the vileness of their mother'.[142] Losing the wife's care of the children could also contribute to the husband's pecuniary loss, especially if the family were large.[143] Children born after the adultery took place presented some difficulty. The presumption of paternity meant that any child born to a married woman was presumed to

137 In *Taaffe v Fitzgerald*, the defendant admitted his guilt and suggested connivance by the plaintiff. This was not proven, but the jury awarded only a quarter of the damages sought.

138 *Hodgens v Mahon* (1835).

139 *Hodgens v Mahon* (1835), p 3. See Chapter 3.

140 *Hodgens v Mahon* (1835), p 28.

141 *Hodgens v Mahon* (1835), p 29.

142 *Fay v Barber* (1797), pp 24–25.

143 In *Fay v Barber* (1797) there were seven or eight children; in *Beaken v Dockeray* (1882) and *Binns v Scott* (1816) there were six.

be her husband's, and he could find himself obliged to financially support the child regardless of suspicions surrounding his or her actual paternity. For example, in *Cloncurry v Piers*, Lady Cloncurry gave birth to a son, presumed to be fathered by Piers, and the solicitor general pointed out during the trial that this boy stood to inherit some of Lord Cloncurry's estate.[144]

Conclusion

Crim con cases peaked in England around the 1790s in the midst of a moral panic.[145] Ireland may have lagged behind in this regard; while crim con actions were described as 'novel'[146] at the turn of the nineteenth century, two decades later they were being described as frequent,[147] 'flagrant'[148] and 'extensively growing to magnitude and depravity'.[149] This may have been a high point in perceptions of the frequency of such cases. The rest of the century was punctuated by statements about the rarity of crim con actions.[150] The moral purity of the Irish, and Irish women in particular,[151] was a popular theme from the mid-nineteenth century onwards;[152] although, as Inglis points out, '[t]he notion that Ireland was a country of virtuous virgins, chaste mothers, and abstemious fathers was mythical',[153] Nevertheless, it was remarked in 1859, for example, that Ireland 'was celebrated not only for the chastity and purity of its women, but also for the honour of its men. It was seldom indeed that [a crim con] action was brought under the notice

144 *Cloncurry v Piers* (1807), p 45.

145 Stone (1993) *Broken Lives*, p 24, links this with the appointment of Lord Kenyon as Chief Justice of the King's Bench: he was '[i]nspired by his own brand of Puritanism, reinforced by the moral panic among the elite aroused by the French Revolution'. See further D Lemmings and C Walker (eds) *Moral Panic, the Media and the Law in Early Modern England* (Basingstoke and New York: Palgrave Macmillan).

146 *Massy v Headfort* (1804), p 2.

147 *Nugent v Norie, Freeman's Journal*, 25 Feb 1818.

148 Anon (1816) *Crim Con William Binns, Plaintiff, John Scott, Defendant, Before the Hon Justice Mayne* (Dublin: Wm Espy), p 3.

149 *Doyle v Brown* (1820), p 42. These statements about the apparent increase in crim con actions may have been linked to a generalized moral panic associated with the mass exodus of nobility and gentry in the decades following the Act of Union. See G O'Brien (2008) 'Visitors' Perceptions of Dublin 1800–30' in G O'Brien, and F O'Kane (eds) *Georgian Dublin* (Dublin: Four Courts Press), p 23. Ó Gráda notes that 'the years 1801–1845 were in many respects years of economic hardship and gloom': C Ó Gráda (1989) 'Poverty, Population and Agriculture 1801–1845' in WE Vaughan (ed) *A New History of Ireland, Volume V: Ireland Under the Union* (Oxford: Oxford University Press), p 108.

150 *Coffey v Magee, Belfast Newsletter*, 23 Mar 1829; *Kinsella v Wingfield, Irish Times*, 24 Apr 1883.

151 The Irish were 'justly proud wherever we go of the purity of our daughters and, as Irishmen, for the respect entertained for the marriage vow': *McCraith v Quinn, Belfast Newsletter*, 2 Aug 1872.

152 See Chapters 4, 9 10 and 11 in this volume.

153 Inglis (2005) 'Origins and Legacies', p 21.

of the public.'[154] Perceptions of the frequency of crim con actions may have depended on whether a particular case occurred in the context of a wider moral panic, and whether the circumstances of a particular case attracted much attention.[155]

Crim con actions were abolished in England by the Divorce and Matrimonial Causes Act 1857.[156] By this time, there was a growing body of opinion that the 'ancient, but not venerable'[157] action of crim con ought to be abolished. Binhammer observes that by the nineteenth century, '[i]ncreasingly, accepting money for one's wife's adultery became morally repulsive. How could a financial sum ever recompense a man for the loss of domestic felicity?'[158] Some viewed the payment of damages by a woman's lover to her husband as effectively allowing husbands to prostitute their wives. Furthermore, the law of the United Kingdom was seen as being increasingly out of step with the rest of Europe.[159] Cornish observes that 'Parliament was from time to time pressed to make adultery a criminal offence'.[160] Damages were difficult to assess, and there appeared to be a lack of consensus as to whether they were to be merely compensatory or also exemplary. Binhammer also argues that the moral foundation of crim con actions was 'eventually eroded by the ideal of companionate marriage'.[161] Furthermore, there was also increasing recognition of the potential unfairness of such actions to women:

> As time went on, more and more thoughtful men and women began to realize that in a crim con suit a wife could be falsely

---

154 *Cashel v Harding, Nenagh Guardian*, 19 Mar 1859.

155 For example, later cases involving middle-class parties and modest damages may have attracted less notice.

156 20 & 21 Vic c 85, s 59. Instead, s 33 allowed a husband to seek damages from a co-respondent who had committed adultery with his wife. These damages were still assessed by a jury. The Law Reform (Miscellaneous Provisions) Act 1970, s 4, abolished this action.

157 JF MacQueen (1860) *A Practical Treatise on the Law of Marriage, Divorce, and Legitimacy: As Administered in the Divorce Court and in the House of Lords*, 2nd edn (London: Maxwell, Sweet, Stevens & Sons), p 129.

158 Binhammer (1996) 'The Sex Panic of the 1790s', p 429.

159 D Urquhart (2012) 'Ireland's Criminal Conversations' *Études Irlandaises,* 37(2), 65–80, p 72, observes that there was no equivalent to crim con in France or Germany. In Scotland, once adultery had been proven against either a husband or a wife, he or she was considered legally dead in relation to the innocent spouse, who was entitled to all property which he or she would have inherited had the spouse actually died. See Leneman (1996) p 468.

160 W Cornish (2010) 'Law of Persons: Family and Other Relationships' in J Baker (ed), *The Oxford History of the Laws of England* (13 vols), (Oxford: Oxford University Press), vol 13, p 732. Binhammer (1996), pp 430–434, for example, discusses Lord Auckland's anti-adultery bill, debated in 1800. In France, the 1810 *Code Napoléon* 'reinvented' the crime of adultery: T MacBride (1992) 'Public Authority and Private Lives: Divorce After the French Revolution', *French Historical Studies* 17(3), 747–768, p 762. Under art 298, a wife who was guilty of divorce could find herself sentenced to up to two years' imprisonment by the same court which granted her divorce.

161 Binhammer (1996) 'The Sex Panic of the 1790s', p 429.

> charged by a husband anxious only to be rid of her, or falsely blamed for enticement, or falsely accused of previous promiscuity by a lover anxious to mitigate the damages against him.[162]

Despite these various problems with crim con, its abolition in England was not followed in Ireland for over a century.[163] It not only existed but evolved over the century, and there was evidently something of a democratization of crim con actions in Ireland. No longer the exclusive preserve of the wealthy elite, lower-middle-class and working-class men increasingly viewed the action as being open to them. The cases reported in newspapers around the turn of the twentieth century lacked much of the glamour associated with cases from a century earlier, and damages awarded were more modest. By the twentieth century crim con had less to do with financially compensating the husband for the loss of his wife,[164] and more to do with public enforcement of private morals.

162 Stone (1990) 'Honour, Morals, Religion', p 300.

163 The action was abolished by section 1 of the Family Law Act 1981. The Law Reform Commission had proposed the abolition of criminal conversation in its *First Report on Family Law*, 1980 (LRC 1-1980). The twentieth-century history of crim con and its ultimate decline has been dealt with thoroughly by Diane Urquhart, who charts the role of feminist groupings in campaigning for crim con's abolition in Urquhart (2012) 'Ireland's Criminal Conversations'.

164 Notwithstanding the comments of Butler J in *Braun v Roche* to the effect that a wife was 'something that the husband owned', and that he ought to be compensated for her loss 'just as you would compensate him for a thoroughbred mare or cow'. *Irish Times*, 22 June 1972.

7

'Divorce Irish style': Marriage Dissolution in Ireland, 1850–1950[1]

Diane Urquhart

Introduction

In 1830 legal commentator and historian, Francis Plowden, claimed that 'the law of marriage bears very hard', and arguably Irish matrimonial provision was harder than most.[2] Although few in Ireland divorced, legally separated or challenged the validity of a marriage with a nullity suit, the longevity of many Irish marriages can be explained not by exalted fidelity, but by the lack of affordable and permanent legal solutions to end unhappy unions.

Until 1922 parliamentary divorce was the sole legal process for ending an Irish marriage to allow remarriage while a spouse was living.[3] This was a costly, complex, gendered and socially restrictive action. In consequence of Ireland's exclusion from the Divorce and Matrimonial Causes Act of 1857,[4] this parliamentary process was also at odds with the court-based divorce system of England, which included Wales in its jurisdiction.[5] This aligned England more closely to the Scottish provision where cheaper and less gender-biased

---

1 The title is adopted from Joseph Cole's article on 'Deserted Wives', *Evening Press*, 4 Apr 1967.

2 F Plowden (1830) *Crim. Con. Biography*, 8 vols, vol 1 (London: Gale reprint (2012)), p iv.

3 On the history of Irish divorce see, for example, D Fitzpatrick (1987) 'Divorce and Separation in Modern Irish History', *Past and Present*, 114(1), 172–196 and J Bergin (2009) 'Irish Private Divorce Bills and Acts of the Eighteenth Century' in J Kelly, J McCafferty and CI McGrath (eds) *People, Politics and Power* (Dublin: University College Dublin Press), 94–121 and D Urquhart (2013) 'Ireland and the Divorce and Matrimonial Causes Act of 1857', *Journal of Family History*, 38(3), 301–320.

4 20 & 21 Vic c 85.

5 See L Stone (1990) *Road to Divorce: England, 1530–1987* (Oxford: Oxford University Press); S Cretney (2005) *Family Law in the Twentieth Century. A History* (Oxford: Oxford University Press); A Horstman (1985) *Victorian Divorce* (London: Croom Helm) and GL Savage (1983) 'The Operation of the 1857 Divorce Act, 1860–1910: A Research Note', *Journal of Social History* 16(4), 103–110.

court divorce prevailed from the time of the Reformation.[6] By the end of the 1860s, Ireland's use of parliamentary divorce was unique as many areas of the empire, like Canada and India, adopted court-based divorce. Other remedies to marital unhappiness such as separation and church and civil nullity were never overly popular. Thus, desertion, which was sometimes consensual and constituted an informal separation, often provided the only escape.[7]

Divorce

Parliamentary divorce was a late seventeenth-century construction. Its origins lie in the demand to allow remarriage during the lifetime of a former spouse and, as Lord Westbury described in the mid-nineteenth century case of *Shaw v Gould*, 'This proceeding was in spirit a judicial, though in form a legislative act ... This house [of Lords] acted as a Court of Justice.'[8] A private divorce bill would therefore be presented to Westminster, evidence would be submitted and petitioner, respondent and witnesses could be cross-examined.[9] From 1780 to the late nineteenth century, a divorce bill also had to be preceded by a criminal conversation suit where a husband sued for damages from a wife's paramour as well as a legal separation which was attained in the Irish ecclesiastical courts until 1870 and subsequently in the High Court.[10] The sexual double standard, and particularly concerns for illegitimate children being held as legitimate issue, shaped the grounds for divorce which varied between the sexes. Men were required to prove a wife's adultery to divorce, but wives needed to prove aggravated adultery: incestuous adultery

6 See L Leneman (1998) *Alienated Affections: Scottish Experience of Divorce and Separation, 1684–1830* (Edinburgh: Edinburgh University Press).

7 For a fuller discussion, see Deirdre McGowan's examination of desertion in Chapter 8 of this volume.

8 Cited in J Roberts (1906) *Divorce Bills in the Imperial Parliament* (Dublin: J Falconer), p 7.

9 Before the Act of Union of 1800 the Irish parliament passed 11 divorce acts. Irish bills were also presented to Westminster. On divorce in the Irish parliament see Bergin (2009) 'Irish Private Divorce Bills'.

10 Stone (1990) *Road to Divorce*, p 325. Amounts awarded in Irish criminal conversations cases ranged from a farthing to £20,000, the sum depending on the alleged purity of the woman and what her infidelity denied her spouse. For examples of higher awards see, for example, the 1759 case of Lord Belvedere against his brother, Arthur Rochfort for adultery with Mary Molesworth, the eldest daughter of the 3rd Viscount of Swords (Anon (1857) *Crim. Con. Actions and Trials and Other Legal Proceedings Relating to Marriage before the Passing of the Present Divorce Act* (London: np), pp 80–83 and S Staves (1982) 'Money for Honour: Damages for Criminal Conversation', *Studies in Eighteenth-Century Culture*, 11, 279–297, p 284). Lord Cloncurry was also awarded £20,000 damages against Sir JB Piers in 1808 (Roberts (1906) *Divorce Bills in the Imperial Parliament*, p 49). By comparison, one farthing was awarded in the Lynch trial of 1890 (*Irish Times*, 2 July 1890) and in Reverend Vanston's trial of 1897 (Roberts (1906) *Divorce Bills in the Imperial Parliament*, pp 92–93). If a criminal conversation case had not been held, an explanation would need to be proffered to Parliament, although the demand lessened from the mid-1880s as a result of the Westropp precedent which is discussed later in this chapter. An unsuccessful separation would not prevent a divorce bill being passed. Howlin discusses the criminal conversation suit at more length in Chapter 6.

or adultery coupled with bigamy or serious cruelty. Rape and unnatural offences such as sodomy and bestiality provided 'sufficient evidence of a man's depravity' to constitute grounds for divorce.[11]

The cost of parliamentary divorce is contested, but it was considerable. Not all would now concur with barrister and author John Fraser Macqueen's 1842 comment that it was a 'truly aristocratic indulgence' which excluded the 'poor, nay even the moderately opulent' to the extent that 'justice is denied to the bulk of the Queen's subjects'.[12] However, although an estimated half of parliamentary divorces cost less than the £500 suggested by the Royal Commission on Divorce in the 1850s, it was still beyond the means of the majority.[13] The cost was due to counsel and house fees and transporting witnesses to Westminster. Clerics, hotel owners, friends and family members could face, at times, bruising cross-examination in the House of Lords. However, testimony was most frequently garnered from servants, some of whom were placed in the position of giving evidence against an employer. Paid testimony, some of it fictitious, was also presented. For instance, in one of a litany of matrimonial suits brought by the Marquess and Marchioness of Westmeath in the nineteenth century, witnesses were paid and three were subsequently sentenced to 18 months for perjury by the Commission Court in Dublin.[14]

The gendered grounds for divorce and the cost of a private bill, as well as widespread press coverage and the publication of divorce trial transcripts, resulted in only four women, none of them Irish, divorcing in Westminster by the time of the passage of the 1857 Divorce and Matrimonial Causes Act in comparison to 321 men.[15] The cost of dissolving a marital union by a private parliamentary act also remained prohibitive; estimated at a conservative

11 The rape of a wife was not illegal in the UK and Ireland until the late twentieth century. The rape of a separated wife was, however, illegal. See Cretney (2005) *Family Law*, p 169. Earner-Byrne discusses the criminalization of marital rape in Chapter 9 in this collection.

12 JF Macqueen (1842) *A Practical Treatise on the Appellate Jurisdiction of the House of Lords and Privy Council Together with the Practice on Parliamentary Divorce* (London: A Maxwell and Sons), p 209.

13 See S Anderson (1984) 'Legislative Divorce; Law for the Aristocracy' in GR Rubin and D Sugarman (eds) *Law, Economy and Society, 1750–1914* (Abingdon: Professional Books), 412–444.

14 The case was heard in 1822. For a fuller discussion of the *Westmeath* case see D Urquhart (2014) 'A Woman's Reply: Irish Female Divorce Law Reformers' in B Walsh (ed) (2014) *Knowing their Place? The Intellectual and Professional Life of Women in 19th-Century Ireland* (Dublin: History Press) and L Stone (1993) *Broken Lives: Separation and Divorce in England, 1660–1857* (Oxford: Oxford University Press).

15 See, for example, Anon (1857) *Divorce in 1857: The Talbot Case. Letters by 'Cujus,' Containing Full Particulars of the Case, with Observations on the Present Unsatisfactory State of the Law* (London: Ward and Lock). The pre-1857 female divorces were granted to Mrs Addison (1810) and Mrs Turton (1830) who divorced on the grounds of incestuous adultery; Mrs Battersby (1840) on the grounds of adultery and cruelty and Mrs Hall (1850) on the grounds of adultery and bigamy, although technically this was an annulment as the parties never cohabited.

minimum of £450 in the 1910s.[16] This placed Irish petitioners at a serious disadvantage in the post-1857 period; the cost of divorce in the new London-based Court for Divorce and Matrimonial Causes was considerably lower than in Parliament, approximated at £40–£45 for an undefended suit if the parties were resident in London, with higher costs incurred if the couple and witnesses had to travel to London or if the suit was defended. Divorce certainly became more accessible in court: it granted an annual average of 202 divorces from the late 1850s to early 1860s and over 800 divorces a year were granted by 1914. A change in the profile of those seeking a divorce in court was also apparent: a growing number of women and members of the middle classes filed for divorce.[17]

There were further variances between Irish and English divorce. In contrast to England, the Irish ecclesiastical courts never granted separation on the ground of desertion, but post-1857, desertion of at least two years' duration was a ground for divorce in court. At the time of the passage of the 1857 Act it was not clear if Parliament would hear cases brought on this ground or apply case law derived from the divorce court. A landmark Irish divorce act, however, clarified this position: Louisa Westropp became the first Irishwoman to divorce in the modern period in 1886 and her Act established the precedent of Parliament embracing any grounds for divorce which were accepted by the divorce court.[18] This was effectively summarized by Lord Chancellor Herschell: 'whatever would justify a divorce and afford a legal ground for it' in court 'will afford sufficient grounds for an application to the Legislature to grant a divorce in that part of the United Kingdom where the Act [of 1857] does not itself operate.'[19] This was significant; desertion and the changing definition of spousal cruelty emerging in court were subsequently applied in parliamentary divorces. In addition, as the 1857 Divorce and Matrimonial Causes Act abolished the need for a criminal conversation action in court-based divorce, the application of the Westropp precedent also began to lessen, although not wholly remove, the prerequisite for this suit in parliamentary divorce. The number of Irish petitioners, especially women, who followed Westropp to Westminster was also striking; five Irishwomen divorced in Parliament from 1886 to 1900 and a further 24 Irishwomen presented divorce bills from 1900 to 1922. This

16 *Royal Commission on Divorce and Matrimonial Causes: Report of the Royal Commission on Divorce and Matrimonial Causes* HC 1912–1913 [C-6478] xviii, 143, p 18.

17 The Royal Commission on Divorce (1912–1913), p 18, estimated that a defended court divorce could cost from £70 to £500. Procedural amendments in 1914, 1920 and 1926 made court-based divorce more affordable with the provision of financial assistance and the ability to hear cases outside of London. See Savage (1983) 'The Operation of the 1857 Divorce Act', 103–110.

18 Louisa Westropp's Divorce Act 1886 (49 & 50 Vic) [Unprinted c 1P].

19 Cited in Roberts (1906) *Divorce Bills in the Imperial Parliament*, p 11.

constituted 45 per cent of all Irish divorce bills presented from 1900 to 1922 and 54 per cent from 1914 to 1922.[20]

The Donovan parliamentary divorce of 1905 was illustrative of the increasing number of bills brought by Irishwomen and the application of the widening definition of marital cruelty beyond serious physical abuse which endangered life and limb.[21] Alice Donovan (nee Rodgers) from Cork sought a divorce on grounds of the 'alleged misconduct and cruelty' of her spouse. She married Daniel Donovan, then a police commissioner in the Gold Coast and later chief of police at Cape Coast castle, in the Roman Catholic Church of the African Mission in Cork in 1895. Her spouse worked in Africa from mid-1895 to 1897 and again from 1898 to 1899, but following his return to Cork 'he began to use violent language, and frequently was guilty of various acts of cruelty' as well as adultery with a nurse in his employ. Alice Donovan withdrew from cohabitation in May 1899 and in the next month successfully separated. There was then a six-year interlude before she sought a parliamentary divorce. Such a delay was not uncommon and was often due to a lack of funds. When Alice Donovan's bill was considered, she was examined in House of Lords with Cork medic Dr Patrick O'Sullivan acting as a witness to her abuse and her father identifying the handwriting and a photograph of his son-in-law who remained in the Cape. Daniel Donovan, however, admitted adultery to his solicitor and showed some remorse: 'Yes, I admit that I did this, but I now ask for forgiveness having done so.'[22]

Although the intent of the Westropp ruling was 'to put persons domiciled in Ireland as near as may be in the same position as those domiciled in England', that was unattainable.[23] The financial implications of parliamentary divorce, for example, not only delayed petitioners like Alice Donovan but could be a deterrent. As Sarah Nesbitt's 1908 correspondence with Joshua Peel and Son Solicitors in Armagh highlighted, 'My sister and I did not understand in taking divorce proceedings she would not get any support. If that is so, she would not wish to follow him in that way as she would think he should support her.'[24] Some Irish petitioners in the post-1857 period also sought to circumvent a parliamentary divorce by presenting cases to court

20 Records of the House of Commons, Minutes of Proceedings on Irish Divorce Bills [1907–1922] (Parliamentary Archives, HC/CL/CO/BF/1-4).

21 See D Urquhart (2013) 'Irish Divorce and Domestic Violence, 1857–1922', *Women's History Review*, 22(5), 820–837.

22 There were two children of this marriage. *Irish Times*, 29 Mar and 31 May 1905; Roberts (1906) *Divorce Bills in the Imperial Parliament*, p 103 and Donovan's Divorce Act 1905 (1905 (5 Edw 7) [Unprinted c 5P]).

23 Roberts (1906) *Divorce Bills in the Imperial Parliament*.

24 Her spouse reportedly sold property to a value of £1,000 and cattle, 9 Oct 1908 (Public Record Office of Northern Ireland [hereafter PRONI], D889/2/358).

although not all could prove English domicile and cases which were heard often faced subsequent legal challenges.[25]

Yet not all petitioners who might be classified as Irish used the court surreptitiously. London residency, for example, allowed Lord and Lady Connemara to divorce in court in 1890 after 27 years of marriage. With the 'usual ... scrabbling for seats in the gallery', the adulterous relationship with a servant of the former governor of Madras and son of Lord Mayo, Lord Connemara, and his cruelty in dispensing medicine which made his wife ill were detailed. He claimed his wife was adulterous, but proffered no evidence. Leaving her spouse in Madras in 1886 but later returning might have been interpreted as condonation on Lady Connemara's part and barred the suit, but a divorce was granted with costs.[26]

An estimated 92 Irish divorces were granted by Westminster from 1857 to 1922, and the number of petitioners was especially marked in the early twentieth century: the highest annual number of bills presented peaked at seven in 1920.[27] Parliamentary divorce remained inaccessible to the majority, but as Westminster discussed equalizing the grounds for divorce in England, Irish divorce provision worsened.[28] Divorce proved quickly controversial in the newly independent Irish Free State. Although not mentioned in the State's first Constitution of 1922, divorce was the subject of governmental and Catholic hierarchical deliberations and charged parliamentary exchanges, which have been depicted as akin to a 'sectarian bear pit', followed.[29] By mid-1924 three divorce bills were waiting to be processed by the Irish parliament, but there was no mechanism to facilitate this. There was stalemate until February 1925 when President of the Executive Council, W. T. Cosgrave, brought a Dáil motion to prevent the introduction of divorce bills.[30] Although successfully challenged in the Irish Senate on the ground that it was unconstitutional, as the right to petition parliament by private bill existed under common law, a revised motion to allow the Irish parliament to process divorce bills was similarly defeated in June 1925.[31] This did not ban divorce in the Irish Free State, but there was no parliamentary process to allow divorce bills to be heard. This

25 See, for example, the cases of domiciled Irishmen Colonel Sinclair and Colonel Malone who divorced in court in 1897 and 1905 respectively. The validity of their divorces was subsequently challenged and problems arose over marriage settlements (see Roberts (1906) *Divorce Bills in the Imperial Parliament*).

26 *Irish Times*, 28 Nov 1890.

27 Figures compiled from Roberts (1906) *Divorce Bills in the Imperial Parliament* and Records of the House of Commons, Minutes of Proceedings on Irish Divorce Bills (1907–22) (4 vols) (Parliamentary Archives HC/CL/CO/BF/1-4).

28 The grounds for divorce in England were equalized between the sexes in 1923.

29 D Ferriter (2004) *The Transformation of Ireland, 1900–2000* (London: Profile Books), p 339.

30 See Cosgrave in the Dáil Éireann debates, vol 10, 11 Feb 1925, cols 156–158. The President of the Executive Council was later known as Taoiseach.

31 See Dáil Éireann debates, vol 10, 25 June 1925.

was confirmed by the 1937 constitutional ban on divorce which remained *in situ* to 1996: article 41 of the 1937 Constitution stated, 'no law shall be enacted providing for the grant of a dissolution of a marriage'.[32] By comparison, the Northern Ireland Parliament embraced the Westminster model of divorce before transferring to a court-based process in 1939. As a regional assembly, divorce was faster and cheaper than in Westminster and female and middle-class petitioners were amongst the 63 divorces passed, but many of the difficulties and the publicity surrounding this procedure remained.[33]

Separation

Separation, formally known as a divorce *a mensa et thoro*, allowed a couple to live apart but not to remarry during a spouse's lifetime. It has thus been described as an 'unnatural and unsatisfactory remedy' to marital unhappiness.[34] The action was, however, the only form of marital dissolution acceptable to the Catholic Church as although nullity was permitted it denied that a valid marriage had occurred. As Father Patrick Dinneen highlighted: '[f]orced by the necessity of a given case, human law can indeed declare a separation, but on such terms only as will preclude a fresh alliance so long as death does not intervene.'[35]

The partial remedy which separation offered helps to explain why, although the number of Irish applications for separation presented in the period from 1840 increased, this was a modest augmentation. From 1840 to 1843, for example, there were 57 applications; from 1901 to 1909 203 applications and from 1970 to 1979 357 applications.[36] The transfer of separation hearings from the Irish ecclesiastical courts to the Irish High Court in 1871 in the wake of the disestablishment of the Church of Ireland also only had a minimal impact on the number of separations.[37] Indeed, the move to the High Court did not alter the grounds for Irish separation; its principles and rules were 'as nearly as may be conformable to ... the ecclesiastical courts of

32 *Bunreacht na hÉireann* – Constitution of Ireland, 1937. This is further explored by Thomas Mohr in Chapter 13.

33 The *Westropp* precedent also impacted to lessen demands for a criminal conversation action and allowed some women to bring divorce bills forward solely on the basis of adultery to the Northern Ireland Parliament.

34 *Report of Royal Commission on Divorce* (1912–1913), p vii and p 11.

35 Dinneen's text was written in c 1915 but was not unpublished. See PS Dinneen (2013) *The Queen of the Hearth* (Dublin: University College Dublin Press), p 74.

36 Fitzpatrick (1987) 'Divorce and Separation', p 174.

37 Up to 1870, separation cases were heard in the consistory courts which were the least powerful of the ecclesiastical courts. There were 27 consistory courts in Ireland organized on a diocesan basis and sitting approximately once per month. H Jefferies (1997) *Priests and Prelates of Armagh in the Age of the Reformations, 1518–58* (Dublin: Four Courts Press), p 108.

Ireland'.[38] In both Ireland and England divorce *a mensa et thoro* was available on the grounds of adultery, cruelty or unnatural practices. These were fault-based grounds; consensual separation was not permitted, although with willing parties, careful negotiation and selective testimony this could occur. However, in contrast to England, desertion in Ireland was remedied by a suit for the restitution of conjugal rights rather than by separation and the move to the High Court did not rectify this position.[39]

The number of marriages affected by legal separation was, however, even lower than the above figures suggest as they include unsuccessful applications, which were manifold. For example, in 1898 of 20 Irish separation petitions, nine were granted; in 1904 of 20 petitions, four were granted; in 1908 of 29 petitions, six were granted. Indeed, in total the Irish High Court only granted 18 per cent of separation petitions submitted between 1901 and 1909.[40] By comparison, the English separation success rate was higher, averaging 33 per cent in the mid-nineteenth century.[41] The Irish figures are also perplexing as, despite the difficulties of the parliamentary divorce procedure and, more pressingly, the non-availability of divorce in independent Ireland from 1922, the number of annual separations granted in the Republic of Ireland remained in single figures as late as the 1960s and 1970s.[42] This contrasts to the English pattern of separations which declined as divorce became

38 W Harris Faloon (1881) *The Marriage Law of Ireland* (Dublin: Hodges and Figgis), p 181.

39 Restitution of conjugal rights forced a spouse to return to the marital home. If a ruling for restitution of conjugal rights was ignored, up to 1813 this could lead to excommunication although it seems that this was rarely enforced. After 1813, such a refusal could lead to imprisonment. After 1857, however, desertion was a ground for divorce in the divorce court and, following the 1886 *Westropp* ruling, in parliamentary divorce. Draft despatch from the Governor General to the Secretary of State for Dominion Affairs, 29 Nov 1926 in response to Belgian ambassador asking for clarification on the Irish Free State's position on divorce and separation (NAI, S4680).

40 Figures from *Return of Judicial statistics, Ireland, 1898. Part II. – Civil Statistics. Statistics Relating to Civil Proceedings in Supreme Courts of Appeal; the Divisions of the High Court of Justice; the Court of the Irish Land Commission; and in Larger and Smaller District Courts – Law Stamps and Taxes – Consolidated Taxing Offices – Registration of Judgments, Titles, Deeds, &c., for the Year 1898*, HC 1899 [C-9494] cviii, Pt ii, 445, p 108; *Return of Judicial Statistics, Ireland, 1904. Part II. – Civil Statistics. Statistics Relating to Civil Proceedings in Supreme Courts of Appeal; the Divisions of the High Court of Justice; the Court of the Irish Land Commission; and in Larger and Smaller District Courts – Law Stamps and Taxes – Consolidated Taxing Offices – Registration of Judgments, Titles, Deeds, &c., for the Year 1904*, HC 1905 [C-2632] xcix, Pt ii, 176, p 99 and *Return of Judicial Statistics, Ireland, 1908. Part II. – Civil Statistics. Statistics Relating to Civil Proceedings in Supreme Courts of Appeal; the Divisions of the High Court of Justice; the Court of the Irish Land Commission; and in Larger and Smaller District Courts – Law Stamps and Taxes – Consolidated Taxing Offices – Registration of Judgments, Titles, Deeds, &c., for the Year 1908*, HC 1909 [C-4793] civ, 176, p 104. 36 of the 203 cases were granted in the period from 1901 to 1909. See also W Duncan (1972) 'Desertion and Cruelty in Irish Matrimonial Law', *Irish Jurist*, VII, 216.

41 English figures refer to the decade of 1858 to 1868. See AJ Hammerton (1992) *Cruelty and Companionship. Conflict in Nineteenth-Century Married Life* (London and New York: Routledge), p 105.

42 K O'Higgins (May 1974) *Marital Desertion in Dublin. An Exploratory Study* (Dublin: Economic and Social Research Institute, Broadsheet, 9), p 123.

more accessible in the post-1857 period. In 1900, for example, the London court received 89 separation petitions and granted 19 separations; by 1939 it heard fewer than 30 separations per annum.[43] A similar shift occurred in Northern Ireland after it moved to a court-based divorce process in 1939; the number of judicial separations fell significantly – only two petitions for separation were presented from 1953 to 1955.[44]

Although instances of separation remained low, there was an early preponderance of Irish separation applications from women. This became a perennial feature of Irish separation. In 1908 of 29 petitions, for example, six were presented by men and 23, representing 79 per cent, by women; in 1914 of 30 petitions, three were presented by men and 27, representing 90 per cent, by women; in 1916 28 petitions were filed, five by men and 23, representing 82 per cent, by women.[45] This female complexion mirrors that of England where women presented an estimated 90 per cent of all separation suits.[46] The proportion of Irish women bringing separation cases may be surprising, but men could more easily leave the marital home, inducing an informal separation and leaving a wife to care for dependents. However, with widespread and sustained poverty in nineteenth- and much of twentieth-century Ireland, the cost of separation was a common constraint and the award of costs was a crucial consideration in petitioning for a separation. The cost could also vary widely. £1,226 was, for example, incurred as a result of Captain E. S. MacGeough Bond's successful separation proceedings against his wife in 1886. She attempted a defence by denying the adultery, charging her spouse with impotency, drunkenness, connivance, cruelty and conduct conducive to her adultery. Her evidence for such a litany of problems was characteristic of many separation suits; it 'depended almost entirely' on servants' testimony, highlighting the middle-class social background of many petitioners.[47]

By comparison, much lower costs were incurred by Jane Hanna of Armagh when she sought to separate from her spouse on the grounds of his cruelty and adultery in 1873. In 1855, aged 40, she married George Hanna. The

43 Cretney (2005) *Family Law*, pp 153 and 281.

44 *Ulster Year Book* (1956) (Belfast: HMSO), p 254.

45 Figures from *Return of Judicial Statistics of Ireland* (1908), p 104; *Return of Judicial Statistics, Ireland, 1914. Part II. – Civil Statistics. Statistics Relating to Civil Proceedings in Supreme Courts of Appeal; the Divisions of the High Court of Justice; in Larger and Smaller District Courts – Law Stamps and Taxes –Consolidated Taxing Offices – Registration of Judgments, Titles, Deeds, &c., for the Year 1914*, HC 1914–1916 [C-8077] lxxxii, pt ii, 170, p 82 and *Return of Judicial Statistics, Ireland, 1916. Part II. – Civil Statistics. Statistics Relating to Civil Proceedings in Supreme Courts of Appeal; the Divisions of the High Court of Justice; in Larger and Smaller District Courts – Law Stamps and Taxes – Consolidated Taxing Offices – Registration of Judgments, Titles, Deeds, &c., for the Year 1916*, HC 1918 [C-9066] xxv, pt ii, 65, p 25.

46 Hammerton (1992) *Cruelty and Companionship*, p 105.

47 The costs were later contested. See MacGeough Bond papers (PRONI, D288/B/14).

abuse she suffered began six or seven years later and consisted of 'striking' and beating. This escalated in 1870 when she was forcibly pulled out of bed:

> knocked ... down on a crock of delph and china and hurt ... very severely ... very frequently ... struck on the face and blacked her eyes, with a whip ... beating her ... threw her violently down on a tiled floor ... would strip her of her bed clothes and let her lie naked ... threw stones at her ... habitually used coars [sic] and violent and threatening language ... and never ... treated as a wife should be treated he having kept almost every article of food and locked up.[48]

The changing strictures regarding a husband's acceptable treatment of a wife emerge strongly in Jane Hanna's testimony. The influential *Kelly v Kelly* case in Liverpool of the preceding year, for instance, determined that a woman should not be deprived of running her own home.[49] Thus, George Hanna's ordering of his wife from the marital home 'as she had no authority there' was regarded as a matrimonial offence. Jane Hanna also claimed to be 'in terror of her life' and prolonged anxiety and fear which damaged health was increasingly accepted as constituting cruel conduct. Her spouse countered that she was mentally unstable, 'violent and excited in her manner and behaviour', treating him with 'insolence and neglect and ... violently assaulted him and spat in his face and threatened him with personal injury'. He also claimed she both condoned and provoked the acts of cruelty while simultaneously denying that many of them had occurred. The case was, however, withdrawn and a private deed of separation was executed whereby they continued to live apart; she received £30 maintenance per annum and £25 costs.[50]

As the Westropp parliamentary divorce and the MacGeough Bond and Hanna separation cases illustrate, the changing definition of marital cruelty provided more women with grounds to end a marriage. In 1902, for example, Mary Orr from Belfast's Shankill Road petitioned the matrimonial division of the Irish High Court. Married aged 19 in 1888, she bore four sons and resided with her husband until 1902. She was, however, subjected to ill-treatment from 1890, including being struck:

> a violent blow in the face with a clenched fist, causing her nose to bleed and her face to swell ... he beat [her] across the left cheek discolouring her face, and used offensive names to her, kicked [her] on the side, and threw her against the wall ... and she

48 Divorce case papers of Jane and George Hanna, Terryhoogan, Co. Armagh, 1873 (Hanna Divorce papers) (PRONI, D1252/2/4).

49 J Mews, CM Chapman, HHW Sparham and AW Todd (1884), *A Digest of the Reported Decisions of the Courts of Common Law, Bankruptcy, Probate, Admiralty, and Divorce, Together with a Selection from those of the Court of Chancery and Irish Courts. From 1756 to 1883 Inclusive. Founded on Fisher's Digest*, vol IV (London: H. Sweet, Stevens and Sons and W Maxwell and Son), p 138.

50 Hanna Divorce papers (PRONI, D1252/2/4).

> suffered pain from the cruelty for some weeks ... emptied a dish of water over [her] ... knocked her down on her back and dragged her by the heels across a rough yard.

She was 'severely wounded' and required medical treatment. Her spouse was bound over to keep the peace towards her for a year in 1899, but after a month 'again became offensive by squirting tobacco spits into her face and eyes'. Within a year he threatened to shoot her and 'violently struck her on the body, and in the face, blackening her eyes ... and has beaten and abused her.' He also failed to support her financially, failing to give her money for clothes or provide clothes for her for five years: 'she has been compelled for long periods to go out and work for her support and that of her children, also to work on his farm, in addition to doing all the work of his house without the assistance of a single servant.' In 1902, after another violent attack, she left the house and went to her mother's, believing 'it would be dangerous to her health and life to live any longer under the same roof ... She has tried to endure his torture and violence for many years, and her health has already suffered by his cruelty'. But her options were limited. If the cruelty could be proven, as the notes on her High Court petition suggest, a separation would be granted on the grounds of cruelty alone, but without adultery a parliamentary divorce would not be possible.[51] Although the grounds for cruelty moved beyond a strict requirement that life and limb must be endangered and now considered, for example, verbal abuse, the threat of violence and its deleterious effect on a woman's health, concerns remained that Orr's grounds could be insufficient.[52]

The need for witnesses or medical evidence to prove cruelty, adultery or unnatural practices, conjoined with the notion of female forbearance in marriage which was held not only by women but also by wider society of which the judiciary, of course, formed a part, cumulatively produced a consistently low Irishwomen's separation success rate. Of six successful separation suits presented in 1908, for example, two were granted to husbands in consequence of their wives' adultery; one was granted due to the cruelty and adultery of the husband with an additional three awarded to wives as a result of the cruelty of their spouses, representing a female success rate of 17 per cent. In 1914 three separations, representing a 100 per cent success rate, were granted to husbands on the grounds of wifely adultery and five to wives, three due to their husband's adultery and two for adultery and cruelty, representing a female success rate of 18 per cent.[53] The English female separation

51 Cruelty needed to be combined with adultery to be considered grounds for female divorce until the law of divorce was equalized between the sexes in the UK in 1923. In consequence of the *Westropp* ruling, this subsequently allowed some female petitioners to divorce on the sole ground of cruelty in the Parliament of Northern Ireland.

52 Copy of petition of Mary Elizabeth Orr, Belfast, 12 Apr 1902 (PRONI, D1824/C/3/3/22).

53 Figures from the *Return of Judicial Statistics of Ireland* (1908), p 104 and (1914), p 82.

success rate was higher and less gender specific: from 1858 to 1868, for instance, 37 per cent of women and 30 per cent of men successfully separated.[54] This discrepancy suggests a long-lived attachment to the view that it was a wife's 'merit ... to bear, and endeavour to reclaim. It is not her duty, 'til compelled by the last extremity, to have recourse to legal remedies'.[55]

The evidence presented could, however, be morally compromising for both men and women. Indeed, as the feminist Irish Women's Reform League's Watching the Courts Committee reported on a 1915 separation case, the judge requested 'all ladies' to leave the court.[56] For those who wished to avoid making their marital problems public, private deeds of separation, like those in the 1873 Hanna case, could be executed. Although controversial, by the 1820s the Irish King's Bench held that such agreements were so engrained that they could not be challenged as contrary to public policy.[57] These agreements could not be drawn up directly by wives until the Married Women's Property Act of 1882,[58] but prior to this private deeds of separation were executed for women by trustees: the Marchioness of Westmeath, for example, had two private deeds of separation executed on her behalf in 1817 and 1818. These were, however, subject to multiple legal challenges and ultimately proved ineffectual in securing custody of her only child and protecting her sizeable annuity.[59] Nor was the execution of private separation deeds a nineteenth-century relic; they were still being drawn up in Ireland in the 1980s.[60]

The financial implications of separation also reached beyond legal costs. Sarah Magowan of Belfast, for example, married her cousin William in 1901 and bore one child. With three rental properties, farms, a five-bedroomed house with one servant and an income of c. £800–1,000 per annum, they were comfortably middle class. A separation case brought by Sarah Magowan in 1910, however, saw her husband raise money on security of property to meet the £175 costs. Like many abused women, Sarah Magowan forgave her

54 Hammerton (1992) *Cruelty and Companionship*, p 105.

55 JP Byrne (1859) *The New Law of Divorce and Matrimonial Causes Applicable to Ireland... Popularly Explained* (Dublin: EJ Milliken), p 36.

56 R Cullen Owens (2001) *A Social History of Women in Ireland, 1870–1970* (Dublin: Gill and Macmillan), p 85.

57 This was the ruling in *MacDonnell v Murphy* (1824) J. Scott Fox and C. Lacey Smith (1887–1895) *Registration Cases. Reports of Cases Argued and Determined on Appeal from the Decisions of the Revising Barristers in the Queen's Bench Division of the High Court of Justice* (London: Stevens and Sons), 2, 279. I am grateful to Kevin Costello for bringing this case to my attention.

58 Under the 1882 Married Women's Property Act married women became feme sole regarding property and had the ability to contract (Fitzpatrick (1987) 'Divorce and Separation', p 176). See also C Baker (1880) *Husband and Wife and the Law of Divorce* (London: F. Warne), p. 130.

59 See Urquhart (2014) 'A Woman's Reply'.

60 M Walls and D Bergin (1997) *The Law of Divorce in Ireland* (Bristol: Jordan's), p 32.

husband's actions for years; the acts of cruelty list presented to court documented abuse from 1905:

> Caught Petr. by the throat and said he would 'crush the life out of her and left black marks'; called Petitioner a bloody whore ... Accused Petitioner of Impropriety with men ... [and] 'threatened to batter out Petitioner brains'; 'Stopped Petitioner allowance and credit'; 'locked Petr. out'...; 'brought his illegitimate daughter to the house'; 'Contemptuous treatment of Petitioner ... before servants'; 'Accused Petitioner of trying to poison him' ... he admitted ... Adultery.[61]

Sarah Magowan feared the ramifications of instituting legal proceedings: 'I bore all this with patience as I did not want people to know and was ashamed to acknowledge it even to myself. My husband told me often I was no use (as a wife) and did not suit him ... I was afraid of his threats.' The legal view of such female perseverance was not, however, sympathetic. This could be seen as condonation and this was reinforced by Sarah Magowan's return to the marital home four months after leaving in 1906. She left permanently in 1909 and separated on basis of William's adultery and cruelty in 1910, but the case went to appeal over a decade later in 1921. The result was an increase in alimony from £4 to £7 per month, but Sarah Magowan resorted to running a boarding house in Belfast and lived on c. £130 per annum.[62] In Ireland there was no statutory provision for a husband to maintain his wife after his death and in this case Sarah Magowan was not mentioned in his will, entitled to continued alimony or able to make a claim on the estate.[63]

Difficulties were also caused by married women's dependent domicile which was determined by that of her spouse. Women like Nita Martin, 'the daughter of a well[-]known gentleman in England', but married to a domiciled Irishman, therefore had to separate in Ireland. In 1917 she sought to separate from Thomas Martin, a Dublin quantity surveyor, on the grounds of his cruelty and misconduct. She married Martin in 1904, but was subjected to abuse: 'Respondent had kicked and beaten the petitioner, and had been persistently cruel to her'. She was deserted in 1905 when her spouse went to Australia.[64] Thomas Martin did not attend the case and a separation was granted.

61 William Magowan had an illegitimate child with a servant who 'killed herself with drugs in trying to do away with the child, when she was pregnant'. Sarah Magowan's statement of 1910 detailed her husband's infidelity (PRONI, D1905/2/19/7).

62 A further appeal over costs came to the High Court of Justice (Ireland), King's Bench Division (Probate) on 8 Apr 1921, but was dismissed: William Magowan had to pay costs. See the papers of L'Estrange and Brett Solicitors, Belfast (PRONI, D1905/2/19/7).

63 PRONI, D1905/2/19/7.

64 She did not see him until 1915 when he was wounded at Sulva Bay and hospitalized in Manchester, but there was no reconciliation. *Irish Times*, 5 May 1917.

A month later she applied for permanent alimony, fixed at £3 per week, pending a divorce bill in the House of Lords which passed in August 1917.[65]

Informal separations were, however, more commonplace. These could be consensual and, as noted, frequently saw men leave the marital home. This situation was drawing comment from the 1960s: 'The fact that many marriages are broken down, although they have not broken up officially, makes them no less of a failure than those who have gone through the ... courts.'[66] The instances of informal separation and desertion also helps to explain why consecutive census returns record tens of thousands of married Irishwomen as living alone while the figure for men in the same circumstances was consistently considerably lower.[67]

Nullity

Akin to other legal remedies for dissolving marriage, the nullity suit was subject to censure. In the mid-nineteenth century, for example, the Catholic Church was labelled both 'very liberal and indulgent' in constructing legal impediments to invalidate marriage:

> the power of dispensation having been for many centuries a fruitful source of ecclesiastical revenue ... the spiritual lawyers – the canonists – invented many ingenious fictions, distinctions, and refinements, which made in most instances [it] not very difficult ... to annul a marriage.

Such claims were not without foundation: increasing the impediments of consanguinity to seventh cousins and decreeing sex with a wife's sister or any of her relations to the seventh degree as incest was beyond the scriptures.[68] In addition to consanguinity, nullity could be granted on grounds such as the non-consummation of marriage, underage marriage, pregnancy with another's child at the time of marriage, duress, fraud, bigamy, idiocy or lunacy to the extent of being unfit to contract. However, children would be made illegitimate when a wife sought nullity on the grounds of non-consummation/impotency so this was never an easy solution.[69] The church could also invoke *vetitum* (prohibition) in nullity cases to deny the right of one or

65 *Irish Times*, 30 June 1917. *Hansard* 5, xxvi [45–46], 26 Jul 1917 (HL), Martin's Divorce Act 1917 (7 & 8 Geo V) [Unprinted c 2P]).

66 D Rohan (1969) *Marriage Irish Style* (Cork: Mercier Press), p 51.

67 The census figures may also include some widowed or unmarried women or those whose husbands were seasonal workers: Fitzpatrick (1987) 'Divorce and Separation', p 179.

68 JF Macqueen (1848) *The Rights and Liabilities of a Husband and Wife at Law and at Equity as Affected by Modern Statutes and Decisions* (London/Charleston: Bibliobazaar repr., 2008), pp 195, 196, 198. For lists of the prohibited degrees of kindred and affinity and of the lesser prohibitions listed in Leviticus, chapters XVIII and XX, see Faloon (1881) *The Marriage Law of Ireland*, pp 224–225.

69 Fitzpatrick (1987) 'Divorce and Separation', p. 176.

both of the parties to remarry in the Catholic Church; *vetitum* was applied in an estimated three-quarters of church annulments.[70] Church annulments also could cost hundreds of pounds, take up to four years to secure and were not recognized as ending a marriage by the State. This pitched civil and canon law against one another; there were prosecutors for bigamy, and Catholics who divorced and remarried in a civil service were seen by the church as living in a state of sin as their first marriage remained valid.[71]

Until 1870, the ecclesiastical (Church of Ireland) courts could also annul marriages but, like their jurisdiction for separation, the Matrimonial Causes and Marriage Law (Ireland) Amendment Act 1870[72] transferred nullity proceedings to the new Court of Matrimonial Causes and Matters. State annulments were expensive, costing approximately £6,000 to £8,000 in the late twentieth century, and in consequence this was an uncommon suit. By the 1960s, for instance, there were between two and 130 State annulments per annum.[73] The grounds also highlight the significance of the church inheritance: one or both of the parties were under age at the time of marriage; non-observance of marriage ordinances; non-consensual marriage including a forced or fraudulent union or where one of the parties or both were incapacitated by mental illness or consanguinity.[74] An existing valid marriage, including remarriage after securing a divorce which was not recognized in Ireland or after a church annulment without a civil divorce, would also provide grounds for a State annulment but the most popular mid-century grounds were insanity and non-consensual marriage or, as the twentieth century progressed, the sexuality of a spouse.[75]

The suggestion that nullity suits were brought in the Republic of Ireland in consequence of the non-availability of divorce is supported by lower nullity figures in Northern Ireland where divorce was available: 21 petitions for nullity were heard in Northern Ireland from 1953 to 1955; 421 divorce petitions were submitted over the same period.[76] By comparison, after the

70 LL Abbate (2002) 'What God Has Joined "Let" Man Put Asunder: Ireland's Struggle Between Canon and Common Law Relating to Divorce', *Emory International Law Review*, 16(2), 583–637. The decisions of church annulments are not publicly available.

71 For Irish bigamy cases see, for example, *The People v Hunt* (1946), *Irish Law Times and Solicitors Journal*, 8, 19 and *Irish Times*, 12 Dec 1945 and *The People v Ballins* (1964), *Irish Jurist* 14. For a fuller discussion see Abbate (2002) 'What God has Joined "Let" Man Put Asunder', 584.

72 33 & 34 Vic c 110.

73 The number of State annulments remained low. O'Brien suggested 20–30 State annulments per year in the mid-1990s, but in some years the figures could be much lower. In 1997, for example, six State annulments were granted in the High Court. M O'Brien (ed) (1995) *Divorce? Facing the Issues of Martial Breakdown* (Dublin: Basement Press), p 117.

74 Same-sex marriage was later a ground for a State annulment.

75 O'Brien (1995) *Divorce?*, p 117.

76 Walls and Bergin (1997) *The Law of Divorce in Ireland*, p 4. Figures from the *Ulster Year Book* (1956), p 254. After divorce was introduced to the Republic of Ireland in 1996, the number of nullity and separation suits both declined.

Second World War, the number of applications for church annulments doubled in the Republic of Ireland.[77] In the 1960s c. 400 petitions for church annulments were presented per annum and the numbers continued to grow. However, like separations, the success rate was low.[78] The rise in demand also failed to ease the difficulty of this process. Indeed, Ferriter claims that some women seeking an annulment 'were humiliated in what was another men's club, the marriage tribunal', often facing questions on the most intimate aspects of their marriage.[79] Presenting evidence to two church tribunals, one regional in Armagh, Dublin, Cork or Galway and then the National Appeals Tribunal, was also a trying and emotional experience for many.[80]

Conclusion

The failure of independent Ireland's legal system to offer any solution to allow remarriage for those experiencing marital breakdown until 1996 was a useful scapegoat for claiming that Irish unions were long-lived and harmonious. Such a view was, however, contested by Dorine Rohan's pioneering work, *Marriage Irish Style,* which sought to answer the 'great unknown ... [the] number of Irishmen and women who would end their marriages if they were permitted to'. Rohan noted that estimates of unhappy Irish marriages varied widely with some as high as 70 per cent and others as low as one per cent, but a quarter of the women that she interviewed favoured divorce and support was higher amongst men. The concept of female forbearance was, however, still to the fore: 'Women feel that a bad marriage is better than a divorce, but on the whole their fears are economic rather than emotional ... Call it resignation, long suffering ... heroism [or] ... the "vale of tears" tradition'.[81] Rohan also supported Joseph Cole's earlier brave assertion that a lack of divorce provision caused desertion:

> Irish husbands ... leave because they want a divorce ... They get around this by simply walking out on their wives and families

77 CP James (1997–1998) 'Céad Míle Fáilte? Ireland Welcomes Divorce: The 1995 Irish Divorce Referendum and the Family (Divorce) Act of 1996', *Duke Journal of Comparative and International Law*, 8, 175–228, pp 175, 190.

78 D Ferriter (2009) *Occasions of Sin: Sex and Society in Modern Ireland* (London: Profile), pp 438–439.

79 Ferriter, *Occasions of Sin*, pp 438–439. In England, the practice of the Catholic Church was not to process applications for annulments unless a court decree has been granted. O'Brien (1995) *Divorce?*, p 122.

80 Both tribunals had to concur for a marriage to be annulled. K Wood and P O'Shea (1997) *Divorce in Ireland. The Options. The Issues. The Law* (Dublin: O'Brien Press), p 116. At the time of writing, the Catholic Church is reforming the annulment procedure without altering the criteria for annulment. *Motu Proprio* is the result of Pope Francis's desire to 'simplify and streamline' the annulment process while 'safeguarding the principle of the indissolubility of marriage' (*Times of Malta*, 8 Sept 2015).

81 Rohan (1969) *Marriage Irish Style*, pp 28, 54 and 88. Such sentiments were still pervasive at the time of the 1986 divorce referendum.

> and disappearing in the large industrial cities of Britain. This has become known as Divorce–Irish Style – nobody has dared publicly to put a name on it. The name is divorce ... it is a disgrace. The Vatican, in trying to keep the family as the most important social unit in society by forbidding divorce, has unwittingly achieved the opposite in Ireland for here, families are being broken up every day.[82]

Migration was so serious and sustained, with an estimated net migration of 119,568 from the Republic of Ireland in the inter-censal period of 1946 to 1951, that the government-sponsored Commission on Emigration considered it a 'population problem'.[83] Yet, how many of Ireland's migrants were motivated less by economics or ambition but by marital strife and whose migration effected a desertion of spouses and dependants endures as another Irish unknown. The stigma attached to marital breakdown also remained and for Rohan this posed the most troubling aspect of a situation which affected 'thousands': 'many of these "deserted wives" are living lives of extreme hardship ... rather than go out to work and let the neighbours know they have been abandoned.'[84]

Other commentators in the mid-twentieth century struggled to understand Ireland's restrictive provisions for the dissolution of marriage. Alexander Humphreys' *New Dubliners*, for example, portrayed a cowering government and a defunct system of family law:

> Fear of hierarchical opposition carries such weight that the government has consistently been conservative in the face of it and has been wary of pressing its constitutional prerogatives ... another institution which instances the conservatism of the Irish revolution – family law ...[is] still fundamentally the common law of England as it was based on Canon Law prior to the Reformation.[85]

Humphreys' case study of John and Joan Dunn also highlighted the prevalent traditionalism and sense of male dominance in Irish marriage. The married state was 'not merely ... contractual but ... sacred, indissoluble, sacramental'.[86] Although a sense of marital partnership was evolving, Joan Dunn recalled that 'many of the mothers were afraid of their husbands.

82 Cole (1967) 'Deserted Wives'.

83 Emigration from Northern Ireland totalled 14,918 in the period 1947–1951. See WE Vaughan and AJ Fitzpatrick (eds) (1978) *Irish Historical Statistics: Population, 1821–1971* (Dublin: Royal Irish Academy), pp 266–267. See also *Eire: Commission on Emigration and Other Population Problems, 1948–54* (1955) (Dublin: Stationery Office).

84 Rohan (1969) *Marriage Irish Style*, p 50.

85 A Humphreys (1966) *New Dubliners. Urbanization and the Irish family* (Dublin: Fordham University Press), pp 53, 55.

86 Humphreys (1966) *New Dubliners*, p 116.

I knew many families where the mother was always hiding things from the father and trying to keep him pleased because she was afraid that he would be hard on the children'.[87] A generational shift was, however, apparent in the Dunn's progeny; more women sought social advantage from marriage and would continue to work post-marriage. Yet the children of the 1950s and 1960s retained 'their parents' conception of marriage in the crucial fundamentals ... they, too, look on marriage as a sacramental, indissoluble state'.[88]

Rohan, Cole and Humphreys were part of a broader mid-twentieth century sociological investigation which cumulatively critiqued the idealization of Irish society. Their controversial and confronting studies also highlight that demands for Irish reform were not wholly externally driven by challenges like that of *Johnston and Others v Ireland* in the European Court of Human Rights in 1986.[89] For those whose marriages broke down, were incompatible, abusive or unhappy, the legal solutions to protect, support and ultimately allow lives to be rebuilt were severely lacking in Ireland in the period from 1850 to 1950 and beyond. Indeed, the factors which would lead to Labour Chief whip and later Minister for Minister for Equality and Law Reform Mervyn Taylor's exasperation at the time of the first referendum on divorce in 1986 were already apparent by the mid-century: 'We have had a constitutional ban on divorce all these years, yet, it has availed us nothing in preventing the break-up of families.'[90]

87 Humphreys (1966) *New Dubliners*, p 122.

88 Humphreys (1966) *New Dubliners*, p 129.

89 [1986] ECHR 17, 9697/82; [1986] 9 EHRR 203 and KM Dillon (1989) 'Divorce and Remarriage as Human Rights: the Irish Constitution and the European Convention on Human Rights At Odds in *Johnston v Ireland*', *Cornell International Law Journal*, 22(1), 63–90.

90 *Irish Press*, 20 May 1986.

8

Class, Criminality and Marriage Breakdown in Post-Independence Ireland

Deirdre McGowan

Introduction

Over the past 50 years private law rules have come to play a central role in our affective lives and law's language defines our social relationship status. We are married or unmarried, civilly partnered, cohabiting, separated or divorced. Marriage breakdown and divorce are accepted as unfortunate, but normal, social events and private law rules govern maintenance, judicial separation and divorce. Telling the history of marriage breakdown in terms of current understanding of legal status and social practice is, however, problematic. This is particularly so in the Irish context where divorce was impossible from 1922 to 1997[1] and the concept of 'marriage breakdown' was largely absent from political and cultural discourse.[2]

Crafting an account of marriage breakdown in the post-independence period is further complicated by a rural bias in existing descriptions of Irish marriage practices. Other than statistics collected in decadal censuses, most existing anthropological or sociological accounts focus on farming families and suggest that marriage breakdown did not occur within this social group.[3] Reported superior court decisions in matrimonial actions during

1 The 1937 Constitution as originally drafted prohibited the enactment of any law facilitating the dissolution of marriage. The provision was replaced, following a referendum, in 1996 to allow divorce on a constitutionally restricted basis. For a detailed account of the family provisions of the 1937 Constitutions see Chapter 13 in this volume

2 The term 'marriage breakdown' first emerged in political debate in the late 1970s. One of the first references to the phenomenon was in the Oireachtas occurred in 1977 when Deputy David Andrews referred to marriage breakdown brought about 'by the spectre and reality of continuous unemployment' in the Dáil during a debate on a social welfare bill. *Dáil Éireann deb*, ccxcvii [1218] 10 Mar 1977.

3 See, for example, C Arensberg and S Kimball (2001) *Family and Community in Ireland* 3rd edn (Clare: Clasp Press); KH Connell (1962) 'Peasant Marriage in Ireland: Its Structure and Development Since the Famine', *The Economic History Review* 14(3), 502–523.

the period also suggest a dearth of marital failure, being few in number and reflecting the experience of atypical middle- and upper-class families. In opposition to these indications of widespread marital harmony, newspaper reports of criminal prosecutions for wife and child desertion, child cruelty and bigamy suggest greater regularity in spousal separation among the urban poor and working class.[4] Accordingly, in order to appreciate how marriage breakdown was regulated in post-independence Ireland, account must be taken of criminal and civil law responses to spousal conflict, as well as social practices that removed marital failures from public view. This essay reviews legal and practical responses to marriage breakdown in the post-independence period, noting how economic security facilitated spousal separation without 'marriage breakdown' among the middle and landowning classes, while criminal prosecutions among the urban poor linked separation and remarriage to female poverty, male transgression and child cruelty. This association between marriage breakdown, poverty and social disorder would later become an essential element of socio-political opposition to divorce.[5]

Rural indissolubility

In the present, we understand marriage as a relationship based on affection, and generally accept spousal conflict and marriage breakdown as a somewhat inevitable feature of social life. For the rural smallholder in post-independence Ireland, however, marriage was principally an economic transaction, and although spousal conflict may have occurred, it was not necessarily considered antithetical to the marital bond. In their study of farm families in 1930s County Clare, Arensberg and Kimball describe how the 'match' system tied marriage to inheritance in a carefully choreographed economic transaction.[6] A farmer nominated one son to succeed to his farm and when he was ready to transfer control a spouse (in possession of a dowry corresponding to the value of the farm) was sought and marriage would result in the transfer of land from father to son. The dowry received was used to 'settle' a daughter, provide a passage to America for a sibling or pay off the father's debts. Connell develops a similar account from records of the folklore commission, describing large families in which only one son and one daughter could be facilitated in ambitions to marry.[7] Gibbon and Curtin challenge the ubiquity of the form of 'the match' described by Connell and

4 Diane Urquhart, in Chapter 7, makes a similar point in relation to nineteenth-century practices.

5 For an account of how these narratives contributed to the 'marriage saving' objectives of later matrimonial legislation see D McGowan (2016) 'Governed by Marriage Law: An Irish Genealogy' *Social and Legal Studies* 25(3), 311–331.

6 Arensberg and Kimball (2001) *Family and Community*.

7 Connell (1962) 'Peasant Marriage in Ireland'.

Arensberg and Kimball in which the groom's parents remained on the land. They use census information to demonstrate a concentration of intergenerational households among families in possession of medium-sized farms. The poor and the wealthy mainly adopted the nuclear form, with just one set of parents and children in each household.[8] Further evidence of diversity is offered by Curtin et al. in their examination of early twentieth-century marriage settlements from County Galway.[9] Settling farmers did not always cede immediate control to their sons, and dowries were not always paid. Occasionally women in possession of land could command dowries in exchange for their suitors' farm labour and there is some evidence of women in this position pursuing men who failed to uphold their part of the bargain. As reported in *The Irish Times* in 1939, for instance, Sarah Burke, a widow with four children in possession of a cottage and 12 acres, married John Burke. He brought a fortune of £26, but the marriage ran into difficulties when she refused to wash his shirts and he refused to support another man's children. Sarah pursued John in the District Court for payment of maintenance, but the court did not rule, adjourning the matter for a number of months to allow the parties to be 'brought together'.[10]

Rural marriage practices thus reflected the needs of the particular families involved, and in the main were contracted in order to secure land for lineal descendants. Despite evidence of diversity in specific practices, farmer marriages were essentially economic transactions involving the transfer of money and spouses from one household to another and the settlement of land for the benefit of future kin.

Such a system did not facilitate marriage breakdown as understood today; the economic transaction at the heart of the marriage contract could not be undone. A wife's dowry was distributed among kin, not retained by her husband, and the division of a landholding to facilitate dissolution of marriage was unimaginable.[11] None of the very few reported matrimonial decisions between 1922 and 1950 involved farming families. Lack of spousal litigation is, however, hardly conclusive. The matrimonial jurisdiction of the

8 P Gibbons and C Curtin (1978) 'The Stem Family in Ireland' *Comparative Studies in Society and History*, 20(3), 429–453.

9 C Curtin, E Devereux and D Shields (1992) 'Replaying "The Match": Marriage Settlements in North Galway', *Irish Journal of Sociology*, 2, 85–95.

10 'Peer's Nephew and Labourer' *Irish Times*, 29 Jul 1939. The title of the article refers to the differing statuses of Sarah Burke's husbands.

11 *Irwin v O'Connell* [1936] 1 IR 44, one of the few reported decisions involving a rural farmer marriage, was a suit by the husband's mother for arrears of an annuity on land, reserved when the tenancy of the farm was transferred to the son on his marriage. The wife brought a dowry of £150, of which £100 was spent on paying off a mortgage on the farm and the rest on discharging ordinary debts. The husband was 22 at the time of marriage and the wife 52; the wedding was clearly an attempt to retain the land within the family. In the event, the husband failed to pay rent and a new tenancy was granted to his wife, who later became the registered owner pursuant to the Land Acts. The Supreme Court held that the husband's tenancy had been extinguished and that the annuity did not attach to the wife's interest.

High Court was derived from that of the ecclesiastical courts of the formerly established church, an institution alien to the mainly Roman Catholic Irish.[12] Further, access to the courts was prohibitively expensive and the ecclesiastical remedies of nullity, divorce *a mensa et thoro*, restitution of conjugal rights and criminal conversation were meaningless to farming spouses performing complementary roles on smallholdings.[13] Gavan Duffy J observed in 1942 that 'the intense feeling of the family for the family' was one of the basic characteristics of Irish country life and 'the family in actual practice' was 'the basic unit of social order'.[14] The judge attributed the centrality of the family to 'Christian feeling', but the economic exigencies of rural life also provided a powerful practical support to family stability. Nonetheless, no more than in the present, personal compatibility was never assured and animosity inevitably defined at least some farmer marriages.

Complete marital breakdown as currently understood may have been rare or non-existent, but rural ways of life provided generous opportunities for marital separation without the necessity of undoing 'the match'.[15] Women who failed to produce children could be returned to their families of origin, men could go away for work either seasonally or on a long-term basis,[16] and the strict division of farm labour allowed spouses to live separate lives under the one roof. Evidence of a practical approach to marital difficulties can be found in Arensberg and Kimball's Clare and Fox's Tory.[17] Arensberg and Kimball recorded cases of women who failed to produce children within a year of marriage being returned to their families of origin. The husband would then transfer his landholding to a brother to facilitate his marriage and thus the succession of land to the next generation.[18] Fox observed the practice of 'natolocal marriage' on Tory Island, in which husbands and wives remained in their parents' household after marriage, achieving the economic objective

12 The matrimonial jurisdiction of the High Court was built directly upon the ecclesiastical rules of the formerly established Church of Ireland. Jurisdiction had been transferred from the Ecclesiastical Courts to the civil courts in 1870 by the Matrimonial Causes and Marriage Law (Ireland) Amendment Act (33 & 34 Vic c 110) which required civil judges to act in accordance with 'the principles and rules' of the ecclesiastical courts.

13 For a full account of matrimonial remedies available in the High Court prior to 1970 see A Shatter (1977) *Family Law in the Republic of Ireland* (Dublin: Wolfhound Press). See also Chapter 7 in this collection.

14 In *Re Estate of Patrick Walsh, dec: Walsh v Walsh* [1942] IR 403, 408.

15 D Fitzpatrick (1987) 'Divorce and Separation in Modern Irish History', *Past and Present*, 114(1), 172–196, p 182.

16 Seasonal and long-term migration to England and Scotland, as well as within Ireland, was a feature of Irish rural life since the eighteenth century. For an account of this phenomenon see C Ó Gráda (1973) 'Seasonal Migration and Post-Famine Adjustment in the West of Ireland' *Studia Hibernica* 13, 48.

17 R Fox (1978) *The Tory Islanders: A People of the Celtic Fringe* (Cambridge: Cambridge University Press).

18 Arensberg and Kimball (2001) *Family and Community*, pp 137–138.

of marriage without necessarily making an interpersonal commitment.[19] Where husbands and wives were older and had established businesses or their own farms, co-residence could be avoided completely. The husband in *Donovan v Croft*[20] was prosecuted for not paying his wife's income tax. He successfully defended the action by demonstrating that he and his wife did not live together. They had agreed upon marriage not to cohabit and each lived and carried on their own businesses in separate towns.

Law reports also provide evidence of rural pragmatism. In *Keelan v Garvey*[21] the plaintiff husband went away to work when he could no longer tolerate his wife, leaving her in possession of his farm from which she earned a living. He supported himself with wage labour and returned to claim the land when news reached him of her death. Brigit Walsh, a minor character in a family dispute over her father's will, was returned to her home place after marriage when she became incapacitated, her children and dowry remaining with her husband's family.[22] Similarly, as recounted in *Lennon v Maguire*, John Lennon maintained his daughter and her four children for 15 years following the breakdown of her marriage.[23] His patience was clearly tested by the experience, and he pursued the husband for the cost of their maintenance in the Circuit Court.[24]

Although living in comparative poverty, farm families with access to land often had the means, however meagre, to house and support a family member whose marriage had ceased to function. The effects of marriage breakdown were absorbed by land ownership, rendering them invisible to the wider community and the institutions of the State. Legal intervention in the form of separation, divorce or maintenance was unnecessary because rural lifestyles and the economic security of land produced similar, and perhaps superior, solutions to interspousal conflict. David Fitzpatrick has argued that a moral code drawn from rural marriage practices shaped Irish ideas about the indissolubility of marriage, and that the curtailment of divorce in Ireland resulted from these social conditions rather than opposition from Catholic Hierarchy or doctrine.[25] Yet, separation did occur among the farming classes;

19 Thus sidestepping the very possibility of marriage breakdown. Fox (1978) *The Tory Islanders*. David Fitzpatrick argues that the ubiquity of natolocal marriage suggested by Fox is not borne out by census reports. D Fitzpatrick (1983) 'Irish Farming Families before the First World War', *Comparative Studies in Society and History*, 25(2), 339–374, pp 367, 368.

20 *Donovan v Croft* [1926] 60 ILTR 115.

21 [1924] 38 ILTR 165.

22 *Walsh v Walsh*, 412 (Gavan Duffy J).

23 [1935] 69 ILTR 67.

24 He did not succeed, the court finding no agreement by the husband to pay for their upkeep.

25 Fitzpatrick (1987) 'Divorce and Separation', p 196.

Fitzpatrick refers to it as 'ubiquitous'.[26] Farming families were clearly not universally opposed to the notion of interpersonal conflict or spousal incapacity making cohabitation impossible. It was the economic transaction of marriage that was indissoluble, not the interpersonal one. Rural marriage practices undoubtedly had an influence on later objections to divorce, but these objections were economic, not moral. The most powerful and perhaps effective arguments against divorce during the 1986 divorce referendum campaign were based on economic concerns, and this was particularly true of the farming lobby which saw civil divorce as a threat to the integrity of landholdings.[27] Divorce had the potential to give in-marrying spouses a legal claim to family farms that had been carefully preserved through several generations.

Marriage breakdown among the middle classes

Most reported marriage law cases involved middle class or wealthy families. The anatomy of their marital difficulties is set out in detail in case reports, but by looking beyond the legal issues we can begin to build a picture of the lived experience of marriage failure among this social group. By extending the analysis to child custody disputes and the wider category of 'family disputes' a clearer picture emerges of how marital conflict was managed outside the courtroom.

The simplest way to remove oneself from the company of an unsatisfactory spouse was, and is, to simply leave the marital home.[28] This was effective and relatively unproblematic if the spouses had adequate means to establish and maintain two households. It is impossible to gauge how common such arrangements were; utmost discretion was necessary to avoid inevitable social disproval. Catholics could achieve some level of post-relationship respectability through a Church annulment. A canon law declaration of nullity did not affect civil status, but did go some way to addressing social and cultural distrust of marital breakdown. The process of obtaining a church annulment was long, arduous, and in the early years of the State, prohibitively expensive. Nonetheless, it was pursued, and in some of the matrimonial cases coming before the courts a church annulment had already been

26 Fitzpatrick (1987) 'Divorce and Separation', p 174. The influence of rural lifestyles and morality on social attitudes is a recurrent theme in accounts of post-independence Ireland. State institutions are accused of 'rural fundamentalism' with government policy focused on supporting the economic interests of rural land owners. Public discourses of nationhood are understood as centring on the idealization of the frugal farm family. Fitzpatrick's assertion of a link between social attitudes and rural practices can thus be seen as part of a more general account of the influence of rural ideology on national policy. For an overview, see M Horgan (2004) 'Anti-urbanism as a Way of Life: Distain for Dublin in the Nationalist imaginary', *Canadian Journal of Irish Studies*, 30(2), 38–47.

27 For a detailed account of discourses surrounding the 1986 divorce referendum see M Dillon (1993) *Debating Divorce: Moral Conflict in Ireland* (Kentucky: University of Kentucky Press).

28 See also Chapter 7.

obtained.[29] The church would remarry parties to a prior annulled marriage, and although not civilly recognized, this did provide the practical benefits of marriage, particularly for women.[30] There was the potential of prosecution for bigamy,[31] but such prosecutions were very rare among the middle classes. Statistics for church annulments are not readily available, although Dooley, writing in *The Furrow* in 1975, noted 'a considerable increase in the number of nullity verdicts passed in recent years'. Dooley notes 15 verdicts in 1970 (either affirmative or negative) and 25 in 1971 and 1972, mostly negative. If these numbers represent an increase, it must be assumed that church annulments were very rare indeed.[32]

The willingness, or perhaps perceived obligation, of families of origin to support daughters and sisters experiencing marriage difficulties emerges as a clear theme in reported cases involving middle-class families. Kenneth McNally's pregnant mother left her husband and went to live with her father.[33] She won custody of her son in the High Court, Haugh J noting that the financial position of husband and wife were equal.[34] The wife in *Re Kevin Isherwood, an Infant*[35] was able to secure employment as a nurse when she left her husband in England. She placed her son with relatives in the countryside and a daughter was subsequently born. The court ordered that the son be returned to his father in England, but no application was made in respect of the daughter. The wife in this instance had means with which to support her children and had secured the assistance of a relative in respect of their practical care. In the nullity case of *RM v MM*[36] the wife went to live with her parents following the breakdown of her marriage.

The return of daughters, and perhaps grandchildren, to their parents' home following marital breakdown, could not have been without difficulties. Familial support was available for Jane Bradley when she left her husband to live, first with her grown-up son, and eventually with her mother whom her husband alleged was 'a woman of substantial means'.[37] Mrs Bradley nonetheless attempted (unsuccessfully), all the way to the High Court,

---

29 See for example the civil nullity cases of *McM v McM* [1936] IR 177; *Griffith v Griffith* [1944] 78 ILTR 95. I have not dealt with nullity in any detail in this chapter because the reported cases from this period mainly involved marriages that did not support a post-ceremony interpersonal relationship reflecting experience of non-marriage rather than breakdown of marriage.

30 For a fuller account of civil and religious nullity see Chapter 7.

31 For an account of the background to mid-nineteenth century reform of the law on bigamy see Chapter 3.

32 M Dooley (1975) 'Marriage Annulments', *The Furrow*, 26(4), 211, 213. Dooley drew his statistics from the *Annuario Statistico 1972* of the Holy See.

33 *Re Kenneth Francis McNally, an Infant* [1950] 84 ILTR 7.

34 *Re Kenneth Francis McNally* [1950], p 10.

35 [1948] 82 ILTR 85.

36 [1942] 76 ILTR 165.

37 *Bradley v District Justice in and for the District of Bray* [1932] 66 ILTR 154.

to enforce a maintenance order obtained against her husband. The wife and mother in *Re NP, an Infant*[38] successfully defended her husband's application for habeas corpus of her six-and-a-half-year-old son. She was in receipt of agreed maintenance from her estranged husband and, despite the scepticism of the court, successfully argued that she could support herself and her child with income from knitting. The father in this case was 74 years of age with an income of £176 per annum. He had brought the action in the hope of placing the child in a children's home. In a different case, Eileen Mitchell was facilitated in leaving her husband by her mother, with whom she went to live.[39] A child was born, and the husband sought an order of habeas corpus seeking her return to his custody. The grandmother swore an affidavit for the court stating that she was willing to continue to support both daughter and granddaughter and that she would care for the child if the mother secured employment.

Middle-class spouses who chose to use the matrimonial jurisdiction of the civil courts were chiefly concerned with interpersonal animosity and the division of matrimonial wealth. In *O'Malley v O'Malley*,[40] following the breakdown of their interpersonal relationship, the wife sought an injunction to restrain her husband from continuing in possession of, and interfering with the sale and disposal of, the matrimonial home of which she was the sole owner. The Supreme Court refused an interlocutory order and the case report evidences significant personal conflict between the spouses. The allocation of resources was also at issue in *Ormsby v Ormsby*[41] in which the wife sought to cease payment of agreed maintenance to her husband because he had begun to associate with another woman. Similarly, in 1923 dissatisfaction with the quantum of a matrimonial settlement led Ella Courtney to commence, ultimately unsuccessful, divorce *a mensa et thoro* proceedings against her husband.[42]

For those with access to a source of income or familial support, the matrimonial jurisdiction of the civil courts added little value, although when conflict arose in respect of children civil actions could assist in dispute resolution. Church annulments provided a degree of respectability to bigamous second marriages with almost no possibility of prosecution. For the middle classes, marriage breakdown was a personal tragedy as well as a practical economic problem. Existing ecclesiastically based law had little to offer estranged spouses, but they were nonetheless able to rely on their social and familial networks to shape post-relationship lives.

---

38 [1944] 78 ILTR 32.

39 *In Re Mitchell, Infant* [1937] IR 767.

40 [1951] 85 ILTR 43.

41 [1945] 79 ILTR 97.

42 *Courtney v Courtney* [1923] 57 ILTR 42.

Marriage breakdown among the urban poor

Urban families, and the families of farm labourers, depended on wages from work to survive, and married people tended to adopt gender-based roles, with women caring for children and the home, and men engaging in wage labour. Just 5.7 per cent of married women were gainfully employed in 1926, falling to five per cent in 1946.[43] Children were an inevitable consequence of marriage, and family sizes were 'extremely large by the standards of virtually all other western countries'.[44] While women from farming families had an economic safety net in the event of marriage breakdown, and de facto separation could be accommodated by rural social practice, marriage breakdown for urban women and children, dependent on a husband's income, was an economic disaster. Social supports were minimal, with discretionary funds disbursed at local level and funded by rate payers. Exchequer-funded unemployment assistance was introduced in 1933, but this was available only to men, leaving married women without male support reliant on 'outdoor relief' or the workhouse.[45] Maguire points out that relieving officers were often reluctant to extend home assistance to separated wives where repayment by their husbands was unlikely, favouring committal to an institution over direct financial support in such cases.[46] Assistance was funded by local ratepayers and relieving officers felt duty bound to disburse it only to the morally deserving or those who might be able to repay it. Deserted wives fell into neither category. The 1938 National Society for the Prevention of Cruelty to Children (NSPCC) report for the Dublin region records that the Board of Assistance was seeking to restrict relief for deserted wives and children to indoor relief (effectively incarceration in the County Home) because it felt that the provision of outdoor relief was encouraging men to desert and resulting in collusive desertion.[47]

Following independence, the Irish State inherited a pre-1857 British legal framework intended to enforce marriage performance among the poor, while facilitating separation among those who could afford to support two

43 C Clear (2000) *Women of the House: Women's Household Work in Ireland: 1922–1961* (Dublin: Irish Academic Press), p 23.

44 Clear (2000) *Women of the House*, p 10.

45 Social Assistance or 'outdoor relief' was reformed by the Public Assistance Act 1939, which built upon Poor Law rules that allowed the payment of assistance outside of the workhouse. The amounts paid were minimal, discretionary and set by local administrations. Although the Minister for Local Government had an oversight role in relation to public assistance he could not direct that any particular person should receive or qualify for relief, this being a matter entirely for local determination. For a comprehensive exposition of how the system operated in practice, see S O'Cinnéide (1971) *A Law for the Poor: A Study of Home Assistance in Ireland* (Dublin: Institute of Public Administration).

46 M Maguire (2009) *Precarious Childhood in Post-Independence Ireland* (Manchester: Manchester University Press), pp 37–40.

47 *Irish Times*, 1 June 1939.

households. British assumptions about a lack of moral fortitude among the urban poor were accepted without question in Ireland and enactment and enforcement of criminal laws penalizing marital breakdown among the poor continued after the foundation of the State. The Irish Vagrancy Act 1847[48] penalized men whose failure to maintain their wives and children created a charge on public funds, and the Irish Public Assistance Act 1939 continued the tradition, imposing a penalty of six months' imprisonment for desertion or wilful neglect of a wife or child.[49] In addition, the Children Act 1908 provided that any person having custody or control of a child, who wilfully ill-treated, neglected, or abandoned such child would be guilty of an offence.[50] For the purposes of the Act 'a parent ... legally liable to maintain a child ... shall be deemed to have neglected him ... if he fails to provide food, clothing, medical aid, or lodging for the child'.[51] A husband who did not financially support his wife and children could thus be charged with desertion under the 1847 or 1939 Acts, or child cruelty under the 1908 Act.

An Irish Branch of the NSPCC was established in 1899 and played a key role in enforcement of desertion and child cruelty legislation in the post-independence period.[52] Although their work was not primarily concerned with the effects of marriage breakdown, the phenomenon of 'desertion' was noted in annual reports as a particular concern.[53] Through its local and international offices, the Society traced husbands who deserted and failed to maintain their wives and children and saw the prevention of desertion as an essential part of its work.[54] The 1940 Waterford Branch report refers to a complaint by the wife of a marine engineer, the father of three small children, with weekly earnings of £4. The report states:

> When the Inspector visited the father was at home. He appeared in a violent temper, but after a warning became calm. At length he consented to give his wife £2 per week for housekeeping which he

48 10 & 11 Vic c 84.

49 s 83.

50 s 12. The Act was adapted with administrative amendments by the Irish Executive Council pursuant to SI 8 of 1928.

51 s 12(1).

52 H Ferguson (1996) 'Protecting Irish Children in Time: Child Abuse as a Social Problem and the Development of the Child Protection System in the Republic of Ireland', *Administration*, 44(2), 5–36, p 7.

53 Annual reports were compiled on a branch basis and not collated at national level at this time. I have not consulted the reports themselves, but contemporaneous newspaper reports detailing their contents. Maria Luddy notes that the Society's archive is not complete. M Luddy (2009) 'The Early Years of the NSPCC in Ireland', *Éire-Ireland* 44 (1 & 2), 62–90, p 64.

54 For a comprehensive account of the work of the NSPCC during this period see S-A Buckley (2013) *The Cruelty Man: Child Welfare, the NSPCC and the State in Ireland, 1889–1956* (Manchester: Manchester University Press).

> handed to the Inspector for her. Since then the Inspector has visited and found the children's condition satisfactory. The mother has nothing to complain regarding the father's conduct. She even received more than £2 per week. In this case the warning had the desired effect.[55]

This was considered a success for the Society: desertion and inevitable poverty for wife and children were averted by the inspector's intervention. The Dublin branch had similar success in 1934 in pursuing, with the assistance of the New York Branch, a merchant seaman who had deserted his wife and children. Following NSPCC intervention the wife received a £5 note monthly by post.[56]

Where these types of mediated arrangements broke down, the Society would proceed to prosecution; jurisdictional boundaries were no impediment. If physical separation had already taken place, the society would pursue and attempt to obtain financial support from the husband. Their approach is demonstrated by the experience of Thomas Myers who left his wife and travelled to England in 1941. He was traced by the NSPCC and paid maintenance to his wife for five years. When payments ceased, Myers was again traced, brought before the District Court and convicted on two charges of desertion and neglect of his wife and three children.[57] The arrest in this case was made in Ireland when the accused returned for a family funeral, but it was not unusual for men to be arrested abroad and escorted back to Ireland to stand trial on desertion charges. Michael Crowley was arrested in Wales in 1935 on a charge of deserting his Irish wife who was being relieved by the Cork County Home.[58] Cornelius Sheehan was arrested in London in 1928 on NSPCC information, and brought to Dublin to face charges of neglecting his seven-year-old child. He had left his wife and child following an affair with a work colleague in Dublin.[59] Indeed, the first appearance of the newly formed Irish government police in London was to take custody of an alleged wife deserter from Scotland Yard officers at Paddington Station.[60]

Prosecution of deserting husbands was also a very effective way to ensure payment of maintenance. Although none of the relevant legislation provided for maintenance in lieu of the statutory penalties,[61] District Justices

55 *Cork Examiner*, 4 Dec 1940.

56 *Cork Examiner*, 26 Mar 1934.

57 *Cork Examiner*, 26 Jan 1950.

58 *Cork Examiner*, 10 May 1950.

59 *Irish Independent*, 4 May 1928.

60 *Irish Times*, 31 Oct 1922.

61 The penalty for wife and child desertion under s 2 of the 1847 Vagrancy Act was committal 'to the common gaol or house of correction, there to be kept to hard labour for any time not exceeding three calendar months.' Fines and imprisonment for up to six months on summary conviction were provided for in the 1908 Children Act, s 12(b).

regularly employed their discretion to, in effect, make maintenance orders backed by threat of imprisonment. Thus, when James Flaherty was convicted under the 1908 Act on information from the NSPCC, District Justice O'Farrell sentenced him to six months' imprisonment with hard labour, not to take effect if he provided for his wife and child to the satisfaction of the Society.[62] Thomas Kavanagh was likewise found guilty of wife desertion and ordered to pay 20s per week to his wife, and Cornelius Sheehan, following conviction for child neglect, was ordered to pay maintenance with six months' jail in default.[63] District Justices also purported to make attachment of earnings orders; Reddin DJ at Kilmainham District Court ordered the deduction of 20s per week from the wages of Christopher Fulton for payment to his wife.[64]

Many NSPCC-instigated prosecutions involved men with very limited or no means. Christopher Halpin was arrested in London and charged in Ireland with deserting his wife and children who had been in receipt of public assistance for seven years. He had neither address nor occupation but was nonetheless sentenced to six months' imprisonment.[65] A number of similar cases appear in newspaper reports and reflect the moral objectives of the NSPCC. There was nothing to be gained in terms of child protection from this type of prosecution, but men were considered to have a moral responsibility to support their families, despite abject poverty, ill-health or homelessness.[66] Prosecution also served as a warning to other men considering a similar route out of an unsatisfactory marriage, and it was no doubt threatened by inspectors in order to encourage maintenance payments.

Some of the greatest cruelties meted out to children in this period were perpetrated in children's homes and industrial schools.[67] Maguire identifies the pervasive use of institutional care for destitute children in the first half of the twentieth century, noting that for children whose parents separated, confinement in a children's home or industrial school was not uncommon.[68] Institutionalization of children following parental economic

62 *Cork Examiner*, 26 Jul 1926.

63 *Irish Independent*, 4 May 1928. The maximum term of imprisonment was three months.

64 *Irish Press*, 4 Jul 1940.

65 *Irish Independent*, 28 Jan 1939.

66 Buckley notes that in the post-independence period desertion was framed as a 'public morality' issue. Buckley (2013) *The Cruelty Man*, p 183.

67 But see M Maguire and S Ó Cinnéide (2005) '"A Good Beating Never Hurt Anyone": The Punishment and Abuse of Children in Twentieth Century Ireland', *Journal of Social History*, 38(3), 635–652, p 636. Also, see Chapter 9 in this collection, for a detailed account of the grounds upon which children were committed to industrial schools.

68 Maguire links resort to institutional care for children to NSPCC distrust of men caring for daughters and a reluctance among local authorities to provide outdoor relief to deserted wives. Maguire (2009) *Precarious Childhood*, p 40.

crisis is also noted by Luddy, who observes that death or desertion of a father often left a mother unable to both hold a job and look after children.[69] The absence of any welfare support beyond public assistance meant that lone parents, married or otherwise, were often left with no option but to commit their children to residential care. Residential institutions, pursuing the reform of parents as much as the support of children, required payment of a maintenance fee. This reflected the belief that poverty was essentially a moral failure, and by requesting a fee institutions promoted the notion of parental responsibility and discouraged reliance on charity.[70] Children were also committed to institutional care by local authorities and the courts, often simply because they were poor. A particularly disturbing account of the means employed to secure their committal is given by Kennedy CJ in *Re Kavanagh, Infants*.[71] John and Annie Kavanagh's children were handed over to the Sacred Heart nuns following Annie's committal to a mental asylum in 1928. When the boys became too old for the convent they were

> put out of the house for the express purpose of Miss McLoughlin's [a welfare officer] meeting them and giving them each a penny ... to found a charge of receiving alms with a view to obtaining from the District Court an order committing them to an Industrial school.[72]

With such determination to confine indigent children, it seems inevitable that poverty brought about by marriage breakdown was a significant contributor to the institutionalization of children.

The connection between marital breakdown and the institutionalization of children is also apparent in reported decisions relating to child custody. A number of such cases were reported, particularly in the 1940s, and many involved the children of working-class parents.[73] At common law, 'the rights of the father to the guardianship and custody of his children were absolute'.[74] A certain degree of rebalancing in favour of the mother was effected by the

69 Luddy (2009) 'The Early Years of the NSPCC', p 68.

70 Luddy (2009) 'The Early Years of the NSPCC,' p 68.

71 [1934] 68 ILTR 110.

72 [1934] 68 ILTR 110, 124 *per* Kennedy CJ.

73 I have been unable to identify where these parents got the means to take legal action, given they were unable to support their own children at home. It seems likely, given that most concerned the religious education of children, that the various churches were behind the litigation although there is no commonality of legal representation to suggest that the churches were directly involved. The issue deserves further investigation.

74 *Re A & B* [1897] 1 Ch 786, 788.

Guardianship of Infants Act 1886[75], section 5 providing that the court could, on the application of the mother of any infant, 'make such order as it thinks fit regarding the custody of such infant, having regard to the welfare of the infant and to the conduct of the parents, and to the wishes of the mother and father.' A father, being entitled to custody as of right, could not make an application under the Act, and when deprived of the custody of his children was required to apply for habeas corpus pursuant to Article 6 of the 1922 Constitution or Article 40.4.2 of the 1937 Constitution. A number of such applications involved institutions holding the children of separated parents and the decisions of the court generally centred on religious education. In *Re Keenan's Infants*[76] two children of separated parents were transferred by order of the High Court from a Protestant to a Catholic children's home on the application of the father. Neither parent had the financial resources to support the children outside an institution. In *Re Frost, Infants*[77] the court accepted that institutionalization of children following desertion by their father was preferable to life with their mother in a Dublin tenement. Financial resources were key to securing the release of children from institutional care. In *Re Tilson: Infants*[78] the children were, unusually, released from a home to the care of their mother. Gavan Duffy J referred to the 'patent objections against consigning the boys to any institutional asylum' and how in refusing the order he would 'make the State complete the final destruction of their home life and rob their childhood of a very precious possession'.[79] Crucially for these children, however, the mother had a place to live, an accommodating aunt ready to assist with childcare, and a steady income from work.

The breakdown of marriage, particularly after the birth of children, could send working-class women and children into destitution, the county home or industrial school. For men suffering unhappy marriages, particularly those without a steady income, there was a strong temptation to seek work, and a new life, abroad. Relationship failure thus manifested itself as 'desertion' which was considered morally reprehensible behaviour and the source of child and female poverty. But this was a crime committed only by the poor, and whose victims were likely already suffering severe economic hardship before the act of desertion. Marriage breakdown was made visible among the urban poor by criminal prosecutions, often instigated by the NSPCC. In the post-independence period, therefore, the principal public manifestation of marriage breakdown associated spousal conflict with urban crime, poverty and immorality.

75 49 & 50 Vic c 27.

76 [1950] 84 ILTR 169.

77 [1947] 1 IR 3.

78 [1952] 86 ILTR 49.

79 [1952] 86 ILTR 49, 58.

Bigamy: divorce for the poor

Prosecutions for bigamy, like those for child abandonment and wife desertion, mainly involved urban working-class defendants.[80] Bigamy was punishable, pursuant to section 57 of the Offences Against the Person Act 1861, by up to seven years' imprisonment and involved marrying another person during the lifetime of an existing spouse. In the reported cases, remarriage emerges as a victimless crime, a fact reflected in the often minimal sentences handed down in the courts. Nonetheless, where defendants demonstrated moral turpitude judges would sentence them to periods of imprisonment with hard labour. The policy reasons for criminalizing bigamy, as opposed to simply treating the second marriage as civilly invalid, are not entirely clear. Morse offers a number of justifications: discouraging the procuring of sexual relationships by fraud, preventing public affront to the first wife, avoiding the risk of desertion and failure to support, and eliminating confusion in property transmission.[81] These suggest a male perpetrator, a female victim, the presence of the means to support, and property to transmit. Only one case of bigamy was heard in the Superior Courts for the period in question and its facts reflect such policy concerns.[82] The vast majority of bigamy prosecutions were dealt with on guilty pleas in the District and Circuit Courts.[83] These cases reveal a very different picture of the crime of bigamy from that offered by Morse. Women and men are equally represented as defendants. The second marriages were often fully consensual with little evidence of deceit; failure to maintain was rarely an issue; the transmission of property was never mentioned. The policy of the law, if there was one, was directed to the protection of a middle-class ideal of marriage and family life. Prosecutions, on the other hand, involved, almost exclusively, working-class people trying to deal with adversity as best they could.

Mary Devers' case illustrates the point. Devers pleaded guilty to bigamy at the Mayo Criminal Sessions in 1925. Her first husband, whom she married aged 15, had joined the British army and was sent to India where he was involved in a mutiny leading to a prison sentence. Upon release he joined the Irish army but had never supported his wife. In the interim, Devers had married a man who 'treated her decently and undertook the cost of her

80 The case of Robert Durdin Vere Hunt is notable exception. Mr Hunt, a 27-year-old farmer, pleaded guilty to bigamy in the Central Criminal Court in 1945. He had left his first wife and two children to live with another woman, but had provided maintenance and a home to his first wife. There was some question over the civil validity of his first marriage which had taken place in a registry office in London. His second marriage was solemnized in a Catholic church, and was valid according to canon law. Haugh J imposed a six-month suspended sentence and a fine of £75, effectively an endorsement of Hunt's living arrangements. *Irish Times*, 11 Dec 1945.

81 CGJ Morse (1976) 'Polygamists and the Crime of Bigamy', *International and Comparative Law Quarterly*, 25, 229–235, p 234.

82 *People v Hunt* (1946) 80 ILTR 19. See n 80.

83 These were widely reported in national and regional newspapers.

defence'. She was sentenced to one day's imprisonment.[84] Similarly, Dubliner Mary Reilly remarried following desertion by her husband. She had first married in 1919, but her husband never lived with nor supported her, enlisting in the British Army as a single man.[85] He returned in 1925, but still refused to support her. She married again when she fell pregnant, and at the time of prosecution had a very young baby. Reilly pleaded guilty and received a six-month suspended sentence.[86] The courts also had sympathy for male parties to failed marriages who formed second relationships. William Henry Smyth's first wife was portrayed in court as a petty criminal who refused to live with her husband, and was thus unworthy of his support. He was a private in the defence forces and had taken a second wife within two years of separating from his first, believing the first marriage to be invalid. Smyth was convicted and sentenced to one day's imprisonment, the judge noting that Smyth 'looked very intelligent and seemed as though he might go far'.[87] Desmond Brennan was looked upon less favourably by the court despite his first wife being 'addicted to drink'. He was sentenced to six months' hard labour on pleading guilty to bigamy.[88]

It is impossible to divine why individuals contracted bigamous marriages, but very few of the cases reported in newspapers involved anything other than serial monogamy. Ginger Frost, in her account of bigamy and cohabitation in Victorian England, argues that second unions were socially accepted if they conformed to certain norms.[89] Leaving a former spouse for good reason and fair treatment of a second spouse earned social acceptance. It is likely that a similar moral weighing occurred in Irish society; certainly the judiciary levied small, sometimes negligible, sentences on those individuals who demonstrated good reasons and fair treatment in their relationship practices. Long sentences were reserved for those engaged in deceit or irrational behaviour. Chef Michael Mc Manus, for example, was sentenced to nine months' imprisonment for bigamy; he had married two women within four days without the knowledge of either.[90]

As with prosecutions for desertion, bigamy cases drew attention to the relationship practices of the poor, labelling as transgressive individual attempts to regularize second relationships. The policy of the law was far removed from its practical application; second unions likely improved both the financial

84 *Irish Times*, 29 Oct 1925.

85 Enlisting as a single man allowed him to nominate a family member to receive his separation allowance. Enlisting as married resulted in the allowance being paid to the wife.

86 *Irish Times*, 11 June 1933.

87 *Irish Times*, 19 Feb 1943.

88 *Irish Times*, 19 Oct 1946.

89 Ginger Frost (1997) 'Bigamy and Cohabitation in Victorian England', *Journal of Family History*, 22(3), 286–306.

90 *Irish Times*, 29 Mar 1939.

position and social standing of the purported spouses with few adverse outcomes for previous spouses. Nonetheless, as with desertion, prosecutions arising from serial monogamy associated marriage breakdown with criminality and suggested social deviance in the relationship practices of the working classes.

Conclusion

In the post-independence period, economic factors were pivotal in determining how spousal incompatibility was managed across the social classes. Existing sociological and anthropological accounts, and reported private law cases, point to an economic explanation for the relative invisibility of marriage breakdown among landowning farmers. Similarly, social practices around middle-class marriage breakdown, as indicated in reported matrimonial and childcare cases, demonstrate that separation was both facilitated and hidden from public view by financial security. Marriage breakdown in the post-independence period was only clearly visible among the poor and working classes, where it resulted in criminal prosecution for desertion, child cruelty or bigamy. When marriage breakdown became a political issue in the 1960s and 1970s it was understood in terms of 'desertion,' a 'pressing social evil' that threatened social order and the welfare of children.[91] Fitzpatrick claims that a moral code drawn from the practice of farmer marriage in the late modern period was the foundation of later moral objections to divorce, but rural economics are only part of the story. Since the foundation of the State, marriage failure had been associated in public discourse with female poverty, male transgression and child cruelty. These narratives emerged clearly in the anti-divorce campaigns of the 1980s and 1990s, evidencing their centrality to Irish cultural resistance to legal divorce.

91 The Irish Constitution, Article 41, emphasizes the centrality of the (marriage-based) family to a well-ordered State, a statement largely taken for granted in Irish political discourse. For an overview of arguments in the 1986 campaign see Dillon (1993) *Debating Divorce*, and in relation to the 1996 poll see C James (1997–1998) '*Cead Míle Fáilte*: Ireland Welcomes Divorce: The 1995 Irish Divorce Referendum and the Family Law (Divorce) Act 1996', *Duke Journal of Comparative and International Law*, 8, 175–228.

9

'Behind Closed Doors': Society, Law and Familial Violence in Ireland, 1922–1990

*Lindsey Earner-Byrne**

From the early stages of political independence, the Irish family came under scrutiny. Its role in the war of independence (1919–1921) and subsequent civil war (1922–1923) brought it to the centre of a narrative of violence. Family homes were used as safe houses, frequently raided and became the site of extreme physical, and on occasion, sexual or gender violence.[1] In the wake of the prolonged period of violence that was the revolutionary period (1913–1923), there was widespread concern that the family had been irreparably damaged. Similar to other post-war societies, Irish contemporaries expressed concern that parental authority – perceived as the bedrock of the family – had been eroded and sexual morality had been destroyed. Hence the foundation years of the Irish Free State witnessed a conscious reaffirmation of the family. The government, philanthropic and voluntary groups, and the various churches, rallied to bolster the family through law, charity and sermon.

The understanding of the family as a patriarchal structure that served to socialize children in Irish values, civic obedience, 'appropriate' gender behaviour and religious observance was widespread until, arguably, the 1970s. At that point the family came, once again, under the spotlight as a result of changes in childcare practices, the emerging Second Wave Women's Movement and increased international influences through various forms of media, in particular the television. This paper examines what evidence there is relating to the family as a site of danger, a place where physical and sexual violence could be, and was, perpetrated. 'Familial violence' is currently understood in its broadest sense to mean violence perpetrated by any member of the

* I would like to thank Carole Holohan and Lesley Byrne for their astute observations relating to this topic and chapter.

1 L Earner-Byrne (2015) 'The Rape of Mary M: A Microhistory of Sexual Violence and Moral Redemption in 1920s Ireland', *Journal of the History of Sexuality*, 24, 75–98.

family upon another member within the domestic environment (see Chapter 10 in this volume). However, this paper deals with male violence directed at women and children because this was (and is) the most common form of domestic violence and it was the main focus of contemporary discussions on the subject prior to 1990.[2] It outlines the evolution of social and legal understandings of violence within the family and discusses how this reality for many women and children was subsumed into a culture of silence and denial that sought to protect the 'integrity' of the family at the expense of its individual members (see Chapters 7 and 8 in this volume). It challenges, however, the argument that the Irish State was non-interventionist in family life by introducing a class analysis into the history of State responses to 'problem families'. Finally, it traces the emergence of a new consciousness regarding violence in the home that resulted, ultimately, in new laws to criminalize the most intimate form of violence – marital rape.

Moral panic, the family and the Irish Free State, 1922–1935

One of the most demanding tasks that befell the new Irish Free State in 1922 was that of restoring law and order. After a decade of political uncertainty and violence, trauma characterized the fragile nation-state. Several official inquiries reiterated profound cultural concern that Ireland had 'lost its way' because parents no longer had authority over their children and illegitimacy and delinquency rates were rising. The Commission on the Relief of the Sick and Destitute Poor, including the Insane Poor, one of the first official inquiries into the state of the country's welfare services, interviewed witnesses from all over the country. It reported in 1927 and reflected much of the contemporary anxiety regarding declining moral standards in the wake of prolonged conflict, in particular the fear that the family was losing its social power. It hoped, for example, that with political stability and 'the gradual tightening of the reins of discipline, both governmental and parental', there would be a decrease in illegitimacy rates.[3] However, when the Committee on the Criminal Law Amendment Acts (known as the Carrigan Committee) reported in 1931, it reiterated the belief that 'the loss of parental control ... during a period of general upheaval' had done long-term damage to the family and the morality of society in general.[4] The Committee heard evidence on sexual

2 The term 'domestic violence' was coined to denote gender or sexual violence perpetrated by men (often husbands) against their female partners (usually wives). It has evolved to include violence against men; indeed, a 2005 study noted that while women are much more frequently the victims of domestic violence, one in 16 men had experienced 'severely abusive behaviour of a physical, sexual or emotional nature from an intimate partner'. See *Domestic Abuse of Women and Men in Ireland: Report on the National Study of Domestic Abuse* (Dublin: ESRI, 2005).

3 *Report of the Commission on the Relief of the Sick and Destitute Poor, including the Insane Poor* (Dublin: Stationery Office 1927), p 73.

4 *Report of the Committee on the Criminal Law Amendment Acts (1880–1885) and Juvenile Prostitution* (Dublin: Stationery Office 1931), p 12.

crimes against children and was informed by the Commissioner of the Civic Guard that 'not 15 per cent of such cases were prosecuted'.[5]

The picture painted by the Committee was so shocking that the Department of Justice concluded:

> Unless these statements are exaggerated ... the obvious conclusion to be drawn is that the ordinary feelings of decency and the influence of religion have failed in this country ... It is clearly undesirable that such a view of conditions in the Saorstát should be given wide circulation.[6]

Its response was to become a default official position for many decades: suppression of the report.[7] However, Susannah Riordan offers a valuable caveat to this interpretation with regard to what was known by wider society. While the report was suppressed, the figures that Eoin O'Duffy, the Garda Commissioner, provided on child sexual abuse referred to convictions and therefore represented 'not evidence of crimes concealed but evidence of crimes reported'.[8] Finola Kennedy offers a thorough critique of the Department's reaction to the report, observing that it objected to the raising of the age of sexual consent from 16 to 18 years of age on the grounds that it would 'produce an enormous increase in the number of crimes committed in the country'. It also queried if women police would be of 'any real value' and, in relation to child sexual abuse, argued that experts had 'grave doubts as to the value of children's evidence'.[9] Despite the recommendations of the Carrigan committee, the Department's reservations appear to have held sway and the Criminal Law Amendment Act 1935 raised the age of sexual consent to 17 years (not 18), and classed unlawful carnal knowledge with girls between 17 and 18 years as a misdemeanour. Furthermore, the Act was phrased in such a way as to imply that attempted carnal knowledge of a child under 15 could be interpreted legally (at the discretion of the District Court) as a 'minor offence'.[10] The wrangling that surrounded the Carrigan Report is significant as it reveals that there were counter-voices that acknowledged the harm sexual abuse did to children under 18 years, and that understood the value of

5 F Kennedy (2001) 'The Suppression of the Carrigan Report: A Historical Perspective on Child Abuse', *Studies: An Irish Quarterly Review*, 89, 354–363, p 355; M Finnane (2001) 'The Carrigan Committee of 1930-31 and the "Moral Condition of the Saorstát"', *Irish Historical Studies*, 23, 519–536; MJ Maguire (2006) 'The Carrigan Committee and Child Sexual Abuse in Twentieth-Century Ireland', *New Hibernia Review*, 11, 79–100.

6 Confidential Department of Justice Report on the Committee on the Criminal Law (Amendment) Acts, p 13 (NAI, Attorney General 2000/10/1235).

7 J Smith (2004) 'The Politics of Sexual Knowledge: The Origins of Ireland's Containment Culture and the Carrigan Report (1931)', *Journal of the History of Sexuality*, 13, 208–233.

8 S Riordan (2011) 'A Reasonable Cause: The Age of Consent and the Debate on Gender and Justice in the Irish Free State, 1922–35', *Irish Historical Studies*, 37, 427–446.

9 Kennedy (2001) 'The Suppression of the Carrigan Report', p 357.

10 Kennedy (2001) 'The Suppression of the Carrigan Report', p 359.

women police in dealing with vulnerable children or young girls in the legal system. Crucially, these concerns were not just silenced, they were rebuffed.[11] Thus within the first decade of independence there was general concern about declining moral standards, the weakening of parental authority and an acknowledgement that sexual crimes, in particular child abuse, went largely unprosecuted. However, this was combined with an official insistence that there was no need for women in the justice system and that children made unreliable victims.[12] The legislation introduced established a legal system with embedded class and gender prejudice that was predisposed to passivity on the issue of child sexual abuse and the abuse of adult women.[13]

'[A] moral institution that possesses inalienable and imprescriptible rights': the family and the State

A common theme in much of this discourse was the idea that the family was vital to re-establishing moral standards and maintaining social cohesion. Many contemporaries also regarded political independence as an opportunity to establish a State based on the principles of Catholic social teaching, which also venerated the family.[14] In 1925, when introducing the proposal to prohibit private member bills for divorce, the President of the Executive Council and head of the government, William T Cosgrave, explained to the Dáil:

> I consider that the whole fabric of our social organisation is based upon the sanctity of the marriage bond and that anything that tends to weaken the binding efficacy of that bond to that extent strikes at the root of our social life.[15]

---

11 Carol Smart notes a similar resistance in Britain to the idea of women being involved in these cases due to the fear that they would be determined to have men convicted. C Smart (2000) 'Reconsidering the Recent History of Child Sexual Abuse, 1910–1960', *Journal of Social Policy*, 29, 64–66.

12 The term 'victim' is used in this paper as Joanna Bourke adopts it in her history of rape, to 'draw attention to the hurt of abuse; it is not a moral judgement, nor an identity. Many "victims" are survivors'. J Bourke (2007) *Rape: A History From 1860 to the Present* (London: Virago), p 7. It is important to note that women had been removed from the jury register and had to apply for inclusion under the Juries Act 1927, despite a vigorous campaign by women against the legislation. See C Beaumont (1999) 'Gender, Citizenship and the State in Ireland, 1922–1990' in S Brewster, C Crossman, F Becket and D Alderson (eds), *Ireland in Proximity: History, Gender, and Space* (London and New York: Routledge), 94–108; MG Valiulis (2009) 'Virtuous Mothers and Dutiful Wives: The Politics of Sexuality in the Irish Free State' in MG Valiulis (ed), *Gender and Power in Irish History* (Dublin: Irish Academic Press), 100–114.

13 Tom O'Malley offers stark figures: between 1927 and 1961 90 people were sent to prison in Ireland for rape. T O'Malley (1993) 'Perceptions of Sexual Violence' in A Byrne et al. (eds), *University College Galway Women's Studies Review*, 11, 131–147.

14 For a good discussion of the morally radical elements of Catholic Action, see M Curtis (2010) *A Challenge to Democracy: Militant Catholicism in Modern Ireland* (Dublin: The History Press Ireland).

15 'Private Bills for Divorce', *Dáil Éireann deb*, x [158] 11 Feb 1925.

These sentiments were given added validity in 1937 when Article 41.1 of the Constitution of Ireland recognized 'the family as the natural primary and fundamental unit group of Society, and as a moral institution possessing inalienable and imprescriptible rights, antecedent and superior to all positive law'. Kennedy points out that while the first Dáil of 1919 had pledged to protect the well-being of children, the 1937 Constitution switched the focus to the family and 'the rights of the family as a unit and [on to] the protection of the family from intervention by the State, rather than on the rights of individual members of the family'.[16]

Ciaran McCullagh concurs that the family played a 'key role in the ideology of Irish society', but he claims that this was necessary to mask or contain deep tensions within and between families.[17] These tensions, he argues, revolved around land, exploitation of family labour by parents and the emergence of the stem family system.[18] Indeed, the amount of domestic crimes and murders that involved these core ingredients lends credence to his theory.[19] However, there is at least one other source of potential conflict in the Irish family to be considered: gender relations. The reality of the lived experience of these gender relations behind closed doors was largely airbrushed from Irish public life on the grounds that the privacy of the family was sacrosanct. One could argue that this was the case with families everywhere during this period; however, there are particular things that should be remembered when thinking about the potential lines of conflict in Irish families that did not necessarily pertain elsewhere, at least not to the same degree. Marriage rates were relatively low in Ireland, thus there were many 'substitute families' of brothers and sisters, aunts and nieces, uncles and nephews, living together into old age.[20] Those that did marry, particularly in rural Ireland (and Ireland was predominantly a rural society until the 1960s), generally had to wait until their parents were happy to hand over the running of the farm or accept a new woman of the house (see Chapter 8). Until at least the 1950s, in 50 per cent of Irish marriages there was an age gap greater than five years, with younger wives marrying men who had been bachelors for many years. These families' lives were framed and shaped overwhelmingly by conservative Catholic values that prohibited artificial contraception

16 F Kennedy (2001) *From Cottage to Crèche: Family Change in Ireland* (Dublin: Institute of Public Administration), p 123.

17 C McCullagh (1991) 'A Tie That Binds: Family and Ideology in Ireland', *The Economic and Social Review*, 22, 199–211, p 200.

18 McCullagh (1991) 'A Tie That Binds', pp 202–205.

19 See Chapter 10 in this volume for a discussion of the key elements involved in serious and fatal violence in the Irish family between 1930 and 1950. For the nineteenth-century context of the same themes, see PM Prior (2008) *Madness and Murder: Gender, Crime and Mental Disorder in Nineteenth-Century Ireland* (Dublin: Irish Academic Press).

20 T Guinnane (1997) *The Vanishing Irish: Households, Migration and the Rural Economy in Ireland 1850–1914* (Princeton: Princeton University Press), pp 193–240.

and frowned upon birth control of any kind. For many men and women this meant child after child irrespective of whether or not their emotional energy, physical health or budget stretched to meet each arrival.[21] There was a direct and accepted connection between large families and childhood poverty and there was also a social understanding that poverty strained family relations.[22] Furthermore, Irish married women had one of the lowest participation rates in the workforce in Western Europe until the 1970s, which meant that they had a greater likelihood of financial dependency on their husbands.[23] Finally, marriage was for life; divorce was unavailable/prohibited in Ireland between 1922 and 1996.[24] This is not to suggest that these factors made the Irish family a more violent domain, but it is essential context when considering how the violence may have manifested itself and how it may have been perceived, approached and resolved. As Linda Gordon cautions, 'family violence cannot be understood outside the context of the overall politics of the family'.[25]

Physical punishment: the child and socially acceptable violence

There was a general public and official acceptance that physical punishment of children was not only acceptable but advisable and there is little evidence of any ground swell against this view until the 1950s. While the Children Act 1908 theoretically protected children from severe and unjustified physical abuse, it also safeguarded parents' rights to physically punish their children.[26] Moira Maguire, Seamus Ó Cinnéide and Mary Daly note a real and consistent resistance on the part of the government (in particular the Department of Education) and the judicial system to defining 'legitimate' corporal

21 The consensus against birth control held relatively strong until the 1960s. However, there is evidence that Irish families were getting smaller from 1911 and certainly by the 1940s many families were spacing their children. For an overview of these issues see ME Daly (2006) 'Marriage, Fertility and Women's Lives in Twentieth-century Ireland', *Women's History Review*, 15, 571–585.

22 See, for example, C Clancy Gore (1943–1944) 'Nutritional Standards of Some Working-Class Families in Dublin, 1943', *Journal of the Statistical and Social Inquiry Society of Ireland*, 17, 241–253. See also the *Dáil and Seanad Debates* on the proposed introduction of children's allowances in 1942–44, for example, *Seanad Éireann deb*, 26 [2571-2572] 14 Oct 1942 and *Dáil Éireann deb*, 92 [188] 24 Nov 1943.

23 ME Daly (1997) *Women and Work in Ireland* (Dundalk: Dundalgan Press), pp 43–45.

24 See Chapter 7 in this book by Diane Urquhart and her insightful article on the history of divorce in Ireland and its relationship to understandings of domestic violence: D Urquhart (2013) 'Irish Divorce and Domestic Violence, 1857–1922', *Women's History Review*, 22, 820–837. Different legislation pertained in Northern Ireland.

25 L Gordon (1989) *Heroes of Their Own Lives: The Politics and History of Family Violence* (London: Virago), p 3.

26 Children Act 1908, s 37. MJ Maguire and S Ó Cinnéide (2005) '"A Good Beating Never Hurt Anyone": The Punishment and Abuse of Children in Twentieth Century Ireland', *Journal of Social History*, 38, 635–652, p 636.

punishment.[27] This reluctance seems to have emerged because there was a general belief that physical chastisement had a place in parenting/caring of minors and a fear of criminalizing parents or teachers if limits were clearly set. When it came to instituting a ban on corporal punishment in schools the Department of Education resisted a parental campaign for 30 years, decrying those parents as 'people reared in an alien and in a completely un-Irish atmosphere' – a common dismissal in Ireland of any person or group that challenged the status quo.[28] There is substantial evidence that the legal system endorsed the view that the physical punishment of children was a testament of good parenting and parents who refused to carry out recommended physical punishment stood to lose custody of their children to the industrial school system. Maguire and Ó Cinnéide note a particularly disturbing case that came before the courts in 1967 of a foster father who had so severely beaten the six-year-old girl in his care that she died of her injuries.[29] Quite apart from the girl's death there are a few aspects of this case that reveal deeper attitudes to violence in the home and child protection. The foster father's evidence appeared on the face of it to be damning: he admitted waking the child at night, punching her several times in the face and head until she lost consciousness, at which stage he put her back in bed and she choked on her vomit. This 'punishment' had been administered because she had left a face cloth in the basin. Despite this testimony, the judge cautioned the jury: '[I]t does not follow from the fact that there was regular punishment that it was necessarily given with the intention of causing serious injury or what was done on this evening was something dangerous.'[30] Carolyn Conley has highlighted the readiness of the Irish courts in the late nineteenth century to place considerable emphasis on the absence of 'responsible agency', arguing that the Irish carried this idea further than the Anglo-American norm, 'viewing the killed and the killer as the victims of uncontrollable emotions'.[31] This she notes often resulted in leniency with incredibly light sentences. Although the foster father was found guilty of manslaughter, he was only sentenced to 12 months' imprisonment. This little girl had only lived in her adopted home for three months and there was another foster child in the family. It was noted in the newspapers that the State pathologist had confirmed there 'had been no evidence of sexual assault', suggesting that the elimination of

27 Maguire and Ó Cinnéide (2005) '"A Good Beating Never Hurt Anyone"'; ME Daly (2009) '"The Primary and Natural Educator"? The Role of Parents in the Education of Their Children in Independent Ireland', *Éire-Ireland: An Interdisciplinary Journal of Irish Studies*, 44, 194–217.

28 Minister for Education, General Mulcahy, *Dáil Éireann deb*, clii(4), [470] 8 Jul 1955.

29 Maguire and Ó Cinnéide, '"A Good Beating Never Hurt Anyone"', p 638.

30 'Glassmaker is accused of killing adopted daughter', *Irish Times*, 2 Jul 1968. It was also noted that the 'girl was coloured'; therefore, racism cannot be ruled out as a factor in this case.

31 C Conley (1999) *Melancholy Accidents: The Meaning of Violence in Post-Famine Ireland* (New York and Oxford: Lexington Books).

sexual abuse was standard practice in such cases. There was also evidence given during this trial that neighbours had noticed the little girl often had bruises and black eyes and they suspected she was being beaten. However, no one reported the man prior to the night of the fatal assault. Thus regular physical punishment was implicitly acceptable when directed at children; the manslaughter of a child did not warrant a severe sentence; sexual assault was routinely considered a possibility; neighbours did not feel empowered and/or willing to raise their suspicions about severe physical abuse of a child with the authorities. Finally, this was a foster child – one has to wonder to what degree this impacted on everybody's approach: as McCaughren and Powell note in Chapter 12, the 'public child' was afforded a disgracefully low status in Irish society.[32]

Harry Ferguson has argued that the history of child protection in Ireland has been complicated by the fact that the National Society for the Prevention of Cruelty to Children (NSPCC) remained the main agency responsible for child protection until 1956.[33] However, after political independence the Irish State operated a policy of leaning heavily on voluntary agencies for various aspects of welfare services, particularly those considered to have a moral dimension.[34] The same was true of legislation in various social areas, for example the Children Act of 1908 was the main piece of childcare legislation in Ireland until the Child Care Act 1991. While Ferguson interprets the State's attitude to child protection as reflective of its non-interventionist stance in relation to the family, this is only partially true. In fact, the Irish State could be aggressively interventionist if the family in question was poor. We have discussed the State's ability to dismiss parental campaigns to end corporal punishment; consider also its attitude to non-attendance at school.[35] The Children Act 1929 extended the grounds for committal to an industrial school to include non-attendance at school, poverty and neglect. This mechanism became the vehicle for the greatest violation of the family unit. Through this act thousands of children were committed for their childhood (until the age of 16) to the brutalizing industrial school system.[36]

32 R Gilligan (2009) 'The "Public Child" and the Reluctant State?' *Éire-Ireland*, 44, 265–290, p 282. This little girl began her life in the mother and baby home run by the Sacred Heart Sisters in Manor House, Castlepollard, County Westmeath, hence she was more than likely born outside marriage.

33 H Ferguson (1993) 'Surviving Irish Childhood: Child Protection and the Death of Children in Child Abuse Cases in Ireland Since 1884' in H Ferguson, R Gilligan and R Torode (eds), *Surviving Childhood Adversity: Issues for Policy and Practice* (Dublin: Social Studies Press), pp 14–26, p 15.

34 L Earner-Byrne (2007) *Mother and Child: Maternity and Child Welfare in Dublin, 1922–1960* (Manchester University Press), pp 24–58, 172–220.

35 Fahey argues this case convincingly. T Fahey (1992) 'State, Family and Compulsory Schooling in Ireland', *The Economic and Social Review*, 21, 369–395.

36 L Earner-Byrne (2011) 'Child Sexual Abuse, History and the Pursuit of Blame in Modern Ireland' in K Holmes and S Ward (eds), *Exhuming Passions: Memory and the Uses of the Past in Australia and Ireland* (Dublin: Irish Academic Press), 51–70.

Furthermore, the first investigative commission into the industrial system in 1936 noted that poverty and neglect provided the grounds for 90 per cent of committals to Irish industrial schools.[37] The idea that the Irish State was reluctant to interfere on principle in the Irish family is a myth.

A site of danger: sexual violence and the home

While physical violence was accepted as a facet of childrearing, both in and outside the home, the presumption in all the debates regarding child sexual abuse was that these crimes were perpetuated by strangers, and there was little consideration of the realities of sexual violence within the home. Incest was only criminalized in Ireland and Britain under the Punishment of Incest Act 1908 and provisions relating to this offence were guided by that piece of legislation in Ireland until 1995. Sarah-Anne Buckley has noted that in 1922, in Britain and Northern Ireland, legislators addressed impediments to the prosecution of incest, for example the hearing of cases in camera ceased and incest was reclassified as a felony.[38] However, in Ireland incest was legally treated as a misdemeanour and cases continued to be heard in camera. This had several implications: obviously, incest was not treated as seriously in terms of crime and punishment in Ireland,[39] but also any public knowledge of and discussion relating to the issue was seriously impeded by the in camera procedure. It literally silenced public discourse for much of the twentieth century and when a society is denied the language that public awareness brings, it is extremely difficult for victims or concerned witnesses to raise the alarm and seek help or protection. It is no coincidence that following the publicity surrounding convictions in relation to rape or sexual abuse, reports of other cases increase: people need a framework in which to place their knowledge, they need precedents.[40] Finally, the removal of incest from public discourse increased the cultural disposition to see the family as a site of inviolate privacy about which no tales could be told.

Several scholars have noted the difficulty in accessing the history of incest or child sexual abuse within the family. Both Ferguson and Buckley have observed the limitations in using the records of the NSPCC. After 1922, for

---

37 *Commission of Inquiry into the Reformatory and Industrial School System 1934–1936: Report* (Dublin: Stationery Office 1936), p 10 (the Cussen Report).

38 S Buckley (2011) 'Family and Power: Incest in Ireland, 1880–1950' in A McElligott, L Chambers, C Breathnach and C Lawless (eds), *Power in History. From Medieval Ireland to the Post-Modern World* (Dublin: Irish Academic Press), 185–206, pp 186, 190.

39 Once incest was classified as a misdemeanour the maximum sentence possible was seven years: after 1922 the average sentence for the crime fell by five years to two years' imprisonment. Buckley (2011) 'Family and Power', p 197.

40 For example, after the Kilkenny Incest case child abuse referrals increased 150 per cent in certain parts of the country. H Ferguson (1993–1994) 'Abuse Inquiries and the Report of the Kilkenny Incest Investigation: A Critical Analysis,' *Administration*, 41, 385–410, p 404.

example, the only references to incest in NSPCC records were to the small numbers of cases investigated annually. Carol Smart suggests that suspected child abuse was coded in order to enable NSPCC officers to secure permission from fathers to have children examined and treated for venereal disease.[41] Other than that the Society talked in oblique terms noting that children were endangered by 'immoral surroundings', 'moral danger' and 'other wrongs'.[42] This terminology reflects the fact that sexual crimes in general, including child sexual abuse, were interpreted as moral crimes that also 'infected' the victim.[43] This belief meant the victims of any form of sexual abuse held a dubious social status and could often end up ostracized or incarcerated in various institutions.[44] Ferguson argues that what took place in Ireland was 'a more subtle process of "knowing"... where the problem of sexual abuse was contained within other categories of abuse, especially neglect, and never came to be seen as a separate social reality.'[45] However, Buckley identifies several cases of incest that reached the Irish courts. Therefore it was identifiable, recognized and, occasionally at least, pursued. She notes that at least 44 cases of incest were investigated between 1927 and 1935 and between 1929 and 1939 there were 21 convictions for incest resulting in prison sentences.

These cases came to the attention of authorities when the family could no longer contain the issue and required public assistance, usually in the wake of a pregnancy, attempted or actual infanticide, or when a perpetrator was caught 'in the very act'.[46] Buckley identified a widespread tendency not to believe the victim's evidence and, even when it was accepted, the victim was often treated as though she (as it was invariably a daughter) was morally implicated in the crime.[47] Moreover, a strong and enduring narrative developed since the 1880s that familial violence and incest were closely linked with poverty and overcrowding; in other words, with the working class. This was driven in large part by social reformers' concerns about the impact of poverty and poor housing on child health and moral purity. Buckley argues that 'the effects of this contextualisation would reverberate throughout the twentieth century in Ireland'.[48] While some historians have accepted this reading, it should be seen as part of reform rhetoric and was based on assumptions

41 C Smart (2000) 'Reconsidering the Recent History of Child Sexual Abuse, 1910–1960', 55–71, p 60.

42 Buckley (2011) 'Family and Power', p 196.

43 Bourke (2007) *Rape,* pp 119–146; E O'Sullivan (2002) '"...Otherwise Delicate Subject": Child Sexual Abuse in Early Twentieth-Century Ireland' in P O'Mahony (ed) *Criminal Justice in Ireland* (Dublin: Institute of Public Administration), 176–201, p 198.

44 Earner-Byrne (2011), 'Child Sexual Abuse', p 59.

45 H Ferguson (2001) '*States of Fear,* Child Abuse, and Irish Society', *Doctrine & Life,* 20–30, p 30.

46 Ferguson (2001) '*States of Fear*', p 198.

47 Ferguson (2001) '*States of Fear*', p 200.

48 Ferguson (2001) '*States of Fear*', p 188.

of working-class inferiority and inherent sexual impurity.[49] Smart notes, for example, that medics went to great lengths to explain gonorrhoea in children along class lines: working-class children were assumed to have caught it in their parents' beds (which they invariably shared), while middle-class children were the victims of their servants' poor hygiene.[50] There is, in fact, no evidence that children were more likely to be sexually abused in poor or working-class cramped households than in spacious middle-class homes. There is only evidence that the former were under constant observation and were therefore more likely to come before the courts.

A case of incest in 1920s Wicklow reflects several themes that emerge in the history of child abuse in Ireland prior to the 1980s. In January 1926, Fr C. of County Wicklow, was asked to investigate a case of incest in his parish. He had initially been unaware of the case of 'incestuous concubinage' and had been visiting the father and daughter in question as 'man and wife for nearly twelve months'.[51] He had been concerned with getting the children to school, but when he discovered the facts he did all he could 'to induce them to separate'. He had managed to get the daughter and her children admitted into the local County Home, but she had returned to her father within a week. The priest's campaign had involved pressurizing the daughter and 'impressing on her *especially*, the fate that awaited her in eternity if she continued her sinful life'. Fr C. displayed absolutely no understanding of child sexual abuse and appeared to hold Mr H.'s daughter equally responsible for the incestuous relationship. He finally succeeded

> in conjunction with the local police, in having three of the children sent to an industrial school and hope tomorrow to bring the mother to High Park [Magdalene asylum] and her infant (aged 7 months) to the Sacred Heart Home [orphanage on the site of the asylum].

Many victims of abuse were dealt with in this way. It seemed easier for Irish society to incarcerate them rather than the perpetrators. Of course, this 'in-house' resolution prevented the scandal of a court case, but it also allowed society to avoid dealing with the needs of its most vulnerable citizens.

---

49 For example, Diarmaid Ferriter repeatedly notes that overcrowding left children vulnerable to sexual abuse, noting but not interrogating the assumption that contemporaries believed such conditions were conducive to child sexual abuse. D Ferriter (2009) *Occasions of Sin: Sex and Society in Modern Ireland* (London: Profile Books), pp 8, 49, 53, 76, 139 and 183.

50 She notes that it was not until the 1980s that doctors were alert to venereal disease in children as an indicator of sexual abuse. She does, however, argue that there was a 'counter-discourse' as early as the 1900s that insisted infection in children was a direct result of rape. Smart (2000) 'Reconsidering the Recent History of Child Sexual Abuse', 58–59.

51 Fr JMC, X, County Wicklow, 9 Jan 1926 (Dublin Diocesan Archives (DDA), Charity Cases Box 1: 1922–1926, Byrne Papers).

Man and wife: physical and sexual violence in intimate relationships

One of the core principles of marriage was that the woman subsumed her *self*; she became a wife and her identity was defined by how well she supported her husband and mothered her children.[52] This was reflected in public discourse, religious doctrine, welfare provision and legislation.[53] A husband remained a *man* after marriage, he was the head of the household and represented the patriarchal system upon which Irish culture and Catholicism placed so much faith and emphasis.[54] This was the prism through which domestic abuse – physical and sexual – was viewed. As Melissa Anderson astutely observes, 'by the time the English reign in Ireland ended in the twentieth century, the nation was firmly entrenched in English common law ideals, and had a constitution firmly based on Catholic beliefs'.[55] If a woman became the property of her husband upon marriage how did she retain any bodily integrity? How could she be assaulted or raped by her husband, if her consent was presumed at the point of marriage? As Anderson notes, various practices 'underscored the theme of women as property' and she links this directly with the legal definition of rape and the spousal exemption for rape, which endured in Ireland until 1990.[56] Of course, this ideology was sustained by a belief in the inherent unreliability of *all* women's claims regarding rape. Just as Irish politicians had feared that women would falsely accuse men of being the fathers of their 'illegitimate' offspring for the purposes of blackmail, so they feared wives would falsely accuse their husbands of rape.[57]

It is, therefore, no surprise that the beginnings of a conversation about domestic violence (even as a concept – the phrase came later) emerged from feminists who were also campaigning for the vote, women's property rights and various other legal entitlements for their sex. Louise Ryan and Elizabeth Steiner-Scott have both tracked the origins of this debate in the pages of the

52 This discourse extended to the idea that a good wife tolerated domestic violence in order to keep her family intact. Urquhart (2013) 'Irish Divorce and Domestic Violence, 1857–1922', p 826.

53 MG Valiulis (2009) 'Virtuous Mothers', 100–114.

54 It should be noted that patriarchy was by no means unique to Ireland, but the dominance of Catholicism presented a particularly watertight version of the ideology.

55 M Anderson (1998) 'Lawful Wife, Unlawful Sex – Examining the Effect of the Criminalization of Marital Rape in England and the Republic of Ireland', *Georgia Journal of International & Comparative Law,* 27, 139–166, p 160.

56 Anderson (1998) 'Lawful Wife, Unlawful Sex', p 145.

57 This fear was expressed throughout the Dáil and Seanad debates on the Illegitimate Children (Affiliation Orders) Bill in 1930. See L Earner-Byrne (2008) 'Reinforcing the Family: The Role of Gender, Morality and Sexuality in Irish Welfare Policy, 1922–44' History of the Family: International Quarterly Journal, 13, 360–379.

Irish Citizen (the main Irish feminist paper founded in 1912).[58] These early feminists did much to interrogate the concept of the public and the private sphere and how this ideology was used to silence and hide women's voices. It was in this context that they framed domestic violence, as an article in the *Irish Citizen* in September 1919 explained:

> An age-old tradition prevails that in matrimonial affairs what transpires in the home must be carefully concealed from the world without ... This natural shrinking from exposure gives a sense of security to the stronger, fiercer, and more dominant partner, the husband, in ill-treating his wife.[59]

The feminist Margaret Connery argued that the judiciary and the police were all men and thus had 'an indulgent tolerance' of male sex offenders reducing the administration of justice to a 'ghastly joke'.[60] They highlighted the impact of the rule that no one could be convicted on the uncorroborated evidence of children and the requirement that judges warn juries in sexual abuse/rape cases that it was dangerous to convict on the evidence of a single witness, the victim.[61] Sandra McAvoy has shown that this campaigning continued into the 1920s and 1930s as these women worked to challenge the assumption that 'as male sexual urges were uncontrollable, male sexual transgressions were excusable'.[62]

Steiner-Scott argues that the Irish Free State was not willing to 'accept new feminist theories about the nature of domestic violence' and so it 'continued to emphasize that the problem stemmed largely from an abuse of alcohol, not power'.[63] As with child abuse and neglect, wife beating was framed as a working-class problem. Indeed, there are many similarities in the social and official responses to child abuse and domestic violence against women: both issues increasingly 'went out of sight'[64] in the new Ireland after 1922, less frequently covered in the press (although there were still reports of convictions for unlawful carnal knowledge in the courts), and coded in the reports of relevant agencies and charities. The cultural idea of the family as a primary unit

58 E Steiner-Scott (1997) '"To Bounce a Boot Off Her Now And Then": Domestic Violence in Post-Famine Ireland' in MG Valiulis and M O'Dowd (eds), *Women and Irish History* (Dublin: Wolfhound Press), 125–143; L Ryan (2007) 'Publicising the Private: Suffragists' Critique of Sexual Abuse and Domestic Violence' in L Ryan and M Ward (eds), *Irish Women and the Vote: Becoming Citizens* (Dublin: Irish Academic Press), 75–89.

59 Cited in Steiner-Scott, '"To bounce a boot off her now and then"', p 142.

60 *Irish Citizen*, Jul 1919. Ryan (2007) 'Publicising the Private', p 82.

61 S McAvoy (2009) 'Sexual Crime and Irish Women's Campaign for a Criminal Law Amendment Act, 1912–35' in Valiulis (2009) *Gender and Power*, p 86.

62 McAvoy (2009) 'Sexual Crime', p 85.

63 Steiner-Scott, '"To Bounce a Boot Off Her Now and Then"', p 143.

64 Ferguson's phrase in relation to child deaths as a result of abuse. Ferguson, 'Surviving Irish Childhood', p 19.

of society afforded a selective policy of avoidance and interference depending on the 'type' of family in question. Undoubtedly, there were many middle-class women trapped behind the veneer of respectability with little choice but to live with violence in their home.[65] For working-class women it was the fear of the authorities (that non-interventionist State) that kept them quiet.[66] Angeline Kearns Blain, in her memoir of a 1930s Dublin childhood, notes her mother refused to get help when her husband began beating her because of 'fear and stigma'.[67] In her memoir Elaine Crowley also records her father's violence against her mother. Crowley's father beat her mother so severely that he broke several ribs and left her unable to consume anything but liquid for several days due to facial injuries. She petitioned for a barring order, which she was denied; instead the judge bound her husband over to keep the peace for two years. It was probably an injunction that Crowley's mother sought because prior to 1976 the only options open to women were to pursue a common law charge of breach of the peace, a criminal charge of assault or an injunction.[68] Crowley's aunt was not impressed with the court and her disbelief was undoubtedly shared by many wives:

> Bound him up and thrown him in the Liffey – that's what he [the judge] should have done. What in the name of Christ is the matter with men like him? Didn't he have all the evidence? What does a husband have to do – kill his wife before a judge sees the light of day?[69]

Criminalizing family violence: child sexual abuse and marital rape

The Second Wave Women's movement, which emerged in the early 1970s, played a crucial role in raising awareness of previously 'hidden' or taboo issues. While the movement has been criticized for failing to challenge

65 Urquhart cites the groundbreaking nature of the Irishwoman Louisa Westropp's divorce case in 1886, in which violence was the main grounds for divorce. In the 19 divorce petitions brought by Irishwomen after this case, adultery and cruelty were the most commonly cited grounds. Due to the cost of the procedure, all of these cases concerned wealthy families. Urquhart (2013) 'Irish Divorce and Domestic Violence, 1857–1922', pp 829–830.

66 Kearns' oral history of Dublin testifies to this fear among working-class women. KC Kearns (2004) *Dublin's Lost Heroines: Mammies and Grannies in a Vanished City* (Dublin: Gill & Macmillan), p 15, pp 81–93.

67 A Kearns Blains (2000) *Stealing Sunlight: Growing up in Irishtown* (Dublin: A & A Farmar), p 29.

68 An injunction was only obtainable in the Circuit Court or High Court and would have been expensive.

69 E Crowley (1996) *Cowslips and Chainies: A Memoir of Dublin in the 1930s* (Dublin: Lilliput Press), p 77 and pp 40, 82.

deeply held cultural assumptions regarding the housewife,[70] it was from this movement that vital resources such as the Rape Crisis Centre and various refuges emerged.[71] Several pieces of legislation introduced in the 1970s recognized the realities of modern family life, for example an unmarried mother's allowance in 1972 and the Family Law (Maintenance of Spouse & Children) Act in 1976, which allowed for a husband to be barred from the family home. However, official resistance remained when it came to extending the definition of rape to include marital rape. For example, when explaining why he was not willing to include marital rape in the Criminal Law (Rape) Act 1981 the Minister for Justice explained:

> I regard marriage as a very stable contract between two people, as provided for in our Constitution and which the very great majority of the people of this land support and adhere to. I feel that in any area where we are going to legislate, particularly an area as sensitive and as delicate as the area of marriage and matters between husbands and wives, we must be satisfied about how we should go about it.[72]

Mary Robinson, an active member of the women's movement and most associated with the campaign to legalize contraception in Ireland, echoed the sentiments of her feminist predecessors at the turn of the century when she asked the Minister:

> if we fail to extend the definition of rape to include marital rape, are we not, as legislators ... turning a blind eye on rape within marriage? Is there not an implication that we are somehow condoning it because it is within the marriage relationship and putting a higher reluctance to intrude on a marriage relationship than the need and the desire to protect a wife in those circumstances?[73]

She argued that recognizing marital rape as a crime was a key objective of the women's movement; however, despite her plea the fictitious sanctity of the family remained intact.

In the 1970s and 1980s various socially constructed issues were renegotiated and reformulated culturally and legally, for example the status of the

---

70 Cassidy notes there was no mention of the battered wife in Report of the Commission on the Status of Women, Dec 1972. M Cassidy (1987) *Domestic Violence Against Women* (Dublin: Social & Organisational Psychology Research Unit UCD), p 7.

71 L Connolly (2002) *The Irish Women's Movement: From Revolution to Devolution* (London: Palgrave Macmillan), p 90.

72 Criminal Law (Rape) Bill: Committee and Final Stages, *Seanad Éireann deb.*, xcv [1734] 29 Apr 1981.

73 Criminal Law (Rape) Bill, 1980: Second Stage, *Seanad Éireann deb,* xcv (14) [1368-1369] 1 Apr 1981.

unmarried mother and the concept of illegitimacy.[74] There were also ferocious debates about abortion and divorce.[75] Throughout the 1980s women's groups, social campaigners and scholars did much to demythologize marital relations and family life in Ireland. In 1987 Maeve Cassidy argued that the refusal to protect wives and children from violence in the home was 'neither good for the institution of marriage nor good for the institution of law'.[76] As the social discourse on the Irish family darkened, contemporaries began to increasingly make a connection between the physical and sexual abuse of women within marriage and the sexual abuse of children.[77] In fact, some contemporaries went as far as to situate abuse in a narrative of an unstable and inherently destructive modern family. For example, in 1988 Imelda Colgan McCarthy and Nollaig O'Reilly Byrne, both involved in family therapy, claimed: 'It is tempting, if alarming, to propose that the phenomenon of incest is the inevitable feature of profound structural changes in the social relations of the modern family'.[78] Indeed, it was a shocking case of child sexual abuse in the early 1990s, known as the Kilkenny incest case, that is generally regarded as pivotal in changing public views on familial violence.[79] Ferguson argues that the Kilkenny case was the 'powerful symbolic event to focus public and political' attention on the issue of violence against women and children.[80] The role played by the victim 'Mary' was also crucial as she appeared on the national television station the day after the trial and spoke of the abuse she suffered at the hands of her father.[81] Ferguson noted that the impact of the case was swift, leading to a reform of the sentencing for incest and an increase of the maximum penalty from seven to 20 years.

Ferguson situates the shift in the response to familial violence in the context of the collapse of the 'family centred ideology' that had hitherto resulted

74 Law Reform Commission (1982) *Report on Illegitimacy* (Dublin: Law Reform Commission) LRC 4/1982.

75 MJ Maguire (2001) 'The Changing Face of Catholic Ireland: Conservatism and Liberalism in the Anne Lovett and Kerry Babies Scandals', *Feminist Studies,* 27, 335–358.

76 Cassidy (1987) *Domestic Violence,* p 25.

77 Cassidy (1987) *Domestic Violence.*

78 I Colgan McCarthy and N O'Reilly Byrne (1988) 'Mis-Take Love: Conversations on the Problem of Incest in an Irish Context', *Family Process,* 27, 181–199.

79 This involved the sexual abuse of a daughter by her father over a 16-year period. See C McGuinness (1993) *The Report of Kilkenny Incest Investigation* (Dublin: Department of Health).

80 Ferguson (1993–1994) 'Abuse Inquiries and the Report of the Kilkenny Incest Investigation,' p 393. There is widespread agreement on the importance of this case to the wider social response to the familial violence. See Anderson (1998) 'Lawful Wife, Unlawful Sex', p 162, n 125; K Sheridan, 'Walls of Fear, Walls of Silence', *Irish Times,* 6 Mar 1993.

81 RTE legal correspondent Kieron Wood's book on the case, published in 1993, became a bestseller.

in the State's unwillingness to intervene in family life.[82] Indeed, a running theme through much of the professional debates on child abuse, incest and family violence was that the constitutional protection of the family had inhibited professionals and authorities when dealing with vulnerable children or women.[83] In her report into the Kilkenny incest case, Justice Catherine McGuinness suggested that 'the very high emphasis on the rights of the family in the Constitution may consciously or unconsciously be interpreted as giving a higher value to the right of parents than to the rights of children.'[84] However, as we have noted, when it wished to do so the State proved more than capable of removing thousands of children from their family home to fill the industrial schools of the country. The answer is more complex and rests at the heart of the cultural reluctance to interrogating heterosexual relations, patriarchal understandings of sex and the status of men and women within the family home. As Caroline Fennell notes, by its nature 'the criminal law and the criminal justice system are concerned with deviance: criminalizing what is a departure from the norm and constructing the reality of what is unacceptable by its definition.'[85] Hence, ideas about the family, appropriate gender roles, parenting norms and heterosexual relations all inform the criminal system every bit as much as they underpin the social and cultural constructions of deviance. While the law does not operate in a vacuum, it is also crucial to explore how the law, the operation of the courts and the words and actions of the judiciary inform wider society. Smart's tentative suggestion that 'it was the criminal trial and its attendant procedures which prevented any wide-scale reconceptualization of the harm of child sexual abuse' has implications for any study of the Republic of Ireland and the role played by the legal forum in the jurisdiction.[86]

Conclusion

Marital rape was finally criminalized in January 1991 with the introduction of the Criminal Law (Rape) (Amendment) Act 1990; however, this piece of legislation continued to treat the victims of rape as suspect. A victim's sexual history could still be admitted as evidence and a judge could still issue a jury with a warning that it was dangerous to rely on a victim's testimony. Moreover, court cases continued to reveal the social and legal propensity to consider violent stranger rape as the most serious form of rape thus, implicitly,

82 Ferguson (1993–1994) 'Abuse Inquiries', p 391.

83 See Chapter 13 in this volume.

84 Cited in Kennedy (2001) *From Cottage to Crèche,* p 123.

85 C Fennell (1993) 'Criminal Law and the Criminal Justice System: Women as Victim' in A Connelly (ed), *Gender and the Law in Ireland* (Dublin: Oak Tree Press), 151–170, p 151.

86 Smart (2000) 'Reconsidering the Recent History of Child Sexual Abuse, 1910–1960', p 66.

imposing a hierarchy in which the raped wife or partner is at the bottom of the scale. Writing several years after its enactment, Anderson concluded,

> effectively ... the wife in Ireland still does not receive the full protection of the law in cases of spousal rape, and the reality is that the husband rapist will probably receive special treatment over that given by the courts to a stranger rapist.[87]

Indeed, it took over 10 years before the first husband was convicted in the Irish courts for marital rape.[88] The endurance of deeply held cultural myths regarding the sanctity of the family is reflected in the 2001 plea by the National Women's Council of Ireland that 'the silence that blankets this pervasive social problem must be broken'. The Council also noted that it was in the civil and criminal justice arena that victims 'experienced the most devastating humiliation and disempowerment'.[89] Women found that the judiciary still reflected the cultural view that the notional integrity of the 'family' should trump the needs of victims of domestic violence. As one woman explained: 'In our local court it is difficult to obtain a barring order. The local judge in his wisdom tries his best to keep the "family" intact, usually requests the perpetrator to stop drinking and assures the victim that this will solve the problem.'[90]

Linda Gordon's groundbreaking 1989 study of the history of family violence in America has yet to be replicated for Ireland. This has serious implications for contemporary understanding of the subject because, as Gordon notes, 'distortions [are] created in the public discussion by the lack of a history'.[91] In the Irish context 'the lack of history' has required each generation of campaigners to restate the same discoveries time and again, while failing to connect the threads of continuity: the role of economic dependence, the voices that tend not to be heard (those of children, wives and the economically disadvantaged), the power of the concept of privacy in enabling abusers, and the role of class in allowing evasion. Only by considering the history of familial violence in its social, cultural and legal contexts can we begin to understand the implications of that history for how Irish society currently responds to crimes that happen behind closed doors.

87 Anderson (1998) 'Lawful Wife, Unlawful Sex', p 165.

88 First conviction did not come until Jul 2002: see *Irish Times,* 19 Jul 2002.

89 National Women's Council of Ireland (2001) *The Heart that Bites: Violence Against Women* (Dublin: National Women's Council), p 3.

90 National Women's Council of Ireland (2001) *The Heart that Bites,* p 19.

91 Gordon (1989) *Heroes of Their Own Lives,* p 2.

10

Murder in the Irish Family, 1930–1945

*Karen Brennan**

This study examines a sample of cases involving charges against persons for the murder of a family member that appeared at the Central Criminal Court during a 15-year period, between 1 January 1930 and 30 December 1944. The study focuses on convictions and sentences, and asks whether there are aspects to the disposition of these cases which indicate that the courts took a unique approach to family murders. This study also explores gendered aspects of the criminal justice response to family murder.

Methodology and overview of outcomes of criminal proceedings

The data for this study was obtained from the State Files and State Books for the Central Criminal Court (hereafter SFCCC and SBCCC respectively) held at the National Archives of Ireland. The SBCCC contains a record of cases where a person appeared at the Central Criminal Court on a charge,[1] providing information on the charge and the outcome of proceedings, including sentence. Potential cases involving family relationships, where the perpetrator and victim shared the same surname,[2] were identified from this record and the SFCCC for each case was consulted. The SFCCCs contain prosecution evidence against the defendant and include: statement(s) of the accused at time of arrest; certain trial exhibits, including photographs and maps of the scene; medical officer's report on the accused while on remand;

* The author expresses her sincere gratitude to staff at the National Archives of Ireland for their assistance and patience while this research was being undertaken and to the anonymous reviewers and Drs Niamh Howlin and Kevin Costello for their comments on earlier drafts.

1 The following SBCCCs were consulted: NAI, ID/33/68 (1927–1933), ID/24/129 (1928–1943), ID/11/92 (1933–1941), & ID/27/1 (1941–1945).

2 The limitations of this methodology are acknowledged, as not all family members will necessarily share the same surname. For example, one such case (Jane O'Brien) was identified when consulting the SFCCCs for other cases. There may be additional cases where the parties did not share the same surname, such as where the perpetrator or victim was a married sister.

and, most importantly, depositions given by witnesses at the preliminary investigation of the murder charge at the District Court.[3] The information in this record, however, is limited: while it indicates the circumstances of the case and the State's evidence against the accused, it provides no insight into what happened at the arraignment or trial stage of the proceedings, and, in particular, provides no indication of the evidence presented by the accused.

There are 27 cases in this sample involving 19 men and eight women charged with murdering a family member. The family relationships covered are cases where the victim was: a spouse; a (legitimate) child aged over one year; and a parent, sibling, or other relative, where the accused and victim resided together. Cases involving children aged under 12 months were excluded from this study, as the topic of infanticide has been covered extensively elsewhere.[4] These cases usually involved unmarried women who had concealed their pregnancies and given birth alone, killing the child at birth,[5] and present unique motivations and circumstances.[6]

Table 10.1 demonstrates the relationships between victims and accused persons. There were 27 victims,[7] a slight majority of whom were female. The adult female victims were all killed by men, usually their husbands and sons. On the other hand, in adult male victim cases the suspect was female in 60 per cent of cases, and was usually the wife of the victim (40 per cent of adult male cases). However, half of the adult male victims were brothers, and in these cases the perpetrator was usually male.

The outcome of criminal proceedings by gender of the perpetrator is provided in Table 10.2, and may be summarized as follows: less than a quarter of those appearing at the Central Criminal Court on murder charges were convicted; five offenders, all female, were acquitted; five offenders (mostly male) were convicted of manslaughter, in three cases following a guilty plea; finally, the most common disposal (40.7 per cent) involved an insanity-related finding, either unfitness to plead or a verdict of 'guilty but insane'.

Forty per cent of the sample was sentenced following either a murder or manslaughter conviction. Those convicted of murder were sentenced to

3 At the preliminary examination, the District Court determined whether the case could proceed to trial based on whether the prosecution had produced evidence upon which a jury could reasonably convict. See D Walsh (2002) *Criminal Procedure* (Dublin: Thomson Round Hall), pp 677–678.

4 See C Rattigan (2012) *'What Else Could I Do?' Single Mothers and Infanticide, Ireland 1900–1950* (Dublin: Irish Academic Press); K Brennan (2013) '"A Fine Mixture of Pity and Justice:" The Criminal Justice Response to Infanticide in Ireland 1922–1949', *Law and History Review*, 31(4), 793–841 and E Farrell (2013) *'A Most Diabolical Deed': Infanticide and Irish Society, 1850–1900* (Manchester: Manchester University Press).

5 For an account of the circumstances in which this offence was committed, see generally Rattigan (2012) *'What Else Could I Do?'* ch 1. See also Chapter 11 in this volume.

6 See Brennan (2013) '"A Fine Mixture of Pity and Justice"'.

7 In two cases involving offences against children, another child had also been targeted by the accused but had survived.

Table 10.1 Category of cases by relationship of victim to perpetrator and gender of perpetrators and victims

Category by relationship to perpetrator	*Total cases*		*Gender of perp*		*Gender of victim*	
	N.	*%*	*M*	*F*	*M*	*F*
Spouses	11	41	7	4	4	7
Child	4	15	2	2	2	2
Parent	5	18	5	0	0	5
Siblings	6	22	5	1	5	1
Other	1	4	0	1	1	0
Total	27	100	19	8	12	15

Percentages have been rounded to the nearest whole number

death, as was mandatory at the time, and the sentence was carried out in all but two cases. Five persons were sentenced for manslaughter, which carried a maximum sentence of penal servitude for life. The most severe sentence, 15 years' penal servitude, was imposed on John Cullen, convicted of manslaughter following a trial for the murder of his wife who had died from a

Table 10.2 Outcome of murder cases by gender of perpetrator

Outcome	*Total*		*Male*		*Female*	
	N.	%	N.	%	N.	%
Convicted	6	22	5	26	1	13
Acquitted	5	18	0	0	5	63
Manslaughter:	5	18	4	22	1	12
Plea	(3*)	(11)	(2)	(11)	(1)	(12)
Convicted	(2)	(7)	(2)	(11)	(0)	(0)
Incapable of pleading	7	27	6	31	1	12
Guilty but insane	4	15	4	21	0	0
Total	27	100	19	100	8	100

Percentages have been rounded to the nearest whole number

*In one case (Sullivan), where a man pleaded guilty to manslaughter on a charge of murdering his mother, his wife, who was co-accused of murder, also pleaded guilty to manslaughter and was given a 12-month prison sentence, suspended on entering into a recognizance to keep the peace and be of good behaviour for two years.

brutal assault.[8] In a similar case, shopkeeper Thomas Curley received five years' penal servitude. He admitted to stabbing his wife in the neck one night with a knife he had been using to cut rashers. He claimed in his statement that during the course of an argument she rushed at him and that he had accidentally stabbed her.[9] The two remaining male offenders were sentenced in connection with the manslaughter of their mothers. Patrick Dalton pleaded guilty having killed his mother as a result of an assault, and received five years' penal servitude.[10] Patrick Sullivan also pleaded guilty, having asphyxiated his mother by a 'violent crushing pressure' to the neck, and received three years' penal servitude.[11] Only one woman was convicted of manslaughter. Kate Reilly, a farmer's wife, pleaded guilty to the manslaughter of her two-year-old daughter. According to her Garda statement, she gave a grain of strychnine to each of her twin daughters in their tea, planning to take the remainder of the poison herself. Only one of her children ingested the poison and when she became ill, Kate immediately took her to a neighbour and admitted to what she had done. She was given a recognizance to keep the peace and be of good behaviour for 12 months and to enter St Mary Magdalene Convent at Donnybrook for 12 calendar months.[12]

Finally, 41 per cent of accused persons were ordered to be detained indefinitely at the Central Mental Hospital following a finding of unfitness to plead or a verdict of 'guilty but insane'.

Explaining the outcome

The context in which these cases were heard was one where murder was a capital offence. Although the death sentences were not always carried out,[13] murder convictions undoubtedly depended on prosecutorial, judicial and juror willingness to expose the defendant to the risk of execution.[14] Thus,

---

8 NAI, SFCCC ID/20/84 (Cullen, 1943); SBCCC ID/27/1 (Kildare, 1943).

9 NAI, SFCCC ID/56/27 (Curley, 1936); SBCCC ID/11/92 (Galway, 1936).

10 NAI, SFCCC ID/75/39 (Dalton, 1934); SBCCC ID/11/92 (Waterford, 1934).

11 NAI, SFCCC ID/11/93 (Sullivan, 1939); SBCCC ID/11/92 (Cork, 1939). His wife, who also pleaded guilty to manslaughter, received a suspended sentence.

12 NAI, SFCCC ID//60/56 (Reilly, 1937); SBCCC ID/11/92 (Cavan, 1937).

13 G O'Brien (2006) 'Capital Punishment in Ireland, 1922–1964' in N Dawson (ed) *Reflections on Law and History: Irish Legal History Society Discourses and Other Papers, 2000–2005* (Dublin: Four Courts Press), 223–258, p 236. The Governor General, and after 1937, the President, had the power to commute the sentence on the advice of the government.

14 Judges' summations of the evidence and instructions with regard to possible verdicts likely had an impact on the outcome in many cases: see T Carey (2013) *Hanged for Murder: Irish State Executions* (Cork: Collins Press), pp 10–11.

there may be cases involving a non-capital disposal where on the evidence the accused had met the requirements for a murder conviction.[15]

Overall, less than a quarter of the cases in this study resulted in a murder conviction. Although it might be suggested that the courts were particularly reticent about convicting of a capital offence in cases of family murder, without information on the overall murder conviction rate, particularly for non-family killings, such a conclusion is highly speculative. In an effort to try to identify whether the courts were influenced by the family context in adjudicating the cases in this sample, the criminal justice response in these cases will be analysed under the following themes: explaining the differences between manslaughter and murder convictions; explaining acquittals; the use of insanity-related disposals; and the use of the death penalty. This analysis will demonstrate that in general decisions in relation to the outcome in these cases were likely affected by factors connected with the circumstances of the killing in a context where murder was a capital offence and the impact of gender on criminal justice outcomes, rather than the relationship between the offender and victim per se. However, some suggestions do emerge from this analysis with regard to the impact of the family context in connection with cases involving pre-existing abuse and in cases involving insanity findings.

Explaining murder and manslaughter convictions

Five cases in the sample resulted in a manslaughter conviction (just over 18 per cent), in three cases following a guilty plea. A comparison of cases resulting in murder convictions against those resulting in manslaughter convictions indicates key factual differences which may explain the outcome. These differences do not necessarily mean that in cases where a manslaughter conviction resulted that the offender had not killed with malice aforethought, a concept which required neither malice, nor forethought, but which was widely construed to cover some reckless as well as intentional killings. They do indicate, however, that the absence or presence of certain aggravating

15 Murder, a common law offence, was defined as the unlawful killing of a 'reasonable creature *in rerum natura*' with malice aforethought: E Coke (1644), *Third Part of the Institutes of the Laws of England Concerning High Treason, and Other Pleas of the Crown, and Criminal Causes* (London), 47. The scope of the offence of murder has varied over time and in the earlier part of the twentieth century was wider than it is currently construed. It covered not only intentional killings, but killings where the defendant had foreseen death or serious harm as a probable outcome of his conduct. It also encompassed killings committed in the course of a felony where the defendant had foreseen death as a possibility. Manslaughter covered unlawful killings without malice aforethought, or murders where the defendant successfully pleaded the defence of provocation. Provocation was available at common law as a partial defence to murder where the defendant had killed 'in a passion', essentially where he lost self-control in response to a provocation that would have been sufficient to have caused a similar reaction in a reasonable man: see F McAuley and P McCutcheon (2000) *Criminal Liability: A Grammar* (Dublin: Round Hall, Sweet and Maxwell), pp 290–293, 849–856.

factors had an impact on perceptions of the moral culpability of the accused and, consequently, whether they deserved a capital conviction.[16]

First, while premeditation was not a requirement for murder, cases resulting in capital convictions tended to have involved circumstances of premeditation and in some cases previous attempts to kill the victim.[17] The evidence tended to suggest that the killing had been committed 'in cold blood'. Only one of the murder convictions in this sample (Griffin) involved an unplanned violent attack committed in a state of intoxication. The fact that the accused left his bedroom to fetch a hatchet from the shed, which he then used to kill his semi-sleeping wife, may, however, have indicated some element of forethought.[18]

In contrast, four out of the five manslaughter convictions involved unpremeditated attacks. Two men were convicted by juries of the manslaughter of their wives. Each case (Cullen and Curley) involved a sudden unplanned attack in the context of an alleged confrontation with their spouse. In both cases, however, the evidence suggested that the accused had previously been violent towards the victim, and in one of these cases the fatal attack was particularly brutal.[19] At least one of the other male manslaughter cases (Sullivan) took place in the context of pre-existing abuse of the victim by the accused. Sullivan pleaded guilty to the manslaughter of his mother, who had been manually strangled. There was medical and other evidence to indicate that the killing took place in the context of sustained abuse against the victim. The accused had also attempted to cover up the killing by not reporting it immediately and claiming, when the death was reported, that his mother had fallen down the stairs.[20]

The fact that the killings in these cases were not premeditated and did not appear to have been committed 'in cold blood' may partly explain the outcome. Such killings may have been interpreted as being less morally blameworthy and thus not deserving of a capital conviction. In this regard, it is worth noting that the partial defence of provocation would have aligned well with such perceptions, the historical rationale for that defence being that a killing arising in the context of a sudden quarrel or a 'chance medley' was less blameworthy than a cold-blooded killing.[21]

16 See the material at n 15.

17 For example, there is evidence in the files that O'Shea and Fleming made previous attempts to kill their wives; NAI, SFCCC ID/22/84 (O'Shea, 1943); SFCCC ID/33/63 (Fleming, 1933). Patrick McDermott had shot his brother dead on the road outside their farmhouse one night, earlier that day procuring a shotgun and cartridges from a neighbour; NAI, SFCCC IC/95/71 (McDermott, 1932). See also Carey (2013), *Hanged for Murder*, for further detail on these cases.

18 NAI, SFCCC ID/22/83 (Griffin, 1943); SBCCC ID/27/1.

19 See NAI, SFCCC ID/20/84 (Cullen, 1943), SBCCC ID/27/1 (Kildare, 1943), SFCCC ID/56/27 (Curley, 1936), SBCCC ID/11/92 (Galway, 1936).

20 See NAI, SFCCC ID/11/93 (Sullivan, 1939), SBCCC ID/11/92 (Cork, 1939).

21 See the material at n 15.

However, at least three of the four male manslaughter cases involved very violent assaults in the context of pre-existing abuse, and while a lack of premeditation may have legitimately led to reluctance to convict of the capital crime, another plausible explanation is that that the courts did not take domestic violence seriously. In the two cases involving a manslaughter conviction following a contested trial (Curley and Cullen), both involved wife-killing. It is unclear from the evidence whether the jury concluded that the defendant did not have the *mens rea* for murder, or had accepted a provocation plea.[22] Given the wide scope of murder at the time, and the nature and level of violence in these cases, it seems implausible that there was no malice aforethought. However, provocation may have been successfully pleaded in these cases if it was accepted that the defendant had killed his wife 'in a passion', during a domestic argument, having lost self-control in response to alleged provocative conduct from the deceased.[23] The gendered nature of the criminal law and its application in the context of wife-killing is well known, particularly with respect to the provocation defence, and has been highlighted by feminist writers.[24] Provocation, as traditionally characterized, has been criticized on the ground that it is inherently 'male' in origin and in nature, its basis being that of righteous male anger in response to provocations which included a wife's unfaithfulness.[25] The defence often allowed controlling, possessive and angry men who killed their wives to be treated leniently, even where the supposed provocation was minor in nature; on the other hand, women who killed their abusive husbands struggled to be accommodated within this defence.[26] Although this Irish sample is very small, it does raise important questions about perceptions of unpremeditated male violence in the domestic setting, particularly in the context of previous abuse, and the gendered operation of the law in this regard.

A second factual difference between manslaughter and murder cases is that murder convictions tended to involve the use of a gun or other weapon,[27] whereas only one manslaughter case (Curley) involved the use of a weapon, a knife, though one other case did involve the use of poison (Reilly).[28] In

22 See the material at n 15.

23 See the material at n 15.

24 For example, see J Radford (1982) 'Marriage Licence or Licence to Kill? Womenslaughter and the Criminal Law', *Feminist Review*, 11, 88–96; S Edwards (1985) 'Male Violence Against Women: Excusatory and Explanatory Ideologies in Law and Society', in S Edwards (ed) *Gender, Sex and the Law* (London: Croom Helm), 183–216.

25 SSM Edwards (2010) 'Anger and Fear as Justifiable Preludes for Loss of Self Control', *Journal of Criminal Law*, 74(3), 223–241, p 226; C Wells (2000), 'Provocation: The Case for Abolition', in A Ashworth and B Mitchell (eds) *Rethinking English Homicide Law* (Oxford: Oxford University Press), 85–106, pp 87–88.

26 Wells (2000), 'Provocation', pp 91–94.

27 In Kirwin's case, no cause of death was established (NAI, SFCCC ID/20/103 (Kirwin, 1942)).

28 See NAI, SFCCC ID//60/56 (Reilly, 1937).

the three remaining cases, the accused had killed in the course of a physical attack.[29] Third, evidence in murder conviction cases tended to suggest that the killing had been done for the purpose of gain, either financial (usually a grievance over inheritance), or to rid the accused of an unwanted relative (usually a wife). None of the manslaughter cases appear to have been committed for personal gain.

Finally, three of the murder conviction cases also involved a cover-up of the crime or denial of guilt by the accused. Three of the manslaughter cases involved a guilty plea. In at least two cases the evidence suggested that the accused would have met the requirements for murder. In one case, the accused had poisoned her daughter with an evident intention to kill; in the other case, the accused had strangled his mother with a 'violent crushing pressure' and had initially tried to disguise his involvement in her death. In the three remaining manslaughter cases, two of which resulted from a jury verdict, the accused had admitted to killing the victim in the immediate aftermath of the crime, though in two of these cases they did try to minimize their blameworthiness in this regard.

The factors identified here as having delineated capital from non-capital convictions were likely also relevant in non-family murder cases. In this regard, the family context in which the killing took place may have had little impact on the outcome. However, given that four of those convicted of manslaughter were men who killed their wives or mothers in the context of violent assault, and that at least three of these cases involved pre-existing domestic abuse, it is suggested that perceptions about the seriousness of domestic abuse and the gendered nature and operation of the criminal law may have played a part in the outcome. Further research is needed on this point.

Explaining acquittals: a question of gender?

Five cases in this sample resulted in an acquittal at trial. Notably, the five acquittals all involved female accused. The fact that 83.3 per cent of women who appeared before a jury on a murder charge at the Central Criminal Court were acquitted, while none of the male defendants were, raises the question of whether the gender of the accused had an impact on the outcome. In this regard, feminist literature has highlighted a tendency towards lenient treatment of *some* female offenders which is linked to the perception of the offender as a woman: while 'good' women can expect lenient outcomes, 'bad' women receive harsher disposals. In connection with violent female offenders, gendered constructions (for example, that she is 'mad', 'bad', 'sad') operate, in a context where women are stereotypically viewed as

29 See NAI, SFCCC ID/20/84 (Cullen, 1943); SBCCC ID/27/1 (Kildare, 1943), SFCCC ID/75/39 (Dalton, 1934), SBCCC ID/11/92 (Waterford, 1934) and SFCCC ID/11/93 (Sullivan, 1939), SBCCC ID/11/92 (Cork, 1939).

being inherently passive and non-violent, to explain their violent acts (e.g. as irrational or evil) and to deny their agency. This serves to preserve notions of ideal womanhood; disguise the social, economic and political causes of female violence; and neutralize the challenge female violence poses to patriarchal structures.[30]

As noted, the Irish criminal justice system was notoriously averse to convicting women charged with murdering their infants. This was certainly related to the offender's gender and her position as an unmarried mother in Irish society.[31] Further, the use of the death penalty in Ireland was highly gendered. Doyle and O'Donnell found that between 1923 and 1964 men were half as likely to be executed as they were to be reprieved; while only one in 10 capital sentences against women were actually carried out.[32] The last Irish execution of a female murderer, Annie Walsh, convicted of murdering her husband, took place in 1925.[33] In the only case involving a murder conviction against a woman in this sample (Jane O'Brien), the jury recommended a reprieve on the death sentence in light of the age and *sex* of the offender.

An analysis of the SFCCCs for the five acquittal cases, however, suggests that while juries, and the trial judges who instructed them, may have been influenced by the sex of the offender, to varying degrees each of these acquittals may be explained on the basis of evidential deficiencies, the most significant of which was establishing that the accused had killed the deceased.[34] First, none of the women acquitted of murder admitted to any involvement in causing the death, whereas four of the seven males convicted by a jury of murder or manslaughter had admitted their involvement. The only woman convicted of murder had admitted to committing the act, and the only woman convicted of manslaughter pleaded guilty. Second, those convicted had caused death through violent acts – shootings, beatings, and attacks with knives, hatchets, and other instruments – and had usually done so in circumstances involving the immediate detection of their crime, because, for

30 For example, see generally, F Heidensohn (1985) *Women and Crime* (London: Macmillan), p 32; F Heidensohn (1989) *Crime and Society* (Basingstoke: Palgrave Macmillan), p 102; SSM Edwards (1984) *Women on Trial: A Study of the Female Suspect, Defendant and Offender in the Criminal Law and the Criminal Justice System* (Manchester: Manchester University Press), pp 80–85 and 91–100; H Allen (1987) *Justice Unbalanced: Gender, Psychiatry and Judicial Decisions* (Open University Press); B Morrissey (2003) *When Women Kill: Questions of Agency and Subjectivity* (London: Routledge); L Seal (2010) *Women, Murder and Femininity: Gender Representations of Women who Kill* (Basingstoke: Palgrave Macmillan); S Weare (2013), '"The Mad", "The Bad", "The Victim": Gendered Constructions of Women Who Kill in the Criminal Justice System', *Laws*, 2, 337–361.

31 See generally literature cited at n 4.

32 DM Doyle and I O'Donnell (2012) 'The Death Penalty in Post-Independence Ireland', *Journal of Legal History*, 33(1), 65–91, pp 73–75.

33 Doyle and O'Donnell (2012) 'The Death Penalty', p 73.

34 See NAI: SFCCC IC/94/55 (Walsh, 1931); ID/44/44 (Conway, 1934); ID/33/66 (Shanley, 1933); ID/44/48 (Hanley, 1934; Doherty, 1934).

example, the offence was committed at or near the victim's home and/or because there were witnesses at or near the scene of the crime. As such, it was difficult (and pointless) to try to disguise their involvement in the victim's death. Four of the acquittal cases involved poisoning – an inherently secretive act – and in the fifth case the body of the victim had been found almost a week after his disappearance at a distance away from his home, the suspected scene of the crime. In each, the method of killing or the disposal of the body meant it would have been more difficult to prove the accused's involvement.

Poisoning cases posed particular difficulties. Even where medical evidence identified poison in the victim's system, this did not always conclusively prove to be the cause of death. In one case the post-mortem examination indicated that the most likely cause of death was heart failure as a result of an existing disease, though the medical expert did note that death *might* have been brought on by poisoning in conjunction with disease.[35] In the remaining three poisoning cases, death was solely attributed to strychnine poisoning. However, difficulties then arose in establishing that it was the accused who had administered the poison, particularly given the absence of a confession. This may have been a crucial factor in the decision to acquit in these cases.

For example, recently married Anne Hanley claimed that her husband, Phelim, had become ill on the evening of his death, and that she had given him a bottle of his usual medicine and then left him alone in the bedroom to take this; when she returned his condition had worsened and he died shortly afterwards. Anne and her husband were alone at the time, and it seems the only possible alternatives were that he had either accidentally or deliberately taken the poison himself or that she had administered it to him. At trial the jury failed to reach a verdict; she was acquitted at a second trial.[36] There was convincing circumstantial evidence of motive to kill in this case. The marriage had been the result of a match[37] which Anne had almost immediately tried to rescind; Phelim, however, had refused to reimburse her the money she had paid out on the marriage settlement. Witness depositions indicate that after the marriage Anne was very unhappy with both her new home and her husband. Prior to the match, she had been involved in a relationship with another man, and it appears that she regretted ending that relationship. Her reaction to her husband's death also appeared to raise suspicions among observers: while Anne behaved in a rather dramatic and hysterical fashion, it seems she failed, according to witnesses, to exhibit true indications of grief and, in particular, did not shed a tear.[38] Overall, there was circumstantial

35 NAI, SFCCC ID/33/66 (Shanley, 1933).

36 NAI, SFCCC ID//44/88 (Hanley, 1934), SBCCC ID/11/92 (Roscommon, 1934).

37 Deirdre McGowan discusses matches in Chapter 8.

38 NAI, SFCCC ID//44/88 (Hanley, 1934); SBCCC ID/11/92 (Roscommon, 1934).

evidence in this case to point to the accused having murdered her husband. Nonetheless, two juries failed to find her guilty of the crime.

The non-poisoning acquittal case also presented evidential difficulties in terms of proving that the accused had killed the victim. The victim, Patrick Doherty, had been found dead in a bog-hole almost a week after he had disappeared from the home he shared with his sister, Mary Kate Doherty. His death resulted from head injuries. The State's case was that Mary Kate had killed Patrick at their home, then disposed of the body with the help of a neighbour (the co-accused). However, the delay between the killing and the discovery of the body, and the fact that the body was not found at the scene of the crime, made it difficult to establish that Mary Kate had been responsible for her brother's murder.[39] The evidence against her centred on her motive to kill Patrick, thought to relate to the consequences of their mother's will. A longstanding family dispute had left Mary Kate, in her early thirties at the time of her brother's murder, unable to claim her £100 inheritance. Like many unmarried women at the time who had remained and worked on the family farm, Mary Kate received pocket money but was unpaid.[40] Without her inheritance, it is likely that she would not have been able to attain financial autonomy and personal independence. It seems that she had previously had the opportunity to emigrate to America, but that her two brothers refused permission on the grounds that she was 'too advanced in her years'. These circumstances certainly indicate a plausible motive. However, during Garda questioning Mary Kate denied any knowledge of the contents of her mother's will and claimed that she and Patrick 'were on the best of terms', and 'as happy as any two in the land'.[41] Other evidence included inconsistencies between Mary Kate's account of Patrick's movements the night before he disappeared and those of other witnesses. Traces of human blood were found on household items, the kitchen floor was 'scrupulously' clean, parts of the kitchen wall had been recently whitewashed, and the kitchen dresser had been recently painted red. Furthermore, she did not report her brother missing.[42]

A review of the five acquittal cases indicates that in general these acquittals were not necessarily against overwhelming evidence of guilt. In this regard, it is important to remember that an acquittal at trial does not necessarily mean that the jury believed the accused to be innocent, and may only indicate that the jury had a reasonable doubt as to guilt. The mode of killing (usually poisoning), or the distance between the crime and the subsequent discovery of

39 NAI, ID/44/48 (Doherty, 1934).

40 C Clear (2004), '"Too Fond of Going": Female Emigration and Change for Women in Ireland, 1946–1961', in D Keogh, F O'Shea and C Quinlan (eds) *The Lost Decade: Ireland in the 1950s* (Cork: Mercier Press), p 139.

41 NAI, ID/44/48 (Doherty, 1934).

42 NAI, ID/44/48 (Doherty, 1934).

the body, were surely problematic and the female acquittals are probably, to a varying degree, attributable to the fact that the evidence failed to convince the jury beyond all reasonable doubt that the accused had committed the offence.

However, there were male murder convictions where the evidence appears to have been no more convincing than in some of the female acquittals. In the case of Bernard Kirwin, who denied killing his brother Laurence, the remains found in a local bog six months after Laurence went missing could not be definitely identified and there was no evidence as to the cause of death.[43] In contrast, in one of the female acquittal cases, the accused, charged with murdering her husband, was acquitted notwithstanding the following pieces of evidence: (1) she admitted to giving her husband a glass of lemonade prior to his death (though she did not admit to putting poison in this); (2) scientific tests established the presence of poison in the glass; (3) she admitted to drinking out of the glass prior to giving it to her husband; (4) the pocket of her coat was also found to contain strychnine; (5) she had forged a letter from her previous employer for the purpose of purchasing strychnine poison at a chemist.[44]

However, while the jury's perception of the offender may have affected their assessment of the evidence, this may not necessarily have been along gender lines. For example, Kirwin's previous conviction, resulting in penal servitude, may have been influential. The problem with reviewing the data in the SFCCC is that it provides no indication of what happened at trial, particularly in terms of what prosecution evidence was admitted; how the defence was conducted; how convincing the witness evidence appeared to be; how persuasive the prosecution's case was as a whole when played out live in court; and how the trial judge directed the jury. In this regard, caution must be taken when assessing the evidence against the accused in the SFCCC. What might appear to be convincing or not convincing on paper in the context of a deposition at the District Court may have had an entirely different hue when presented during testimony at trial.

Based on the limited evidence available in the SFCCC, these five cases suggest that evidential deficiencies were a key factor in the female acquittals. However, it is possible that gender, as well as other factors, played a part in the assessment of the evidence. For example, constructions of women murder accused as 'good' or 'bad', or difficulties in acknowledging female agency, rationality and violence, may have impacted on how the judge and jury responded to and interpreted the evidence, leading to a greater tendency to acquit women in cases where the evidence was not conclusive of guilt. Further research is needed.

43 NAI, SFCCC ID/20/103 (Kirwin, 1942).

44 NAI, SFCCC IC/94/51 (Walsh, 1931). Possibly, however, some of this evidence was not admitted at trial.

Insanity and fitness to plead

The most significant factor in accounting for the low number of murder convictions in this sample is the number of insanity-related disposals. Forty per cent of the sample was disposed of either on a finding of unfitness to plead or 'guilty but insane'.[45] Indeed, a quarter were not tried for murder because they were found 'insane and incapable of pleading' (unfit to plead); almost a quarter of those who were tried were found 'guilty but insane'. The extensive use of insanity-related disposals may appear surprising. However, this was not an uncommon response to murder charges in Ireland. Kilcommins et al. refer to a 1962 Department of Justice memorandum in relation to the abolition of capital punishment which indicated that just over half of murder charges during the period from the end of the Second World War to 1962 were disposed of on the basis of an insanity finding.[46] While the overall use of the unfitness to plead procedure declined significantly after 1920, it remained an attractive option in murder cases.[47]

The high proportion of insanity-related findings in this and other studies raises the prospect that unfitness to plead and the insanity defence operated as devices to secure a more lenient outcome in capital cases. In this regard, the circumstances of the killing in most of the insanity cases in this sample were different to those in the manslaughter and murder cases: they usually involved extreme violence with the use of a weapon, but without evidence of premeditation or motive; and while these were generally not 'cold-blooded' killings, neither could it be said that they took place in a context which might have justified a manslaughter conviction based on the absence of *malice aforethought* or the provocation defence. As such, if it was thought that the offender did not deserve a capital conviction, possibly an insanity finding presented a suitable alternative. The question then arises: were these insanity-related disposals justified on the law and the evidence, or were both manipulated to avoid a capital conviction?

In relation to the insanity defence, though the English McNaghten Rules applied in Ireland,[48] the Court of Criminal Appeal had stated in 1935 that

---

45 A finding of unfitness to plead was concerned with the accused's ability to stand trial. A finding of 'guilty but insane' related to the use of the insanity defence at trial. See below at n 48 and 51.

46 S Kilcommins, I O'Donnell, E O'Sullivan and B Vaughan (2004) *Crime, Punishment and the Search for Order in Ireland* (Dublin: Institute of Public Administration), p 55, n 58.

47 P Gibbons, N Mulryan, A McAleer and A O'Connor (1999) 'Criminal Responsibility and Mental Illness in Ireland 1850-1995: Fitness to Plead', *Irish Journal of Psychological Medicine,* 16(2), 51–56, p 54. See also RJ O'Hanlon (1968), 'Not Guilty Because of Insanity', *Irish Jurist,* 3(1) (ns), 61–77, p 63.

48 *R v McNaghten* (1843) 10 Cl & F 200. Under these rules, the defence is available where the defendant: (1) had a defect of reason; (2) caused by a disease of the mind; (3) where this caused him to not know the nature and quality of his act, or to not know that his act was wrong. English authorities interpreted these rules very narrowly. See generally: F McAuley (1993) *Insanity, Psychiatry and Criminal Responsibility* (Dublin: Round Hall), pp 31–44; McAuley and McCutcheon (2000) *Criminal Liability*, pp 644–666.

they did not constitute a comprehensive account of the law governing insanity as a defence.[49] However, the scope of the Irish insanity defence remained undefined and, though juries were possibly being directed in terms falling outside the McNaghten Rules, it is unclear how far judges went in this regard.[50] Unlike the defence of insanity, which is concerned with the defendant's responsibility for the crime, unfitness to plead focuses on the accused's mental state at the time of trial, not at the time the offence was committed, and their ability, in light of any physical or mental condition, to follow and engage with the criminal trial. A finding of unfitness to plead meant that the trial could not take place at that time. However, while the criteria for unfitness to plead were well established, these may not have been strictly applied in practice.[51]

The documents found in the SFCCCs analysed in this study do not include detailed medical reports, and information on the accused's mental condition is limited to brief comments made by the prison medical officer and/or the observations of non-medical witnesses. It is impossible, therefore, to consider the extent to which these insanity findings were justified on the basis of the legal requirements for fitness to plead/insanity. In only two of the seven cases involving a finding of unfitness to plead did the prison medical officer's report indicate that the accused was unfit;[52] in one of these cases the accused had a pre-existing mental condition, having spent time as an inpatient at a mental asylum.[53] In another case, where a woman had killed her young child, the medical officer noted in his report that she was depressed and suffered from goitre, a physical condition which could produce mental abnormality. Her behaviour on the night of the killing also indicated that she had committed the act in a mentally disturbed state. One witness observed: 'she was wild and hysterical her hair was all astray' and another noted: 'her eyes starting going in and out. They were like glass in her head'.[54] Another man, charged with shooting his brother dead one Sunday afternoon at their home after Mass, also, according to family members, had an existing mental health condition for which he had been receiving treatment.[55] In another case involving the killing of a brother, another brother of the accused indicated that he

49 *Attorney General v O'Brien* [1936] IR 263.

50 See generally, F McAuley (1993) *Insanity, Psychiatry and Criminal Responsibility*, pp 42–44; O'Hanlon (1968), 'Not Guilty Because of Insanity', pp 69–77.

51 See McAuley (1993) *Insanity, Psychiatry and Criminal Responsibility*, pp 139–140. According to *R v Pritchard* (1836) 7 C & P 303, the question of a defendant's fitness to plead focused on their ability to: (1) plead to the indictment; (2) understand the course of the proceedings; (3) instruct counsel; (4) challenge jurors; (5) understand the evidence.

52 NAI, SFCCC IC/94/53 (BP, 1933); ID/56/23 (TA, 1935). The names of those found unfit to plead or guilty but insane have not been revealed to preserve anonymity.

53 ID/56/23 (TA, 1935).

54 NAI, SFCCC ID/19/7 (EM, 1938).

55 NAI, SFCCC ID/56/26 (CD, 1938).

may have been suffering from an undiagnosed mental health condition. The behaviour of the accused on the day of the killing also indicated that he was not fully cognizant of what he had done, and a Garda witness stated that he had not taken a statement from the accused in light of his assessment of his mental condition at the time.[56] There was less obvious evidence of physical or mental disability in the remaining two unfitness to plead cases. However, the accused in one case, who had killed his young son one afternoon in what appears to have been an act of random violence, said at arrest 'my nerves got the better of me'.[57] The other man, accused of killing his wife one afternoon after she refused to give him a cigarette, behaved in a violent manner at the time of arrest and had to be restrained; he was also charged with attempted suicide.[58]

In only one of the four 'guilty but insane' verdicts is there an indication that the accused had a mental condition. In that case the accused, who killed his mother, had a history of mental illness and had spent time as an inpatient in a mental hospital.[59] In another case involving a 'guilty but insane' verdict the accused, who had also killed his mother, was violent and in a highly excited state at the time of arrest; he had to be restrained.[60] In the two remaining cases there is little evidence in the SFCCC to suggest that the accused had a mental abnormality, though presumably, medical evidence was provided at trial to support the insanity defence. Interestingly, unlike in the other insanity cases in the sample, the accused in both cases had attempted to conceal the killing; their relationship with their victim (a wife and a mother) appears to have been fractious; and they had a clear motive to kill in terms of what they would gain from the victim's death.[61]

Prior notes the possibility of nineteenth-century defendants being able to feign temporary mental illness in order to successfully plead insanity, thus securing an order for indefinite detention rather than a conviction for a capital offence.[62] Possibly some offenders in this sample were similarly able to manipulate the law. As indicated above, whatever the precise legal requirements for either the defence of insanity or a finding of unfit to plead, the courts may have stretched the law in some cases, and this may have been linked with the objective of avoiding a capital trial or conviction. This is not to say, however, that most or all of these offenders did not warrant an insanity finding. On the whole, while the evidence in the SFCCC is clearly

56 NAI, SFCCC ID/20/103 (EL, 1940).

57 NAI, SFCCC ID/19/7 (TM, 1940).

58 NAI, SFCCC IC/95/72 (JB, 1932); SBCCC ID/33/68 (Galway, 1932).

59 NAI, SFCCC ID/95/73 (HF, 1932)

60 NAI, SFCCC ID/94/67 (MMcC, 1931)

61 NAI, SFCCC ID/22/83 (TF, 1943); ID/56/26 (EB, 1936).

62 P Prior (2005) 'Murder and Madness: Gender and the Insanity Defence in Nineteenth-Century Ireland', *New Hibernia Review*, 9(4), 19–36, pp 29–31.

limited in terms of what it indicates about the accused's mental state, it does appear that many of the insanity findings had some basis in the sense that the accused appears to have had some kind of mental abnormality or history of mental illness. Further, most of these cases appeared to have involved random and inexplicable acts of violence, something which may have helped to support the conclusion that the killing was the result of a disturbed mental state. However, the high number of insanity findings does indicate that there was possibly some manipulation of the evidence and the law in order to avoid the death penalty.

The high number of insanity-related disposals must be viewed in the wider context of extensive institutionalization of the general population in mental institutions at that time.[63] Institutionalization in mental asylums intensified with the foundation of the Irish Free State.[64] Indeed, in the 1930s, Ireland had the highest rate of institutionalization for the 'insane and mentally defective' in Europe.[65] The institutionalization of non-criminal members of the population says something about how the State, families and communities dealt with troublesome and vulnerable individuals, namely through medicalization and institutional control.[66] It is thus not surprising that some kinds of violent criminal behaviour were also understood and managed in this way. Further, in this context, where a significant portion of the non-criminal population were institutionalized in mental hospitals, an order for indefinite detention may not have appeared a particularly harsh outcome and, since it involved the potential for early release,[67] may have presented a lenient course where the alternative was a capital conviction.

Only one woman was found unfit to plead; none successfully relied on insanity at trial. In contrast, slightly more than half of the male sample was disposed of on an insanity finding. This appears to be part of a continued trend in the disposition of male homicide offenders in Ireland. Gibbons et al., in their study of committals following a verdict of 'guilty but insane' to the Central Mental Hospital during the period 1850–1995 found a five to

63 See also Chapter 8.

64 I O'Donnell and E O'Sullivan (eds) (2012) *Coercive Confinement in Ireland: Patients, Prisoners and Penitents* (Manchester: Manchester University Press), p 10. See also Gibbons et al. (1999) 'Criminal Responsibility and Mental Illness', pp 53–54; BD Kelly (2008) 'Poverty, Crime and Mental Illness: Female Forensic Psychiatric Committal in Ireland, 1910–1948', *Social History of Medicine*, 21(2), 311–328, p 314. See generally M Finnane (1981) *Insanity and the Insane in Post-Famine Ireland* (London: Croom Helm).

65 O'Donnell and O'Sullivan (2012) *Coercive Confinement*, p 10.

66 See generally, O'Donnell and O'Sullivan (2012) *Coercive Confinement.*

67 P Gibbons, N Mulryan and A O'Connor (1997) 'Guilty but Insane: The Insanity Defence in Ireland', *British Journal of Psychiatry*, 170, 467–472, p 469; Prior (2005) 'Murder and Madness', p 31. However, see Gibbons et al. (1999) 'Criminal Responsibility and Mental Illness', p 53, which shows that average length of detention for those following an unfitness to plead finding was 14.3 years, with almost 50 per cent of the sample remaining at the Central Mental Hospital until their death.

one male to female ratio in terms of insanity verdicts.[68] Prior, in her study of the insanity defence in Ireland during the late nineteenth century, states, '[t]he main conclusion to be drawn is that the use of the insanity defence was highly gendered'.[69] In particular, men tended to have successfully relied on this defence in connection with the killing of a female family member; women who killed men usually did not rely on this defence.[70] Gibbons et al. have also noted the tendency to use the insanity defence in family killings: 60 per cent of their sample had committed a crime against a family member.[71] They also found that 44 per cent of men committed to the Central Mental Hospital following an unfitness to plead procedure between 1850 and 1995 had been charged with a crime against a family member; 93 per cent of the female cases involved a crime of violence against their family, usually a child.[72]

Contemporary analyses of female violence note a tendency to 'medicalize' female offenders. Constructing the violent woman as 'mad' means her violence is interpreted as irrational and non-agentic, and attention is thus diverted from the social, economic and political causes of her offending.[73] While infanticide statutes are considered a classic example of this medicalization thesis,[74] it is of interest to note that unfitness to plead/insanity were rarely used in infanticide cases in the decades preceding the enactment of the Irish Infanticide Act 1949.[75] The findings in this study, which indicate that slightly over half of the male killers in this sample were disposed of on the basis of an insanity-related verdict, raise a question about whether some male killers were similarly medicalized, particularly in the context of family violence.

Due to the size of this sample and the fact that no non-family comparator sample is available it is impossible to draw any reliable conclusion on this issue. However, it might be suggested that insanity/unfitness operated to explain what might otherwise have appeared, to the 'rational' observer, to be an inexplicable act of male violence against a family member. In this regard,

68 Gibbons et al. (1997) 'Guilty But Insane', p 470.

69 Prior (2005) 'Murder and Madness', p 35.

70 Prior (2005) 'Murder and Madness', p 35. Where women relied on insanity it tended to be in relation to the killing of a child.

71 Gibbons et al. (1997) 'Guilty But Insane', p 469. The use of insanity acquittals in relation to crimes against children was mainly concentrated during the nineteenth century: there were no insanity acquittals for infanticide in Gibbons et al.'s sample from 1920 onwards: Gibbons et al. (1997) 'Guilty But Insane', p 470.

72 Gibbons et al. (1999) 'Criminal Responsibility and Mental Illness', p 52.

73 See generally, Edwards (1984) *Women on Trial*, pp 80–85 and 91–100; H Allen (1987) *Justice Unbalanced*; and material cited above at n 30.

74 Allen (1987) *Justice Unbalanced*, p 27. See K Brennan (2013) '"Traditions of English Liberal Thought": A History of The Enactment of an Infanticide Law in Ireland', *Irish Jurist*, 50, 100–137, pp 123–133.

75 See Brennan (2013) '"A Fine Mixture of Pity and Justice"', pp 814–816.

the insanity cases in this sample tended to involve random and apparently purposeless acts, often committed with excessive brutality involving the use of weapons. Unlike some of the manslaughter cases, the context for the killing did not suggest pre-existing abuse or a 'domestic dispute'. For example, both men who killed their children, in apparently sudden, motiveless, and very violent attacks involving, in one case, a hatchet, and, in the other, a frying pan and hockey stick, were found incapable of pleading.[76] Three of the five men in this sample who killed their mothers were found either incapable of pleading or 'guilty but insane'; two of these cases appeared to involve a sudden unpremeditated and unprovoked attack.[77] Similarly three of the five men accused of murdering a sibling were also disposed of on an insanity finding. These cases similarly involved a random attack without any apparent calculated motive.[78]

The death penalty

In the early 1940s, the Secretary of the Department of Justice, Stephen Roche, observed that three out of every five capital convictions resulted in a reprieve, adding that the figure would be 'more striking' had juries and the Attorney General not made efforts to 'mitigate the severity of the law'.[79] According to Doyle and O'Donnell's figures, 54 per cent of death sentences issued between 1930 and 1945 were reprieved.[80] Overall, two-thirds of death sentences imposed in this sample of family murders were executed, which seems high in comparison with general figures on the execution of this penalty. It is worth bearing in mind, however, that two of these executions (Kirwin and O'Shea) were performed during 'the Emergency', a time when there was an increase in executions and the only time where executions exceeded reprieves in the independent Irish State.[81]

In the cases in this sample where the death sentence was carried out (Fleming, O'Shea, McDermott, Kirwin), a number of aggravating factors, including premeditation, previous attempts, motives involving financial/economic gain and the disposal of an unwanted wife, and cover-ups of the crime, were involved, which may account for the decision to carry out the death sentence in these cases.[82] The case of Jane O'Brien, who lay in wait for her nephew

76 NAI, SFCCC IC/94/53 (BP, 1933); ID/19/7 (TM, 1940).

77 NAI, SFCCC ID/94/67 (MMcC, 1931); IC/95/73 (HF, 1932).

78 NAI, ID/56/23 (TA, 1935).

79 Letter entitled 're trials for murder', SA Roche (Department of Justice) to PP O'Donoghue (Office of Attorney General), dated 25 Aug 1941, p 3 (NAI, Department of Taoiseach s7788(a)).

80 Doyle and O'Donnell (2012) 'The Death Penalty', pp 72–73.

81 Ibid.

82 NAI, SFCCC ID/33/63 (Fleming, 1933); ID/22/84 (O'Shea, 1943); IC/95/71 (McDermott, 1932); ID/20/103 (Kirwin, 1942).

and shot him dead as he returned home one night, also involved aggravating factors and consequently caused difficulty for the government. The jury had recommended a reprieve on the basis of her age and sex, but the Department of Justice noted that while special features were involved in other cases of convicted female murderers, in the case of Jane O'Brien it was unable to 'recollect any case in which there appears to be have been so complete an absence of extenuating circumstances'.[83] However, as noted, the use of the death penalty was highly gendered; the Irish government was not inclined towards executing women, and Jane O'Brien's sentence was reprieved. Ultimately, as Gerard O'Brien concludes, '[i]t is clear the prospect of executing a woman filled both officials and minister with a particular horror'.[84] The only male in the sample to have his death sentence commuted had killed his sleeping wife with a hatchet while in an intoxicated state. He claimed that he was 'so sick from drink' he 'did not know what [he] was doing'. After hiding the hatchet in a manure heap, he immediately turned himself in to the guards.[85]

It is evident from this sample that there was little reticence about carrying out a capital penalty in cases involving the murder of family members, and that the use of this penalty was not limited to politically motivated killings or to cases where the offender posed a threat to the wider public.

Conclusion

Less than one-quarter of the cases in this sample resulted in a conviction for murder. The most common disposal involved an insanity-related finding, with the remaining cases being equally split between acquittals and manslaughter convictions. The wider context for this analysis of the criminal justice response to family murders is the fact that murder was a capital offence, something which undoubtedly had an impact on the way the cases in this small sample were disposed of. In terms of whether the family relationship between the victim and offender had, in this context, an impact on the outcome, some suggestions may be made.

First, only one of the four offenders in this sample who killed their children was convicted; the remaining three cases did not proceed to trial due to an unfitness to plead finding. This may indicate that the courts were inclined to view these killings as manifestations of madness. The only conviction in relation to a child victim followed a plea of guilty to manslaughter. That, plus the fact that a non-custodial sentence was imposed, might indicate, particularly in light of the treatment of infanticide cases at this time, that the courts

83 O'Brien (2006) 'Capital Punishment in Ireland', p 233, referring to NAI, Department of Taoiseach S.8653.

84 O'Brien (2006) 'Capital Punishment in Ireland', p 233.

85 NAI, SFCCC ID/22/83 (Griffin, 1943).

were very reluctant to expose parents who killed their children to the full extent of the criminal law.

Second, there seems to have been a reluctance to subject men who killed wives and other family members in the context of domestic abuse to a capital conviction. The cases in this sample suggest that factors relating to whether the killing was a cold-blooded act done for the purpose of gain played an important part in persuading decision makers towards a capital or non-capital disposal, and these factors were likely relevant in non-family cases too. However, the cases also raise the possibility that killings that took place in the context of pre-existing domestic violence were not viewed as being as serious as other kinds of killings, particularly if it could be suggested that the killer had been provoked, and that the law operated in a gendered way to ensure that men who killed in this context were not convicted of murder.

Third, the high number of insanity findings suggest that unfitness to plead and the insanity defence operated as devices for avoiding a capital conviction in certain cases, particularly where, given the context for and nature of the violence, manslaughter was not a viable option for extending mercy. These insanity cases may have been viewed as falling outside the 'manslaughter' and 'murder' categories evident in the rest of the sample – they were more than a fatal physical assault in the context of a 'domestic dispute' and/or long-term abuse but less than a premeditated cold-blooded killing committed for an evident purpose. However, further research is needed with regard to whether, for example, insanity disposals were also widely used for other offenders and whether they continued to be extensively used after 1964 when capital punishment had been abolished for most murders.[86] The sample also indicates that there was a gendered aspect with regard to the use of insanity findings in cases involving male killers which may have played a particular role in the context of family killings. One possibility is that men were medicalized in an effort to explain their sudden, extreme and motiveless acts of violence against family members, particularly their children and mothers. An insanity finding possibly offered a logical explanation for an otherwise incomprehensible act. This is not to say that none of these men were suffering from mental abnormalities at the time of the killing or at arraignment. There is evidence in many of the cases to suggest that the accused had some kind of mental disturbance, and clearly the defence was able to adduce some evidence to support the plea. Nonetheless, the high number of insanity disposals does indicate willingness to apply the law flexibly in certain cases.

Finally, questions also arise in connection with the impact of gender in the female cases, particularly with respect to acquittals and sentencing. First, the high number of acquittals may suggest that gendered constructions played a part in the way judges and juries assessed guilt in cases involving female offenders. An analysis of the facts in acquittal cases indicates that evidential

86 Criminal Justice Act 1964, s 1.

deficiencies played an important part, though the gender of the offender may have affected the assessment of the weight of the evidence against her. Second, there are too few cases in this sample to make any significant comment on whether female offenders were subject to differential sentencing outcomes in comparison with males. The case of Jane O'Brien clearly reflects the State's aversion to executing women murderers, something noted by other researchers. One woman (Kate Reilly) was sentenced for manslaughter. While the four men convicted of manslaughter in this sample received a custodial sentence, Reilly was given a disposal under the Probation of Offenders Act 1907, which included a requirement to reside at a religious institution for 12 months. The sentence follows exactly the approach taken in many infanticide cases during this period,[87] and may, therefore, reflect an unwillingness to expose women who killed their children in distressing circumstances to harsh criminal sanctions.

In summary, this exploration of the criminal justice response to family murders tends to raise more questions than it answers; as such, these matters, particularly those relating to treatment of domestic abuse by the courts and the use of insanity-related verdicts for male killers require further research.

The court documents considered in this study provide a fascinating insight into the family and community in Ireland during this period, revealing glimpses of the daily lives of ordinary people and the personal struggles they faced. In particular, many of these cases involved households of adults forced, through economic necessity, to live together with their parents or their adult siblings, sometimes in very cramped living conditions where grown men and women shared bedrooms and even beds with other adult family members. Many were, due to inheritance arrangements, trapped in this situation being unable to achieve financial or indeed personal independence: their entire economic security rested on another family member. Discontent, frustration and resentment surely bubbled under the surface in many of these homes. In some of these cases, the motive or suspected motive was clearly linked to inheritance arrangements and/or the accused's consequential lack of economic and indeed personal autonomy. In others, the living situation simply provided the context in which a person one day suddenly lashed out in a violent act against a family member, for no obvious reason. Unfortunately, it has not been possible within the scope of this study to assess these issues, but it is noted that the socio-economic context in which these killings occurred and the motivations involved have potential for fruitful exploration in the future.

87 K Brennan (2013) 'Punishing Infanticide in the Irish Free State', *Irish Journal of Legal Studies* 1–35.

11

Interrogating the Charge of Concealment of Birth in Nineteenth-Century Irish Courts

Elaine Farrell

Due to her ill-health, Jane Irvine was not present at the coroner's inquest on her newborn baby daughter on the afternoon of 20 August 1870. In her absence, a number of witnesses were questioned about their interactions with the young woman in the days leading up to the alleged death. Agnes McClure recounted that on the afternoon of 18 August she was summoned to a water-closet in Ewart's mill on Belfast's Crumlin Road where she and Irvine were both employed. On seeing Irvine, who had allegedly been in the water-closet for almost two hours by that stage, McClure suggested that she get a sick pass to leave work. Irvine, who kept her back to the witness during their conversation, insisted that there was nothing wrong with her, pinned her loose clothes back into place, and picked up a parcel, which she concealed in her clothing. McClure, who admitted on cross-examination that she was aware that Irvine 'was in the family way', denied that she had seen or heard a baby but acknowledged that she saw 'the traces which attend the birth of a child'.[1] A witness, Mary Walker, picked up the story where McClure left off. She deposed that at the request of Irvine's mother she had allowed Jane to sleep that night in the house where she lived with her husband and three young children. Early the next morning, Walker questioned Irvine about her condition: 'I said to her, "Jane, there is a great rumour that you had a baby in the factory last night." She said nothing. I then asked her to tell me the truth, and she said she would.'[2] Irvine subsequently showed Walker the naked body of a dead newborn infant.

As was common in suspected infanticide or concealment of birth cases, rumours of alleged pregnancies and births soon reached the local police

1 *Belfast Newsletter*, 22 Aug 1870.

2 *Belfast Newsletter*, 22 Aug 1870.

station.[3] Local constable Andrew Doherty arrested Irvine and cautioned her that any information that she subsequently provided could be used as evidence against her. In response, Irvine asserted: 'If I bury the child, sure there'll be nothing done to me.'[4] This attitude suggests an ignorance of the law that criminalized the act of concealing the birth of an infant who was subsequently found dead. Concealment of birth was not an unusual charge in the Irish legal landscape; between 1841 and 1893, the years for which concealment of birth figures are provided in annual records, 2,284 cases were reported to the police.[5] However, Irvine was not alone in her ignorance. Despite its relatively frequent appearance in the courts, lawyers also at times demonstrated a lack of familiarity with concealment of birth legislation. Using case law, newspapers and court records, this chapter will argue that particular aspects of nineteenth-century legislation relating to the offence of concealment of birth caused difficulties and confusion for prosecution and defence counsel, as well as judges and juries.

Understanding unlawful concealment

In 1707, an Act 'to Prevent the Destroying and Murthering of Bastard Children'[6] drew attention to a situation where 'many lewd women that have been delivered of bastard Children, to avoyd their shame and to escape punishment, doe secretlie bury, or conceale the Death of their Children'. Such women it was claimed, subsequently

---

3 For infanticide in eighteenth- to twentieth-century Ireland, see K Brennan (2013) '"A Fine Mixture of Pity and Justice": The Criminal Justice Response to Infanticide in Ireland 1922–1949' in *Law and History Review,* 31(4), 793–841; C Conley (1999) *Melancholy Accidents: The Meaning of Violence in Post-Famine Ireland* (New York and Oxford: Lexington Books), ch 4; E Farrell (2013) *'A Most Diabolical Deed': Infanticide and Irish Society, 1850–1900* (Manchester: Manchester University Press); BD Kelly (2007) 'Murder, Mercury, Mental Illness: Infanticide in Nineteenth-Century Ireland', *Irish Journal of Medical Science* clxxvi, 149–152; J Kelly (1992) 'Infanticide in Eighteenth-Century Ireland', *Irish Economic and Social History,* xix, 5–26; J Kelly (2012) 'Responding to Infanticide in Ireland, 1680–1820' in E Farrell (ed), *'She Said She Was in the Family Way': Pregnancy and Infancy in Modern Ireland* (London: Institute of Historical Research), 189–203; D McLoughlin (2002) 'Infanticide in Nineteenth-Century Ireland', in A Bourke, S Kilfeather, M Luddy, M MacCurtain, G Meaney, M Ní Dhonnchadha, M O'Dowd and C Wills (eds), *Field Day Anthology of Irish Writing,* iv (Cork: Cork University Press), 915–922; PM Prior (2008) *Madness and Murder: Gender, Crime and Mental Disorder in Nineteenth-Century Ireland* (Dublin: Irish Academic Press), ch 5; C Rattigan (2012) *'What Else Could I Do?' Single Mothers and Infanticide, Ireland 1900–1950* (Dublin: Irish Academic Press); L Ryan (2004) 'The Press, Police and Prosecution: Perspectives on Infanticide in the 1920s' in A Hayes and D Urquhart (eds), *Irish Women's History* (Dublin: Irish Academic Press), 137–151; L Ryan (1996) '"The Massacre of Innocence": Infanticide in the Irish Free State', *Irish Studies Review,* xiv, 17–20.

4 *Belfast Newsletter,* 22 Aug 1870.

5 *Irish Crimes Records Return of Outrages, 1841–1893* (National Archives of Ireland, Chief Secretary's Office Papers).

6 6 Ann c 4.

> alleadge that the said children were born dead; wheras it falleth out sometimes (although hardlie it is to be proved) that the said child or children were murthered by the said women their lewd mothers, or by their assent or procurement.

In response to such alleged occurrences, the Act legislated:

> That if any woman ... be delivered of any issue of the Body, Male or Female, which being born alive, should by the Lawes of this Realm be a bastard, and that she endeavour privatlie either by drowning or secrett burying thereof, or any other way, either by herselfe of the procuring of others, soe to conceale the death thereof, as that it may not come to light, whether it be borne alive or not, but be concealed, in every such case the mother soe offending shall suffer Death as in the case of murther except such mother can make proffer by one witness at the least, that the Child (whose death was by her soe intended to be concealed) was borne dead.[7]

This Act essentially rendered the woman who had given birth to the infant responsible for her or his subsequent death.[8] She too would be killed unless she could prove herself innocent of any involvement in her baby's death. Similar acts came into force in England and Scotland in 1624 and 1690 respectively and were in operation in particular regions of Canada by the early nineteenth century.[9]

This Act proved difficult to implement in practice and was replaced almost 100 years later in 1803 by an act that placed the onus on the Crown rather than the women who had given birth to prove that their infants had been born alive.[10] Jackson and Kilday have warned that the 1803 Act should not necessarily be regarded as more sympathetic towards the post-parturient woman than its predecessor. The Act retained the death sentence for those found guilty of murder, removed the clauses that had frequently led to not

---

7 6 Ann c 4.

8 Kelly (1992) 'Infanticide in Eighteenth-Century Ireland', p 6.

9 L Abrams (2002) 'From Demon to Victim: the Infanticidal Mother in Shetland, 1699–1899' in Y Galloway Brown and R Ferguson (eds), *Twisted Sisters: Women, Crime, and Deviance in Scotland Since 1400* (East Linton: Tuckwell Press), 180–203; CB Backhouse (1991) *Petticoats and Prejudice: Women and Law in Nineteenth-Century Canada* (Toronto: Women's Press), p 114; A-M Kilday (2013), *A History of Infanticide in Britain, c1600 to the Present* (New York: Palgrave Macmillan), pp 17–18; M Francus (1997) 'Monstrous Mothers, Monstrous Societies: Infanticide and the Rule of Law in Restoration and Eighteenth-Century England', *Eighteenth Century Life,* xxi(2), 133–156.

10 An Act for the Further Prevention of Malicious Shooting and Attempting to Discharge Loaded Fire-arms, Stabbing, Cutting, Wounding, Poisoning and the Malicious Using of Means to Procure the Miscarriage of Women (43 Geo III c 58) (Lord Ellenborough Act); Francus (1997) 'Monstrous Mothers', p 141. For a discussion of a similar Scottish act in 1809, see A-M Kilday and KD Watson (2008) 'Infanticide, Religion and Community in the British Isles, 1720–1920: Introduction', *Family and Community History*, xi(2), 93.

guilty verdicts, and introduced a new offence, that of concealment of birth, which could be returned as a verdict in the case of women found not guilty of murder.[11] A sentence of up to two years in 'the common gaol or house of correction' would be imposed on women found guilty of the crime of concealment of birth.[12] The Offences Against the Person (Ireland) Act 1829[13] extended the Act to include infants born within as well as outside marriage.[14] Those found guilty would be punished with a term of imprisonment of up to two years with or without hard labour. Concealment of birth, however, was not a standalone charge until criticisms that a woman charged with one offence (murder) could be found guilty of another (concealment of birth) were addressed by the Offences Against the Person Act 1861.[15]

The concealment of birth charge caused confusion in Irish courtrooms because it was unclear how the Act and the requirement of 'concealment' was to be understood and interpreted.[16] Using a number of case studies, this chapter interrogates concealment of birth legislation across the century.[17] It explores the debates that ensued throughout the nineteenth century about the validity of the concealment of birth charge: firstly, when childbirth had been acknowledged, secondly, when temporary methods of disposal had been employed, and thirdly, when there was no body.

'I'll not deny it to you': acknowledging childbirth

Neither the 1803 Act nor its 1829 successor specified if an acknowledgement of an imminent or recent birth would nullify a 'concealment' of birth charge. This was debated in the Murphy case, which featured in the line-up of trials at the Downpatrick Spring Assizes in 1836.[18] A witness explained that he had observed that a woman named Murphy was pregnant and that on 'coming past her mother's house one day he saw a blind drawn across the window of the sleeping-room'.[19] Some time later, he noticed that Murphy's

---

11 M Jackson (1996) *New Born Child Murder: Women, Illegitimacy and the Courts in Eighteenth-Century England* (Manchester: Manchester University Press), pp 176–177; Kilday (2013) *A History of Infanticide*, p 19.

12 43 Geo III c 58.

13 10 Geo IV c 34.

14 The terms of this act were introduced in England in 1828 (9 Geo IV c 31).

15 24 & 25 Vic c 100. D Seaborne Davies (1945) 'Child Killing in English Law' in L Radzinowicz and JWC Turner (eds), *The Modern Approach to Criminal Law* (London: Macmillan), 301–343, p 314.

16 For a detailed overview of criminal proceedings and trials in Ireland, see WE Vaughan (2009) *Murder Trials in Ireland, 1836–1914* (Dublin: Four Courts Press).

17 For a discussion of the twentieth-century Irish legislation, see K Brennan (2013) '"Traditions of English Liberal Thought": A History of The Enactment of an Infanticide Law in Ireland', *Irish Jurist*, 50, 100–137.

18 The suspect's forename was not provided in the case law and the case did not appear in the *Belfast Newsletter* account of trials at the Down Spring Assizes: *Belfast Newsletter*, 18 Mar 1836.

19 *R v Murphy* (1836) 5 Law Rec (ns) 98.

physical appearance had changed and she was smaller in shape. His suspicions aroused, he initiated his own search and discovered the body of an infant buried in a nearby field. The unnamed witness's actions in this case are not particularly unusual; some neighbours in the nineteenth century appear to have been quite keen to instigate their own investigations to verify suspicions about sexual activity, childbirth or criminal behaviour.[20] By his own admission, the witness 'believed the whole family was aware of the circumstance, and that, for aught he knew, the mother herself might have assisted at the interment'.[21] Chief Baron Joy advised that this 'was not the case contemplated by the statute'.[22] Given that the birth and subsequent death of the infant had not been concealed, since the woman's family were evidently aware of the situation, a verdict of not guilty was returned.[23]

In the late 1830s, however, the same concern featured in the case of Biddy Fennell in Queen's County. The only evidence was provided by a witness who had heard a baby cry. On entering a room where Fennell was seated with her sister, the witness had coaxed: '"Come tell me the truth." The prisoner replied, ["]*Sally*, I'll not deny it to you, I was confined of a dead child"'.[24] Fennell then produced the dead body of an infant, upon which she appeared to have been lying. At the subsequent trial in the spring of 1838, counsel for the defence suggested that there was no evidence that Fennell had tried to conceal the birth and subsequent death of the infant because at least one person, Fennell's sister, was aware that a baby had been born. Tickell for the prosecution claimed otherwise and Justice Johnston instructed the jury that there was sufficient evidence to show that Fennell had attempted to conceal the birth of her infant. She was accordingly found guilty of the offence.[25]

The presiding judge in the Murphy case was evidently swayed by the fact that Murphy did not attempt to hide her pregnancy from her family at a time when significant shame was attached to pregnancy and birth outside

---

20 Farrell (2013) *'A Most Diabolical Deed'*, ch 4; L Gowing (1997) 'Secret Births and Infanticide in Seventeenth Century England', *Past and Present*, clvi, 87–115; AN May (1995) '"She at First Denied It": Infanticide Trials at the Old Bailey' in V Frith (ed), *Women and History: Voices of Early Modern England* (Toronto: Coach House Press), 19–50; J McShane-Galley (2006) 'For Shame: Accusations of Infanticide and Coroner's Inquests Into the Deaths of Legitimate Infants in Victorian Ontario' in BH Bechtold and D Cooper Graves (eds), *Killing Infants: Studies in the Worldwide Practice of Infanticide* (Lewiston: Edwin Mellen Press), 282–309; R Schulte (1994) *The Village in Court: Arson, Infanticide and Poaching in the Court Records of Upper Bavaria, 1848–1910* (Cambridge: Cambridge University Press).

21 *R v Murphy* (1836) 5 Law Rec (ns) 98.

22 *R v Murphy* (1836).

23 For a discussion of the similar case of Anne Glennan in Galway in 1850, see Farrell (2013) *'A Most Diabolical Deed'*, p 82. Glennan was acquitted on the grounds that she had openly admitted to her work colleague that she was the mother of a dead baby discovered in the vicinity.

24 Emphasis in the original.

25 *R v Fennell* (1838) Cr & Dix, Ab Not Cas 301.

marriage. In the latter case, only Fennell's sister, rather than her family as a whole, seems to have been aware of the pregnancy and subsequent childbirth. While studies of infant murder, and Earner-Byrne's examination of domestic violence in this volume (Chapter 9), reveal the family home as a place of danger, a close reading of individual concealment of birth case studies illustrate that the family unit or individual family members could also protect the pregnant and post-parturient woman. The Offences Against the Person Act 1861 legislated for the punishment of 'every person who shall, by any secret disposition ... endeavour to conceal the birth', even if the post-parturient woman had not been charged with murder or concealment of birth or had been found not guilty by the jury.[26] This essentially ended debates about the role of accomplices and the validity of a concealment of birth charge when others were aware of the birth and subsequent death of the infant. In subsequent years, it was not uncommon for family members, particularly mothers and sisters of the pregnant woman, to be charged with the offence.[27]

'Secret burying, or otherwise'

The method of concealing the dead body of a newborn baby, defined as 'secret burying, or otherwise' in 1803, was further clarified in 1829 as the 'secret burying or otherwise disposing of the dead body of the said child'.[28] Despite the amendment, the wording of the 1829 Act, like its predecessor, resulted in much debate in Irish courtrooms and, consequently, different verdicts for the same offence. The case of Bridget Doran came before the Wicklow Spring Assizes in 1842. The presiding judge, Baron Brady, interpreted that the words of the legislation 'clearly imply an absolute and permanent disposal, tantamount to a burial'.[29] Doran had evidently not permanently disposed of her child, having hidden her newborn offspring underneath the stuffing of her bed. Brady B insisted: 'I do not think the mere circumstance of a temporary concealment, such as has been proved in this case, brings the offence within the terms of the act.' Doran was accordingly acquitted.[30]

A similar case involving 19-year-old Mary Gogarty came before the Dublin Commission Court in October 1855. Gogarty was accused of concealing the birth and subsequent death of her newborn son. Those around her had suspected that she was pregnant on account of her changing physical form and thus, despite Gogarty's repeated denials, the inevitable childbirth was

26 24 & 25 Vic c 100, s 60.

27 For accomplices in infanticide cases, see C Rattigan (2008) '"Done to Death by Father or Relatives": Irish Families and Infanticide Cases, 1922–50', *History of the Family*, xiii, 370–383.

28 Offences Against the Person Act 1829 (10 Geo IV c 34).

29 *R v Doran* (1842) 2 Leg Rep 163.

30 *R v Doran* (1842).

anticipated. On the night in question, Gogarty was found in her bedroom, sitting at the side of her bed, with what appeared to be blood smeared on the floor. A policeman was summoned to the house, 'who, on arriving, found the prisoner's door fastened, and was obliged to break into the room'.[31] Gogarty several times denied that she had given birth but the policeman who conducted a search of her room found the body of a male infant concealed in the bed near the wall. Presiding Chief Justice Monahan addressed the jury: 'The only question for you is, whether there was a concealment intended by the prisoner? If delivered according to the course of nature, or laid there without the design of concealing, there would be no offence.'[32] The placement of the body, on top of the bed sheets but covered over by a quilt, was thus the focus of attention. Pieces of straw were stuck to the body but this appeared to be unintentional. Monahan also placed little importance on Gogarty's repeated denials that she had given birth: 'The fact of the prisoner's not answering or telling where the child was, does not constitute any offence.' Instead, he repeated: 'The only question for you, as I have already said, is, was concealment the object of the prisoner in placing the child where it was?'[33] The jury considered that Gogarty had indeed intended to conceal her newborn infant under the blanket and thus found her guilty of concealment of birth. She was accordingly sentenced to three months in prison.[34] Although the Doran and Gogarty cases were quite similar in that neither suspect could be regarded as having permanently disposed of the bodies of their infants, they resulted in different verdicts. While both women had placed their infants in their beds, Doran was acquitted of any wrongdoing whereas Gogarty was convicted. Evidently, the differing opinions of the presiding judges impacted on the verdicts.

In 1861, the Offences Against the Person Act enacted an amendment to the ambiguous wording of the concealment of birth charge and clarified that 'any secret disposition of the dead body of the said child' would be punishable by up to two years in prison with hard labour.[35] Therefore, the potentially temporary location at which a dead baby's body was found would not nullify a concealment of birth prosecution. The legislature may have anticipated that the 1861 Act would bring to an end debates in the courtroom about the placement of the dead body and the motives of the accused. However, the case of Jane Irvine, mentioned at the outset of this chapter, highlights the fact that individual cases of concealment of birth continued to cause confusion in Irish courtrooms for precisely the same reasons as before the legislative amendment.

---

31 *R v Gogarty* (1855) 7 Cox CC 107.

32 *R v Gogarty* (1855).

33 *R v Gogarty* (1855).

34 *Freeman's Journal*, 27 Oct 1855.

35 24 & 25 Vic c 100, s 60.

Having been arrested at Mary Walker's house, where she had slept after giving birth at Ewart's mill in Belfast, Jane Irvine was sent to be tried at the Antrim Spring Assizes of 1871. She pleaded not guilty to the charge that she 'on the 18th of August last, endeavoured to conceal the birth of a child, by having secretly concealed its dead body, and carried it away'. Dr Seeds, counsel for the defence, argued that the 'indictment was bad, inasmuch as it did not state there was any final disposition of the body anywhere'. In his address to the jury, he insisted that 'there was no secret disposition of the body at all'.[36] After some time, the jury returned with a unanimous verdict that Irvine was not guilty of the charge of concealment of birth but that 'she wished to conceal the fact from her fellow-workers'. Counsel for the prosecution pointed out that this was in fact a guilty verdict. The presiding judge, Baron Deasy, questioned the foreman:

> Do you agree that she conveyed the body from the mill concealed in her handkerchief[?]. The foreman – We do. His Lordship – That sustains the indictment. You had better consult again.[37]

The jury returned to the deliberation room for a second time. In the interim, Dr Seeds for the defence insisted that 'in his judgment, the opinion of the jury that the girl wished merely to avoid exposure in the mill, could not be taken as one that she intended to make a secret disposition of the body according to the Act of Parliament'. He suggested that if Deasy B disagreed, the case would be referred to the Court of Crown Cases Reserved. Deasy B insisted that 'he would himself dispose of the case' but 'would hear any argument Dr Seeds had to address to him on the point'.[38] In any case, the jury returned with a verdict of guilt, 'subject to the opinion they had already expressed'.[39] After pausing to contemplate a verdict, Deasy B released Irvine from custody on the grounds that 'she had already suffered enough'.[40] While this might appear to be a very lenient sentence for a guilty verdict, the maximum sentence of two years in prison with hard labour was generally only resorted to when there was a strong suspicion that the accused was guilty, not only of concealment of birth, but of the more serious offence of murder.[41]

The jury in the Irvine case was evidently confused about the definition of unlawful concealment. The jury comprised a panel of propertied men aged between 21 and 60 years of age,[42] and given that they would not necessarily have been well-versed in legal matters, their uncertainty is not surprising.

36 *Belfast Newsletter*, 10 Mar 1871.

37 *Belfast Newsletter*, 10 Mar 1871.

38 *Belfast Newsletter*, 10 Mar 1871.

39 *Belfast Newsletter*, 10 Mar 1871.

40 *Freeman's Journal*, 13 Mar 1871.

41 Farrell (2013) *'A Most Diabolical Deed'*, pp 87–88.

42 Vaughan (2009) *Murder Trials*, p 121.

However, a close reading of concealment of birth cases also reveals evidence of ignorance on the part of Ireland's criminal lawyers with regard to the legislation, even after the terms were clarified by the Offences Against the Person Act 1861. Belfast's Crumlin Road was the site of another suspected infanticide case in 1896. A barman at Robert Turner's public house had been turning over empty barrels in the back yard of the premises when he discovered an object wrapped in a pillow case concealed in one of the barrels. The dead body of a baby girl was found inside. In the aftermath of the discovery, Olivia Fisher, who had been employed as a domestic servant in the house for the previous six weeks, 'appeared very excited' and 'went about the house wringing her hands'.[43] Fisher admitted on arrest that she had given birth to the infant without assistance about a fortnight previously but was not certain that the baby had been born alive. She also identified the father of the child but his name was not recorded in the surviving court documents.[44] The doctor's physical examination, undertaken with Fisher's consent, verified that she had recently given birth.[45] The post-mortem examination finding that the baby had been stillborn meant that Fisher was tried for concealing the birth of the infant rather than murder.

In advance of the trial, JS Finnegan, counsel for the defence, argued that the prosecution had to prove the birth of the child and the secret burial of the dead body. Finnegan cited three English case law examples taken from Henry Roscoe's *Digest of the Law of Evidence in Criminal Cases* in support of his contention: *R v Snell*,[46] *R v Bell*,[47] and *R v Opie*.[48] The case of Sarah Snell in 1837 ended with an acquittal because the suspect's supposed attempt to dispose of the body of her infant in the privy was interrupted and the offence was not actually committed. It was determined that the 'body of the child must be completely disposed of: a prisoner found with the body still in her possession, though about to dispose of it, cannot be convicted'.[49] The 1841 *Bell* case in Northumberland resulted in an acquittal at the direction of the presiding judge because the suspect had placed her baby in a box in her bedroom, a temporary location that did not seem to constitute the 'burial' specified

43 *Belfast Newsletter*, 18 June 1896.

44 It was not particularly unusual for the father's name to be excluded from the evidence in nineteenth-century Irish infant murder or concealment of birth cases. See E Farrell (2012) '"The Fellow Said It Was Not Harm And Only Tricks": The Father in Suspected Cases of Infanticide In Ireland, 1850–1900' *Journal of Social History* 45(4), 990–1004.

45 Deposition of Richard Purdon, 18 June 1896 (PRONI, Crown records for County Antrim, ANT/1/2/C/6/77). For medical examinations in English infanticide cases, see DJR Grey (2013) '"What Woman is Safe...?": Coerced Medical Examinations, Suspected Infanticide, and the Response of the Women's Movement in Britain, 1871–1881', *Women's History Review*, xxii(3), 403–421.

46 (1837) 2 M & Rob 44.

47 (1841) 2 M & Rob 294.

48 (1860) 8 Cox CC 332.

49 *R v Snell* (1837) 2 M & Rob 44.

by the legislation.[50] The third case, tried in St Austell in November 1859, involved the suspected murder of an infant by unwed domestic servant Sarah Opie. It was alleged that 'whilst her mistress was out, she was delivered of a child, which she put in the boot-hole on a washing-tray'.[51] There it was found by another servant, who did not examine it. He later noticed the baby's body in a tub behind the privy door. On the grounds that there was insufficient evidence to determine that Opie intended to conceal the birth, a verdict of not guilty was returned.[52] If the newspaper account of the discussions is accurate, it seems to have entirely escaped the legal practitioners present in the magistrates' court on this occasion that these three cited examples preceded the Offences Against the Person Act 1861.[53] Debates about the burial of the body, therefore, were entirely irrelevant because the 1861 Act defined 'any secret disposition of the dead Body' as unlawful. In the end, Fisher pleaded guilty to an indictment charging her with concealment of birth and she was sentenced to one month in prison from the date of her arrest, meaning that she walked free from court, her sentence already served. [54]

'Precision is essential': the dead body

The 1803 Act punished a woman where 'it shall so appear in evidence that the prisoner was delivered of Issue of her body, male or female, which, if born alive, would have been Bastard'.[55] In 1829, it was further clarified that 'it shall not be necessary to prove whether the Child died before, at, or after its Birth'.[56] In contrast to the requirements for a murder charge, therefore, the Crown did not need to prove that the infant had been alive at birth or had been fully born in order to find a woman guilty of concealment of birth. The Offences Against the Person Act 1829 allowed for a prosecution in the case of the 'secret burying or otherwise disposing of the dead Body of the said child', but it still had to be proven that there was a dead body to dispose of in some manner.[57] In 1840, domestic servant Jane McKenna was charged with concealing the birth of an infant, sex unknown. McKenna's employer had observed a change in her physical appearance and was evidently monitoring what she perceived to be a progressing pregnancy. She would later testify that McKenna frequently suffered from stomach pains and could be heard moaning one night, as if in great pain, but had recovered the following day and went about her duties as usual. A few days later, a doctor summoned to the

50 *R v Bell* (1841) 2 M & Rob 294.

51 *R v Opie* (1860) 8 Cox CC 332.

52 *R v Opie* (1860) 8 Cox CC 332.

53 *Belfast Newsletter*, 19 June 1896.

54 *Belfast Newsletter*, 19 June 1896.

55 43 Geo III c 58.

56 10 Geo IV c 34.

57 10 Geo IV c 34.

house confirmed from a physical examination that McKenna had recently given birth. Despite an intensive search of the vicinity, however, the body of an infant was never located.

Counsel for the defence argued for an acquittal for two reasons: firstly that the sex of the child was indeterminable and secondly that the manner by which the dead body was concealed or discarded had not been proven. The Crown prosecutor, Thomas Staples, disputed the claim that both pieces of information were required to sustain the charge; the indictment had included three counts which stated the child to be firstly, male, secondly, female and thirdly, of a sex unstated. Justice Burton, however, was not convinced by the prosecution's arguments relating to the concealment and disposal of the body nor by the case law examples cited in support. He insisted that the words of the 1829 Act 'are in my mind conclusive, that proof of the manner in which the dead body has been disposed of, and whether by burying or otherwise, is an essential part of the evidence in cases of this description'. However, given the complete lack of evidence of the body having been disposed of, because remains were never located, an acquittal was in order. The jury accordingly agreed.[58]

A similar case came to public attention some years later in 1874. Jane McClelland deposed that she stayed in the house of James Symes in County Antrim on the night of 31 March of that year, where Jane Bell was employed as a domestic servant. Highlighting the realities of post-Famine Irish homes, even in those households that employed live-in servants, McClelland explained that she slept in the same bed with Bell in a room that lacked a light. McClelland had a fitful night's sleep. Bell rose from the bed a quarter of an hour after retiring, complaining that she felt nauseous. She opened the bedroom door to go for a drink but did not leave and instead returned to the room to sit on a chair. She discouraged McClelland from seeking assistance and eventually retired to bed. At around five or six o'clock in the morning, McClelland awoke to find that she was now alone in the bedroom. She noticed blood smeared on the bed clothes and on the floor in a manner that suggested that an attempt had been made to wipe it up. Blood was also visible on the chair on which Bell had sat a few hours earlier. McClelland recounted that Bell 'appeared to be quite strong the next day, and went about her business as usual'.[59] The similar claim in the above case of Jane McKenna demonstrates the resilience of women who had recently given birth and their determination to proceed as if little had occurred. Like other women mentioned in this chapter, those who encountered Bell regularly suspected that she was pregnant. Her employer, James Symes, had questioned her about her condition, noticing her 'thick and swelled', but she denied any suggestion of pregnancy.[60]

---

58 *R v McKenna* (1840) 1 Cr & Dix C 399.

59 *R v Bell* (1874) IR 8 CL 542.

60 *R v Bell* (1874).

McClelland was not the only witness to have seen Bell during the early hours of 1 April. Matthew Mason, a servant in the same household, had seen Bell coming down the stairs at around four o'clock and witnessed her again about an hour later emerging from the pig house. Most homes during this period would have lacked clocks and thus depositions frequently make reference to time estimates. Mason considered Bell's actions to be unusual because she typically fed the pigs around eight o'clock each morning. He noticed on this occasion that she appeared 'ill and pale'. A doctor was called several days later and confirmed that Bell had recently given birth.[61]

Jane Bell, described by the reporter for the *Belfast Newsletter* as 'a rather prepossessing young girl',[62] was initially charged that she

> was delivered of a child, and that the said Jane Bell, being so delivered of the said child as aforesaid, did then unlawfully endeavour to conceal the birth of the said child by secretly burying the dead body of the said child against the form of the statute, &c.[63]

At her trial at the Antrim summer assizes, the judge agreed with the counsel for the defence that the evidence presented did not sustain the indictment. Presiding Justice Fitzgerald thus directed that the indictment be amended so that the words 'by secretly burying the dead body of the said child' be replaced with 'a certain secret disposition of the dead body of the said child in a manner to the jurors aforesaid unknown'.[64] Henry Tracy, whom Fitzgerald had assigned as counsel for the defence (because Bell was undefended), argued that the judge had no authority to replace the wording on the indictment. Tracy argued that the amendment was not in line with the statute but the judge forged ahead regardless, insisting that there was sufficient evidence to sustain a charge. He instructed the jury to find a verdict of guilty if they reckoned that Bell had given birth to an infant who was subsequently found dead and that she had endeavoured to conceal the birth. The jury accordingly found Bell guilty of concealment of birth and she was released from custody to appear at the following assizes for sentencing.[65]

In the interim, Fitzgerald referred the case to the Court of the Crown Cases Reserved for consideration, firstly as to whether he had the authority to amend the indictment, and secondly as to whether the evidence was sufficient to maintain the guilty verdict. Tracy, for the defence, insisted before the seven presiding justices that the judge had no legal authority to amend the indictment and that the mode by which the concealment of birth was alleged to have occurred should have been specified rather than vaguely hinted at by

61 *R v Bell* (1874).

62 *Belfast Newsletter*, 22 Jul 1874.

63 *R v Bell* (1874) IR 8 CL 542.

64 *R v Bell* (1874).

65 *R v Bell* (1874).

the phrase 'a certain secret disposition'.[66] Tracy argued that the verdict was resolutely unfair to Bell because the present case was almost identical to the case of *R v McKenna*, which he cited and which had ended with an acquittal. Counsel for the prosecution pointed out that the *McKenna* case, and other cases used as examples, were irrelevant because they preceded the Offences Against the Person Act 1861. Tracy's actions may be further evidence of ignorance with regards to the law on the concealment of birth offence or he may simply have been attempting to utilize examples at his disposal to convincingly argue his case, despite the fact that they preceded the changes enacted by the 1861 act.

Having considered the two questions put by Justice Fitzgerald, Chief Justice Whiteside affirmed Tracy's argument that the conviction had to be quashed because there was not sufficient evidence to prove that a dead infant's birth had been concealed. He explained that to sustain the charge, Bell 'must have done the secret act of disposing of the body of the child after it was dead'. He also highlighted the fact that there was insufficient evidence to show that the child had been born in the first instance, that this baby had been born alive, and therefore that she or he had died. He pointed out that Bell's offspring,

> may, if born alive, be running about in the country at this moment. There is no evidence whatever of its death. ... It must be the very offence of disposing of a dead body that is to be established, and you must have a dead body before you can obtain a conviction for the crime alleged.[67]

He commended the defence counsel for a very well-argued case and concluded: 'Precision is essential in proving the very crime imputed. ... Nobody can be convicted under our criminal law where the case is left in obscurity and doubt.'[68] Without a body, or evidence of the alleged infant's death having taken place, Jane Bell could not be convicted of concealment of birth.

Conclusion

Case law examples often provide little detail on the individual women on whose trials they are based. Suspects' ages and occupations, their reactions to arrests, and information about witnesses are frequently excluded from the narratives. Newspaper accounts of concealment of birth cases, particularly in the pre-Famine period, often offer few details to fill such gaps. The destruction of the vast majority of crown file records relating to the years before 1880 similarly restricts the sources upon which an analysis of problematic

66 *Freeman's Journal*, 24 Nov 1874.

67 *R v Bell* (1874) IR 8 CL 542.

68 *R v Bell* (1874).

concealment of birth cases can be based.[69] Yet a close analysis of case law examples or those that caused debate in the courtroom reveals the difficulties posed by changing legislation for the concealment of birth offence, particularly in the three decades between 1829 and 1861. A study of such cases can also highlight how the different opinions of presiding judges could influence juries' deliberations and verdicts. As this chapter has illustrated, contrasting interpretations meant that almost identical cases could have quite different results. The Offences Against the Person Act 1861 did much to eradicate the vagaries of its predecessors. Interpretations became more uniform as the century progressed. The prosecution of accomplices in concealment of birth crimes rendered moot discussions about the extent of family or close friends' knowledge. Discussions about the placement of the body, the nature of the concealment and the perpetrator's motive likewise faded from courtrooms. Nonetheless, some individual cases continued to cause disagreement and confusion for lawyers as well as the selected men of nineteenth-century Irish juries.

69 See Elaine Farrell (ed) (2012) *Infanticide in the Irish Crown Files at Assizes, 1883–1900* (Dublin: Irish Manuscripts Commission), pp xv–xvii; Brian Griffin (2005) *Sources for the Study of Crime in Ireland, 1801–1921* (Dublin: Four Courts Press), p 40.

12

The Fate of the 'Illegitimate' Child: An Analysis of Irish Social Policy, 1750–1952

Simone McCaughren and Fred Powell

> *I know I have vexed the Superior a good many times because I did not punish the boys severely enough for his taste. He told me hundreds of times never to spare them. I will give you his own words in brackets. What are they but 'illegitimates and pure dirt'?*[1]

Adoption enables adult citizens to construct a family through a legal and social process, as opposed to a natural biological process. For children, adoption entails a permanent change in family affiliation and often identity. According to Roman law 'adoption imitates nature'.[2] The ancient Greeks viewed adoption as 'a method of demanding from religion and law that which nature had denied.'[3] In ancient Ireland there was legal provision for adoption through the payment of an adoption fee (*lóg fóesma*) or by invitation, in which case the adopted child is described as *fine thacair* or 'kinsman by summoning'. The word adoption (*fóesam*) in ancient Irish is constructed within the discourse of personal welfare, meaning 'taking into protection'.[4] Modernity led to the discovery (or arguably the rediscovery) of childhood. It also reframed childhood within a sociological discourse, in which it is argued that childhood is culturally and socially constructed. Childhood is a product of the adult imaginary, which seeks to represent it as a universal social status, offering care and protection in a fictionalized and idealized world of safety and innocence. The social reality of childhood is more diverse. Plural childhoods (arising from poverty, abuse or migration) challenge the idealized notion of childhood as a universal age stage characterized by security.

1 S Ryan (2009) *Commission to Inquire into Child Abuse* (Dublin: Government Publications), para 1:8.65 (*Ryan Report*).

2 A Kadushin (1980) *Child Welfare Services*, 3rd edn (New York: Macmillan), p 465.

3 Kadushin (1980) *Child Welfare Services*, p 465.

4 F Kelly (2009) *A Guide to Early Irish Law* (Dublin: Dublin Institute of Advanced Studies), p 105.

The status of illegitimacy defined the 'othered' child in modern Irish society as a social outcast. As detailed by Elaine Farrell in Chapter 11, the single mother and her child were stigmatized, ostracized and institutionalized, as a shameful family secret to be hidden from the world. In this chapter, we seek to locate and contextualize illegitimacy within modern Irish society, through a sociological analysis. We commence our analysis with a focus on the meaning of childhood, child abandonment within the early modern city and its rural hinterlands, institutionalization and forced child migration during the eighteenth, nineteenth and twentieth centuries – often linked to overseas adoptions. We then discuss the background and debate surrounding the introduction of the Adoption Act 1952 and the subsequent evolution of adoption policy in Ireland as a social phenomenon and cultural practice.

The discovery of childhood

The 'Discovery of Childhood' thesis in modern society was originally propagated by influential French historian Philippe Aries in 1973. *Centuries of Childhood*[5] argued that the 'invention of childhood' began with the aristocracy during the sixteenth and seventeenth centuries. However, he argued that this transformation in the 'identity' of childhood amongst the 'popular classes' did not occur until the late eighteenth century, and in some societies even later. Aries' central argument is that in medieval society children, perceived as 'miniature adults', were absorbed into that adult world by the age of seven. Mass compulsory primary school education (which followed the invention of the printing press) in modern urban society changed public consciousness of children's identities, needs and place in society. Aries' theoretical analysis was supported by de Mause in 1976,[6] and while there were some later revisions by medievalist scholars,[7] the thesis of childhood as the invention of modern society has been widely accepted by scholars. However, the meaning of childhood is fraught with complexity.

The experience of childhood has varied between social classes in modern society. The city transformed social attitudes. In the context of the eighteenth-century sexual revolution, illegitimacy became a major social problem, leading to infanticide and child abandonment.[8] Urban child abandonment, which was particularly common during the eighteenth century, involved abandoning the child in the streets, or more scandalously, on church steps, leaving the infant at the mercy of fate. It caused a major public reaction,

5 P Aries (1973) *Centuries of Childhood* (London: Penguin).

6 L de Mause (1976) *History of Childhood* (London: Souvenir).

7 R O'Day (1994) *The Family and Family Relationships 1500–1900: England, France and the United States* (Basingstoke: Macmillan); J Pollock (1983) *Forgotten Children: Parent Child Relations 1500–1800* (Cambridge: Cambridge University Press).

8 See Chapter 11 in this volume.

which led to both legal and policy responses. Infanticide became a major public scandal, placing the onus of responsibility for unwanted pregnancies on the mother. Robins notes that between 1695 and 1707 there were a series of unsuccessful attempts to pass legislation outlawing infanticide.[9] As Farrell explains in Chapter 11, it was not until 1707 that legislation made 'the destroying and murdering of bastard children' a capital crime. It also prescribed the death penalty for women convicted of concealing the death of their child. This draconian measure in the era of 'the Bloody Code' produced a reaction in the form of attempts to provide an ostensibly more humane response. Society was cajoled by Jonathan Swift's 1729 pamphlet *A Modest Proposal*,[10] in which he satirically engaged in public derision of prevailing social hypocrisy in relation to 'illegitimate' children, and suggested that the slaughtering of these children and the sale of their carcases in butchers' shops (as 'baby meat') would provide a rational solution to the disposal of the unwanted child.[11] Provocatively, Swift advocated a return to cannibalism, which he viewed as morally equivalent to the status quo. As it turned out, social policy proved equally surreal in its response to the crisis of illegitimacy, in which social taboos were sacrificed in the interests of protecting public morality and property interests, with 'raw economics' defining the agenda.[12]

Child abandonment, foundling hospitals and angel-makers

The foundling hospital, which dates from fourteenth-century Europe, provided an institution whereby unwanted children could be disposed of without fear of prosecution.[13] While some forms of infanticide, such as overlaying (smothering the child in bed), provided a convenient fiction of natural death, the foundling hospital obviated the need for such deception regarding the unwanted child's disposal. The foundling hospital provided secrecy for the mother (using a swivel or revolving basket to anonymously deposit the child) and kept the child's abandonment a private matter. However, there was little difference between infanticide and abandonment in terms of the child's ultimate fate. Shorter concludes that 'abandonment was tantamount to infanticide'.[14] The rationale behind Shorter's conclusion lay in the extremely high mortality rates amongst children placed in foundling hospitals throughout Europe. The mortality figures for the Dublin Foundling Hospital, opened

9 J Robins (1980) *The Lost Children: a Study of Charity Children in Ireland 1700–1900* (Dublin: Institute of Public Administration), p 12.

10 J Swift (1729) *A Modest Proposal* in P Pinkus (1965) *Jonathan Swift: A Collection of his Works* (London: Macmillan), 478–494.

11 Swift (1729) *A Modest Proposal.*

12 E O'Sullivan and I O'Donnell (2012) (eds), *Coercive Confinement in Ireland: Patients, Prisoners and Penitents* (Manchester: Manchester University Press), p 273.

13 J Boswell (1998) *The Kindness of Strangers* (Chicago: Chicago University Press).

14 E Shorter (1975) *The Making of the Modern Family* (Huntington, NY: Fontana), p 175.

in 1730, were consistent with its European counterparts: over a hundred-year period, its mortality rate varied between 70 and 80 per cent.[15] Those children who survived the institution were placed with 'wet-nurses' in the countryside, known throughout Europe as 'angel-makers', in whose care most perished through neglect or by design.

In a sardonic comment on the latent purpose of the European foundling hospital, the distinguished social anthropologist, Margaret Mead, observed that these bizarre institutions were 'only a prolonged, ritualized method of disposing of the infant for whom nobody wished to care'.[16] Why was society so cruel to foundling children, who were not the authors of their misfortune? Why 'other' them? Why did society conspire in their deaths? The answer cannot simply be found in social hypocrisy. While social hypocrisy clearly was a factor, public attitudes were also shaped by sociogenetic fear. Fear of 'illegitimate' children, who were socially constructed as 'syphilitic children', shaped social attitudes and property relations. They were publicly perceived as the products of prostitution and the carriers of 'bad' genes. Thus labelling was the cause of their social tragedy and the primary explanation for a barely concealed policy of euthanasia. Inglis observes that 'sexual morality became a major issue, but it was wrapped in a veil of silence'.[17] As discussed in other chapters in this volume, sexual morality and the nuclear family became fundamentally interconnected as the pillars of Irish society.[18] Transgression involved shaming and the social exclusion of both single mothers and their children. They were socially constructed in a patriarchal traditional society as having dishonoured their families.

While the foundling hospital was gradually replaced by the workhouse after the introduction of the Irish Poor Law Act 1838,[19] the institutionalization of children continued while the grotesque mortality rates somewhat abated. Middleton notes that 'those [children] who received the least support, the "illegitimate" children, had a death rate twice that of children born in wedlock'.[20] He further comments that the Poor Law philosophy, rooted in its Darwinistic principles, was not designed to eradicate poverty; all it achieved 'was to practise its socially destructive policies on women of little education, living in mean houses, struggling to keep the family together on a pittance, often not greatly helped by a husband and overtaxed by work to the

15 F Powell and M Scanlon (2015), *Dark Secrets of Childhood: Media Power, Child Abuse and Public Scandals* (Bristol: Policy Press), pp 236–241.

16 Quoted in Kadushin (1980) *Child Welfare Services*, p 36.

17 T Inglis (1987) *Moral Monopoly: The Catholic Church in Modern Irish Society* (Dublin: Gill and Macmillan), p 141.

18 See Chapters 6 and 11.

19 1 & 2 Vic c 56.

20 N Middleton (1971) *When Family Failed* (London: Victor Gollancz Ltd), p 138.

point of ill-health'.[21] In turn the workhouses were replaced by a penal system of industrial schools and reformatories during the 1860s and 1870s, which continued to stigmatize their child populations as 'illegitimates and pure dirt'.[22] Illegitimacy and social genetics also continued to inform the Darwinistic project of child institutionalization.[23] Luddy argues that illegitimacy was socially constructed as a moral issue but in reality it was a means of protecting inheritance rights in a land-based economy which sought to protect the gene pool.[24] According to Ferriter 'by 1924 there were more children in industrial schools in the Irish Free State then there were in all the industrial schools, in England, Scotland, Wales and Northern Ireland combined'.[25]

Cillín

The immense secrecy that surrounded the births and deaths of 'fallen women' was deeply rooted in Irish tradition, going back hundreds of years. Priests would not allow children who had not been baptized to be buried in consecrated ground. The mothers were, therefore, forced to bury them in unofficial graveyards, usually a *rath* (an earthen ring fort) or in and around the ruins of an ancient church.[26] Such a burial place was known in Irish as a *cillín*, which Dinneen's Irish-English dictionary defines as 'a place set apart for the burial of unbaptized children'.[27] Children were not baptized because they were either stillborn, died at birth, were orphaned or born to single mothers. When the children of single mothers died, they were buried in these unofficial graveyards in great secrecy so as to conceal the births.

Criminalizing single mothers and problematizing 'illegitimate' children in the Free State

During the period 1765–1914 at least 33 refuges or asylums were established in Ireland to remoralize 'fallen' women.[28] Ireland became 'the Free State' in 1922. It was a victory for political independence, but, as Thomas Mohr points

21 Middleton (1971) *When Family Failed*, p 138.

22 *Ryan Report* (2009), para 1:8.65.

23 J Barnes (1989) *Irish Industrial School 1868–1908: Origins and Development* (Dublin: Irish Academic Press); Powell and Scanlon (2015), *Dark Secrets of Childhood*, pp 251–253.

24 M Luddy (1995) *Women and Philanthropy in Nineteenth Century Ireland* (Cambridge: Cambridge University Press) and M Luddy (1997) 'Abandoned Women and Bad Characters: Prostitution in Nineteenth Century Ireland', *Women's History Review*, 6(4), 485–504.

25 D Ferriter (2005) *The Transformation of Ireland 1900–2000* (London: Profile Books), p 325.

26 RH Aldridge (1969) 'Notes on Children's Burial Grounds in Mayo' *Journal of the Royal Society of Antiquaries of Ireland*, 99(1) 83–87; S Ó Sulleabháin (1939) '*Adhlacadh leanbhaí* (the Burial of Children)' *Journal of the Royal Society of Antiquaries of Ireland* 143–151.

27 PS Dinneen (1904) *Foclóir Gaeilge agus Béarla: An English-Irish Dictionary* (Dublin: Irish Texts Society).

28 F Powell, M Geoghegan, M Scanlon and K Swirak (2012) *Youth Policy, Civil Society and the Modern Irish State* (Manchester: Manchester University Press), pp 31–55.

out, socially the Free State was a deeply Catholic, conservative regime;[29] Lindsey Earner-Byrne and Deirdre McGowan demonstrate how it criminalized single mothers and problematized their children.[30] They were socially and culturally constructed as outcasts and subjected to 'othering' in its cruellest forms through ostracization, beatings, neglect and sexual abuse.[31] Ferriter observes that 'the State appeared to get much more exercised about 'immoral girls' than it did about child abuse'.[32]

Illegitimacy was, for a large part of the early twentieth century, frowned upon. Women who had children outside of marriage were regarded as stigmatized women, pathological, mentally unbalanced and deviant.[33] Their 'moral lapse' was something that was regarded as having 'interrupted the proper functioning of social processes, and revealed a failure of social control, the control of individual behaviour by family and kin, by political and educational authority, by all the influences which persuade most people to obey established norms.[34] In a singularly patriarchal society defined by uncompromising Catholic principles, 'fallen women' bore the brunt of public rebuke. They were regarded in a traditional society as having dishonoured their families. Illegitimacy was imagined as a 'heritable moral weakness, passed down through the blood like a tendency to drink or thievery' and was perceived as evidence of 'bad blood'.[35] This, and the fact that children also came with little or no history discouraged many couples from taking in children.[36] Very often children born to single mothers were disguised as the offspring of relatives; in other cases they were hidden from society by the simple expedient of being put into institutions.[37] Secrecy pervaded responses to illegitimacy and framed the law and adoptive process. Cohen observes in this regard, that 'at a time when illegitimacy was construed as evidence of "bad blood" and a symbol of degeneracy, adoptive parents regarded it as a defect that did not matter so long as it could be hidden'.[38] It was not until 1987 that the status of illegitimacy was finally abolished, primarily due to the efforts

29 See Chapter 13.

30 See Chapters 8 and 9.

31 Powell and Scanlon (2015) *Dark Secrets of Childhood*, pp 229–264.

32 D Ferriter (2009) *Occasions of Sin: Sex and Society in Modern Ireland* (London: Profile Books), p 227.

33 P Laslett (1980) 'Preface' in K Oosterveen and RM Smith (eds), *Bastardy and its Comparative History: Studies in the History of Illegitimacy and Marital Nonconformism in Britain, France, Sweden, North America, Jamaica, and Japan* (London: Edward Arnold).

34 Laslett (1980) *Bastardy and its Comparative History*, p 2.

35 D Cohen (2013) *Family Secrets* (London: Penguin Group), pp 113–114.

36 Middleton (1971) *When Family Failed.*

37 S McCaughren (2010) *A Study of Open Adoption in Ireland through the Narratives of Adoptive Parents* (Unpublished PhD thesis, School of Applied Social Studies, University College Cork). See Earner-Byrne's discussion of the high rates of incarceration in Ireland (Chapter 9).

38 Cohen (2013) *Family Secrets*, p 114.

of Mary Robinson (subsequently President of Ireland and UN Commissioner for Human Rights).[39] Robinson had campaigned on the issue of illegitimacy since 1974. There was a deep cultural resistance to law reform in relation to the status of illegitimacy, not just on grounds of sexual immorality but also because moral conservatives viewed support for single parents as an unjustifiable drain on the resources of the welfare state.[40] Nonetheless, State support for single parents rose from 2,000 in 1974 to over 11,000 in 1985 and 37,215 in 1996. In 1973 approximately 95 per cent of 'illegitimate' babies in Ireland were given up for adoption compared with five per cent in Denmark.[41] Gradually non-relative adoption rates in Ireland declined as illegitimacy became 'normalized' in Irish society, or at least more tolerated.

The welfare of single mothers revealed a particularly patriarchal dimension in the deliberations of the *Commission on the Relief of the Sick and Destitute Poor* in 1927.[42] Its report advocated a series of recommendations that effectively conferred a criminal status on single women with children born out of wedlock. The position adopted by the Commissioners did not endorse the County Home (workhouse) as a suitable place for the reception of single mothers.[43] Furthermore, they observed,

> in dealing with the problem of accommodation for unmarried mothers it must be recognized that there were two classes to be provided for, namely, (1) those who may be amenable to reform and (2) those who for one reason or another are regarded as less hopeful cases.[44]

They included in the second category of 'less hopeful cases' married mothers with children 'who subsequent to desertion had children not the offspring of their husbands'.[45] Single mothers who entered mother and baby homes were automatically stripped of their identities. On entering a mother and baby home, each girl was given a 'home name'.[46] This was a new name given to each new entrant in order to 'protect' their identity and that of their families. Philomena Lee spent three-and-a-half years working in the laundry of the Roscrea Mother and Baby Home, and recently recalled:

---

39 Ferriter (2009) *Occasions of Sin*, p 524.

40 Ferriter (2009) *Occasions of Sin*, p 524.

41 Ferriter (2009) *Occasions of Sin*, pp 437–438.

42 (1927) *Report of the Commission on the Relief of the Sick and Destitute Poor, Including the Insane Poor* (Dublin: Stationery Office). See Chapter 9 in this volume.

43 *Report of the Commission on the Relief of the Sick and Destitute Poor*, paras 96, 227.

44 *Report of the Commission on the Relief of the Sick and Destitute Poor*, para 228.

45 *Report of the Commission on the Relief of the Sick and Destitute Poor*, para 229

46 P Lee (2014) Keynote Address, *Her Story in Her Own Words*, Conference (University College Cork): Redefining Adoption in a New Era, Opportunities & Challenges for Law and Social Work Practice, 4–5 Sept 2014. Available at: https://www.youtube.com/watch?v=KgrkzwaXsZc (accessed 11 April 2107).

> when you went in there you had to lose your identity. I couldn't be called Philomena Lee anymore. I was called Marcella ... so I was only ever known as Marcella.[47]

With regard to the number of women in homes at the inception of the Free State the 1927 Commissioners commented:

> it is difficult to arrive with any degree of accuracy at the numbers that would have to be dealt with, but we find that on 27 March, 1926, there were in the County Homes and Dublin Workhouse 629 unmarried mothers classed as first offenders, and 391 women who had fallen more than once.[48]

They estimated that the number of deserted women with 'illegitimate' children was predictably 'small'.[49] By 1940, Ferriter estimates there were 5,600 women and children at a given time in homes with a further 2,349 children between the ages of two and 15 years boarded out in foster homes.[50]

The 1927 Commission advocated separate modes of treatment for single parents which intended to differentiate 'first offenders' from 'less hopeful cases'. It suggested that the treatment of the former

> must necessarily be in the nature of a moral up building and, while requiring firmness and discipline, must be characterized by and blended with a certain amount of individual charity and sympathy which can only be given when a true estimate of the character of each girl or young woman has been made by those in charge.[51]

Cohen, remarking on the treatment of women in English workhouses, notes that women were criminalized if they had 'fallen twice' and were 'forced to wear special uniforms to denote their crime'.[52] There was already a prototype mother and baby home, Bessborough, in Cork, opened by the Sacred Heart nuns in 1922. The Department of Local Government and Public Health noted in its 1929 report that Bessborough was 'intended primarily for young mothers who have fallen for the first time and who are likely to be influenced towards a useful and respectable life'.[53] The 75 women resident at Bessborough were trained in domestic work, cookery, needlework, dairy work, poultry keeping and gardening. Religious instruction was also a basic element in their training. The report concluded: 'there is a pressing need for homes of a type similar to that at Bessborough, and the aim should be to have these

47 Lee (2014) Keynote Address.

48 *Report of the Commission on the Relief of the Sick and Destitute Poor,* para 231.

49 *Report of the Commission on the Relief of the Sick and Destitute Poor,* para 229.

50 Ferriter (2009) *Occasions of Sin,* pp 251–252.

51 *Report of the Commission on the Relief of the Sick and Destitute Poor,* para 230.

52 Cohen (2013) *Family Secrets,* p 117.

53 *Department of Local Government and Public Health, Fourth Report, 1928–9* (Dublin: Stationery Office).

women removed from Poor Law Institutions altogether'.[54] By 1932 little progress had been achieved apart from the opening of Shan Ross Abbey Roscrea which accommodated 85 young women and is the site of the Philomena Lee narrative. The only other separate facilities for unmarried mothers, in the first offender category, were operated by the Poor Law Authorities at Pelletstown, Co Dublin and Tuam, Co Galway. Pelletstown had provision for 85 women and Tuam 33. On 31 March 1932 there were in all 868 unmarried mothers in Poor Law institutions of one kind or another.[55] These institutions have recently become the centre of intense media scrutiny and are the focus for an official commission, established in 2015, to explore the 'hidden histories' of mother and baby homes.[56]

The 'architecture of containment': policing illegitimacy

The Magdalene laundries, Smith argues, formed part of Ireland's 'architecture of containment'[57] which was based on an assortment of interlinked institutions, including mother and baby homes, reformatories, industrial schools, mental asylums and adoption agencies. All of these institutions were linked together in two important ways.[58] Firstly, many of the religious congregations who managed the reformatory and industrial schools also operated Magdalene laundries. Secondly, these institutions helped sustain each other – girls from the reformatory and industrial schools were sometimes sent to the Magdalene laundries to boost their workforce.[59] Similarly, the children of the 'Magdalenes' (as inmates were sometimes called) ended up in industrial and reformatory schools if no other home could be found for them, where they were stigmatized as 'orphans' and 'conventors', and targeted for abuse. Thus a vast institutional network concealed women and children who appeared to belie the idealized picture of Catholic morality and family life which Church and State wished to construct. The single mother, above all, had to be concealed behind the closed doors of religious-run institutions:

> In a society where even the faintest whiff of scandal threatened the respectability of the normative Irish family, the Magdalene asylums existed as a place to contain and/or punish the threatened embodiment of instability.[60]

---

54 *Fourth Report, 1928–9*, pp 113–115.

55 *Department of Local Government and Public Health, Annual Report, 1931–2* (Dublin: Stationery Office), pp 128–129.

56 The Commission of Investigation into Mother and Baby Homes and certain related matters, established in 2015 (www.mbhcoi.ie).

57 J Smith (2007) *Ireland's Magdalene Laundries and the Nation's Architecture of Containment* (Notre Dame: University of Notre Dame Press), p 2.

58 M Raftery and E O'Sullivan (1999) *Suffer the Little Children* (Dublin: New Island Books), pp 18–19; Smith (2007) *Ireland's Magdalene Laundries*, p 25.

59 Raftery and O'Sullivan (1999) *Suffer the Little Children*, pp 18–19

60 Smith (2007) *Ireland's Magdalene Laundries*, p xviii.

In addition to single mothers, the Magdalene homes admitted a range of other unwanted women, including those deemed to be 'wayward', 'backward' or 'mentally defective', those on remand from courts and those who were simply 'in the way'.[61] The survivors describe a life of hard physical work, long hours and strict discipline within the laundries:

> Seven (7) female witness reports related to continuous hard physical work in residential laundries, which was generally unpaid. Two (2) witnesses said that the regime was 'like a prison', that doors were locked all the time and exercise was taken in an enclosed yard. Working conditions were harsh and included standing for long hours, constantly washing laundry in cold water, and using heavy irons for many hours. One witness described working hard, standing in silence and being made to stand for meals and kneel to beg forgiveness if she spoke. Another witness stated that she was punched and hit as a threat not to disclose details of her everyday life working in the laundry to her family.[62]

Two women who attended mother and baby homes provided a similarly bleak picture of life within institutions. Both described 'a regimented "prison-like" atmosphere, where they were made wear uniforms and punished for talking and laughing'.[63] They described suffering humiliation at the hands of nuns who were both verbally and physically abusive. Both women felt that they had been emotionally traumatized during their time in the home. Pre- and post-natal care was described as being non-existent. Maguire has noted the 'alarmingly high' rate of infant mortality in mother and baby homes,[64] which inevitably raises questions about conditions in these institutions. Recent (undocumented) media reports on Tuam Mother and Baby Home during 2014 put this issue in the public eye.[65]

Not surprisingly many single mothers decided to leave the country. The Department of Local Government and Public Health, in its annual report for 1931–1932, noted that several complaints had been received from the English Rescue Societies because of 'the number of girls who having got into trouble leave the Free State and go to England'.[66] A conference was duly arranged between representatives of these societies and an inspector from the Department at which it was agreed 'that every effort should be made to discourage

61 Smith (2007) *Ireland's Magdalene Laundries*, p xviii.

62 Ryan Report (2009), vol. 3, para 18.25.

63 Ryan Report (2009), vol. 4, para 5.145.

64 MJ Maguire (2009) *Precarious Childhood in Post-Independence Ireland* (Manchester: Manchester University Press), p 88.

65 For example *The Guardian*, 4 June 2014; *Irish Times*, 7 June 2014.

66 *Department of Local Government and Public Health, Annual Report, 1931–2* (Dublin: Stationery Office), pp 129–130.

girls going to England in such circumstances and to bring them back where possible'.[67] Kornitzer observed that efforts to repatriate Irish single mothers were not conspicuously successful, creating a surplus of Catholic babies available for adoption in Britain.[68] The explanation for this failure to repatriate single parents was the mothers' fear of stigmatization, institutionalization and losing their child. As O'Sullivan and O'Donnell put it:

> the mother, if she did not (or could not) emigrate was placed in a mother and baby home or county home, and her children if confined in a mother and baby home were generally adopted in Ireland, or in the US.[69]

Such a failure cannot have been wholly displeasing to the Irish authorities since it served to distort the nation's illegitimacy rate by artificially pushing it downwards. It was, therefore, possible for Church and State to take comfort in Ireland's relatively low official illegitimacy rate, which stood at 2.68 per cent in 1925.[70] The statistics provided propagandistic 'evidence' (however spurious) of the virtuous adherence of Irish women to traditional sexual mores. However, by 1945 the Irish illegitimacy rate had risen to 3.93 per cent, its highest annual rate between 1864 and 1977.[71]

The term 'Magdalene' captures the 'othered' status of the single mother as a 'sinner'. It also reflects on the children of single mothers, referred to in the Ryan Report euphemistically as 'orphans', who were picked out for particularly severe abuse.[72] The Report comments that 'the sons of lone mothers, "orphans or conventors", were reported as particular targets for such abuse [denigration of family of origin], being told their mothers were "sinners", "slags" or "old whores."'[73] The practice of stigmatizing illegitimacy was, Luddy argues, driven by economic considerations.[74] Property rights were paramount. Single mothers were socially constructed as 'prostitutes' and 'offenders'. Chastity was elevated in Irish culture to a totemic status through the cult of motherhood. Inglis observes that the Irish mother 'creates and maintains the supervision and discipline of the Church within the home'.[75] This rigid Victorian sexual ethic could not be defended as society gradually modernized and the cultural oppression of women came to be challenged in liberal civil society, by organizations like the Joint Committee of Women's Societies and

67 *Annual Report, 1931–2*, pp 129–130.

68 M Kornitzer (1952) *Child Adoption in the Modern World* (London: Putnam), p 52.

69 O'Sullivan and O'Donnell (2012) *Coercive Confinement*, p 273.

70 (1927) *Report of the Commission on the Relief of the Sick and Destitute Poor*, App. table v.

71 Ferriter (2009) *Occasions of Sin*, p 252.

72 Ryan Report (2009).

73 Ryan Report (2009), para 3:7.236.

74 Luddy (1995) *Women*; Luddy (1997) 'Abandoned Women and Bad Characters'.

75 Inglis (1987) *Moral Monopoly*, p 68.

Social Workers (JCWSSW), founded in 1935. The introduction of adoption legislation became inevitable in the post-Second World War era.

Overseas placements or 'forced adoptions'?

The post-Second World War era saw an increase in the numbers of 'illegitimate' and orphaned children. In the period preceding the enactment of the Adoption Act 1952, 'illegitimate' children (as argued above) were constructed as one of society's social problems. In a society whose Constitution framed the family as the basic unit of society,[76] the fate of the 'illegitimate' child was at best tenuous. A number of unsatisfactory, highly questionable and illegal practices were improvised in order to provide so-called 'solutions'. Irish society did not tolerate single mothers, with no humane support proffered. Financial assistance was not introduced until the 1970s. The moral mindset of exclusion remained resolute in its dogmatic Catholic ideology. The authority of the Catholic Church remained firmly embedded in State relations and, as a result, the fate of the 'illegitimate' child rested with both Church and State.[77] It has been remarked that 'no child was more disregarded, in policy and practice, than the 'illegitimate'' child'.[78] Indeed society did not view 'illegitimate' children as valuable future citizens worthy of care and protection. Instead,

> the State with the assistance and co-operation of the local authorities, religious orders, and Catholic philanthropic organisations, used institutionalisation, boarding-out and overseas adoption as the most effective and inexpensive means of controlling potentially deviant, immoral and delinquent 'illegitimate' children.[79]

Some children were 'boarded out' to foster parents in what became known as informal de facto adoptions. However, in reality this often became a 'euphemism for child labour'.[80] The informal nature of such de facto adoptions 'suited the haphazard, patriarchal, father-centred concept of family life; if the child turned out badly he could be disowned' and so there was no need to formalize this arrangement.[81]

Another 'solution' that was practised was the removal of children from the State who were placed with American Catholic families. These 'illegitimate' children were seen as dispensable and America, particularly in the post-war

---

76 See Chapter 13 in this volume.

77 Inglis (1987) *Moral Monopoly*, pp 140–142.

78 Maguire (2009) *Precarious Childhood*, p 49.

79 Maguire (2009) *Precarious Childhood*, p 49.

80 M Milotte (2012) *Banished Babies: The Secret History of Ireland's Baby Export Business* (rev. ed, Dublin: New Island).

81 Middleton (1971) *When Family Failed*, p 236.

era, was seen as the land of opportunity.[82] Church and State worked alongside one another in sanctioning the export of children; 'it was regulated by the Catholic Archbishop of Dublin Dr John Charles McQuaid, and facilitated by the Department of Foreign Affairs which issued passports so that children could be taken out of the country'.[83]

It is very difficult to establish the exact numbers of children who were sent abroad for informal adoptions, although it has been noted by Cooney that by 1951 over 300 children per annum were being 'sold' overseas.[84] However, what is clear is that there were very few questions asked about the practice at the time. While the custom of sending children abroad for adoption provided children with an alternative to a life of institutionalization, it was also thought that the practice provided an optimal solution for all parties. It remedied the overcrowding often experienced in mother and baby homes and relieved local authorities of the financial costs associated with industrial schools and foster care.[85] What did become a priority, however, was that children were being sent to Catholic homes, and in fact this seems to have taken precedence over the suitability of adopters. With very little paperwork required, often a letter from a Catholic priest sufficed and there was also evidence of large sums of money passing hands between adoptive parents or their agents and the orphanages, which were run by religious orders.[86] It appears that some children were removed from the State without a passport while other 'illegitimate' children were wrongly registered as the biological children of their 'adopters'.[87] Ireland's ad hoc response to catering for the needs of 'illegitimate' children meant that their fate was sealed and had far-reaching consequences for their future lives. In 1950 Archbishop John McQuaid introduced guidelines for international adoptions where prospective adopters had to fulfil six conditions. One condition was that adopters had to swear an affidavit that they were Catholics and guarantee to bring up the adopted child as a Catholic. They also had to swear to undertake to educate the adopted child in a Catholic school and university.[88] In the lead-up to making legal provision for adoption, it appears that a preoccupation with Catholic values remained foremost in the minds of legislators.

---

82 M Milotte (1997) *Banished Babies: The Secret History of Ireland's Baby Export Business* (Dublin: New Island), p 23.

83 Milotte (2012) *Banished Babies*, pp 7–8.

84 J Cooney (1999) *John Charles McQuaid: Ruler of Catholic Ireland* (Dublin: The O'Brien Press).

85 M Maguire (2002) 'Foreign Adoptions and the Evolution of Irish Adoption Policy 1945–52', *Journal of Social History*, 36(2), 387–404.

86 Cooney (1999) *John Charles McQuaid*; Milotte (2012) *Banished Babies*.

87 M Milotte (2011) *Banished Babies: The Secret History of Ireland's Baby Export Business* 2nd edn (Dublin: New Island); Maguire (2009) *Precarious Childhood*.

88 Cooney (1999) *John Charles McQuaid*.

The lead-up to the enactment of the Adoption Act 1952

The lead-up to the enactment of the Adoption Act 1952 highlights the outlandish way in which the Irish government was cornered into producing adoption legislation. While one would have thought that legislation was introduced to protect the best interests of the children, this was far from the minds of those involved. Instead, legislation was primarily enacted in response to media reports and civil society pressures, which highlighted the ease with which Irish children were being sent abroad for adoption.[89] This left both the Church and State with little or no choice but to take action. There were a number of incidents that drew special attention to the shortcomings of Ireland's adoption policy in the early 1950s.

One such incident was when American actress Jane Russell set her sights on adopting a child. On her arrival to Britain she realized that, under British law, it would not be that straightforward. Adoption had been legalized there since 1926. However, when the opportunity arose of adopting an Irish child from Britain, there appeared to be very few legal barriers to stop her. While Milotte notes that the whole transaction was in fact illegal[90] (a contention supported by the advice of the Attorney General, cited below), the authorities, without question, issued the child with a passport for a 'three-month holiday' knowing full well the long-term implications. Russell, therefore, adopted a three-year-old Irish child whose parents were living and working in Britain. Little Tommy Kavanagh flew back to America with Russell on an Irish passport.[91]

The establishment of a legal framework for adoption in Ireland – Adoption Act 1952

The international press attention that the Jane Russell story attracted was unwelcome for both the Catholic hierarchy and the government. Following this international exposé of Ireland's baby trade, the government was left with no option but to consider legislating for adoption. The sluggish pace at which adoption legislation was finally introduced meant that 'lawmakers placed church-state relations above the well-being and best interests of thousands of 'illegitimate' Irish children who would have benefited enormously from having stable, loving adoptive homes'.[92]

By the time Ireland came to legislating for adoption, there were only eight countries in the Western world that had no provision for adoption.[93] Adoption became a legal process in England and Wales in 1926, in Scotland in 1930 and in Northern Ireland in 1929. According to Cooney the question

89 Maguire (2009) *Precarious Childhood*; Milotte (2012) *Banished Babies.*

90 Milotte (2012) *Banished Babies.*

91 Milotte (2012) *Banished Babies;* Maguire (2009) *Precarious Childhood.*

92 Maguire (2009) *Precarious Childhood*, p 135.

93 Kornitzer (1952) *Child Adoption.*

of making adoption legal was first asked in the Dáil in 1939 with further questions being asked in the mid-1940s.[94] With high rates of illegitimacy at this time and a general dissatisfaction amongst 'adopters' of their legal position, there was growing need to put this issue on the political agenda. In the mid-1940s there was also a move towards placing children in foster homes (which were regarded as de facto adoptions) rather than institutions which was overseen by an organization called the Catholic Protection and Rescue Society.[95] However, as noted by Downing, the issue of introducing adoption legislation rumbled on in the Dáil at various points in the mid-1940s with Ministers providing both vague and unsatisfactory responses.[96] Ireland's remarkable reluctance to legislate for adoption was broadly based on three primary concerns: that it would interfere with the natural bloodline and as a result it would have a direct impact on inheritance rights; it would be unconstitutional; and the 'true faith' would be compromised.

In 1950 the Minister for Justice, General Séan Mac Eoin, in a response relayed by Minister for Defence, Dr T. F. O'Higgins, indicated a strong reluctance to introduce proposals for legislation that 'would provide for the irrevocable transfer of parent's rights and duties in respect of a child to any other person'.[97] There was strong sentiment that the issue of inheritance played on the minds of government. There was a long custom, especially in rural Ireland, of keeping property within the family and passing land down through the family bloodline.[98] Adoption was regarded as a distinct threat to the natural bloodline, and one that would have direct consequences for inheritance. According to Whyte, one official of the Adoption Society recalled a rural Deputy (Member of Parliament) remarking that to interfere with the line of succession was 'like interfering with a stud-book'.[99]

Some of the concerns questioned the constitutionality of introducing legislation on adoption, with particular reference to Articles 40, 41 and 42 of the Irish Constitution.[100] The family cell was seen as an organic part of civil society. Its responsibilities are set out in the 1931 papal encyclical *Quadragesimo Anno*. This encyclical advocated the principle of subsidiarity which put the family and voluntary organizations at the centre of an ethical civil society. The State was consigned to last resort for welfare provision. Article 41.1 of the 1937 Constitution declared that:

---

94 Cooney (1999) *John Charles McQuaid*.

95 Cooney (1999) *John Charles McQuaid*.

96 M Downing (1986) *Adoption Policy in Ireland* (Unpub. Masters thesis, School of Social Science, University College Cork).

97 *Dáil Éireann deb*, cxxiii [9] 29 Nov 1950.

98 See Chapter 8 in this volume.

99 JH Whyte (1971) *Church and State in Modern Ireland 1923–1970* (Dublin: Gill and Macmillan), p 187.

100 See Downing (1986) *Adoption Policy in Ireland*.

> The State acknowledges that the primary and natural educator of the child is the Family and guarantees to respect the inalienable right and duty of parents to provide, according to their means, for the religious and moral, intellectual, physical and social education of their children.

In defending the decision (by General Mac Eoin in 1950) not to introduce adoption legislation, Attorney General Charles Casey, who provided legal advice to the Cabinet, pointed out a number of difficulties in relation to the constitutional position.[101] With reference to Article 42 of the Irish Constitution he asserted that:

> This Article requires very careful consideration. It is clearly binding on both parents of the ordinary family and in my opinion equally binding on the mother of the 'illegitimate' child. What does this mean? If the word inalienable is to be given any meaning at all, it may mean that no mother of an 'illegitimate' child can alienate her right and duty to provide according to her means for the religious and moral, intellectual, physical and social education of her child. In other words, if she cannot allow her child to be irrevocably adopted can the State pass legislation enabling her to do so?[102]

While Article 42.5[103] provided for exceptional cases in which the State could intervene and supply the place of the parents, it was with due regard for the 'natural and imprescriptible rights of the child'.

The refusal to legislate for adoption in 1950 was not well received, especially in light of the staunch efforts of the Adoption Society which worked tirelessly on this issue. Indeed the question of an alternative to adoption was addressed by the assistant editor of the *Irish Times*, W. A. Newman. According to Newman, in the absence of legal adoption the 'illegitimate' child was destined to one for four fates: (1) That it may be 'adopted' by Irish 'adopters' without any legal safeguards and could be removed from their care at any time, and with no legal property rights; (2) 'It may be adopted by foreign adopters under the law of [their] country, in which case it enjoys all the rights and privileges of a child of their body. This is the lucky child'. (3) It may be farmed out to foster parents where the State would pay a contribution or (4) 'It can be lumped into an institution, a home or whatever you call it'.[104] His final remark was that 'not a man or woman in this State would deny that an Act legalising adoption would be the fitting alternative to those four dooms

101 Downing (1986) *Adoption Policy in Ireland.*

102 *Irish Times*, 14 Feb 1951, quoted in Downing (1986) *Adoption Policy in Ireland*, p 30.

103 Which has now been replaced by Article 42A 2.1°.

104 Downing (1986) *Adoption Policy in Ireland*, p 32.

for the unwanted child'.[105] These observations highlight the unease in the media and civil society with regard to the slow pace at which adoption was being progressed.

Irish legislators, therefore, had to do their best not to displace the traditional nuclear family. Unlike British law, unmarried people were practically prohibited from adopting. They could only adopt in exceptional and specific circumstances.[106] Indeed, Catholic principles filtered through the Adoption Act 1952 and adopting parents were to be 'of the same religion as the child and his parents or, if the child is illegitimate, his mother'.[107] This meant that couples of mixed marriages were ineligible to adopt. What is particularly worthy of note is that adoption legislation was circumscribed to illegitimate children only. The Minister for Justice Gerald Boland referred to the 'danger that the bill would be held to be unconstitutional if it provided for the adoption of legitimate children whose parents are alive'.[108] He further remarked:

> the Constitution declares the rights and duties of parents towards their children to be inalienable, and any provision for the permanent transfer of those rights and duties, even with the consent of the parents, might be unconstitutional. The main need for adoption arises in connection with orphans and 'illegitimate' children. The Bill provides adequately for them, and I think it is better to deal with them only than to risk making the Bill unconstitutional and perhaps shipwrecking the whole proposal.[109]

This highlights the contention that the same Constitutional rights did not apply to unmarried mothers or their 'illegitimate' children.

The reality was that the Catholic hierarchy opposed adoption on a number of grounds, and government officials were not in a position to go against the wishes of the Catholic Church.[110] The subject of religion was a recurring one and 'the question of legal adoption was unsuccessfully raised in the Dáil eleven more times between June 1947 and October 1950'.[111] Indeed, the unwillingness to legalize adoption lay primarily in the fear that it would lead to proselytism, as many homes catering for single mothers were run by Protestant organizations.[112] Maguire notes the distinct differences that existed between the debates on adoption in the British Parliament in 1925–1926

---

105 WA Newman (1951) 'Legal adoption', *The Bell*, XVI: 4, 59–66.

106 Adoption Act 1952, s 11.

107 s 21(2).

108 *Dáil Éireann deb*, cxxxii, [8] 11 June 1952.

109 *Dáil Éireann deb*, cxxxii, [8] 11 June 1952.

110 Maguire (2009) *Precarious Childhood.*

111 Downing (1986) *Adoption Policy in Ireland*, p 24.

112 Whyte (1971) *Church and State*, p 191.

and the Dáil in 1952.[113] The debates on adoption in the British Parliament[114] focused on the numerous benefits that would stem from legalizing adoption. There was also recognition given to the State's responsibility in caring for its vulnerable children. The tone, therefore, of the British debates contrasted sharply with 'the obsessive concern among Irish lawmakers with questions of religion and faith, at the expense of the rights and interests of children and their biological parents'.[115] Although there were a number of attempts made to put a legal framework in place for adoption, the final push did not come about until 1950. An external pressure group known as the Legal Adoption Society of Ireland was central in lobbying for legal adoption. This group was founded in 1948 and the aims of the organization were 'the introduction in Eire (Ireland) of an act legalising the adoption of children' and the 'the reform of birth certificates'.[116] An entry in the Adoption Society papers on 5 March 1948 reads as follows:

> An address was made by Mr James in opening the meeting introducing Mr Hartford who gave a very commendable speech on the real necessity for legal adoption. This was followed by another address by Mr Ryan giving a touching outline of the hardships entailed by children in the absence of legal adoption and giving an approximate figure of 20,000 children inside the last 20 years as being in need of legal adoption.[117]

It was this group who recognized the real need for legalizing adoption and that produced a private member's bill.

Finally, the Adoption Act 1952 was passed. The Act regulated the practice of adoption and established An Bord Uachtála[118] whose role would be to oversee all adoptions. Under the Act, adoption societies had to be registered with the Adoption Board. The Act did not bring to an end the practice of sending children overseas. The only restrictions introduced were that only children aged between one and seven years would be eligible for overseas placements. The child's mother or guardian had to consent to an overseas adoption and the practice of donations was not prohibited.[119]

The Adoption Act 1952 was a very limited piece of legislation being confined to 'illegitimate' children. The legacy of Ireland's adoption history remained distinctly visible in the Adoption Act 1952. Adoption was regarded as providing a clean slate for everyone. Single mothers could forget the

113 Maguire (2009) *Precarious Childhood.*

114 Maguire (2009) *Precarious Childhood.*

115 Maguire (2009) *Precarious* Childhood, p 138.

116 National Library of Ireland (NLI), Adoption Society Papers, 1948, MS 19.349.

117 NLI, Adoption Society Papers, 1948, MS 19.349.

118 The Adoption Board; now known as the Adoption Authority of Ireland.

119 Milotte (2012) *Banished Babies*, p 64.

'mistakes' of their past and reintegrate into Catholic Irish society wearing a veil of 'normality'. Their veneer of chastity 'protected' them and their families from the harshness of a dogmatic Catholic ideology. The children would become part of a two-parent Catholic family and the adopters would have the legal safeguards to 'own' the child as if it had been born to them in wedlock. The influence of the culture of secrecy was evident in the closed nature of the adoption process that cut the adopted child off permanently from their origins. Indeed, 'secrecy permitted adoptive parents to banish their children's origins. Openness by contrast meant that illegitimacy stayed near the surface'.[120]

Conclusion

The fate of the 'illegitimate' child in Irish social policy reveals a narrative pervaded by secrecy, the influence of blood and genes in protecting property rights and obsession with preserving sexual mores. This, for many years, resulted in the problematization and institutionalization of both single mothers and their children. In a patriarchal culture there were no 'fallen men'. Women were socially constructed as Magdalenes bearing sole moral responsibility for the illegitimacy of their children. They had to carry the burden of their 'sin' with them for the rest of their lives in the form of stigmatization and ostracization, with many carrying their secret to the grave. The children were problematized, institutionalized and made into social outcasts. A trade in children existed in the form of overseas adoptions. The scale of this practice remains to be documented. The absence of records makes it virtually impossible for these children (now adults) to establish their origins as the Philomena Lee case has demonstrated to a large public audience. This has helped to highlight the plight of many women who experienced the trauma of having to give up a child. The legacy of Ireland's adoption history has created second-class citizens. While the Adoption Act 2010 is now the principal statute, there is a strong residue of its predecessor in its discourse, philosophy and practical application.

120 Cohen (2013) *Family Secrets*, p 137.

13
Embedding the Family in the Irish Constitution

Thomas Mohr

Introduction

The Irish Constitution of 1937 devotes a substantial part of its provisions on fundamental rights to the position of the family in Irish society. Article 41 of the 1937 Constitution has proved to be one of the most controversial provisions in that document. Some commentators accuse it of reflecting Catholic social values, providing unwelcome stereotypes on the position of women in Irish society and promoting the marital family at the expense of an increasing number of non-marital families.[1] Others argue that these provisions are typical of constitutions of the 1920s and 1930s from all parts of Europe and, consequently, should not necessarily be seen as the product of Catholic social teachings.[2]

No equivalent to Article 41 is found in the earlier Irish Free State Constitution of 1922. There were many proposals to enshrine similar provisions in the 1922 Constitution but all were finally rejected. Although the drafters of the 1922 Constitution had broadly similar attitudes towards the place of the family in Irish society to their counterparts in 1937 they concluded that these were not appropriate matters to be enshrined in a national constitution.

The contents of Article 41 have been the subject of frequent debate and analysis. Yet the decision as to whether or not the position of the family was a suitable matter to enshrine in the text of a constitution has received less attention. The absence of any provisions concerning the family in the

1 For example, see JH Whyte (1980) *Church and State in Modern Ireland,* 2nd edn (Dublin: Gill & Macmillan), pp 51, 188–189. For a range of views on the provisions of Article 41 see the 2006 All Party Oireachtas Committee on the Constitution, Tenth Report: *The Family*. Available at: https://www.constitution.ie/Documents/Oireachtas%2010th-Report-Family%202006.pdf (accessed 20 Jul 2015).

2 G Hogan (2014) 'Some Thoughts on the Origins of the 1937 Constitution' in FM Larkin and NM Dawson (eds) *Lawyers, the Law and History* (Dublin: Four Courts Press), 209–232 and the foreword by the same author to D Keogh and A McCarthy (2007) *The Making of the Irish Constitution 1937* (Cork: Mercier Press), 13–37.

1922 Constitution proved to be a major source of criticism for an already controversial document. Yet the provisions on the family that were finally enshrined in its successor have, in turn, proved to be among the most contested provisions of the 1937 Constitution.

Differences in drafting the 1922 and 1937 Constitutions

The shared values of the drafters of Irish Constitutions of 1922 and 1937 far outweigh any differences between them. Most of the drafters of both documents were devout Catholics, held strong nationalist principles and wished to advance the sovereignty of the Irish State as much as possible. There were, however, differences in the political contexts of 1922 and 1937 that resulted in a number of important divergences between the two texts. The drafters of the 1922 Constitution were required to enshrine key provisions demanded by the 1921 Anglo Irish Treaty in their text. By contrast the 1937 Constitution was drafted after a series of constitutional amendments had largely dismantled the Treaty settlement. Another major difference between the Irish Constitutions of 1922 and 1937 concerns the place of religion in the two texts. There are no references to God in the substantive provisions of the 1922 Constitution and references to religion only appear in provisions designed to maintain freedom of religious worship.[3] By contrast references to 'God', 'Jesus Christ', the 'Holy Trinity' and other aspects of Christian belief appear throughout the text of the 1937 Constitution.

This chapter is concerned with a third noticeable difference between the two Irish Constitutions. The 1922 Constitution focuses on establishing the machinery of governance such as the executive, national parliament and system of courts and also details a number of fundamental rights. There are relatively few statements in the 1922 text that might be considered 'directive principles', meaning that they had no immediate or obvious legal impact on state institutions or the rights of citizens but were primarily intended as matters of guidance along a desired path of development for the State.[4] These directive principles cannot be directly enforced by the courts but have been used as interpretative instruments.[5] The exclusion of directive principles from the 1922 Constitution was no accident but the result of deliberate policy.

The 1937 Constitution also provides sustained attention to the machinery of government in provisions that are broadly similar to those of the 1922

3 There was a recognition that 'all lawful authority comes from God to the people' but this appeared in the Preamble of the Irish statute intended to bring the 1922 Constitution into force. See Constitution of the Irish Free State (Saorstát Éireann) Act 1922.

4 Possible exceptions include brief expressions of hope for Irish unity in the preamble to the statute that brought the Free State Constitution into force. Constitution of the Irish Free State (Saorstát Éireann) Act 1922.

5 The use of Article 45's directive principles of social policy as interpretative instruments is outlined in Gerard Hogan and Gerry White (2003) *The Irish Constitution*, 4th edn (Dublin: LexisNexis Butterworths) pp 2080–2086.

Constitution. Yet the 1937 Constitution also contains far more directive principles than its predecessor that can be seen as reflecting philosophical and social values commonly associated with the Catholic Church. For example, Article 44.1.1° declares 'The State acknowledges that the homage of public worship is due to Almighty God. It shall hold His Name in reverence, and shall respect and honour religion'. Article 44.1.2° of the original text provided 'The State recognises the special position of the Holy Catholic Apostolic and Roman Church as the guardian of the Faith professed by the great majority of the citizens' and also recognized the existence of other named religions. These can be termed 'directive principles' as they had no obvious and immediate impact on the governance of the State or the rights of its citizens but were intended as guidance along a desired path of development for the future state. Article 45 of the Constitution contains provisions that are officially known as 'directive principles of social policy'. These are expressly intended to provide guidance to the Oireachtas and their provisions are not cognizable by the courts. Article 45 includes directive principles declaring a commitment to support 'the infirm, the widow, the orphan, and the aged', that 'the tender age of children shall not be abused and that citizens shall not be forced by economic necessity to enter avocations unsuited to their sex, age or strength' and the establishment 'on the land in economic security as many families as in the circumstances shall be practicable'. The 1937 Constitution also contains numerous references to the natural law, a concept that enjoyed particular popularity with Catholic theologians and philosophers in the early twentieth century. Although these references may also have been intended as directive principles they would later have a direct impact on the development of Irish law in the form of recognition of unenumerated rights.[6]

Directive principles were consciously omitted from the 1922 Constitution of the Irish Free State in contrast to the stance adopted in 1937. The drafters of the 1922 Constitution maintained this stance in the face of intense domestic lobbying and the example set by several foreign constitutions that contained numerous directive provisions on the subject of the family.[7] The contrasting approach towards the position of the family within the texts of the two Constitutions was not the result of differing social or religious values between 1922 and 1937. As mentioned earlier, most of the drafters of the 1922 Constitution and members of the provisional government shared the values and attitudes towards the family of their successors in 1937. These contrasting approaches could be attributed to the different circumstances in which the two Constitutions were drafted, an active British government and

6 *Ryan v Attorney General* [1965] IESC 1; [1965] IR 294 and *McGee v Attorney General* [1973] IESC 2; [1974] IR 284.

7 For example, see F O'Reilly, Catholic Truth Society to A O'Rahilly, 1 Apr 1922 (UCD Archives, Kennedy papers, P178/27).

a passive Catholic Church in 1922 with a passive British government and an active Catholic Church in 1937. Yet the fundamental reason for the different approach was differing attitudes as to what a national constitution should be and what purpose it should serve. Those responsible for the drafting and enacting of the 1922 Constitution wanted a short and simple document that focused primarily on establishing the mechanics of governance for the infant State. In these circumstances they were determined to keep directive principles to an absolute minimum in the text. This resulted in a policy of rejecting draft provisions containing directive principles concerning the role and position of the family notwithstanding broad agreement with their contents.

This chapter examines the provisions concerning the family in the 1937 Constitution and analyses whether they were consistent with the values of those responsible for the enactment of the 1922 Constitution. It also examines the proposals to embed the family in the 1922 Constitution and explains why these efforts were unsuccessful notwithstanding broad agreement with their contents. Finally, it explains why the drafters of the 1922 Constitution insisted on producing as short and simple a document as possible that consciously kept directive principles, including declarations on the position of the family in Irish society, out of the text.

The position of the family

Eamon de Valera, who came to power as President of the Executive Council of the Irish Free State in 1932, considered the very word 'home' to have sacred qualities.[8] Recognition of the role of the family in society and as a buttress to the State was considered fundamental by the drafters of the 1937 Constitution, an approach supported by numerous papal encyclicals. For example, according to Leo XIII's *Sapientiae Christianae* (1890), '[t]he family may be regarded as the cradle of civil society, and it is in great measure within the circle of family life that the destiny of the State is fostered'.[9]

Other papal encyclicals also provided important sources of inspiration, in particular Leo XIII's *Rerum Novarum* of 1891 and Pius XI's *Casti Connubii* of 1930. A number of existing constitutions from Catholic countries also proved influential, for example the 1933 Constitution of Portugal.[10] The institution of the family was seen as being older than all other human communities including sovereign states and their institutions. It was seen as an institution supported and protected by eternal and unchanging natural law. This point was emphasized by the clerical advisers to the government on the drafting

8 *Dáil Éireann deb* lxvii [1866] 4 June 1937.

9 John Charles McQuaid, notes on 'articles on the family', Mar 1937, quoting Leo XIII *Sapientiae Christianae* (UCD Archives, de Valera papers, P150/2408).

10 For example, George Gavan Duffy to de Valera, 7 Apr 1935 (UCD Archives, Gavan Duffy papers, P152/39).

of the 1937 Constitution including the future archbishop of Dublin, John Charles McQuaid, and a special committee of Jesuits. It is no coincidence that the institution of the family inspired McQuaid to write a lengthy philosophical disquisition on the nature and contents of natural law that drew on the works of St Thomas Aquinas and various papal encyclicals. McQuaid wrote that the family was 'an institution of nature, a moral institution in the sense that, on the analogy of the human person, it possesses rights and is bound by obligations'.[11]

All these considerations ensured that the family was seen as entitled to protection from interference from the State in all but the most extreme circumstances. This area of protection intersected with many other fundamental rights including those of religion, property and education.[12] Many contributors to the drafting of the 1937 Constitution also believed that the institution of the family could be utilized to improve the governance of the State. For example, proposals were made during the drafting of the 1937 Constitution that an extra vote be given in Dáil elections to heads of families intended to emphasize 'a family outlook in political affairs as compared to an irresponsible individualistic outlook'.[13] It was also proposed that the 1937 Constitution should follow the example of the 1933 Constitution of Portugal and establish rural parochial committees that would be elected by heads of families. This was advocated by Edward Cahill who argued that such committees 'being founded on the natural basis of the family and the parish, would be saved from the corruption and the jobbery, which apparently prevailed in the previous rural councils'.[14] The Irish government rejected all these proposals. Instead, the 1937 Constitution focused on enshrining principles that reflected the right of the family to protection from State interference in all but the most extreme circumstances.

The opening provisions of Article 41 of the 1937 Constitution are very similar to a number of drafts offered by the Jesuit advisory committee.[15] They begin by recognizing the importance of the family to society and the State. They also recognize the position of the family under natural law:

> 41.1.1 The State recognises the Family as the natural primary and fundamental unit group of Society, and as a moral institution possessing inalienable and imprescriptible rights, antecedent and superior to all positive law.

---

11 John Charles McQuaid, notes on 'articles on the family', Mar 1937 (UCD Archives, de Valera papers, P150/2408).

12 McQuaid, notes on 'articles on the family'.

13 See *Dáil Éireann deb*, lxvii [1327-1334] 1 June 1937.

14 Edward Cahill SJ to de Valera, 21 Oct 1936 and 13 Nov 1935 (UCD Archives, Gavan Duffy papers, P152/39) and Article 17 of the 1933 Constitution of Portugal.

15 Suggestions for a Catholic constitution, Oct 1936 (UCD Archives, de Valera papers, P150/2393).

> 41.1.2 The State, therefore, guarantees to protect the Family in its constitution and authority, as the necessary basis of social order and as indispensable to the welfare of the Nation and the State.

It is unlikely that the Irish government in power in 1922 would have disagreed with any of the principles outlined in Article 41 of the 1937 Constitution. Of course, *Rerum Novarum* and other relevant papal encyclicals were also available in this period. Kevin O'Higgins, Minister for External Affairs and Minister for Justice, associated the family with the natural law at the Imperial Conference of 1926 when he joined the South African delegation in opposing a change to the nationality law common to all members of the Commonwealth. The current state of the law provided that a woman who married an alien lost her nationality irrespective of whether or not she was entitled to receive the nationality of her husband. O'Higgins objected to the proposal that women should have the right to choose whether or not to keep their original nationality on marriage to an alien. He argued that facilitating a position in which husband and wife might have different nationalities would be to create a 'national frontier' within the family. He used natural law principles and evoked the works of St Thomas Aquinas to justify this stance.[16]

The common values between those responsible for the creation of the two Irish Constitutions were also evident during the 1937 parliamentary debates on the provisions concerning the family that appeared in de Valera's draft Constitution. Members of Fine Gael, which included most of the Cumann na nGaedheal administration that had held power between 1922 and 1932, did not disagree with the concept of the family as 'the natural primary and fundamental unit group of Society'. Instead they attacked the vagueness of these provisions and their suitability for inclusion in a national constitution.[17]

The position of women

Article 41.2.1° of the 1937 Constitution provides 'the State recognises that by her life within the home, woman gives to the State a support without which the common good cannot be achieved'. Although many European constitutions in the 1920s and 1930s contained provisions for the protection of maternity, Article 41 of the 1937 Irish Constitution recognized the place of 'woman' instead of 'mothers' in the home. De Valera refused to replace the word 'woman' in Article 41.2.1° notwithstanding arguments that it would make the article far more acceptable.[18] The papal encyclical *Rerum Novarum*

16 Imperial Conference 1926, committee on nationality (NAI, Department of Foreign Affairs, 1/20). See also Department of Justice memorandum, undated (UCD Archives, Blythe papers, P35/217) and *Dáil Éireann deb,* liv [1462–1464] 15 Dec 1934 and liv [398] 28 Nov 1934.

17 For example, *Dáil Éireann deb,* lxvii [1582] (2 June 1937) and lxvii [1887] (4 June 1937).

18 *Dáil Éireann deb,* lxvii [1867–1868] 4 June 1937.

provided 'a woman is by nature fitted for home-work, and it is that which is best adapted at once to preserve her modesty and to promote the good bring-up of children and the well-being of the family'.[19]

Women's organizations made unfavourable comparisons between these provisions of Eamon de Valera's draft Constitution and those of the 1922 Constitution. The National University Women Graduates' Association passed a resolution that presented the 1922 Constitution as a document reflecting principles of 'equal rights and opportunities'. The text produced in 1922 was contrasted with the draft Constitution of 1937 which was presented as a 'sinister and retrogressive' measure.[20] The 1922 Constitution has long served as a useful foil to be used against its successor with respect to its treatment of women. Many of these eulogies of the 1922 Constitution were based on what it did not say rather than on what it did. The 1922 Constitution did not attempt to stereotype the place the place of women in society. It did not speak of life or duties within the home. It did not speak of preventing people from entering avocations unsuited to their sex, age and strength. Nevertheless, the attitudes of the administrations in power in 1922 and 1937 were almost identical on these points.

The assumption that a woman's place was in the home surfaced again and again in legislation passed by the government that had overseen the enactment of the 1922 Constitution. This is evident in legislation permitting the exclusion of women from certain types of employment, the maintenance of the marriage bar in the civil service and the gradual removal of women from juries.[21] The undesirability of women being employed in certain professions, for example as customs officers, was raised on many occasions in the Oireachtas.[22] Kevin O'Higgins, as Minister for Justice, even excluded women stenographers from the Circuit Court and from the Central Criminal Court on the basis that these courts often dealt with matters 'which one would not like to discuss with the feminine members of one's own family'.[23] O'Higgins' position on the place of women in Irish society was almost identical to that enshrined in Article 41.2, as illustrated when he told the Dáil: 'It is the normal and natural function of women to have children. It still is the normal and natural function of women to have charge of households'.[24]

19 Quoted in John Charles McQuaid, notes on 'articles on the family', Mar 1937 (UCD Archives, de Valera papers, P150/2408).

20 *Irish Times*, 11 May 1937.

21 Civil Service Regulation (Amendment) Act 1926; Local Authorities (Officers and Employees) Act 1926; Juries (Amendment) Act 1924 and the Juries Act 1927.

22 For example, see *Dáil Éireann deb*, xiii [503-4] 18 Nov 1925 and *Seanad Éireann deb*, vi [261] 17 Dec 1925.

23 *Dáil Éireann deb*, xviii [469] 15 Feb 1927.

24 *Dáil Éireann deb*, xviii [766] 23 Feb 1927.

The position of marriage

In Article 41.3.1° 'The State pledges itself to guard with special care the institution of Marriage, on which the Family is founded, and to protect it against attack'. Other provisions in Article 41.3 go beyond the status of being directive principles. In particular, the prohibition in the original wording of 41.3.2° that 'No law shall be enacted providing for the grant of a dissolution of marriage' had more obvious practical implications than other provisions of Article 41. Yet these provisions also attracted considerable controversy during their lifetime. The absolute prohibition on divorce was finally removed in 1995 and was replaced by a new Article 41.3.2° containing details of the conditions required for granting a dissolution of marriage that are more suitable as legislative provisions than being embedded in the text of a national constitution.[25] The provisions of the revised Article 41.3.2° erect formidable obstacles to those seeking dissolution of marriage and reflect a continuing sense of hostility to the institution of divorce.

Early drafts of the 1937 Constitution listed grounds for annulment and provided for the dissolution of the marriages of unbaptized persons under certain circumstances. These detailed provisions threatened considerable controversy and the position was simplified by forbidding any law that would provide for dissolution of marriage irrespective of the religious status of the married partners.[26] There were also some additional provisions concerning marriage that were considered during the drafting process. The Jesuit advisory committee recommended that the law on betrothal and marriage for Catholics be made identical with canon law.[27] No such provision was included in the final text of the 1937 Constitution meaning that marriages recognized by the State and those recognized by the Catholic church would never be entirely identical. The early drafts also included provisions intended to repress the practice of contraception:

> Contraception and the advocacy of the practice of contraception are prohibited and the possession, use, sale and distribution of contraceptives shall be punishable by law.[28]

The most likely reason for the removal of this provision from the draft version of the 1937 Constitution was that a ban on the sale and importation of contraceptives and the prohibition of publications advocating their use were already enshrined in recently enacted legislation.[29]

25 Fifteenth Amendment of the Constitution Act 1995.

26 The final version of Article 41.3.2° was settled in the third revise of the draft 1937 Constitution. (NAI, Department of the Taoiseach, S10160, 24 Apr 1937).

27 Suggestions for a Catholic constitution, Oct 1936 (UCD Archives, de Valera papers, P150/2393).

28 First draft, undated 1936, Article 34.2.3° (UCD Archives, de Valera papers, P150/2385)

29 Censorship of Publications Act 1929, s 16 and Criminal Law Amendment Act 1935, s 17.

Attitudes towards marriage were broadly similar in 1922. Although the Irish courts had never been empowered to grant divorce *a vinculo matrimonii* it was still possible before 1922 for the wealthy to obtain a full divorce by means of a private bill passed through parliament. This narrow outlet was closed after 1922 when the Oireachtas refused to enact any such measure. A dispute between the two houses of the Oireachtas erupted in 1925 when WT Cosgrave and Kevin O'Higgins proposed changing the standing orders in order to prevent private bills requesting divorce from even being placed before the Irish legislature.[30] Many senators including the Cathaoirleach, Lord Glenavy, argued that citizens could not be prevented by parliamentary standing orders from exercising their legal right at common law to petition the Oireachtas for a private bill even if, in practice, there was little chance of that private bill being accepted.[31] Even the theoretical possibility of the Oireachtas granting a divorce proved unacceptable to the Cosgrave administration and a proposed procedural compromise only worsened the dispute.[32] Although the Cosgrave government never introduced legal or administrative measures that formally closed the theoretical possibility of gaining a divorce *a vinculo matrimonii* by means of a private bill no such bill was ever passed in the lifetime of the Irish Free State.

There can be no doubt that the attitude of the Cosgrave administration to the institution of divorce was virtually identical with the drafters of the 1937 Constitution. In 1925 Cosgrave told the Dáil:

> I have no doubt but that I am right in saying that the majority of people of this country regard the bond of marriage as a sacramental bond which is incapable of being dissolved. I personally hold this view. I consider that the whole fabric of our social organisation is based upon the sanctity of the marriage bond and that anything that tends to weaken the binding efficacy of that bond to that extent strikes at the root of our social life.[33]

This shared attitude towards divorce was also apparent when James Dillon, a leading Fine Gael politician, declared during the debates on the 1937 Constitution that protecting the sanctity of marriage 'is a purpose that will command the assent of every Deputy in this House'.[34] Kevin O'Higgins' assertion in 1926 that allowing a husband and wife to have different nationalities was inconsistent with the concept of 'Christian marriage' went far beyond anything asserted in the 1937 Constitution.[35]

30 *Dáil Éireann deb,* x [156-82] 11 Feb 1925.

31 *Seanad Éireann deb,* iv [929-45] 5 Mar 1925.

32 D O'Sullivan (1940) *The Irish Free State and its Senate* (London: Faber and Faber), pp 166–171.

33 *Dáil Éireann deb,* x [158] 11 Feb 1925.

34 *Dáil Éireann deb,* lxvii [251] 12 May 1937.

35 Imperial Conference 1926, committee on nationality (NAI, Department of Foreign Affairs, 1/20).

A preparatory draft of the 1937 Constitution would have added the following words to Article 41: 'propaganda directed against the sanctity of marriage and family life are prohibited'. This provision appears to have been directed against material providing information or advice on contraception and abortion. These provisions were removed from the final text of Article 41 but, once again, it is possible to provide examples of similar values held by those responsible for bringing the 1922 Constitution into existence. In 1922 Kevin O'Higgins rejected a draft constitutional provision proposed by the Labour party that would have provided: 'The secrecy of correspondence and communication by post, telegraph, telephone, or other common means is guaranteed and is inviolable'.[36] O'Higgins rejected this proposal on the grounds that it would prevent the government from limiting correspondence aimed at facilitating illegal gambling and 'indecent and immoral circulars and advertisements'. According to O'Higgins the latter included '[a]dvertisements, encouraging the limitation of childbirth and advertising all kinds of immorality, and all kinds of indecent devices are sent through the post'.[37]

It is also worth noting that the limitation of fundamental rights as being 'subject to public order and morality' that appears in many provisions of the 1937 Constitution was originally inserted in the 1922 Constitution in connection with the institution of marriage. The Catholic bishops were concerned that the original provisions in the draft 1922 Constitution on the free profession and practice of religion would permit 'Mormonism with plurality of wives'. The insertion of 'public order and morality' was intended to prevent such deviations from the accepted form of marital relations.[38]

The role of the family in education

The drafters of the 1937 Constitution were convinced that the position of the family intersected with fundamental rights outside the confines of the institution of marriage and the autonomy of the family. For example, the institution of the family was frequently raised in connection with property rights.[39] Consequently, the Jesuit advisory committee advocated the inclusion of special provisions on rural families and their property rights.[40] Other important areas influenced by the institution of the family included the provisions on education that were finally enshrined in Article

36 *Dáil Éireann deb,* i [1432] 10 Oct 1922.

37 *Dáil Éireann deb,* i [1433] 10 Oct 1922.

38 Article 8, Copy of memorandum after conference with bishops at Maynooth, Sept 1922 (UCD Archives, Kennedy papers, P4/349).

39 For example, see notes by John Charles McQuaid on 'articles on the family', Mar 1937 (UCD Archives, de Valera papers, P150/2408).

40 G Hogan (2012) *The Origins of the Irish Constitution, 1928–1941* (Dublin: Mercier), p 252.

42 of the 1937 Constitution.[41] Once again, this position was supported by papal encyclicals, in particular Pius XI's *Divini Illius Magistri* (1929).[42] The Jesuit committee wrote 'the primary responsibility and control of the education of the young belong inalienably to the parents and the Church'.[43] An early official draft of the Constitution included a duty on parents 'to maintain discipline in the home'.[44] The final text of Article 42 omitted any reference to the Church or maintaining discipline but did place the family at the heart of rights to education. In particular in Article 42 the State 'acknowledges that the primary and natural educator of the child is the Family'. It also provides that 'Parents shall be free to provide this education in their homes or in private schools or in schools recognised or established by the State.'

The provisions on the right to education in the 1922 Constitution were far less elaborate than those in the 1937 Constitution. Article 10 of the 1922 Constitution provided: 'All citizens of the Irish Free State (Saorstát Éireann) have the right to free elementary education' which was later incorporated into the wider provisions of Article 42 of its successor. An initiative to place a more detailed provision on education into the 1922 Constitution was sponsored by the Labour party that, among other things, would have provided: 'The right of the children to food, clothing, shelter and education, sufficient for their proper physical welfare and training as citizens of Saorstát Éireann is guaranteed'.[45] The Labour proposal went on to provide details on the nature of education and for state control of all schools. These detailed provisions were seen as incompatible with the provisional government's aim of producing as short and simple a constitution as possible. Hugh Kennedy wrote that it contained 'a large amount of controversial matter' that was more properly the subject of ordinary legislation.[46] The opposition in the constituent assembly had by this time become familiar with the provisional government's opposition to enshrining directive principles in the draft Constitution. Consequently, it agreed to consolidate these detailed provisions into a single sentence:

> Provision shall be made by Saorstát Éireann for the free education of the young, and for their compulsory attendance at school up

41 Supplementary Suggestions for the New Constitution of the Irish Free State, 13 Nov 1936 (UCD Archives, de Valera papers, P150/2393).

42 Draft Constitution, 1937 (UCD Archives, de Valera papers, P150/2414)

43 Later Jesuit texts removed reference to the Church. See Hogan (2012) *Origins of the Irish Constitution*, p 249.

44 Draft Constitution, 1937 (UCD Archives, de Valera papers, P150/2414).

45 *Dáil Éireann deb*, i [696] 25 Sept 1922 and [1693] 18 Oct 1922.

46 Amendment to Constitution, Article 10, undated (UCD Archives, Kennedy papers, P4/341).

> to such an age, and to such a stage of instruction as shall be prescribed by law.[47]

This provision was also rejected on grounds that illustrate that the main difference between the drafters of the 1922 and 1937 Constitutions was their drafting approach. Professor Eoin MacNeill, Minister for Education, made clear his view:

> my position is that the right of education, in the first place and fundamentally, belongs to the parents of the children, or those who are in *loco-parentis*, so long as the children are properly under that parental control: in the first place, and fundamentally, that that is the higher right, a more fundamental right, than any right possessed by the State.[48]

Although MacNeill was convinced that the State should intervene in cases of dereliction of duty he was convinced that it was wrong to compel every child to make use of provisions for education supplied by the State and emphasized the right of parents to educate their children at home.[49]

George O'Brien, a barrister who acted as an external adviser on the drafting of the 1922 Constitution, argued that if rights to education were included in the text 'the fact should be emphasised that the State's duty to provide education for children only arises on the failure or incapacity of the parents' doing so. The primary duty of the State in the matter is one of supervision'.[50] Darrell Figgis and other members of the constitution committee declined to accept this recommendation during the drafting of the 1922 Constitution: 'This, we believe, is a matter rather for legislation. Details of such a controversial kind must be avoided in a Constitution'.[51] Once again, it is apparent that the values of most of the drafters and sponsors of the 1922 Constitution were similar to those of the 1937 Constitution. The main difference concerned their approach to drafting and their perceptions of the primary purpose of a national constitution.

The 1922 Constitution as the 'mechanics of governance'

The drafters of the 1922 Constitution took a much more restrained approach to creating constitutional provisions than their counterparts in 1937. The provisional government's desire for a short and uncluttered constitution was

47 *Dáil Éireann deb,* i [1698] 18 Oct 1922.

48 *Dáil Éireann deb,* i [1698–1699] 18 Oct 1922.

49 *Dáil Éireann deb,* i [1700] 18 Oct 1922.

50 Memorandum on the draft Constitution, George O'Brien, 5 Apr 1922 (NAI, Department of the Taoiseach, S6541).

51 Figgis to Collins, 13 Apr 1922 (NAI, Department of the Taoiseach, S8953).

stressed at the very first meeting on 24 January 1922. Michael Collins, the official chairman, instructed the rest of the committee that the Constitution 'should be as simple as possible'.[52] One of the earliest drafts produced in 1922 contained a mere 10 articles.[53] Although later drafts were much longer it became clear from the outset that the emphasis was on producing a constitution that would, in the words of Irish ministers, provide the basic 'mechanics of government' for the new State.[54] Later drafts did include provisions on matters such as free expression, free assembly, freedom of religion and a right to free elementary education but these were drafted in concise and general terms.[55] This approach was bolstered by the contributions of two external advisers, George O'Brien and T. M. Healy, who both recommended a simple and concise Constitution.[56]

Once a draft was finally selected as the basis for a future Constitution, Michael Collins, W. T. Cosgrave, George Gavan Duffy and Eoin MacNeill wrote assessments that concluded that the draft was too long and required cutting down.[57] MacNeill also made clear his disapproval of 'declaratory statements' such as the statements of national and social principles set out in one of the unsuccessful drafts proposed as the basis of the Constitution.[58] He concluded, 'Some actual constitutions contain such declaratory statements, and I doubt if they amount to much as constitutional provisions'.[59] George Gavan Duffy was the most vehement member of the government in insisting that the draft Constitution needed cutting down in length. He believed that the text was 'too difficult for the man on the street' who would have to vote on it. Duffy also advocated the removal of directive principles that were contained in the opening provisions and elsewhere in the chosen draft.[60] Darrell Figgis took umbrage at criticism as to the length of the

52 Enclosure to letter from Collins to James Douglas, 20 Jan 1922 (NAI, Department of the Taoiseach, S8952). James Douglas confirms in his memoirs that these instructions, which were attached to an outline Constitution drafted by an unnamed solicitor, were authored by Collins himself. JG Douglas (1998) *Memoirs of Senator James G Douglas (1887–1954) Concerned Citizen* (Dublin: University College Dublin Press), pp 85–86.

53 Enclosure with letter from Michael Collins to James Douglas, 20 Jan 1922 (NAI, Department of the Taoiseach, S8952).

54 *Dáil Éireann deb*, i [360] 18 Sept 1922; [1704] 18 Oct 1922 and [1907] 25 Oct 1922.

55 Document No 28 (UCD Archives, Kennedy papers, P4/323).

56 NAI, Cabinet Minutes, G1/1 15 Mar 1922 and NAI, Department of the Taoiseach, S6541 and S8953.

57 For the views of Collins and Duffy, see Duffy to Collins, 6 Apr 1922 and Collins to Duffy, 7 Apr 1922 (UCD Archives, Duffy papers, P152/199). For those of WT Cosgrave, see NAI, Department of the Taoiseach, S8953.

58 E MacNeill, memorandum, 21 Mar 1922 (NAI, Department of the Taoiseach, S8953). The draft in question was Draft C supported by Professors Alfred O'Rahilly and James Murnaghan.

59 MacNeill, memorandum, 21 Mar 1922.

60 G Gavan Duffy, memorandum on suggested amendments to the proposed Constitution, 11 Apr 1922 (NAI, Department of the Taoiseach, constitution committee V13)

draft Constitution and produced figures to show that it was relatively succinct when compared to the constitutions of existing States. He pointed out that the current draft could be reproduced on a single page of newspaper.[61] Nevertheless, in April 1922 the provisional government began the process of paring down its provisions although the cuts were not as radical as had been proposed by Duffy.

Additional cuts were made at the insistence of the British government in June 1922. These included rare examples of provisions that might be considered directive principles that had survived the drafting process in 1922. These provisions extended sovereignty to the nation's wealth, natural resources and other material possessions in addition to its human population. They were taken from the works of Patrick Pearse and provided useful links to the 1916 Rising and the 1919 Democratic Programme.[62] The provisions were considered undesirable by several of the provisional government's own advisers and also met with hostility from the British government once they saw the draft Constitution. Consequently these opening provisions were removed despite their obvious propaganda value.[63]

The desire for a short and simple constitution in 1922

Why was there such a determination among the drafters to produce a short constitution that kept directive principles to a minimum in 1922? There are a number of possible explanations. These include considerations based on the position that the Irish Free State was intended to be a British Dominion under the 1921 Treaty. The Constitutions of the Dominions focused on the mechanics of government and contained few provisions that could be described as directive principles. This argument cannot be considered conclusive as Collins and Griffith had made it clear to the constitution committee that it was not to be considered as being bound by Dominion precedents when drafting the text.[64]

A more convincing consideration that assists in explaining the different approaches to drafting a constitution in 1922 and 1937 concerns differences in the dominant personalities behind the two Irish Constitutions. Although de Valera's role in creating the 1937 Constitution has been exaggerated in the past it cannot be denied that he did play a major role in the drafting process. De Valera certainly favoured the insertion of directive principles in a constitution

61 Figgis to Collins, 13 Apr 1922 (NAI, Department of the Taoiseach, S8952).

62 H Kennedy, memorandum, 11 June 1922 (NAI, Department of the Taoiseach, S8955).

63 See G O'Brien, memorandum on the draft Constitution, 5 Apr 1922 (NAI, Department of the Taoiseach, S6541); T Mohr (2008) 'British Involvement in the Creation of the Constitution of the Irish Free State', *Dublin University Law Journal*, 30, 166–186, pp 171–172.

64 Enclosure to letter from Collins to James Douglas, 20 Jan 1922 (NAI, Department of the Taoiseach, S8952); Constitution committee, report of first meeting, 24 Jan 1922; Padraic Colum (1959), *Arthur Griffith* (Dublin: Brown & Nolan), p 356.

in order to inspire and elicit loyalty from the Irish people.[65] This approach was also encouraged by the submissions made by his clerical advisers, John Charles McQuaid, Edward Cahill and the special Jesuit advisory committee.

Although some scholars argue that the Free State Constitution was intended to be 'Michael Collins' Constitution', this never became reality.[66] Collins never had the time or luxury for involvement in the drafting process to the extent enjoyed by de Valera in 1937. Although Collins was appointed chairman of the committee that drafted the 1922 Constitution he had many other responsibilities that ensured that he only attended two meetings during the initial drafting process. Yet he was involved in later revisions of the draft Constitution and led the Irish delegation along with Arthur Griffith in negotiating key amendments with the British government. Most important of all, Collins did establish the important principle at the very first meeting of the 1922 constitution committee that the document they produced 'should be as simple as possible'.[67] Collins also oversaw the drafting of a brief outline of a Constitution that dealt entirely with matters of governance and contained little material that could be described as directive principles.[68] Collins' practical approach that insisted on a concise and functional text was maintained after his death by his successors in the provisional government.

The only significant voice of dissent on this point came from Professor Alfred O'Rahilly, a maverick member of the 1922 constitution committee, who was convinced that it was proper if not essential to include directive principles on important social and spiritual matters in a national constitution. According to O'Rahilly, the constitution committee was amenable to the inclusion of 'basic social principles' in the Constitution but 'there was a decided difference as to what principles should be included'.[69] Failure to agree at this early stage is likely to have contributed to the emergence of a document that contained a minimum of directive principles. O'Rahilly considered the text finally selected and amended by the provisional government was a 'meagre' document because it avoided such declarations. He complained to government officials in 1922: 'I may, for instance, point out that the draft does not mention God, the Family, religious education, that it contains no democratic social or labour ideals'.[70] He believed that a constitution should serve as a source of inspiration and guidance for its citizens and considered

65 For example, see transcript of radio broadcast, 30 Apr 1937 (NAI, Department of the Taoiseach, S9868).

66 DH Akenson and JF Fallin (1970) 'The Irish Civil War and the Drafting of the Free State Constitution', *Éire-Ireland,* 5(1), 10–26, p 13.

67 Enclosure to letter from Collins to James Douglas, 20 Jan 1922 (NAI, Department of the Taoiseach, S8952).

68 Collins to Douglas, 20 Jan 1922.

69 *Irish Independent*, 15 May 1937.

70 A O'Rahilly to Michael McDunphy, Secretary General, 2 Sept 1922 (UCD Archives, O'Rahilly papers, P178/48).

directive principles to be the most characteristic aspect of a national constitution.[71] These attitudes were shared in common with de Valera and other drafters of the 1937 Constitution. Consequently, O'Rahilly's vision of the nature and purpose of a constitution deserve examination as a link between the drafting of the 1922 and 1937 Constitutions. His views on the position of the family in a national constitution also merit particular attention.

Alfred O'Rahilly: a link between the 1922 and 1937 Constitutions

The constitution committee appointed to draft the 1922 Constitution produced three alternative drafts for consideration by the Irish provisional government. Drafts A and B were very similar apart from their provisions on the composition of the executive. Draft B was finally chosen as the basis for the future Constitution of the Irish Free State. The third draft, known as Draft C, was very different from the other two. It was drafted by Alfred O'Rahilly, professor of mathematical physics at University College Cork and won the support of James Murnaghan, professor of jurisprudence, Roman law and international law at University College Dublin, the only other academic on the 1922 constitution committee.

O'Rahilly, a polymath of inexhaustible energy, has been described by biographers as a 'controversialist', 'pugnacious polemicist', 'flamboyant, extrovert, disputatious and dynamic'.[72] Poor health and a number of personality clashes with other members of the constitution committee ensured that he was absent from many of the drafting meetings. This isolation permitted the production of a draft Constitution that was very different from Drafts A and B. O'Rahilly distanced himself from most members of the constitution committee in order that he be free to draft a document imbued with his own ideas on the place of religion, natural law and the family in Irish society.

Chapter 8 of Draft C dealt with 'Family, Education, Religion' which O'Rahilly and others considered the most distinctive aspect of his draft Constitution.[73] Highlights of these lengthy provisions include the recognition that 'Marriage, as the basis of family life and national wellbeing, is under the special protection of the State'.[74] These detailed provisions also recognized

71 Footnotes to the draft Constitution of 1922, undated 1922 (UCC Archives, O'Rahilly papers, U. 118, Box 6) and memorandum on Draft C by Murnaghan and O'Rahilly, 7 Mar 1922 (NAI, Department of the Taoiseach, S8953).

72 J McGuire and J Quinn (eds) (2009) *Dictionary of Irish Biography* (Cambridge: Cambridge University Press), vol 7 pp 825–826.

73 Footnotes to the draft Constitution of 1922, undated 1922 (UCC Archives, O'Rahilly papers, U. 118, Box 6).

74 O'Rahilly originally included the following words at this point: 'Resting on the equal rights of both sexes marriage shall be monogamous'. Handwritten corrections to Draft C, undated 1922 (UCC Archives, O'Rahilly papers, U. 118, Box 6). These words were deleted from the text submitted to the provisional government. Draft C submitted 7 Mar 1922 and Department of the Taoiseach S8953, Draft C submitted 7 Mar 1922 (NAI, constitution committee, B6).

that 'Parents have the right and duty of rearing and educating their children, so as to make them good citizens'. In addition, they recognized that 'Maternity shall be under the special protection of the law'. O'Rahilly was convinced that his provisions on the family represented the views of the 'vast majority of the people of Ireland'. He concluded: 'Any government in this country, which fancies that it can ignore all this in our Constitution, is under some peculiar delusion'.[75]

O'Rahilly's arguments were rejected and his Draft C was never seriously considered as a possible basis for the Free State Constitution by the provisional government. There were a number of reasons why O'Rahilly's Draft C was not given greater consideration. The most important of these was that O'Rahilly had very different ideas concerning the purpose of a national constitution to the provisional government and other members of the constitution committee. O'Rahilly wished to produce a constitution that would 'educate and stimulate the people'.[76] This ensured that it was vital to include 'expressions of guiding ideals to direct and inspire future legislation'.[77] By contrast the provisional government wanted a short and simple constitution that focused on the 'mechanics of government' that could face the challenges of an uncertain future.

O'Rahilly's disappointment ensured that he proved one of the most persistent critics of 1922 Constitution in the years that followed. At the heart of his impression that the 1922 Constitution was a 'false start' was the position that 'neither parent nor family is so much as mentioned in our present Constitution'. O'Rahilly concluded that in terms of enumerating 'fundamental principles' the 'present Constitution is a lamentable failure'.[78] In place of a recital of fundamental principles, natural rights and social ideals the State had been given 'a woefully meagre, barren and inaccurate Constitution, which is ... out of touch with the living ideals of our people'.[79] For O'Rahilly these ideals certainly included the family as the oldest and most basic social institution. He maintained, 'It is ridiculous ... to argue that the present Constitution protects the family (which it does not mention)'.[80] O'Rahilly went further when he insisted: 'At the present moment we really have no Constitution at all ... On fundamental questions like Family, Marriage, Education, Private Property, Social Structure, we have failed to enunciate a single clear principle'. His preferred solution was to ditch the 1922 text and produce a

75 Footnotes to the draft Constitution of 1922, undated 1922 (UCC Archives, O'Rahilly papers, U. 118, Box 6). See also *Irish Independent*, 13 Oct 1922.

76 Footnotes to the draft Constitution of 1922, undated 1922 (UCC Archives, O'Rahilly papers, U. 118, Box 6).

77 Footnotes to the draft Constitution of 1922.

78 A O'Rahilly (1936) 'The Constitution and the Senate', *Studies* 25, 1–19, p 18.

79 O'Rahilly (1936) 'The Constitution and the Senate', p 2.

80 A O'Rahilly, 'Introduction to Thoughts on the Constitution', 1937 (UCD Archives, O'Rahilly papers, P178/57).

new constitution 'based on Catholic principles of natural right and social justice'.[81] What was needed was 'a Constitution safeguarding natural rights and moral principles, enunciating social ideals, in consonance with the professed tenets of our people'.[82] In the 1930s an entirely new constitution was produced that attempted to fulfil these goals.

O'Rahilly's assistance was soon required by the new Fianna Fáil government that came to power in 1932. He provided advice on the legal means of removing the controversial parliamentary oath imposed by the 1921 Treaty.[83] The oath was duly removed from the substantive articles of the Constitution in 1933.[84] This proved to be an important first step in a process of removing the influence of the 1921 Treaty from the text of the 1922 Constitution. The entirely new Constitution of 1937 was intended as the final step in achieving this goal. O'Rahilly sent the text of Draft C along with other materials to the Irish government during the drafting process.[85]

Although there is no evidence that O'Rahilly had anything more than an indirect role in the drafting of the 1937 Constitution, his influence remained significant. For example, Article 55 of O'Rahilly's Draft C declared that 'maternity shall be under the special protection of the law' and further provided that 'industrial night work of women shall be forbidden by law'. These provisions reflect a similar spirit to that contained in Articles 41.2 and 45.4 of de Valera's Constitution. Another provision of Draft C that is echoed in the 1937 Constitution is the declaration that:

> Marriage, as the basis of family life and national well-being, is under the special protection of the State; and all attacks on the purity, health and sacredness of family life shall be forbidden.[86]

The draft produced by O'Rahilly also committed the State to recognizing the 'inviolable sanctity of the marital bond' that was mirrored in the original version of Article 41.3.2° of the 1937 Constitution.[87] O'Rahilly's own reaction to the 1937 Constitution was broadly supportive: 'The Family and Motherhood Article 41 is in many ways excellent, and at last removes a glaring defect of the present Constitution which calmly ignores the Family'. However, O'Rahilly was quite clear that the provisions on the family in the draft 1937 Constitution could be improved. For example, he was disappointed that de

81 O'Rahilly (1936) 'The Constitution and the Senate', p 19.

82 O'Rahilly (1936) 'The Constitution and the Senate', p 3. See also the first of three opinion pieces written by O'Rahilly on the draft 1937 Constitution. *Irish Independent*, 11 May 1937.

83 Conor Maguire to O'Rahilly, 23 Mar 1932 (UCD Archives, P178/60).

84 Constitution (Removal of Oath) Act 1933.

85 De Valera to O'Rahilly, 27 Mar 1934 (UCD Archives, P178/63).

86 Article 53 of Draft C (NAI, Department of the Taoiseach, S8953). See Article 41.3.1 of the 1937 Constitution.

87 Article 53 of Draft C (NAI, Department of the Taoiseach, S8953).

Valera had declined to include the 'family vote' guaranteeing extra votes for married people.[88] Although he approved of the principle contained provision in Article 41.2.2° that 'the State shall endeavour to ensure that mothers shall not be obliged by economic necessity to engage in labour to the neglect of duties in the home', he felt that the word 'endeavour' created imprecision and, in any case, felt that such provisions were unnecessary in a national constitution and were best left to legislation.[89]

The greatest similarity between O'Rahilly's Draft C and the 1937 Constitution concerned their attitudes to the purpose of a national constitution which was utterly different to that of the provisional government in 1922. De Valera revealed his approach to drafting a constitution in a radio address made on 30 April 1937. He emphasized that the new Constitution was designed to provide a firm foundation for an ordered life and peaceful political development within the community, but added 'the ideals which ought to inspire and direct that development are rightly emphasized'.[90] He continued:

> I know that there are many theorists who take the view that a written Constitution should contain nothing more than the legal machinery necessary for the establishment and control of the organs of State. Whilst agreeing that a Constitution should be as simple as possible, I cannot altogether share that view. In my judgment a Constitution ought to do more than define the character of the legislative, executive and judicial regime, and if it be based on the democratic principle it ought to do more, for example, than prescribe how the representative institutions should function, how the parliamentary responsibility of the Executive is to be secured, the independence of the Judiciary maintained, or the principle of universal suffrage applied. It should inspire as well as control, elicit loyalty as well as compel it.[91]

This approach to drafting a Constitution was similar to that adopted by O'Rahilly in 1922. O'Rahilly may not have been in entire agreement with all of de Valera's provisions in relation to safeguarding and buttressing the position of the family in Irish society but he insisted that the differences were largely matters of wording and detail. O'Rahilly concluded that de Valera should be 'sincerely congratulated on his courageous exposition of Catholic social principles'.[92]

---

88 *Irish Independent*, 15 May 1937.

89 *Irish Independent*, 15 May 1937.

90 Transcript of radio broadcast, 30 Apr 1937 (NAI, Department of the Taoiseach, S9868).

91 Transcript of radio broadcast, 30 Apr 1937.

92 *Irish Independent*, 15 May 1937.

The largest opposition party, Fine Gael, did not attack the contents of the constitutional provisions on the family but did criticize their aspirational character. John A. Costello made this clear when he told the Dáil:

> You cannot, by merely inserting a principle which everybody agrees with and putting it down on paper, pretend that you have carried out in practice some laudable purpose which we all would wish to see achieved. Merely writing down high principles in this Constitution is not going to see that these things are, in fact, achieved in practice. There is a lot of theory in this Constitution.[93]

The independent TD Robert Rowlette told the Dáil in 1937 that a constitution is essentially a legal document and should be declaratory of the structure of the State and the rights of individual citizens. He complained that instead of taking this approach the proposed 1937 Constitution 'consists largely of a moral homily in which various directions are given as to the lines on which the State should work in the future'.[94]

The opposition in the Dáil, which tended to stereotype the 1937 Constitution as the work of de Valera alone, labelled the aim of educating the Irish people as part a wider agenda of political control. John A. Costello condemned this with unrestrained sarcasm: 'Public opinion must be educated until it coincides with the whim, will and pleasure, the peculiar views and the constitutional pirouetting of the particular President'.[95] Nevertheless de Valera made no apology and revealed his vision of a constitution when he told the Dáil:

> it is not being narrowed down to a mere framework, merely giving you the institutions of the State. That is the view that some people hold of what it should be. This is intended to do more. It is intended to offer directions in which the State, as a whole, should move.[96]

Conclusion

The 1922 Constitution is often praised for its secular nature. Despite drafting errors arising from inexperience, the simplicity of its text and its minimal inclusion of directive principles has ensured that the 1922 Constitution has aged relatively well. It has been described as 'a typical liberal-democratic

93 *Dáil Éireann deb*, lxvii [1859] 4 June 1937.

94 *Dáil Éireann deb*, lxviii [386-387] 14 June 1937.

95 *Dáil Éireann deb*, lxvii [315] 12 May 1937.

96 *Dáil Éireann deb*, lxvii [425] 13 May 1937.

document which would have suited a country of any religious complexion'.[97] By contrast the directive principles of the 1937 Constitution, including the provisions on the family, women and marriage, have aged badly and damaged its reputation. Although the provisions recognizing the special position of the Catholic Church and the ban on divorce have since been removed, many directive principles remain in the 1937 Constitution that continue to cause offence and damage its popular image.[98]

The case law that has followed the enshrinement of the provisions on the family into the 1937 Constitution has increased rather than decreased their controversial nature. Examples include decisions that the provisions on the family only protects families based on the institution of marriage,[99] the striking down of legal measures intended to ensure equal ownership of a marital home,[100] decisions that prioritized the rights of parents over the best interests of the child,[101] the upholding of laws that discriminated against men,[102] the upholding of discrimination against illegitimate children,[103] justification for denying the decriminalization of homosexuality in 1984[104] and the original determination that the right to marry was confined to couples of the opposite sex that required the insertion of the 34th amendment in 2015.[105] The provisions on the position of women in the home have been described as 'probably the most contentious provisions in the Constitution'[106] but have been interpreted by the courts in a manner that provides little, if any, benefit to women working in the home.[107] Of course it can be argued that Article 41 has inspired positive decisions too. For example, it is argued that Article 41 has curbed some of the excesses of state intervention in family life experienced in other jurisdictions.[108] However, this does not alter the reality that directive principles such as

97 Whyte (1980) *Church and State in Modern Ireland,* p 51.

98 Fifth Amendment of the Constitution Act 1972 and Fifteenth Amendment of the Constitution Act 1995.

99 *The State (Nicolaou) v An Bord Uchtála* [1966] IR 567; *G v An Bord Uchtála* [1980] IR 32 and *W O'R v EH (Guardianship)* [1996] IESC 4, [1996] 2 IR 248.

100 *L v L* [1989] ILRM 528 (HC) and *Re Art 26 and the Matrimonial Home Bill 1993* [1994] IESC 5, [1994] 1 IR 305.

101 For example, *Northwestern Health Board v HW* [2001] IESC 90, [2001] 3 IR 622.

102 For example, *The State (Nicolaou) v An Bord Uchtála* [1966] IR 567 (SC) and *Dennehy v Minister for Social Welfare,* unreported, High Court, 26 Jul 1984.

103 *O'B v S* [1984] IR 316 (SC).

104 *Norris v Attorney General* [1984] IR 36 (SC).

105 *Zappone v Revenue Commissioners* [2006] IEHC 404

106 O Doyle (2009) *Constitutional Law: Text, Cases and Materials* (Dublin: Clarus Press), p 249.

107 (1996) *Report of the Constitution Review Group* (Dublin: Stationery Office), pp 319–337. Article 41.2 was used by O'Higgins CJ to support the effective exclusion of women from juries although a majority of his colleagues on the Supreme Court disagreed. *De Búrca v Attorney General* [1976] IR 38 (SC).

108 W Duncan (1996) 'The Constitutional Protection of Parental Rights' in (1996) *Report of the Constitution Review Group* (Dublin: Stationery Office), 612–626.

those found in Article 41, which recognizes that the family has special status in Irish society but provides little guidance as to the legal consequences of this declaration, gives unelected judges interpretative guidance that may influence the evolution of Irish law in directions that may not always enjoy popular support.

Would the inclusion of significant amendments or the drafting of an entirely new Irish constitution in the early twenty-first century ameliorate these difficulties? There is some evidence to support the suggestion that the spirit of constitution drafting in early twenty-first century Ireland is actually closer to that of 1937 than that of 1922. Of course, there is greater support for secularism and different conceptions of the meaning of 'family' in the early twenty-first century than existed a century earlier.[109] Nevertheless the reports of bodies appointed to advise on the revision of the Constitution indicate support for enshrining a substantial number of new provisions that are likely to be drafted in the form of directive principles. One example concerns calls to enshrine the 1916 proclamation's commitment to 'cherishing the children of the nation equally' in the text of the Constitution. A slightly amended version of this wording was recommended by an Oireachtas committee on constitutional reform in 2010.[110] It is doubtful whether a provision of this nature would create any directly enforceable rights. Another example concerns proposals to enshrine provisions in the Constitution offering support for affirmative action policies that were recommended by a substantial portion of the Constitution Review Group convened in the 1990s.[111] A third example can be found in the proposal to include declarations on economic, social and cultural rights in the text of the Constitution that won the support of 85 per cent of the Constitution Convention that reported in 2014.[112] These included matters related to housing, social security and essential health care. The question of whether these matters would actually be enshrined as enforceable rights or as directive principles would, of course, be entirely dependent on the wording of the final provisions. A future government would have a powerful incentive to enshrine these matters in the text of the Constitution as directive principles in a similar form to the existing

109 However the Convention on the Constitution concluded in 2014 'In the case of the family, the committee takes the view that an amendment to extend the definition of the family would cause deep and long-lasting division in our society and would not necessarily be passed by a majority'. *Eighth Report of the Convention on the Constitution* (Jan 2014). Available at: https://www.constitution.ie/AttachmentDownload.ashx?mid=5333bbe7-a9b8-e311-a7ce-005056a32ee4 (accessed 5 Aug 2015).

110 The final report of the Joint Committee on the Constitutional Amendment on Children published on 16 February, 2010 recommended the insertion of a new Article 42.1.1° that would provide 'The State shall cherish all the children of the State equally'. Available at: https://oireachtas.ie/viewdoc.asp?fn=/documents/Committees30thDail/J-ConAmendChildren/Reports_2008/FinalReport2010.pdf (accessed 25 Feb 2016).

111 (1996) *Report of the Constitution Review Group* (Dublin: Stationery Office), p 242.

112 *Eighth Report of the Convention on the Constitution* (Jan 2014). Available at: https://www.constitution.ie/AttachmentDownload.ashx?mid=5333bbe7-a9b8-e311-a7ce-005056a32ee4 (accessed 5 Aug 2015).

provisions of Article 45. The alternative would be to overturn the existing structure of the doctrine of separation of powers by giving the courts substantial powers over the allocation of finite resources that have traditionally belonged to executives and legislatures that are responsible to the electorate.

The 1922 Constitution was deliberately drafted to be as short and simple a document as possible with an absolute minimum of directive principles. Although constitutions drafted along these lines might be accused of being plain and austere they also date better and tend to survive longer than constitutions that try to freeze the values of a particular point in time in their pages. Examples of constitutions that have largely avoided these pitfalls include the 1789 Constitution of the United States of America, the 1867 Constitution of Canada and the 1901 Constitution of Australia. This approach does not require abandonment of important provisions on human rights that, unlike directive principles, are directly and openly enforceable before the courts. In the aforementioned Constitutions the human rights provisions are spared any risk of being confused with directive principles by being enshrined in a different form or even in a different instrument from the other constitutional provisions.

It is true that directive principles are often the most interesting provisions of any national constitution and to cut them down to an absolute minimum might be seen as creating an insipid constitution that would fail to inspire its citizens. Yet directive principles can repel citizens and discredit a constitution just as easily as they can inspire citizens and elevate the reputation of its provisions. In no part of the 1937 Constitution is this reality more apparent than in the provisions concerning the family, marriage and the position of women.

The greatest difference between the drafters of the 1922 and 1937 Constitutions concern their attitudes towards the future. The drafters of the 1922 Constitution drafted their document at a time of uncertainty when the limbs of the infant State were still supple. The future development of the new State could not easily be predicted and most of the drafters were well aware of this reality. By contrast, de Valera openly admitted that the 1937 Constitution enshrined provisions intended to create a 'Christian polity'.[113] These provisions were intended to point out 'directions in which the State, as a whole, should move' in the future.[114] Patrick Hogan, a Labour TD, reminded the Dáil in 1937 that values change with the passage of time. He warned, 'I think it is very bad to put so much into the present Constitution, to make a rigid Constitution now when so much of the ideals and hopes and aspirations of our people are in flux'.[115]

113 Transcript of radio broadcast, 30 Apr 1937 (NAI, Department of the Taoiseach, S9868).

114 *Dáil Éireann deb*, lxvii [425] 13 May 1937.

115 *Dáil Éireann deb*, lxvii [259] 12 May 1937.

The reality that social values change with the passage of time is most apparent in the provisions of the 1937 Constitution concerning the family, marriage and women. Indeed, Article 41 had long-term consequences that would have alarmed and run contrary to the values of those who drafted it or inspired its drafting. The most obvious example of this is the case of *McGee v Attorney General*[116] in which legislative provisions preventing a married couple from making use of contraceptives were found to be inconsistent with rights of marital privacy. It may be recalled that the drafters of the 1937 Constitution had originally considered an express provision outlawing the use or importation of contraceptive products.[117]

It can be argued that the 1937 Constitution was not exceptional in the interwar world in enshrining a significant number of directive principles in its text, including those related to the family, religion, marriage and the position of women in society. Yet this argument ignores the position that there were also many constitutions in existence in the 1920s and 1930s, as indicated above, that did not follow this course. Both approaches had their advocates and many working examples in foreign constitutions in 1922 and in 1937. In 1922 the drafters consciously chose to create a short and functional constitution that kept directive principles to an absolute minimum. In 1937 the drafters consciously chose to differentiate their Constitution from its predecessor by enshrining a substantial amount of directive principles that reflected the values held by many, though not all, Irish citizens at that date. Many of these provisions, in particular those connected with the family, have dated badly and have damaged the reputation of the 1937 Constitution in the eyes of many living in the early twenty-first century. Yet the reports of expert groups continue to advocate replacing dated directive principles with others that might appear equally dated in an uncertain future. The idea that a national constitution should be built around a substantial number of directive principles is based on the fundamental assumption that these are desirable and even essential subjects for inclusion in the substantive provisions. This assumption is, perhaps, among the greatest legacies of the Constitution drafted in 1937.

116 [1973] IESC 2; [1974] IR 284.

117 First draft, undated 1936, Article 34.2.3° (UCD Archives, de Valera papers, P150/2385)

Bibliography

Archival material

Adoption Society Papers (NLI)
Attorney General's files (NAI)
Blythe Papers (UCD Archives)
Cabinet minutes (NAI)
Civil Bill Books (NAI)
Cork District Registry Will Book (NAI)
Court of Prerogative Will Book (NAI)
Crown records for County Antrim (PRONI)
De Valera Papers (UCD Archives)
Department of An Taoiseach Files (NAI)
Department of Foreign Affairs files (NAI)
Down and Conor Will Book (NAI)
Down Presbytery Minutes (Presbyterian Historical Society Belfast)
Dublin Consistory Court Cause Papers (NAI)
Dublin Diocesan Archives (DDA)
Gavan Duffy Papers (UCD Archives)
Hanna divorce papers 1873 (PRONI)
Kennedy Papers (UCD Archives)
Killaloe Court and Register Book 1707–1868 (NAI)
MacGeough Bond papers (PRONI)
National Library of Ireland (NLI)
O'Rahilly papers (UCD Archives)
Papers of L'Estrange and Brett Solicitors, Belfast (PRONI)
Papers of the Consistory Court of Killaloe, 1671–1824 (BL)
Papers of the Galway Diocesan Archive (GDA)
Praxis Parochi Kerry Diocesan Archive (KDA)
Prerogative Wills Ireland 1777 (NAI)
Public Record Office of Northern Ireland (PRONI)
Records of the Belfast Court of Bankruptcy (BANK)
Records of the House of Commons (Parliamentary Archives)
Registry of Deeds
State Files and State Books for the Central Criminal Court (NAI)
Tuam Consistory Court Book 1740–42 (NAI)

Published books and pamphlets

Allen, H (1987) *Justice Unbalanced: Gender, Psychiatry and Judicial Decisions* (Open University Press)

Andrew, DT (2013) *Aristocratic Vice: The Attack on Duelling, Suicide, Adultery, and Gambling in Eighteenth-Century England* (Yale: Yale University Press)

Anon (1793) *The Proceedings Against Major Hook for Criminal Conversation with his Own Niece Mrs Campbell, Wife of Captain Campbell, Wife of Captain Campbell, before Lord Kenyon and a Special Jury. At Westminster, Feb 26th, 1793* (London: np)

Anon (1797) *The Trial of William Barber, for Criminal Conversation with Jane Fay, Wife of Lawrence Fay, In His Majesty's Court of King's Bench in Ireland; Before the Right Honourable Earl Clonmell, and a Special Jury*, 2nd edn (Dublin: J Whitworth)

Anon (1804) *A Report of the Trial on an Action for Damages Brought by the Reverend Charles Massy Against the Most noble the Marquis of Headfort for Criminal Conversation with Plaintiff's Wife* (Dublin: MN Mahon)

Anon (1804) *The Proceedings on the Trial of Captain J Caulfield for Criminal Conversation with the Wife of Captain George Chambers, Daughter of the late Lord Rodney. Before Lord Ellenborough, in the Court of King's Bench, on the 3rd Dec 1804* (London: np)

Anon (1805) *The Proceedings against Henry Jadis, Esq. for Criminal Conversation with the Wife of the Hon Allan Hyde Gardner, Captain in his Majesty's Navy, and Son to Lord Gardner, Before Lord Ellenborough, In the Court of King's Bench, Guildhall, on Saturday the 2nd of Mar 1805* (London: np)

Anon (1807) *A Full and Accurate Report of the Trial of Sir John Piers for Criminal Conversation with Lady Cloncurry: Taken in Shorthand by an Eminent Barrister Concerned in the Cause* (Dublin: C La Grange)

Anon (1807) *The Trial of J. Hacket, Esquire, for Adultery with Mrs Mansergh. In the Irish Court of Exchequer on Dec the 10th, 1807* (London: J. Day)

Anon (1815) *Crim Con. Court of Common Pleas, Friday, June 9, 1815. John Guthrie, Esq, Plaintiff; WPBD Sterne, Esq, Defendant* (Dublin: W Espy)

Anon (1816) *Crim Con William Binns, Plaintiff, John Scott, Defendant, Before the Hon Justice Mayne* (Dublin: Wm Espy)

Anon (1816) *Crim Con. Report of a Trial, in the Court of Common Pleas, on Saturday, Dec 14, 1816. John Hinds, Gentleman Attorney, Plaintiff. Philip Perry Price Myddleton, Defendant* (Dublin: R Conolly)

Anon (1820) *Crim. Con. A Full, Faithful and Impartial Report of the Trial, wherein Sir John M. Doyle, KCB & KTS was Plaintiff, and George Peter Brown, Esq, Defendant. For Criminal Conversation with the Defendant's Wife* (Dublin: James Charles)

Anon (1835) *Court of Exchequer, Feb 22nd, 1835. Crim. Con. New Trial before the Chief Baron. Hodgens v Mahon* (Dublin: D Scott)

Anon (1857) *Crim. Con. Actions and Trials and Other Legal Proceedings Relating to Marriage before the Passing of the Present Divorce Act* (London: np)

Anon (1857) *Divorce in 1857: The Talbot Case. Letters by 'Cujus,' Containing Full Particulars of the Case, with Observations on the Present Unsatisfactory State of the Law* (London: Ward and Lock)

Anon (1880) *Authentic Report of the Crim Con Trial of Joynt v Jackson in the Exchequer Court, Dublin, Commencing May 10th, 1880* (Dublin: Edward Smith)

Arensberg, C and S Kimball (2001) *Family and Community in Ireland*, 3rd edn (Clare: Clasp Press)

Aries, P (1973) *Centuries of Childhood* (London: Penguin)

Atiyah, P (2003) *The Rise and Fall of Freedom of Contract* (Oxford: Oxford University Press)

Backhouse, CB (1991) *Petticoats and Prejudice: Women and Law in Nineteenth-Century Canada* (Toronto: Women's Press)

Bailey, J (2003) *Unquiet Lives: Marriage and Marriage Breakdown in England, 1660–1800* (Cambridge: Cambridge University Press)

Baker, C (1880) *Husband and Wife and the Law of Divorce* (London: F. Warne)

Baker, JH (2002) *An Introduction to English Legal History*, 4th edn (London: Sweet and Maxwell)

Barnes, J (1989) *Irish Industrial School 1868–1908: Origins and Development* (Dublin: Irish Academic Press)

Betjeman, J (1940) *New Light for Old Chancels* (London: John Murray)

Blackstone, W (1796) *Commentaries on the Laws of England* vol 3, 13th edn (Dublin: White, Bryne and Rice

Blackstone, W (1800) *Commentaries on the Laws of England* vol 3, 13th edn (London: A Strahan)

Boswell, J (1998) *The Kindness of Strangers* (Chicago: Chicago University Press)

Bourke, J (2007) *Rape: A History From 1860 to the Present* (London: Virago)

Browne, A (1803) *A Compendious View of the Ecclesiastical Law of Ireland*, 2nd edn (Dublin: Mercier)

Buckley, S-A (2013) *The Cruelty Man: Child Welfare, the NSPCC and the State in Ireland,* 1889–1956 (Manchester: Manchester University Press)

Buller, F (1806) *An Introduction to the Law Relative to Trials at Nisi Prius: Containing Additions to the Present Time* (New York: Riley & Co)

Buller, F (1817) *An Introduction to the Law, Relative to Trials at Nisi Prius*, 7th edn (London: Bridgman)

Byrne, JP (1859) *The New Law of Divorce and Matrimonial Causes Applicable to Ireland... Popularly Explained* (Dublin: EJ Milliken)

Calendar of Grants of Probate and Letters of Administration from 1 Jan 1868 to 31 Dec 1868 (Dublin: Alex Thom)

Carey, T (2013) *Hanged for Murder: Irish State Executions* (Cork: Collins Press)

Cassidy, M (1987) *Domestic Violence Against Women* (Dublin: Social & Organisational Psychology Research Unit UCD)

Chitty, J (1834) *A Practical Treatise on the Law of Contracts* (London: Milliken and Son)

Chitty, J (1844) (H Greening (ed)), *Chitty's Treatise on Pleading and Parties to Actions: with Second and Third Volumes Containing Modern Precedents of Pleading and Practical Notes*, 3 vols, 7th edn (London: Sweet)

Clancy, J (1819) *An Essay on the Equitable Rights of Married Women: With Respect to Their Separate Property and also on their Claim to a Provision Called the Wife's Equity: To Which is Added the Law of Pin-Money, Separate Maintenance, and of the other Separate Provisions of Married Women*, 2nd edn (Dublin: C Hunter)

Clancy, J (1827) *A Treatise of the Rights, Duties and Liabilities of Husband and Wife at Law and in Equity*, 3rd edn (London: J Butterworth)

Clear, C (2000) *Women of the House: Women's Household Work in Ireland: 1922–1961* (Dublin: Irish Academic Press)

Cohen, D (2013) *Family Secrets* (London: Penguin Group)

Coke, E (1644) *Third Part of the Institutes of the Laws of England Concerning High Treason, and Other Pleas of the Crown, and Criminal Causes* (London)

Colum, P (1959) *Arthur Griffith* (Dublin: Brown & Nolan)

Committee for Promoting the Married Women's Property Bill. Annual Report 1869 (Manchester: A Ireland)

Committee for Promoting the Married Women's Property Bill. Annual Report 1879 (Manchester: A Ireland)

Conley, C (1999) *Melancholy Accidents: The Meaning of Violence in Post-Famine Ireland* (New York and Oxford: Lexington Books)

Connolly, L (2002) *The Irish Women's Movement: From Revolution to Devolution* (London: Palgrave Macmillan)

Cooke, E (1839) *A Treatise upon the Law and Practice of the Court for Relief of Insolvent Debtors* (London: Henry Butterworth, Bookseller and Publisher)

Cooney, J (1999) *John Charles McQuaid: Ruler of Catholic Ireland* (Dublin: The O'Brien Press)

Cosgrave, A (1985) *Marriage in Ireland* (Dublin: College Press)

Council of Trent, Decree *Tametsi* Concerning the Reform of Matrimony (1563)

Cretney, S (2005) *Family Law in the Twentieth Century. A History* (Oxford: Oxford University Press)

Crowley, E (1996) *Cowslips and Chainies: A Memoir of Dublin in the 1930s* (Dublin: Lilliput Press)

Cullen Owens, R (2001) *A Social History of Women in Ireland, 1870–1970* (Dublin: Gill and Macmillan)

Daly, ME (1997) *Women and Work in Ireland* (Dundalk: Dundalgan Press)

de Mause, L (1976) *History of Childhood* (London: Souvenir)

Deacon, EE (1847) *The Law and Practice of Bankruptcy* (London: Shaw and Sons)

Dicey, AV (1905) *Lectures on Relations between Law and Public Opinion* (London: Macmillan)

Dillon, M (1993) *Debating Divorce: Moral Conflict in Ireland* (Kentucky: University of Kentucky Press)

Dinneen, PS (2013) *The Queen of the Hearth* (Dublin: University College Dublin Press)

Dinneen, PS (1904) *Foclóir Gaeilge agus Béarla: An English-Irish Dictionary* (Dublin: Irish Texts Society)

Divini Illius Magistri (1929)

Douglas, JG (1998) *Memoirs of Senator James G Douglas (1887–1954) Concerned Citizen* (Dublin: University College Dublin Press)

Doyle, O (2009) *Constitutional Law: Text, Cases and Materials* (Dublin: Clarus Press)

Earner-Byrne, L (2007) *Mother and Child: Maternity and Child Welfare in Dublin, 1922–1960* (Manchester University Press)

Edwards, SSM (1984) *Women on Trial: A Study of the Female Suspect, Defendant and Offender in the Criminal Law and the Criminal Justice System* (Manchester: Manchester University Press)

Espinasse, I (1794) *A Digest of the Law of Actions and Trials at Nisi Prius*, 2nd edn (Dublin: E Lynch and others)

Farrell, E (ed) (2012) *Infanticide in the Irish Crown Files at Assizes, 1883–1900* (Dublin: Irish Manuscripts Commission)

Farrell, E (2013) *'A Most Diabolical Deed': Infanticide and Irish Society, 1850–1900* (Manchester: Manchester University Press)

Ferguson, WD (1841–1842) *A Treatise on the Practice of the Queen's Bench, Common Pleas, and Exchequer of Pleas in Ireland, in Personal Actions and Ejectments* vol 2 (Dublin: A Milliken)

Ferriter, D (2009) *Occasions of Sin: Sex and Society in Modern Ireland* (London: Profile Books)

Ferriter, D (2005) *The Transformation of Ireland 1900–2000* (London: Profile Books)

Finnane, M (1981) *Insanity and the Insane in Post-Famine Ireland* (London: Croom Helm)

Fox, R (1978) *The Tory Islanders: A People of the Celtic Fringe* (Cambridge: Cambridge University Press)

Foyster, E (2005) *Marital Violence: An English Family History, 1660–1857* (Cambridge: Cambridge University Press)

Gaughan, JA (1986–1993) *Alfred O'Rahilly* (Dublin: Kingdom Books)

Gordon, L (1989) *Heroes of Their Own Lives: The Politics and History of Family Violence* (London: Virago)

Gossan, NJ (1876) *A Plea for the Ladies* (Dublin: William J Dunbar)

Griffin, B (2005) *Sources for the Study of Crime in Ireland, 1801–1921* (Dublin: Four Courts Press)

Guinnane, T (1997) *The Vanishing Irish: Households, Migration and the Rural Economy in Ireland 1850–1914* (Princeton: Princeton University Press)

Hammerton, AJ (1992) *Cruelty and Companionship. Conflict in Nineteenth-Century Married Life* (London and New York: Routledge)

Harris Faloon, W (1881) *The Marriage Law of Ireland* (Dublin: Hodges and Figgis)

Hastings, GW (1868) *Transactions of the National Association Belfast Meeting 1867* (London: Longmans)

Hastings, GW (1869) *Transactions of the National Association 1868* (London: Longmans)

Heidensohn, F (1985) *Women and Crime* (London: Macmillan)

Heidensohn, F (1989) *Crime and Society* (Basingstoke: Palgrave Macmillan)

Herring, J (2012) *Criminal Law: Text, Cases and Materials* 5th edn (Oxford: Oxford University Press)

Hogan, G (2012) *The Origins of the Irish Constitution, 1928–1941* (Dublin: Mercier)

Hogan, G and G White (2003) *The Irish Constitution*, 4th edn (Dublin: LexisNexis Butterworths)

Holcombe, L (1983) *Wives and Property. Reform of the Married Women's Property Law in Nineteenth Century England* (Toronto: University of Toronto Press)

Holmes, A (2006) *The Shaping of Ulster Presbyterian Belief and Practice, 1770–1840* (Oxford: Oxford University Press)

Horstman, A (1985) *Victorian Divorce* (London: Croom Helm)

Howlin, N (2017) *Juries in Ireland: Laypersons and Law in the Long Nineteenth Century* (Dublin: Four Courts Press)

Humphreys, A (1966) *New Dubliners. Urbanization and the Irish family* (Dublin: Fordham University Press)

Ibbetson, D (1999) *A Historical Introduction to the Law of Obligations* (Oxford: Oxford University Press)

Inderwick, FA (1866) *The Law of Wills as Administered in the Court of Probate in England* (London: William Maxwell)

Inglis, T (1987) *Moral Monopoly: The Catholic Church in Modern Irish Society* (Dublin: Gill and Macmillan)

Jackson, M (1996) *New Born Child Murder: Women, Illegitimacy and the Courts in Eighteenth-Century England* (Manchester: Manchester University Press)

Jebb, R (1841) *Cases Chiefly Relating to the Criminal and Presentment Law, Reserved for Consideration, and Decided by the Twelve Judges of Ireland, from May 1822, to November 1840* (Dublin: Andrew Milliken)

Jebb, R (1843) *Reports of Cases Argued and Determined on Six Circuits in Ireland: Taken During the Assizes, in the Years 1841, 1842, 1843* (Dublin: Andrew Milliken)

Jefferies, H (1997) *Priests and Prelates of Armagh in the Age of the Reformations, 1518–58* (Dublin: Four Courts Press)

Kadushin, A (1980) *Child Welfare Services*, 3rd edn (New York: Macmillan)

Kearns, KC (2004) *Dublin's Lost Heroines: Mammies and Grannies in a Vanished City* (Dublin: Gill & Macmillan)

Kearns Blains, A (2000) *Stealing Sunlight: Growing up in Irishtown* (Dublin: A & A Farmar)

Kelly, F (2009) *A Guide to Early Irish Law* (Dublin: Dublin Institute of Advanced Studies)

Kennedy, F (2001) *From Cottage to Crèche: Family Change in Ireland* (Dublin: Institute of Public Administration)

Kilcommins, S, I O'Donnell, E O'Sullivan and B Vaughan (2004) *Crime, Punishment and the Search for Order in Ireland* (Dublin: Institute of Public Administration)

Kilday, A-M (2013) *A History of Infanticide in Britain, c1600 to the Present* (New York: Palgrave Macmillan)

Kisbey, WH (1871) *The Law and Practice of the Court for Matrimonial Causes and Matters* (Dublin: W M'Gee)

Kornitzer, M (1952) *Child Adoption in the Modern World* (London: Putnam)

Korpiola, M (2011) (ed) *Regional Variations in Matrimonial Law and Custom in Europe, 1150–1600* (Leiden: Brill)

Lee, P (2014) Keynote Address, *Her Story in Her Own Words*, Conference (University College Cork): Redefining Adoption in a New Era, Opportunities & Challenges for Law and Social Work Practice, 4–5 Sept 2014

Lemmings, D and C Walker (2009) (eds) *Moral Panic, the Media and the Law in Early Modern England* (Basingstoke and New York: Palgrave Macmillan)

Leneman, L (1998) *Alienated Affections: Scottish Experience of Divorce and Separation, 1684–1830* (Edinburgh: Edinburgh University Press)

Lettmaier, S (2010) *Broken Engagements: The Action for Breach of Promise of Marriage and the Feminine Ideal, 1800–1940* (Oxford: Oxford University Press)

Levy, J (1859) *The Law and Practice of Bankruptcy and Insolvency: Embracing the Irish Bankrupt and Insolvent Act 1857*, 3rd edn (Dublin: Hodges, Smith)

Luddy, M (1995) *Women and Philanthropy in Nineteenth Century Ireland* (Cambridge: Cambridge University Press)

Luddy, M (2011) *Matters of Deceit: Breach of Promise to Marry Cases in Nineteenth- and Twentieth-Century Limerick* (Dublin: Four Courts Press)

Luddy, M and M O'Dowd (forthcoming, 2017), *A History of Marriage in Ireland, 1660–1925.*

Macqueen, JF (1842) *A Practical Treatise on the Appellate Jurisdiction of the House of Lords and Privy Council Together with the Practice on Parliamentary Divorce* (London: A Maxwell and Sons)

Macqueen, JF (1848) *The Rights and Liabilities of a Husband and Wife at Law and at Equity as Affected by Modern Statutes and Decisions* (London/Charleston: Bibliobazaar repr., 2008)

Macqueen, JF (1860) *A Practical Treatise on the Law of Marriage, Divorce, and Legitimacy: As Administered in the Divorce Court and in the House of Lords*, 2nd edn (London: Maxwell, Sweet, Stevens & Sons)

Maguire, MJ (2009) *Precarious Childhood in Post-Independence Ireland* (Manchester: Manchester University Press)

Married Women's Property Association. Annual Report 1880 (Manchester: A Ireland)

Matheson, R (1888) *A Digest of the Irish Marriage Law* (Dublin: HMSO)

Mayne, JD (1872) *A Treatise on the Law of Damages: Comprising their Measure, the Mode in which they are Assessed and Reviewed, the Practice of Granting New Trials, and the Law of Set-Off*, 2nd edn (Lumley Smith (ed), London)

McAuley, F (1993) *Insanity, Psychiatry and Criminal Responsibility* (Dublin: Round Hall)

McAuley, F and P McCutcheon (2000) *Criminal Liability: A Grammar* (Dublin: Round Hall, Sweet and Maxwell)

McGuire, J and J Quinn (eds) (2009) *Dictionary of Irish Biography* (Cambridge: Cambridge University Press)

Meenan, J (1980) *George O'Brien: A Biographical Memoir* (Dublin: Gill & Macmillan)

Mews, J, CM Chapman, HHW Sparham and AW Todd (1884) *A Digest of the Reported Decisions of the Courts of Common Law, Bankruptcy, Probate, Admiralty, and Divorce, Together with a Selection from those of the Court of Chancery and Irish Courts. From 1756 to 1883 Inclusive. Founded on Fisher's Digest*, vol IV (London: H. Sweet, Stevens and Sons and W Maxwell and Son)

Middleton, N (1971) *When Family Failed* (London: Victor Gollancz Ltd)

Milotte, M (1997) *Banished Babies: The Secret History of Ireland's Baby Export Business* (Dublin: New Island)

Milotte, M (2011) *Banished Babies: The Secret History of Ireland's Baby Export Business* 2nd edn (Dublin: New Island)

Milotte, M (2012) *Banished Babies: The Secret History of Ireland's Baby Export Business* (rev. edn, Dublin: New Island)

Milward, CR (1847) *Reports of Cases Argued and Determined in The Court of Prerogative in Ireland and in the Consistory Court of Dublin during the time of the Late Hon. John Radcliffe, LLD* (Dublin: Hodges and Smith)

Morrissey, B (2003) *When Women Kill: Questions of Agency and Subjectivity* (London: Routledge)

Murphy, JA (1995) *The College: a History of Queen's/University College Cork 1845–1995* (Cork: Cork University Press)

National Women's Council of Ireland (2001) *The Heart that Bites: Violence Against Women* (Dublin: National Women's Council)

O'Brien, G (2008) 'Visitors' Perceptions of Dublin 1800–30' in G O'Brien and F O'Kane (eds) *Georgian Dublin* (Dublin: Four Courts Press)

O'Brien, M (ed) (1995) *Divorce? Facing the Issues of Martial Breakdown* (Dublin: Basement Press)

Ó'Cinnéide, S (1971) *A Law for the Poor: A Study of Home Assistance in Ireland* (Dublin: Institute of Public Administration)

O'Day, R (1994) *The Family and Family Relationships 1500–1900: England, France and the United States* (Basingstoke: Macmillan)

O'Donnell, I and E O'Sullivan (eds) (2012) *Coercive Confinement in Ireland: Patients, Prisoners and Penitents* (Manchester: Manchester University Press)

O'Higgins, K (May 1974) *Marital Desertion in Dublin. An Exploratory Study* (Dublin: Economic and Social Research Institute, Broadsheet, 9)

O'Sullivan, D (1940) *The Irish Free State and its Senate* (London: Faber and Faber)

Pearse, P (1922) *Collected Works of Padraic H Pearse – Political Writings and Speeches* (Dublin and London: Maunsell and Roberts)
Pindar, P (1817) *The Humorous Speech of Charles Phillips, Esq. in Blake v Wilkins* (London: William Hone London)
Plowden, F (1830) *Crim. Con. Biography*, 8 vols, vol 1, (London: Gale reprint (2012))
Pollock, J (1983) *Forgotten Children: Parent Child Relations 1500–1800* (Cambridge: Cambridge University Press)
Powell, F and M Scanlon (2015), *Dark Secrets of Childhood: Media Power, Child Abuse and Public Scandals* (Bristol: Policy Press)
Powell, F, M Geoghegan, M Scanlon and K Swirak (2012) *Youth Policy, Civil Society and the Modern Irish State* (Manchester: Manchester University Press)
Prior, PM (2008) *Madness and Murder: Gender, Crime and Mental Disorder in Nineteenth-Century Ireland* (Dublin: Irish Academic Press)
Probert, R (2009) *Marriage Law and Practice in the Long Eighteenth Century: A Reassessment* (Cambridge: Cambridge University Press)
Probert, R (2012) *The Changing Legal Regulation of Cohabitation: From Fornicators to Family, 1600–2010* (Cambridge: Cambridge University Press)
Raftery, M and E O'Sullivan (1999) *Suffer the Little Children* (Dublin: New Island Books)
Rattigan, C (2012) *'What Else Could I Do?' Single Mothers and Infanticide, Ireland 1900–1950* (Dublin: Irish Academic Press)
Report of the Married Woman's Property Committee 1882 (Manchester: A Ireland)
Roberts, J (1906) *Divorce Bills in the Imperial Parliament* (Dublin: J Falconer)
Robins, J (1980) *The Lost Children: a Study of Charity Children in Ireland 1700–1900* (Dublin: Institute of Public Administration)
Rohan, D (1969) *Marriage Irish Style* (Cork: Mercier Press)
Rowbotham, J (1989) *Good Girls Make Good Wives: Guidance for Girls in Victorian Fiction* (London: Blackwell)
Schulte, R (1994) *The Village in Court: Arson, Infanticide and Poaching in the Court Records of Upper Bavaria, 1848–1910* (Cambridge: Cambridge University Press)
Seal, L (2010) *Women, Murder and Femininity: Gender Representations of Women who Kill* (Basingstoke: Palgrave Macmillan)
Shatter, A (1977) *Family Law in the Republic of Ireland* (Dublin: Wolfhound Press)
Shatter, A (1997) *Family Law* (Dublin: Butterworths)
Shorter, E (1975) *The Making of the Modern Family* (Huntington, NY: Fontana)
Smith, J (2007) *Ireland's Magdalene Laundries and the Nation's Architecture of Containment* (Notre Dame: University of Notre Dame Press)
Spencer Dix, E (1842) *Report of the Cases of Regina v Millis, et Regina v Carroll, in the Queen's Bench in Ireland, in Easter and Trinity Terms, 1842* (Dublin)
Staves, S (1990), *Married Women's Separate Property in England, 1660–1833* (Cambridge, Massachusetts: Harvard University Press
Stone, L (1990) *Road to Divorce: England 1530–1987* (Oxford: Oxford University Press)
Stone, L (1993) *Broken Lives: Separation and Divorce in England, 1660–1857* (Oxford: Oxford University Press)
Swain, W (2015) *The Law of Contract 1670–1870* (Cambridge: Cambridge University Press)
Valiulis, MG (ed) (2009) *Gender and Power in Irish History* (Dublin: Irish Academic Press)

Vaughan, WE (2009) *Murder Trials in Ireland, 1836–1914* (Dublin: Four Courts Press)
Vaughan, WE and AJ Fitzpatrick (eds) (1978) *Irish Historical Statistics: Population, 1821–1971* (Dublin: Royal Irish Academy)
Wall, M (1967) *The Penal Laws 1691–1760* (Dundalk: Dundalgan Press)
Walls, M and D Bergin (1997) *The Law of Divorce in Ireland* (Bristol: Jordan's)
Walsh, D (2002) *Criminal Procedure* (Dublin: Thomson Round Hall)
Westminster Confession of Faith (1646)
Westminster Assembly (1764) *The Assembly's Shorter Catechism Explained, By Way of Question and Answer. Part Second. Of the Duty Which God Requires of Man* (Belfast: Daniel Blow)
Whyte, JH (1971) *Church and State in Modern Ireland 1923–1970* (Dublin: Gill and Macmillan)
Whyte, JH (1980) *Church and State in Modern Ireland,* 2nd edn (Dublin: Gill & Macmillan)
Wilson, D (2009) *Women, Marriage and Property in Wealthy Landed Families in Ireland, 1750–1850* (Manchester University Press)
Wood, K and P O'Shea (1997) *Divorce in Ireland. The Options. The Issues. The Law* (Dublin: O'Brien Press)

Chapters in books

Abrams, L (2002) 'From Demon to Victim: the Infanticidal Mother in Shetland, 1699–1899' in Y Galloway Brown and R Ferguson (eds), *Twisted Sisters: Women, Crime, and Deviance in Scotland Since 1400* (East Linton: Tuckwell Press)
Anderson, S (1984) 'Legislative Divorce; Law for the Aristocracy' in GR Rubin and D Sugarman (eds), *Law, Economy and Society, 1750–1914* (Abingdon: Professional Books)
Beaumont, C (1999) 'Gender, Citizenship and the State in Ireland, 1922–1990' in S Brewster, C Crossman, F Becket and D Alderson (eds), *Ireland in Proximity: History, Gender, and Space* (London and New York: Routledge)
Bergin, J (2009) 'Irish Private Divorce Bills and Acts of the Eighteenth Century' in J Kelly, J McCafferty and CI McGrath (eds), *People, Politics and Power: Essays on Irish History in Honour of James I McGuire* (Dublin: University College Dublin Press)
Buckley, S (2011) 'Family and Power: Incest in Ireland, 1880–1950' in A McElligott, L Chambers, C Breathnach and C Lawless (eds), *Power in History. From Medieval Ireland to the Post-Modern World* (Dublin: Irish Academic Press)
Clear, C (2004), '"Too Fond of Going": Female Emigration and Change for Women in Ireland, 1946–1961' in D Keogh, F O'Shea and C Quinlan (eds), *The Lost Decade: Ireland in the 1950s* (Cork: Mercier Press)
Connolly, SJ (1985) 'Marriage in Pre-Famine Ireland' in A Cosgrove (ed), *Marriage in Ireland* (Dublin: College Press)
Cosgrove, A (1985) 'Marriage in Medieval Ireland' in A Cosgrove (ed), *Marriage in Ireland* (Dublin: College Press)
Cornish, W (2010) 'Law of Persons: Family and Other Relationships' in J Baker (ed), *The Oxford History of the Laws of England* (13 vols), (Oxford: Oxford University Press), vol 13
Duncan, W (1996) 'The Constitutional Protection of Parental Rights' in (1996) *Report of the Constitution Review Group* (Dublin: Stationery Office)

Earner-Byrne, L (2011) 'Child Sexual Abuse, History and the Pursuit of Blame in Modern Ireland' in K Holmes and S Ward (eds), *Exhuming Passions: Memory and the Uses of the Past in Australia and Ireland* (Dublin: Irish Academic Press)

Edwards, S (1985) 'Male Violence Against Women: Excusatory and Explanatory Ideologies in Law and Society', in S Edwards (ed), *Gender, Sex and the Law* (London: Croom Helm)

Fennell, C (1993) 'Criminal Law and the Criminal Justice System: Women as Victim' in A Connelly (ed), *Gender and the Law in Ireland* (Dublin: Oak Tree Press)

Ferguson, H (1993) 'Surviving Irish Childhood: Child Protection and the Death of Children in Child Abuse Cases in Ireland Since 1884' in H Ferguson, R Gilligan and R Torode (eds.), *Surviving Childhood Adversity: Issues for Policy and Practice* (Dublin: Social Studies Press)

Fitzpatrick, D (1985) 'Marriage in post-famine Ireland' in A Cosgrove (ed) *Marriage in Ireland* (Dublin: College Press)

Geoghegan, PM (2009) 'Lawless, Valentine Browne (Baron Cloncurry)' in J McGuire and J Quinn (eds) *Dictionary of Irish Biography* (Cambridge: Cambridge University Press)

Hogan, G (2007) 'Foreword' in D Keogh and A McCarthy, *The Making of the Irish Constitution 1937* (Cork: Mercier Press)

Hogan, G (2014) 'Some Thoughts on the Origins of the 1937 Constitution' in FM Larkin and NM Dawson (eds), *Lawyers, the Law and History* (Dublin: Four Courts Press)

Kelly, J (2011) 'The Historiography of the Penal Laws' in J Bergin et al. (eds), *New Perspectives on the Penal Laws* (Eighteenth Century Ireland Special Issue, Dublin)

Kelly, J (2012) 'Responding to Infanticide in Ireland, 1680–1820' in E Farrell (ed), *'She Said She Was in the Family Way': Pregnancy and Infancy in Modern Ireland* (London: Institute of Historical Research)

Laslett, P (1980) 'Preface' in K Oosterveen and RM Smith (eds), *Bastardy and its Comparative History: Studies in the History of Illegitimacy and Marital Nonconformism in Britain, France, Sweden, North America, Jamaica, and Japan* (London: Edward Arnold)

Lemmings, D (2009) 'Introduction: Law and Order, Moral Panics, and Early Modern England' in D Lemmings and C Walker (eds) *Moral Panic, the Media and the Law in Early Modern England* (Basingstoke and New York: Palgrave Macmillan)

Lobban, M (2010) 'Tort' in J Baker (ed), *The Oxford History of the Laws of England*, 13 vols, vol 12 (Oxford: Oxford University Press)

May, AN (1995) '"She at First Denied It": Infanticide Trials at the Old Bailey' in V Frith (ed), *Women and History: Voices of Early Modern England* (Toronto: Coach House Press)

McAvoy, S (2009) 'Sexual Crime and Irish Women's Campaign for a Criminal Law Amendment Act, 1912–35' in MG Valiulis (ed), *Gender and Power in Irish History* (Dublin: Irish Academic Press)

McLoughlin, D (2002) 'Infanticide in Nineteenth-Century Ireland', in A Bourke, S Kilfeather, M Luddy, M MacCurtain, G Meaney, M Ní Dhonnchadha, M O'Dowd and C Wills (eds), *Field day Anthology of Irish Writing*, iv (Cork: Cork University Press)

McShane-Galley, J (2006) 'For Shame: Accusations of Infanticide and Coroner's Inquests Into the Deaths of Legitimate Infants in Victorian Ontario' in BH

Bechtold and D Cooper Graves (eds), *Killing Infants: Studies in the Worldwide Practice of Infanticide* (Lewiston: Edwin Mellen Press)

O'Brien, G (2006) 'Capital Punishment in Ireland, 1922–1964' in N Dawson (ed) *Reflections on Law and History: Irish Legal History Society Discourses and Other Papers, 2000–2005* (Dublin: Four Courts Press)

O'Dowd, M (forthcoming 2017) 'Men, Women, Children and the Family 1550–1730' in J Ohlmeyer (ed), *Cambridge History of Ireland,* vol 2 (Cambridge: Cambridge University Press)

Ó Gráda, C (1989) 'Poverty, Population and Agriculture 1801–1845' in WE Vaughan (ed), *A New History of Ireland, Volume V: Ireland Under the Union* (Oxford: Oxford University Press)

O'Sullivan, E (2002) '"...Otherwise Delicate Subject": Child Sexual Abuse in Early Twentieth-Century Ireland' in P O'Mahony (ed), *Criminal Justice in Ireland* (Dublin: Institute of Public Administration)

Ryan, L (2004) 'The Press, Police and Prosecution: Perspectives on Infanticide in the 1920s' in A Hayes and D Urquhart (eds), *Irish Women's History* (Dublin: Irish Academic Press)

Ryan, L (2007) 'Publicising the Private: Suffragists' Critique of Sexual Abuse and Domestic Violence' in L Ryan and M Ward (eds), *Irish Women and the Vote: Becoming Citizens* (Dublin: Irish Academic Press)

Seaborne Davies, D (1945) 'Child Killing in English Law' in L Radzinowicz and JWC Turner (eds), *The Modern Approach to Criminal Law* (London: Macmillan)

Steiner-Scott, E (1997) '"To Bounce a Boot Off Her Now And Then": Domestic Violence in Post-Famine Ireland' in M Gialanella Valiulis and M O'Dowd (eds), *Women and Irish History* (Dublin: Wolfhound Press)

Stone, L (1990) 'Honour, Morals, Religion and the Law: The Action for Criminal Conversation in England 1670–1857' in A Grafton and A Blair, *The Transmission of Culture in Early Modern Europe* (Philadelphia: University of Pennsylvania Press)

Swift, Jonathan (1729) *A Modest Proposal* in P Pinkus (1965) *Jonathan Swift: A Collection of his Works* (London: Macmillan)

Urquhart, D (2014) 'A Woman's Reply: Irish Female Divorce Law Reformers' in B Walsh (ed), *Knowing their Place? The Intellectual and Professional Life of Women in 19th-Century Ireland* (Dublin: History Press)

Valiulis, MG (2009) 'Virtuous Mothers and Dutiful Wives: The Politics of Sexuality in the Irish Free State' in MG Valiulis (ed), *Gender and Power in Irish History* (Dublin: Irish Academic Press)

Wells, C (2000) 'Provocation: The Case for Abolition' in A Ashworth and B Mitchell (eds), *Rethinking English Homicide Law* (Oxford: Oxford University Press)

Articles in journals

Abbate, LL (2002) 'What God Has Joined "Let" Man Put Asunder: Ireland's Struggle Between Canon and Common Law Relating to Divorce', *Emory International Law Review*, 16(2), 583–637

Akenson, DH and JF Fallin (1970) 'The Irish Civil War and the Drafting of the Free State Constitution', *Éire-Ireland*, 5(1), 10–26

Aldridge, RH (1969) 'Notes on Children's Burial Grounds in Mayo', *Journal of the Royal Society of Antiquaries of Ireland,* 99(1), 83–87

Anderson, M (1998) 'Lawful Wife, Unlawful Sex – Examining the Effect of the Criminalization of Marital Rape in England and the Republic of Ireland', *Georgia Journal of International & Comparative Law*, 27, 139–166

Anon (1889) 'Remedies in Respect of Married Women's Liabilities', *Irish Law Times and Solicitors Journal*, 585, 598

Binhammer, K (1996) 'The Sex Panic of the 1790s', *Journal of the History of Sexuality* 6(3), 409–434

Brennan, K (2013) '"A Fine Mixture of Pity and Justice": The Criminal Justice Response to Infanticide in Ireland 1922–1949', *Law and History Review*, 31(4), 793–841

Brennan, K (2013) 'Punishing Infanticide in the Irish Free State', *Irish Journal of Legal Studies* 1–35

Brennan, K (2013) '"Traditions of English Liberal Thought": A History of The Enactment of an Infanticide Law in Ireland', *Irish Jurist*, 50, 100–137

Clancy Gore, C (1943–1944) 'Nutritional Standards of Some Working-Class Families in Dublin, 1943', *Journal of the Statistical and Social Inquiry Society of Ireland*, 17, 241–253

Cole, J (1967, 4 Apr) 'Deserted Wives', *Evening Press*.

Colgan McCarthy, I and N O'Reilly Byrne (1988) 'Mis-Take Love: Conversations on the Problem of Incest in an Irish Context', *Family Process*, 27, 181–199

Connell, KH (1962) 'Peasant Marriage in Ireland: Its Structure and Development Since the Famine' *The Economic History Review* 14(3), 502–523

Costello, K (2013) 'Imprisonment for Debt in early Nineteenth Century Ireland, 1810–1848', *UCD Working Papers in Law, Criminology & Socio-Legal Studies* Research Paper No 9

Curtin, C, E Devereux and D Shields (1992) 'Replaying "The Match:" Marriage Settlements in North Galway', *Irish Journal of Sociology*, 2, 85–95

Curtis, M (2010) *A Challenge to Democracy: Militant Catholicism in Modern Ireland* (Dublin: The History Press Ireland)

Daly, ME (2006) 'Marriage, Fertility and Women's Lives in Twentieth-century Ireland', *Women's History Review*, 15, 571–585.

Daly, ME (2009) '"The Primary and Natural Educator"? The Role of Parents in the Education of Their Children in Independent Ireland', *Éire-Ireland: An Interdisciplinary Journal of Irish Studies*, 44, 194–217

Dillon, KM (1989) 'Divorce and Remarriage as Human Rights: the Irish Constitution and the European Convention on Human Rights At Odds in *Johnston v Ireland*', *Cornell International Law Journal*, 22(1), 63–90

Dooley, M (1975) 'Marriage Annulments', *The Furrow*, 26(4), 211, 213

Doyle, DM and I O'Donnell (2012) 'The Death Penalty in Post-Independence Ireland', *Journal of Legal History*, 33(1), 65–91

Duncan, W (1972) 'Desertion and Cruelty in Irish Matrimonial Law', *Irish Jurist*, VII, 213–240

Earner-Byrne, L (2008) 'Reinforcing the Family: The Role of Gender, Morality and Sexuality in Irish Welfare Policy, 1922–44', *History of the Family: International Quarterly Journal*, 13, 360–379

Earner-Byrne, L (2015) 'The Rape of Mary M: A Microhistory of Sexual Violence and Moral Redemption in 1920s Ireland', *Journal of the History of Sexuality*, 24, 75–98

Edwards, SSM (2010) 'Anger and Fear as Justifiable Preludes for Loss of Self Control', *Journal of Criminal Law*, 74(3), 223–241

Fahey, T (1992) 'State, Family and Compulsory Schooling in Ireland', *The Economic and Social Review*, 21, 369–395

Farrell, E (2012) '"The Fellow Said It Was Not Harm And Only Tricks": The Father in Suspected Cases of Infanticide In Ireland, 1850–1900', *Journal of Social History* 45(4), 990–1004

Ferguson, H (1993–1994) 'Abuse Inquiries and the Report of the Kilkenny Incest Investigation: A Critical Analysis,' *Administration*, 41, 385–410

Ferguson, H (1996) 'Protecting Irish Children in Time: Child Abuse as a Social Problem and the Development of the Child Protection System in the Republic of Ireland', *Administration*, 44(2), 5–36

Ferguson, H (2001) '*States of Fear*, Child Abuse, and Irish Society', *Doctrine & Life*, 20–30

Finnane, M (2001) 'The Carrigan Committee of 1930–31 and the "Moral Condition of the Saorstát"', *Irish Historical Studies*, 23, 519–536

Fitzpatrick, D (1983) 'Irish Farming Families Before the First World War', *Comparative Studies in Society and History,* 25(2), 339–374

Fitzpatrick, D (1987) 'Divorce and Separation in Modern Irish History', *Past and Present,* 114(1), 172–196

Francus, M (1997) 'Monstrous Mothers, Monstrous Societies: Infanticide and the Rule of Law in Restoration and Eighteenth-Century England', *Eighteenth Century Life,* xxi(2), 133–156

Frost, G (1997) 'Bigamy and Cohabitation in Victorian England', *Journal of Family History,* 22(3), 286–306

Gibbons, P and C Curtin (1978) 'The Stem Family in Ireland', *Comparative Studies in Society and History*, 20(3), 429–453

Gibbons, P, N Mulryan and A O'Connor (1997) 'Guilty but Insane: The Insanity Defence in Ireland', *British Journal of Psychiatry*, 170, 467–472

Gibbons, P, N Mulryan, A McAleer and A O'Connor (1999) 'Criminal Responsibility and Mental Illness in Ireland 1850–1995: Fitness to Plead', *Irish Journal of Psychological Medicine,* 16(2), 51–56

Gilligan, R (2009) 'The "Public Child" and the Reluctant State?' *Éire-Ireland*, 44, 265–290

Gordon, E (2013) 'Irregular Marriage: Myth and Reality', *Journal of Social History*, 47(2), 507–525

Gowing, L (1997) 'Secret Births and Infanticide in Seventeenth Century England', *Past and Present*, clvi, 87–115

Grey, DJR (2013) '"What Woman is Safe...?": Coerced Medical Examinations, Suspected Infanticide, and the Response of the Women's Movement in Britain, 1871–1881', *Women's History Review*, xxii(3), 403–421

Harding, M (2012) 'The Curious Incident of the Marriage Act No 2 1537 and the Irish Statute Book', *Legal Studies*, 32(1), 78–108

Hart, WG (1924) 'The Origin of the Restraint upon Anticipation', *Law Quarterly Review,* XL, 221–226

Horgan, M (2004) 'Anti-urbanism as a Way of Life: Distain for Dublin in the Nationalist Imaginary', *Canadian Journal of Irish Studies,* 30(2), 38–47

Inglis, T (2005) 'Origins and Legacies of Irish Prudery: Sexuality and Social Control in Modern Ireland' *Eire-Ireland* 40(3 & 4), 9–37

James, C (1997–1998) '*Cead Míle Fáilte*: Ireland Welcomes Divorce: The 1995 Irish Divorce Referendum and the Family Law (Divorce) Act 1996', *Duke Journal of Comparative and International Law*, 8, 175–228

Kelly, BD (2007) 'Murder, Mercury, Mental Illness: Infanticide in Nineteenth-Century Ireland', *Irish Journal of Medical Science*, clxxvi, 149–152

Kelly, BD (2008) 'Poverty, Crime and Mental Illness: Female Forensic Psychiatric Committal in Ireland, 1910–1948', *Social History of Medicine*, 21(2), 311–328

Kelly, J (1992) 'Infanticide in Eighteenth-Century Ireland' *Irish Economic and Social History*, xix, 5–26

Kennedy, F (2001) 'The Suppression of the Carrigan Report: A Historical Perspective on Child Abuse', *Studies: An Irish Quarterly Review*, 89, 354–363

Kilday, A-M and KD Watson (2008) 'Infanticide, Religion and Community in the British Isles, 1720–1920: Introduction', *Family and Community History*, xi(2), 84–99

Larkin, E (1962) 'Church and State in Ireland in the Nineteenth Century', *Church History* 31(3), 294–306

Larkin, E (1972), 'The devotional revolution in Ireland 1850–1875', *American Historical Review*, 77, 625–652

Leneman, L (1996) '"Disregarding the Matrimonial Vows": Divorce in Eighteenth and Early Nineteenth Century Scotland', *Journal of Social History*, 30(2), 465–482

Luddy, M (1997) 'Abandoned Women and Bad Characters: Prostitution in Nineteenth Century Ireland', *Women's History Review*, 6(4), 485–504

Luddy, M (2009) 'The Early Years of the NSPCC in Ireland' *Éire-Ireland*, 44 (1 & 2), 62–90

MacBride, T (1992) 'Public Authority and Private Lives: Divorce After the French Revolution' *French Historical Studies*, 17(3), 747–768

Maguire, M (2002) 'Foreign Adoptions and the Evolution of Irish Adoption Policy 1945–52' *Journal of Social History*, 36(2), 387–404

Maguire, MJ (2001) 'The Changing Face of Catholic Ireland: Conservatism and Liberalism in the Anne Lovett and Kerry Babies Scandals', *Feminist Studies*, 27, 335–358

Maguire, MJ (2006) 'The Carrigan Committee and Child Sexual Abuse in Twentieth-Century Ireland', *New Hibernia Review*, 11, 79–100

Maguire, M and S Ó Cinnéide (2005) '"A Good Beating Never Hurt Anyone": The Punishment and Abuse of Children in Twentieth Century Ireland', *Journal of Social History*, 38(3), 635–652

McCullagh, C (1991) 'A Tie That Binds: Family and Ideology in Ireland', *The Economic and Social Review* 22, 199–211

McGowan, D (2016) 'Governed by Marriage Law: An Irish Genealogy' *Social and Legal Studies*, 25(3), 311–331

Mohr, T (2008) 'British Involvement in the Creation of the Constitution of the Irish Free State', *Dublin University Law Journal*, 30, 166–186

Morse, CGJ (1976) 'Polygamists and the Crime of Bigamy', *International and Comparative Law Quarterly*, 25, 229–235

Newman, WA (1951) 'Legal adoption', *The Bell*, XVI(4), 59–66.

O'Dwyer, C (1975) (ed), 'Archbishop Butler's Visitation Book', *Archivium Hibernicum*, XXXIII, 1–90; XXXIV, 1–49

Ó Gráda, C (1973) 'Seasonal Migration and Post-Famine Adjustment in the West of Ireland', *Studia Hibernica*, 13, 48–76

O'Hanlon, RJ (1968), 'Not Guilty Because of Insanity', *Irish Jurist*, 3(1) (ns), 61–77

O'Malley, T (1993) 'Perceptions of Sexual Violence' in A Byrne et al. (eds), *University College Galway Women's Studies Review*, 11, 131–147

O'Rahilly, A (1936) 'The Constitution and the Senate', *Studies,* 25, 1–19
Ó Sulleabháin, S (1939) '*Adhlacadh leanbhaí* (the Burial of Children)' *Journal of the Royal Society of Antiquaries of Ireland,* 143–151
Prior, P (2005) 'Murder and Madness: Gender and the Insanity Defence in Nineteenth-Century Ireland', *New Hibernia Review,* 9(4), 19–36
Probert, R (2008) '*R v Millis* Reconsidered: Binding Contracts and Bigamous Marriages', *Legal Studies* 28, 337–355
Probert, R (2009) 'Control Over Marriage in England and Wales, 1753–1823: The Clandestine Marriages Act of 1753 in Context', *Law and History Review,* 27(2), 413–450
Radford, J (1982) 'Marriage Licence or Licence to Kill? Womenslaughter and the Criminal Law', *Feminist Review,* 11, 88–96
Rattigan, Cl (2008) '"Done to Death by Father or Relatives": Irish Families and Infanticide Cases, 1922-50', *History of the Family,* xiii, 370–383
Riordan, S (2011) 'A Reasonable Cause: The Age of Consent and the Debate on Gender and Justice in the Irish Free State, 1922-35' *Irish Historical Studies,* 37, 427–446
Ryan, L (1996) '"The Massacre of Innocence": Infanticide in the Irish Free State', *Irish Studies Review,* xiv, 17–20
Savage, GL (1983) 'The Operation of the 1857 Divorce Act, 1860–1910: A Research Note', *Journal of Social History* 16(4), 103–110
Sheridan, K (6 Mar 1993) 'Walls of Fear, Walls of Silence', *Irish Times.*
Sievens, MB (2001) '"The Wicked Agency of Others": Community, Law, and Marital Conflict in Vermont, 1790–1830,' *Journal of the Early Republic,* XXI, 20–21
Smart, C (2000) 'Reconsidering the Recent History of Child Sexual Abuse, 1910–1960' *Journal of Social Policy,* 29, 55–71
Smith, J (2004) 'The Politics of Sexual Knowledge: The Origins of Ireland's Containment Culture and the Carrigan Report (1931)' *Journal of the History of Sexuality,* 13, 208–233
Staves, S (1982) 'Money for Honour: Damages for Criminal Conversation', *Studies in Eighteenth-Century Culture,* 2, 279–297
Sumner Holmes, A (1995) 'The Double Standard in the English Divorce Laws, 1857–1923' *Law and Social Inquiry,* 20(2), 601–620.
Swain, W (2010) 'The Classical Model of Contract: The Product of a Revolution in Legal Thought?', *Legal Studies,* 30(4), 513–532, 524–525
Urquhart, D (2012) 'Ireland's Criminal Conversations' *Études Irlandaises,* 37(2), 65–80
Urquhart, D (2013) 'Ireland and the Divorce and Matrimonial Causes Act of 1857', *Journal of Family History,* 38(3), 301–320
Urquhart, D (2013) 'Irish Divorce and Domestic Violence, 1857–1922' *Women's History Review,* 22(5), 820–837
Weare, S (2013) '"The Mad", "The Bad", "The Victim": Gendered Constructions of Women Who Kill in the Criminal Justice System', *Laws,* 2, 337–361
Wolfram, S (1985) 'Divorce in England', *Oxford Journal of Legal Studies,* 5, 155–186

Unpublished theses

Barkley, JM (1952) *History of the Ruling Eldership in Irish Presbyterianism* (unpub MA thesis, Queen's University Belfast)

Coffey, D (2010) *Irish Constitutional History 1936–1937* (unpub PhD thesis, University College Dublin)
Downing, M (1986) *Adoption Policy in Ireland* (unpub Masters thesis, University College Cork)
McCaughren, S (2010) *A Study of Open Adoption in Ireland through the Narratives of Adoptive Parents* (unpub PhD thesis, University College Cork)

Government publications

All Party Oireachtas Committee on the Constitution, Tenth Report: The Family (Dublin 2006)
Commission of Inquiry into the Reformatory and Industrial School System 1934–1936: Report (Dublin: Stationery Office 1936)
Committee on Court Practice and Procedure (1974) *Nineteenth Interim Report: Desertion and Maintenance*, (Prl 3666, Dublin: Stationery Office)
Dáil Éireann debates
Department of Local Government and Public Health, Annual Report, 1931–2 (Dublin: Stationery Office)
Department of Local Government and Public Health, Fourth Report, 1928–9 (Dublin: Stationery Office)
Domestic Abuse of Women and Men in Ireland: Report on the National Study of Domestic Abuse (Dublin: ESRI 2005)
Eighth Report of the Convention on the Constitution (Jan 2014)
Eire: Commission on Emigration and Other Population Problems, 1948–54 (1955) (Dublin: Stationery Office)
Final Report of the Joint Committee on the Constitutional Amendment on Children (16 February 2010)
Hansard's Parliamentary Debates
Irish Crimes Records Return of Outrages, 1841–1893 (National Archives of Ireland, Chief Secretary's Office Papers)
Law Reform Commission, *Working Paper on the Law Relating to Breach of Promise of Marriage* (LRC 4-1978)
Law Reform Commission, *First Report on Family Law*, 1980 (LRC 1-1980)
Law Reform Commission, *Report on Illegitimacy* (Dublin: Law Reform Commission), 1982 (LRC 4/1982)
McGuinness, C (1993) *The Report of Kilkenny Incest Investigation* (Dublin: Department of Health)
Report of the Commission on the Relief of the Sick and Destitute Poor, including the Insane Poor (Dublin: Stationery Office 1927)
Report of the Commission on the Status of Women, Dec 1972
Report of the Committee on the Criminal Law Amendment Acts (1880–1885) and Juvenile Prostitution (Dublin: Stationery Office 1931)
Report of the Constitution Review Group (Dublin: Stationery Office 1996)
Ryan, S (2009) *Commission to Inquire into Child Abuse* (Dublin: Government Publications)
Seanad Éireann debates
Ulster Year Book (1956) (Belfast: HMSO)

Parliamentary papers

Tenth Report from the Select Committee on the Poor Laws. HC 1849 (301), 12

Special Report from the Select Committee on Married Women's Property Bill, Together with the Proceedings of the Committee, Minutes of Evidence, Appendix and Index. HC 1867–1868 (441), 76

Census of Ireland, 1871. Part III. General Report. HC 1876 [C-1377]

Return of Judicial Statistics, Ireland, 1898. Part II. Civil Statistics. HC 1899 [C-9494] cviii, Pt ii, 445

Thirty-Third Report of the Deputy Keeper of the Public Records and Keeper of the State Papers in Ireland, HC 1901 [C-729] xxxiii, 763

Thirty-Fourth Report of the Deputy Keeper of the Public Records and Keeper of the State Papers in Ireland HC 1902 [C-1176] xlix, 779

Return of Judicial Statistics, Ireland, 1904. Part II. Civil Statistics. HC 1905 [C-2632] xcix, Pt ii, 176

Return of Judicial Statistics, Ireland, 1908. Part II. Civil Statistics. HC 1909 [C-4793] civ, 176

Royal Commission on Divorce and Matrimonial Causes: Report of the Royal Commission on Divorce and Matrimonial Causes HC 1912–1913 [C-6478] xviii, 143

Return of Judicial Statistics, Ireland, 1914. Part II. Civil Statistics. HC 1914–1916 [C-8077] lxxxii, pt ii, 170

Return of Judicial Statistics, Ireland, 1916. Part II. Civil Statistics. HC 1918 [C-9066] xxv, pt ii, 65

Newspapers and periodicals

Anglo-Celt
Belfast Newsletter
Cork Examiner
Dublin Evening Mail
Dublin Gazette
Dundalk Democrat
Ennis Chronicle and Clare Advertiser
Evening Press
Finn's Leinster Journal
Freeman's Journal
Irish Citizen
Irish Independent
Irish Press
Irish Times
Nation
Nenagh Guardian
Northern Whig
Stubbs Gazette
The Guardian
Times of Malta
Weekly Irish Times
Women's Suffrage Journal

Constitutions

The Constitution of the Irish Free State 1922
Constitution of Portugal 1933
The Constitution of Ireland (Bunreacht na hÉireann) 1937

Legislation (acts and bills)

Marriage Act (No 1) 1537 (28 Hen VIII c 2 [Ire])
Marriage Act (No 2) 1537 (28 & 29 Hen VIII c 17 [Ire])
Marriage Act 1542 (33 Hen VIII c 6 [Ire])
An Act to Restrain all Persons from Marriage until their Former Wives and Former Husbands be Dead 1603 (1 Jac I c 11)
Statute of Uses 1634 (10 Car I sess 2 c 1)
An Act for the Punishment of Such as Shall Take Away Maidens that be Inheritors Being Within the Age of 16 Years or Marry them Without Consent of Their Parents 1635 (10 Cha I c 17 [Ire])
An Act for the Restraining of all Persons from Marriage till their Former Wives and Former Husbands be Dead 1635 (10 Car I c 21 [Ire])
Statute of Frauds 1677 (29 Car II c 3)
An Act to Prevent Protestants from Intermarrying with Papists 1697 (9 Will c 3 [Ire])
An Act for Banishing all Papists Exercising any Ecclesiastical Jurisdiction, and all Regulars of the Popish Clergy out of the Kingdom 1698 (9 Will III c 1 [Ire])
An Act for Registering the Popish Clergy 1703 (2 Ann c 7 [Ire])
An Act to Explain and Amend an Act, Intituled An Act for Registering the Popish Clergy 1704 (4 Ann, c 2 [Ire])
An Act to Prevent the Destroying and Murthering of Bastard Children 1707 (6 Ann c 4)
An Act for the More Effectual Preventing the Taking Away and Marrying Children Against the Wills of their Parents or Guardians 1707 (6 Ann c 16 [Ire])
An Act to Prevent the Further Growth of Popery 1707 (2 Ann c 6) [Ire])
Registration of Deeds Act 1707 (6 Ann c 2 [Ire])
An Act for Explaining an Act to Prevent the Further Growth of Popery 1709 (8 Ann c 3 [Ire])
Marriage Act 1725 (12 Geo I c 3 [Ire])
An Act for the More Effectual Preventing of Clandestine Marriages 1735 (9 Geo II, c 11 [Ire])
An Act for Allowing Further Time to Persons in Offices to Qualify Themselves Pursuant to an Act Entitled 'An Act to Prevent the Further Growth of Popery; and for Giving Further Ease to Protestant Dissenters with Respect to Matrimonial Contracts' 1737 (11 Geo II c 10 [Ire])
An Act for Annulling all Marriages to be Celebrated by any Popish Priest Between Protestant and Protestant, or Between Protestant and Papist 1745 (19 Geo II c 13 [Ire])
An Act for the More Effective Preventing of Clandestine Marriages 1749 (23 Geo II, c 10 [Ire])
Marriage Act 1753 (26 Geo II c 33)
Catholic Relief Act 1777 (17 & 18 Geo III, c 49)

An Act for the Relief of Protestant Dissenters in Certain Matters Therein Contained 1782 (21 & 22 Geo III, c 25 [Ire])
An Act to Remove Certain Restraints and Disabilities Therein Mentioned, to which His Majesty's Subjects Professing the Popish Religion are now Subject 1792 (32 Geo III c 21 [Ire])
An Act to Repeal Certain Penal Enactments made in the Parliament of Ireland Against Roman Catholic Clergymen for Celebrating Marriages Contrary to the Provisions of Certain Acts Made in the Parliament of Ireland 1793 (33 Geo III c 21)
An Act for the Further Prevention of Malicious Shooting and Attempting to Discharge Loaded Fire-arms, Stabbing, Cutting, Wounding, Poisoning and the Malicious Using of Means to Procure the Miscarriage of Women 1803 (43 Geo III c 58)
Marriage of Lunatics Act 1811 (51 Geo III c 37)
Infant Executors (Ireland) Act 1818 (58 Geo III c 81)
Offences Against the Person Act 1828 (9 Geo IV c 31)
Offences Against the Person (Ireland) Act 1829 (10 Geo IV c 34)
Roman Catholic Relief Act 1829 (10 Geo IV c 7)
Marriages by Roman Catholics (Ireland) Act 1833 (3 & 4 Will IV c 102)
Dower Act 1833 (3 &4 Will IV c 105)
Marriage Act 1835 (5 & 6 Will IV c 54)
Poor Law (Ireland) Act 1838 (1 & 2 Vic c 56)
Insolvent Debtors (Ireland) Act 1840 (3 & 4 Vic c 105)
Marriages (Ireland) Act 1844 (7 & 8 Vic c 81)
Marriages (Ireland) Act 1846 (9 & 10 Vic c 72)
Vagrancy (Ireland) Act 1847 (10 & 11 Vic c 84)
A Bill to Amend the Law Regarding Actions for Criminal Conversation 1854, HC 1854 (61) ii, 121.
Divorce and Matrimonial Causes Act 1857 (20 & 21 Vic c 85)
Offences Against the Person Act 1861 (24 & 25 Vic c 100)
Registration of Marriages (Ireland) Act 1863 (26 & 27 Vic c 90)
Married Women's Property (Ireland) Act 1865
Married Women's Property Bill HC 1867–1868 (89)
Married Women's Property Bill 1868 (HC 1868–1869 (20))
Irish Church Act 1869 (32 & 33 Vic c 42)
Evidence Further Amendment Act 1869 (32 & 33 Vic c 68)
Matrimonial Causes and Marriage Law (Ireland) Amendment Act 1870 (33 & 34 Vic c 110)
Married Women's Property Act 1882
Guardianship of Infants Act 1886 (49 & 50 Vic c 27)
Westropp's Divorce Act 1886 (49 & 50 Vic) [Unprinted c 1P]
Donovan's Divorce Act 1905 (1905 (5 Edw 7) [Unprinted c 5P])
Probation of Offenders Act 1907
Children Act 1908
Punishment of Incest Act 1908
Martin's Divorce Act 1917 (7 & 8 Geo V) [Unprinted c 2P]
Constitution of the Irish Free State (Saorstát Éireann) Act 1922
Juries (Amendment) Act 1924
Civil Service Regulation (Amendment) Act 1926

Local Authorities (Officers and Employees) Act 1926
Juries Act 1927
Censorship of Publications Act 1929
Children Act 1929
Constitution (Removal of Oath) Act 1933
Criminal Law Amendment Act 1935
Public Assistance Act 1939
Infanticide Act 1949
Adoption Act 1952
Criminal Justice Act 1964
Law Reform (Miscellaneous Provisions) Act 1970 (UK)
Fifth Amendment of the Constitution Act 1972
Family Law (Maintenance of Spouse & Children) Act 1976
Criminal Law (Rape) Act 1981
Family Law Act 1981
Criminal Law (Rape) (Amendment) Act 1990
Child Care Act 1991
Fifteenth Amendment of the Constitution Act 1995
Family Law (Divorce) Act 1996
Adoption Act 2010

Table of cases

Addis v Gramophone [1909] AC 488
Allen v Field, *Freeman's Journal*, 10, 16 Dec 1872
Anonymous case, *Belfast Newsletter*, 18 Aug 1789
Arthur v Arthur [1848] 11 Ir Eq Rep 511
Atkins v Packford, *Irish Times*, 27 Jan 1887
Attorney General v Mc Manus, *Irish Times*, 29 Mar 1939
Attorney General v O'Brien [1936] IR 263
Attorney General v Reilly, *Irish Times*, 11 June 1933
Attorney General v Smyth, *Irish Times*, 19 Feb 1943
Attorney General v Vere Hunt, *Irish Times*, 11 Dec 1945
Aylward v Morrisson, *Belfast Newsletter*, 10 Sept 1813
Bardon v Douglas, *Irish Times*, 21 Nov 1888
Beaken v Dockeray, *Irish Times*, 22 Feb 1882
Beamish v Longley, *Belfast Newsletter*, 23, 25 Mar 1875
Berbick v Byrne, *Freeman's Journal*, 23 Jul 1814
Binns v Scott (1816) *Crim Con William Binns, Plaintiff, John Scott, Defendant, Before the Hon Justice Mayne* (Dublin: Wm Espy)
Birket v Bates, *Freeman's Journal*, 6 Mar 1838; *Belfast Newsletter*, 9 Mar 1838
Blachford v Latouche, *Freeman's Journal*, 13 Jan 1811
Blake v Daly, *Belfast Newsletter*, 13 Apr 1821
Blake v Wilkins, *Freeman's Journal*, 31 Mar 1817; *Belfast Newsletter*, 8 Apr 1817
Bowers v Morris, *Freeman's Journal*, 13 Mar 1840
Bradley v District Justice in and for the District of Bray [1932] 66 ILTR 154
Brandon v Robinson (1811) Ves Jun Rep 429, 34 ER 379
Braun v Roche, *Irish Times*, 22 June 1972
Brown v Ibbetson, *Freeman's Journal*, 13 Nov 1845

Browne v Blake in Browne, M (1817), *Irish Gallantry! Fairburn's Edition of the Unprecedented Trial between Mark Browne and Joseph Blake for Adultery*, 4th edn (Dublin)
Butterworth v Butterworth and Englefield [1920] P 126
Caila v McNamara, *Freeman's Journal*, 11, 12, 13 Dec 1820
Calcraft v Earl of Harborough (1831) 4 C & P 499
Campbell v Hook (1793) *The Proceedings Against Major Hook for Criminal Conversation with his Own Niece Mrs Campbell, Wife of Captain Campbell, before Lord Kenyon and a Special Jury. At Westminster, Feb 26th, 1793* (London: np)
Campion v Drew, *Freeman's Journal*, 14, 16 Aug 1841
Cashel v Harding, *Nenagh Guardian*, 19 Mar 1859
Chute v Blennerhassett, *Freeman's Journal*, 12, 13 Dec 1865
Cloncurry v Piers (1807) *A Full and Accurate Report of the Trial of Sir John Piers for Criminal Conversation with Lady Cloncurry: Taken in Shorthand by an Eminent Barrister Concerned in the Cause* (Dublin: C La Grange)
Cobbe v Garaton (1841) Milward 529
Coffey v Magee, *Belfast Newsletter*, 23 Mar 1829
Conyers v Westropp, *Belfast Newsletter*, 20 May 1834
Connemara v Connemara, *Irish Times*, 28 Nov 1890
Copperthwaite v Tuite (1848) 13 Ir Eq Rep 68
Courtney v Courtney [1923] 57 ILTR 42
Cronin v Murphy, *Belfast Newsletter*, 17 May 1897
Dalrymple v Dalrymple (1811) 2 Hag Con 54; 161 ER 665
De Búrca v Attorney General [1976] IR 38 (SC)
Dennehy v Minister for Social Welfare, unreported, High Court 26 Jul 1984
Devlin v Davy, *Irish Times*, 7 Jan 1888
Donovan v Croft [1926] 60 ILTR 115
Doyle v Brown (1820) *Crim. Con. A Full, Faithful and Impartial Report of the Trial, wherein Sir John M. Doyle, KCB & KTS was Plaintiff, and George Peter Brown, Esq, Defendant. For Criminal Conversation with the Defendant's Wife* (Dublin: James Charles)
Dunlevie v Barry, *Belfast Newsletter*, 29 Mar 1833
Dunlop v Johnson, *Belfast Newsletter*, 22 Jul 1886
Dunlop v Wallace, *Anglo-Celt*, 6 Jul 1849
Echlin v Brady (1865) 10 *Irish Jurist* (ns) 188
Ennis v Butterly [1996] 1 IR 426, 436 (IEHC)
Ex p Hodgens (1847) 11 Ir Eq Rep 99
Fay v Barber (1797) *The Trial of William Barber, for Criminal Conversation with Jane Fay, Wife of Lawrence Fay, In His Majesty's Court of King's Bench in Ireland; Before the Right Honourable Earl Clonmell, and a Special Jury* (2nd edn, Dublin: J Whitworth)
Fitzgerald v Hawkesworth (1811) *Speeches of John Philpot Curran, Esq.* Vol. II (I Riley: New York)
Fleming v Purcell, *Belfast Newsletter*, 23 Feb 1893
Forrest v O'Brien, *Freeman's Journal*, 21, 22 Mar 1845
Fortune v Conolly, *Freeman's Journal*, 1 Mar 1806
Francis v Wigzell (1816) 1 Madd 258, 56 ER 96
G v An Bord Uchtála [1980] IR 32
G v H, *Belfast Newsletter*, 28 Apr 1843
Garvey v Lindsay, *Freeman's Journal*, 21, 22, 24, 25 June 1872
Geoghegan Nowlan v Glentworth, *Freeman's Journal*, 10 Jul 1822

Glerawley v Burn, *Belfast Newsletter,* 4 June 1820

Goodin v Smith (1831) Milward 236

Goodwin v Holden, *Freeman's Journal,* 18 Mar 1847; *Belfast Newsletter,* 19 Mar 1847

Grace v Grace (1768) (Dublin Consistorial Court Cause Papers, NAI)

Graham v Pattison, *Irish Times,* 23 June 1935

Griffith v Griffith [1944] 78 ILTR 95

Guthrie v Sterne (1815) *Crim Con. Court of Common Pleas, Friday, June 9, 1815. John Guthrie, Esq, Plaintiff; WPBD Sterne, Esq, Defendant* (Dublin: W Espy)

Hadley v Baxendale (1854) 1 Ex 410

Harding's Case, *Nation,* 25 Mar 1865

Harrison v Hooks, *Belfast Newsletter,* 14 Jan, 8, 10 Feb 1862; *Cork Examiner,* 10 Feb 1862

Hartnett v O'Neill, *Irish Press,* 15 Nov 1977

Head v Purdon, *Belfast Newsletter,* 20 June 1837; *Freeman's Journal,* 24 June 1837

Herbert v Nalty, *Freeman's Journal,* 8 Nov 1839

Hewitt v Lyttle, *Irish Times,* 16 Dec 1886

Hodgens v Mahon (1835) *Court of Exchequer, Feb 22nd, 1835. Crim. Con. New Trial before the Chief Baron. Hodgens v Mahon* (Dublin: D Scott)

Hulme v Tenant (1778) 1 Bro CC 16

Hurst v McDonnell, *Belfast Newsletter,* 16 June 1891

Irwin v O'Connell [1936] 1 IR 44

James v Biddington (1834) 6 C & P 589

Johnston and Others v Ireland [1986] ECHR 17, 9697/82; [1986] 9 EHRR 203

Joynt v Jackson (1880), *Authentic Report of the Crim Con Trial of Joynt v Jackson in the Exchequer Court, Dublin, Commencing May 10th, 1880* (Dublin: Edward Smith)

Kavanagh v McGarry, *Belfast Newsletter,* 12 Nov 1820

Keelan v Garvey [1924] 38 ILTR 165

Keenan v Pringle, *Irish* Times, 5 Feb 1891

Kelly v Gannon, *Freeman's Journal,* 18 Dec 1812

Kingsley v Peile, *Weekly Irish Times,* 20 Jan 1883

Kinsella v Wingfield, *Irish Times,* 24 Apr 1883

Knox v Arnold, *Dundalk Democrat,* 30 Nov 1872

L v L [1989] ILRM 528 (HC)

Legeyt v O'Brien (1834) Milward 325

Lemon v Lemon (1841) Cr & Dix 498

Lennon v Maguire [1935] 69 ILTR 67

Leonard v Hartford, *Freeman's Journal,* 6, 12 Aug 1823; *Belfast Newsletter,* 19 Aug 1823

Lessee of Kirwan v Kirwan (1826) Batty 712

Lismore v Bingham, *Freeman's Journal,* 21 Apr 1825

Little v Lynch, *Freeman's Journal,* 26 Oct 1831; *Belfast Newsletter,* 1 Nov 1831

Little v Newenham, *Belfast Newsletter,* 19 Aug 1845; *Freeman's Journal,* 19 Aug 1845

Lowry v Bustard, *Irish Times,* 16 Apr 1885

Lynch v Cork and Macroom Railway (1879) *Irish Law Times and Solicitors Journal* 260

Lynch v Macan, *Irish Times,* 2 July 1890

MacDonnell v Murphy (1824) in J. Scott Fox and C. Lacey Smith (1887–1895) *Registration Cases. Reports of Cases Argued and Determined on Appeal from the Decisions of the Revising Barristers in the Queen's Bench Division of the High Court of Justice* (London: Stevens and Sons), 2, 279

Madden v McEgan, *Freeman's Journal,* 15 Dec 1809

Maher v Collins [1974] 1 IR 232
Mallon v Barnwell, *Irish Times*, 25 Jan 1889
Mansergh v Hacket (1807) *The Trial of J. Hacket, Esquire, for Adultery with Mrs Mansergh. In the Irish Court of Exchequer on Dec the 10th, 1807* (London: J. Day)
Massy v Headfort (1804) *A Report of the Trial on an Action for Damages Brought by the Reverend Charles Massy Against the Most Noble the Marquis of Headfort for Criminal Conversation with Plaintiff's Wife* (Dublin: MN Mahon)
Matthews v Moniali, *Freeman's Journal*, 14 Jul 1866
Maxwell v Maxwell (1832) Milward 290
McCraith v Quinn, *Belfast Newsletter*, 1–2 Aug 1872
McDonnell v Weddick, *Freeman's Journal*, 21 June 1873
McGee v Attorney General [1973] IESC 2; [1974] IR 284
McLaren v Osborne, *Freeman's Journal*, 29 July 1868
McM v McM [1936] IR 177
Mitchell v Spread (1799), Rowe's Popery Cases 208
Montray v McCartney, *Freeman's Journal*, 6 Nov 1840
Moore v Thompson, *Belfast Newsletter*, 3 Aug 1841
Moriarty v Moriarty in Browne, A (1803) *A Compendious View of the Ecclesiastical Law of Ireland*, 2nd edn (Dublin: Mercier)
Morrison v Roberts, *Irish Times*, 30 Jul 1892
Morrow v Menzies, *Freeman's Journal*, 16 Jul 1846
Morrow v Morrow [1914] 2 IR 183
Mulvaney v Collins, *Irish Times*, 10 Nov 1979
Murdock v Rynn, *Belfast Newsletter*, 2–7 May 1894
Murray v Redmond, *Belfast Newsletter*, 10 Aug 1847
Norris v Attorney General [1984] IR 36 (SC)
Northwestern Health Board v HW [2001] IESC 90; [2001] 3 IR 622
Nowlan v Sullivan, *Freeman's Journal*, 23, 24 June 1851
Nugent v Norie, *Freeman's Journal*, 25 Feb 1818
O'B v S [1984] IR 316 (SC)
O'Connor v McCann Milward (1829) 204
O'Malley v O'Malley [1951] 85 ILTR 43
O'Reilly v McCan, *Belfast Newsletter*, 15 Jul 1828
O'Reilly v McKay, *Irish Times*, 22 Oct 1954
Ormsby v Ormsby [1945] 79 ILTR 97
Patterson v Pullen, *Freeman's Journal*, 2 Dec 1800
People v Ballins (1964) *Irish Jurist* 14
People v Hunt (1946) ILTR 8; *Irish Times*, 12 Dec 1945
Pepper v Kelly [1843] 6 Ir Law Rep 530
Pybus v Smith (1791) 3 Bro CC 329
R v Bell (1841) 2 M & Rob 294
R v Bell (1874) IR 8 CL 542
R v Charleton (1839) Jebb CCR 267; (1839) 2 Jebb & Symes 54; (1841) Crawford & Dix 315
R v Doran (1842) 2 Leg Rep 163
R v Fennell (1838) Cr & Dix, Ab Not Cas 301
R v Gogarty (1855) 7 Cox CC 107
R v McKenna (1840) 1 Cr & Dix C 399

R v McLaughlin (1841) Crawford & Dix 315
R v McNaghten (1843) 10 Cl & F 200
R v Millis (1844) 10 Cl & F 534
R v Murphy (1836) 5 Law Rec (ns) 98
R v Opie (1860) 8 Cox CC 332
R v Pritchard (1836) 7 C & P 303
R v Sandys (1835) Jebb CCR 166
R v Smith (1843) Cr & Dix 318; *R v Smith* (1842) Jebb & Bourke, App i
R v Snell (1837) 2 M & Rob 44
R v Stonage (1832) Jebb CCR 121
Re A & B [1897] 1 Ch 786, 788
Re Art 26 and the Matrimonial Home Bill 1993 [1994] IESC 5; [1994] 1 IR 305.
Re Brennan, *Irish Times,* 19 Oct 1946
Re Devers, *Irish Times,* 29 Oct 1925
Re Estate of Patrick Walsh, dec: Walsh v Walsh [1942] IR 403, 408
Re Frost, Infants [1947] 1 IR 3
Re Hogg, *Women's Suffrage Journal,* 1 Oct 1879
Re Hunt, *Freeman's Journal,* 23 Oct 1850
Re Hunt, *Irish Times,* 11 Dec 1945
Re John Johnston, *Freeman's Journal,* 7 May 1838
Re Kavanagh, Infants [1934] 68 ILTR 110
Re Keenan's Infants [1950] 84 ILTR 169
Re Kenneth Francis McNally, an Infant [1950] 84 ILTR 7
Re Kevin Isherwood, an Infant [1948] 82 ILTR 85
Re Mitchell, Infant [1937] IR 767
Re NP, an Infant [1944] 78 ILTR 32
Re Smith, *Irish Times,* 19 Feb 1943
Re Tilson: Infants [1952] 86 ILTR 49
Re Train, *Freeman's Journal,* 24 June 1868
RM v MM [1942] 76 ILTR 165
Rollfe v Budder (1724) Bunb 187, 134 ER 642
Rubie v Foley, *Belfast Newsletter,* 7 Aug 1838; *Freeman's Journal,* 7 Aug 1838
Ryan v Attorney General [1965] IESC 1; [1965] IR 294
Ryan v Ryan, in Browne, A (1803) *A Compendious View of the Ecclesiastical Law of Ireland,* 2nd edn (Dublin: Mercier)
Sargent v Spring, *Freeman's Journal,* 24 Aug 1810
Savage v Carse, *Belfast Newsletter,* 9, 12 Mar 1847
Scott v Morley (1887) 20 QBD 120
Sheehan v Stack, *Cork Examiner,* 19 Jul 1870
Smith v Dillon, *Freeman's Journal,* 1 Jul 1815
Smith v Kearon, *Irish Times,* 13 Feb 1957
Smith v Smith (1821) Milward 120
St Lawrence v Skehan, *Cork Examiner,* 27 June 1870; *Freeman's Journal,* 27 June 1870
Steele v Braddell (1838) Milward 1
Sullivan v Lackney, *Freeman's Journal,* 2 Apr 1812
Sutter v Courtney, *Freeman's Journal,* 20 Mar 1841
Taaffe v Fitzgerald, *Belfast Newsletter,* 1 Mar 1816
The State (Nicolaou) v An Bord Uchtála [1966] IR 567

Todd v Alexander, *Irish Times*, 20 Jan 1917
Toner v Bullick, *Belfast Newsletter*, 9 Jul 1900
Townley v Lyle, *Irish Times*, 6 Feb 1886
Vanston v Whitecroft (1897) *Belfast Newsletter,* 11 June 1897
W O'R v EH (Guardianship) [1996] IESC 4; [1996] 2 IR 248
Wallace v Mulvey, *Cork Examiner,* 29 June 1870
Walsh v Lacken, *Freeman's Journal,* 4 Feb 1852
Wetherall v Gamble, *Belfast Newsletter,* 10 Mar 1815
Whittaker v Berry, *Irish Times,* 12 Feb 1894
Wilson v Leonard (1852) 5 *Irish Jurist* (os) 101
Wilton v Webster (1835) 7 C & P 198, 202: 173 ER 87
Winsmore v Greenbank (1745) Willes 577: 125 ER 1330
Worrall v Snow, *Belfast Newsletter*, 12 Aug 1874
Wynn v Warner, *Freeman's Journal,* 19, 20, 22 Aug 1823; *Belfast Newsletter,* 22 Aug 1823
Wytham v Waterhouse (1596) Tothill 91
Zappone v Revenue Commissioners [2006] IEHC 404

Index

Lightning Source UK Ltd.
Milton Keynes UK
UKOW06f2238021217
313515UK00002B/19/P